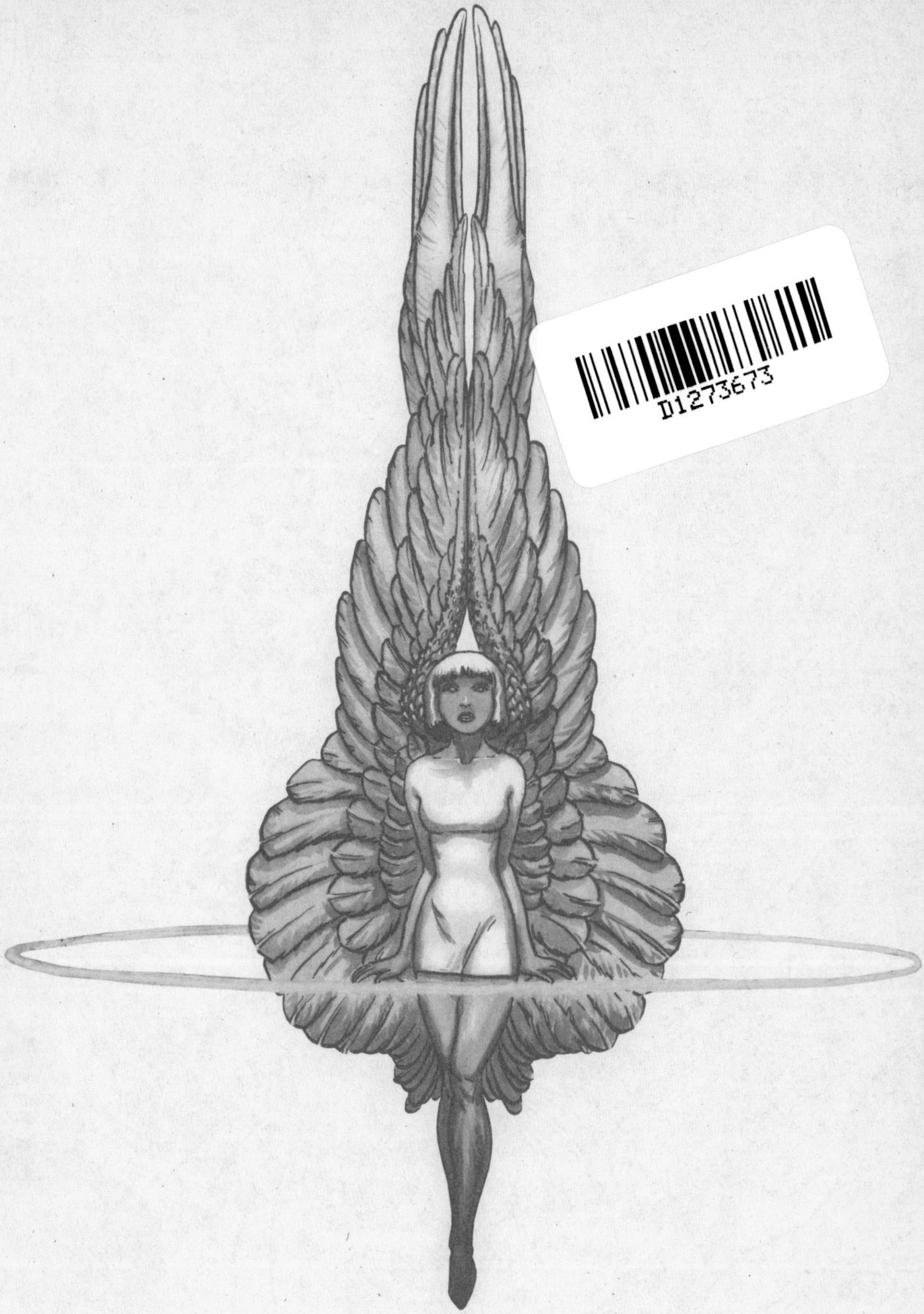

Lucifer

Crux

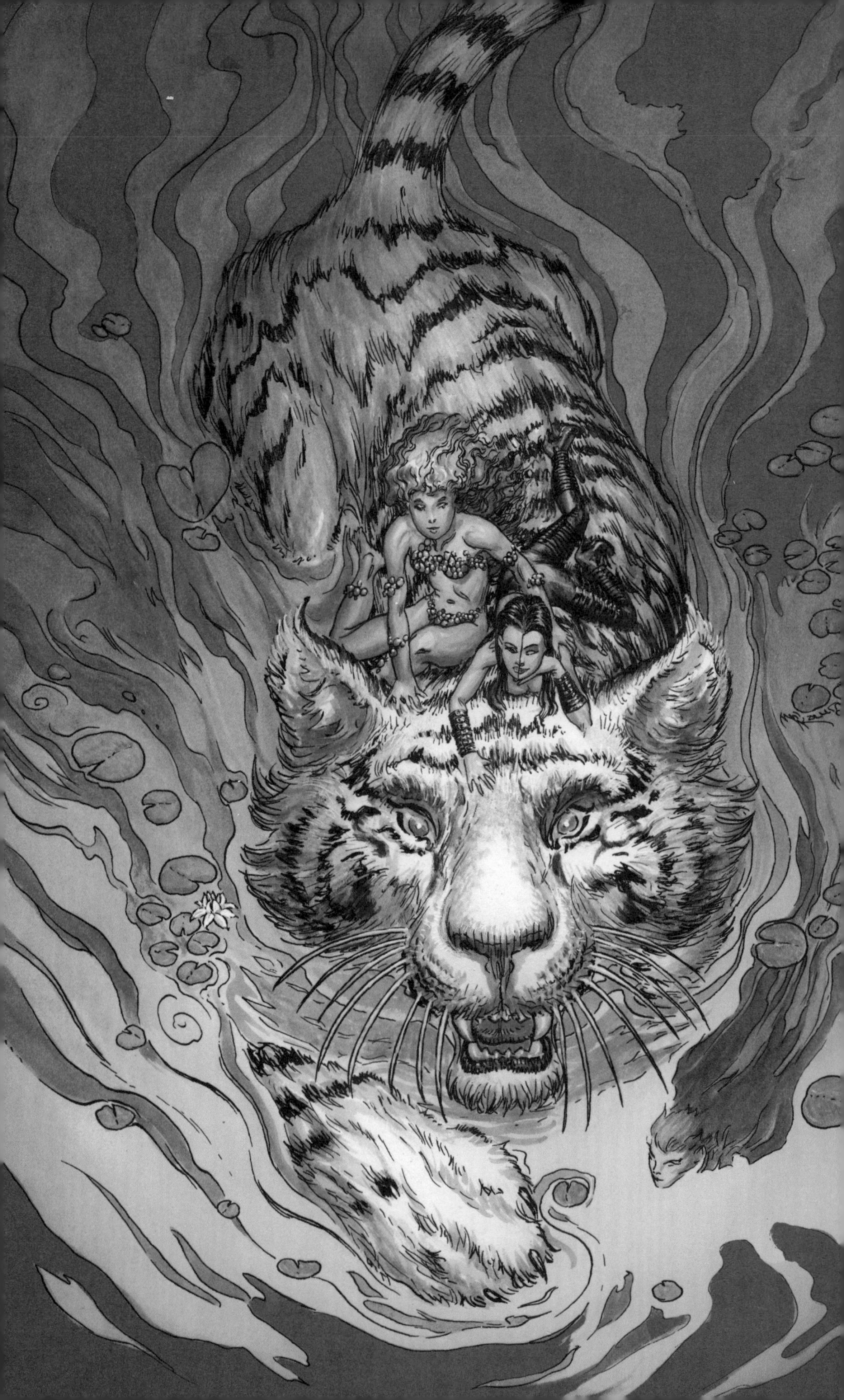

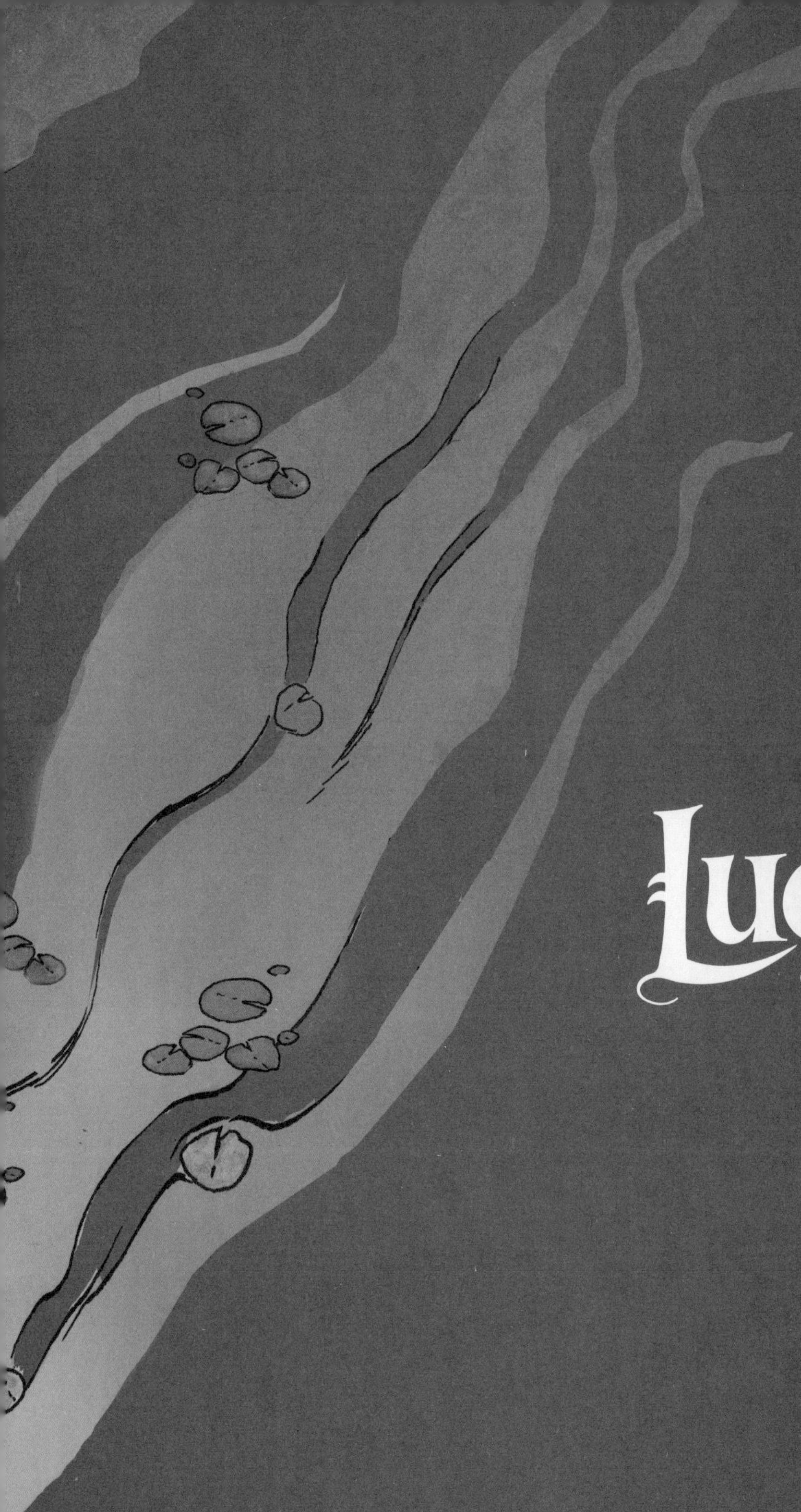

Lucifer

Crux

Mike Carey
Writer

Peter Gross
Ryan Kelly
Marc Hempel
Ronald Wimberly
Artists

Daniel Vozzo
Colorist

Jared K. Fletcher
Letterer

Michael Wm. Kaluta
Original Series Covers

Based on characters created by
Neil Gaiman, Sam Kieth and Mike Dringenberg

Karen Berger VP-Executive Editor

Mariah Huehner Editor-original series

Scott Nybakken Editor-collected edition

Robbin Brosterman Senior Art Director

Paul Levitz President & Publisher

Georg Brewer VP-Design & Retail Product Development

Richard Bruning Senior VP-Creative Director

Patrick Caldon Executive VP-Finance & Operations

Chris Caramalis VP-Finance

John Cunningham VP-Marketing

Terri Cunningham VP-Managing Editor

Stephanie Fierman Senior VP-Sales & Marketing

Alison Gill VP-Manufacturing

Rich Johnson VP-Book Trade Sales

Hank Kanalz VP-General Manager, WildStorm

Lillian Laserson Senior VP & General Counsel

Jim Lee Editorial Director-WildStorm

Paula Lowitt Senior VP-Business & Legal Affairs

David McKillips VP-Advertising & Custom Publishing

John Nee VP-Business Development

Gregory Noveck Senior VP-Creative Affairs

Cheryl Rubin Senior VP-Brand Management

Jeff Trojan VP-Business Development, DC Direct

Bob Wayne VP-Sales

LUCIFER: CRUX

Published by DC Comics. Cover and compilation copyright
© 2006 DC Comics. All Rights Reserved.

Originally published in single magazine form as LUCIFER 55-61.
Copyright © 2004, 2005 DC Comics. All Rights Reserved.
All characters, their distinctive likenesses and related elements
featured in this publication are trademarks of DC Comics.
The stories, characters and incidents featured in this publication
are entirely fictional. DC Comics does not read or accept
unsolicited submissions of ideas, stories or artwork.

DC Comics, 1700 Broadway, New York, NY 10019
A Warner Bros. Entertainment Company
Printed in Canada. Second Printing.
ISBN: 1-4012-1005-8
ISBN 13: 978-1-4012-1005-2
Cover illustration by Christopher Moeller.
Logo design by Alex Jay.

Table of Contents

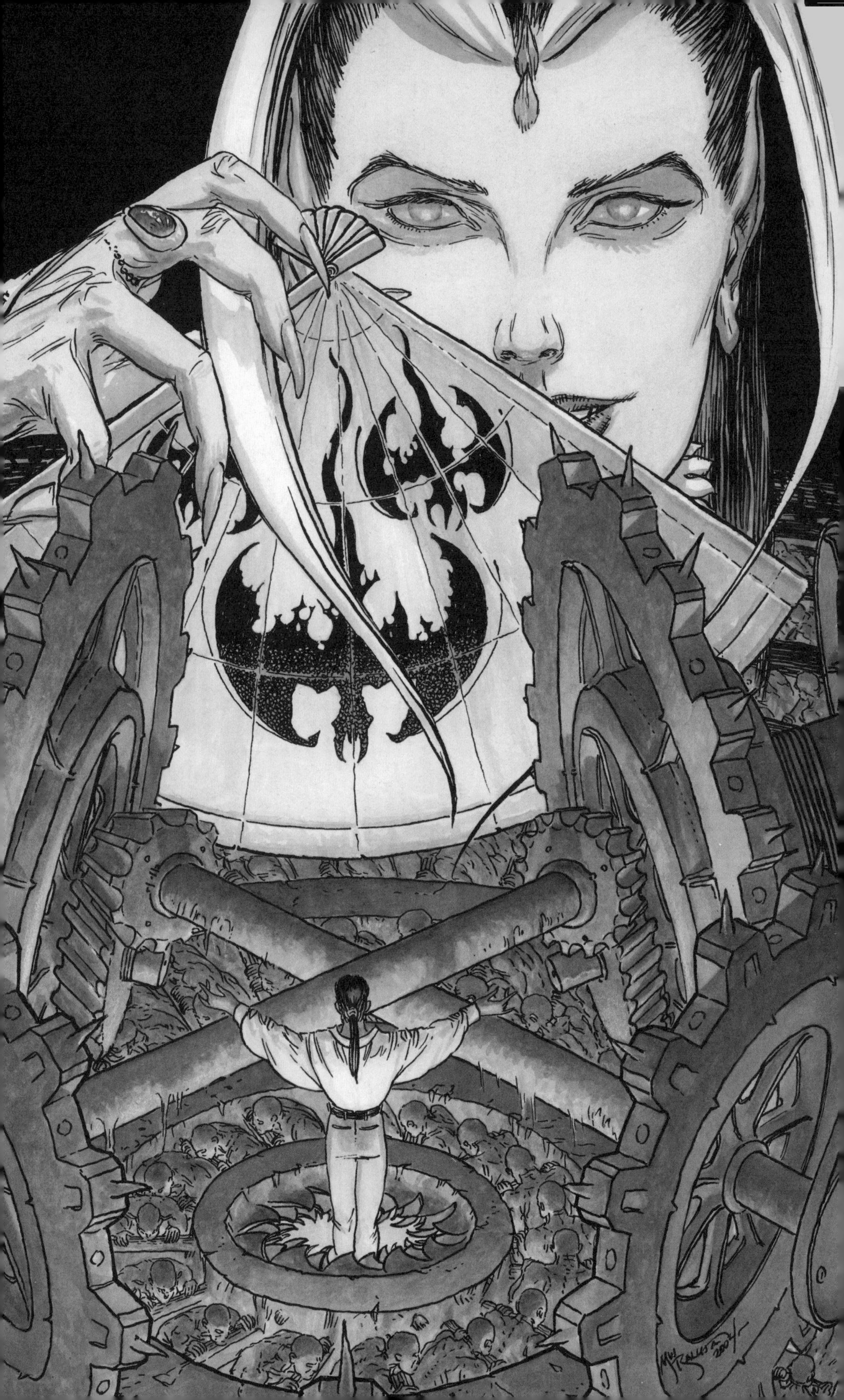

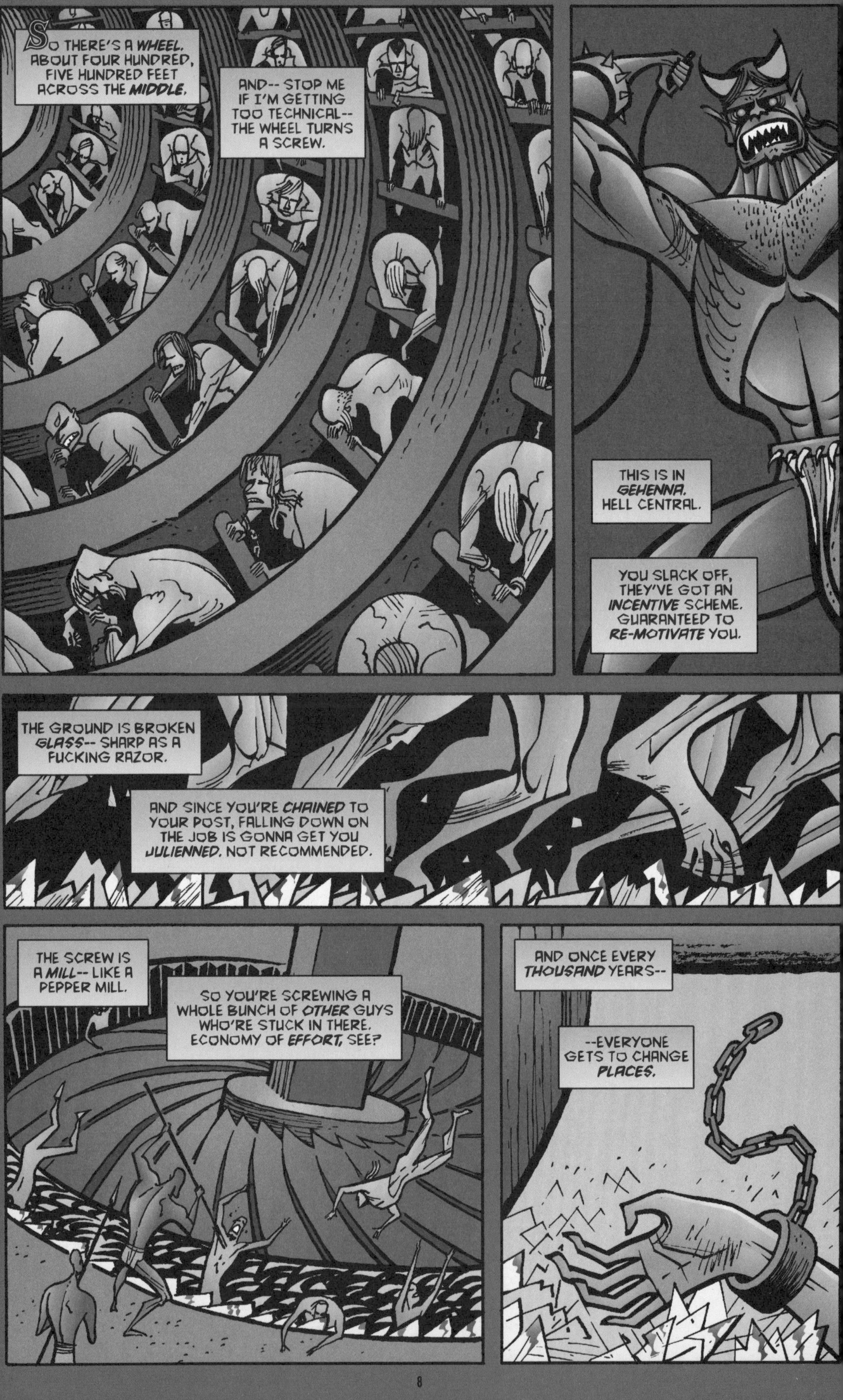
SO THERE'S A WHEEL, ABOUT FOUR HUNDRED, FIVE HUNDRED FEET ACROSS THE MIDDLE.
AND-- STOP ME IF I'M GETTING TOO TECHNICAL-- THE WHEEL TURNS A SCREW.
THIS IS IN GEHENNA. HELL CENTRAL.
YOU SLACK OFF, THEY'VE GOT AN INCENTIVE SCHEME. GUARANTEED TO RE-MOTIVATE YOU.
THE GROUND IS BROKEN GLASS-- SHARP AS A FUCKING RAZOR.
AND SINCE YOU'RE CHAINED TO YOUR POST, FALLING DOWN ON THE JOB IS GONNA GET YOU JULIENNED. NOT RECOMMENDED.
THE SCREW IS A MILL-- LIKE A PEPPER MILL.
SO YOU'RE SCREWING A WHOLE BUNCH OF OTHER GUYS WHO'RE STUCK IN THERE. ECONOMY OF EFFORT, SEE?
AND ONCE EVERY THOUSAND YEARS--
--EVERYONE GETS TO CHANGE PLACES.

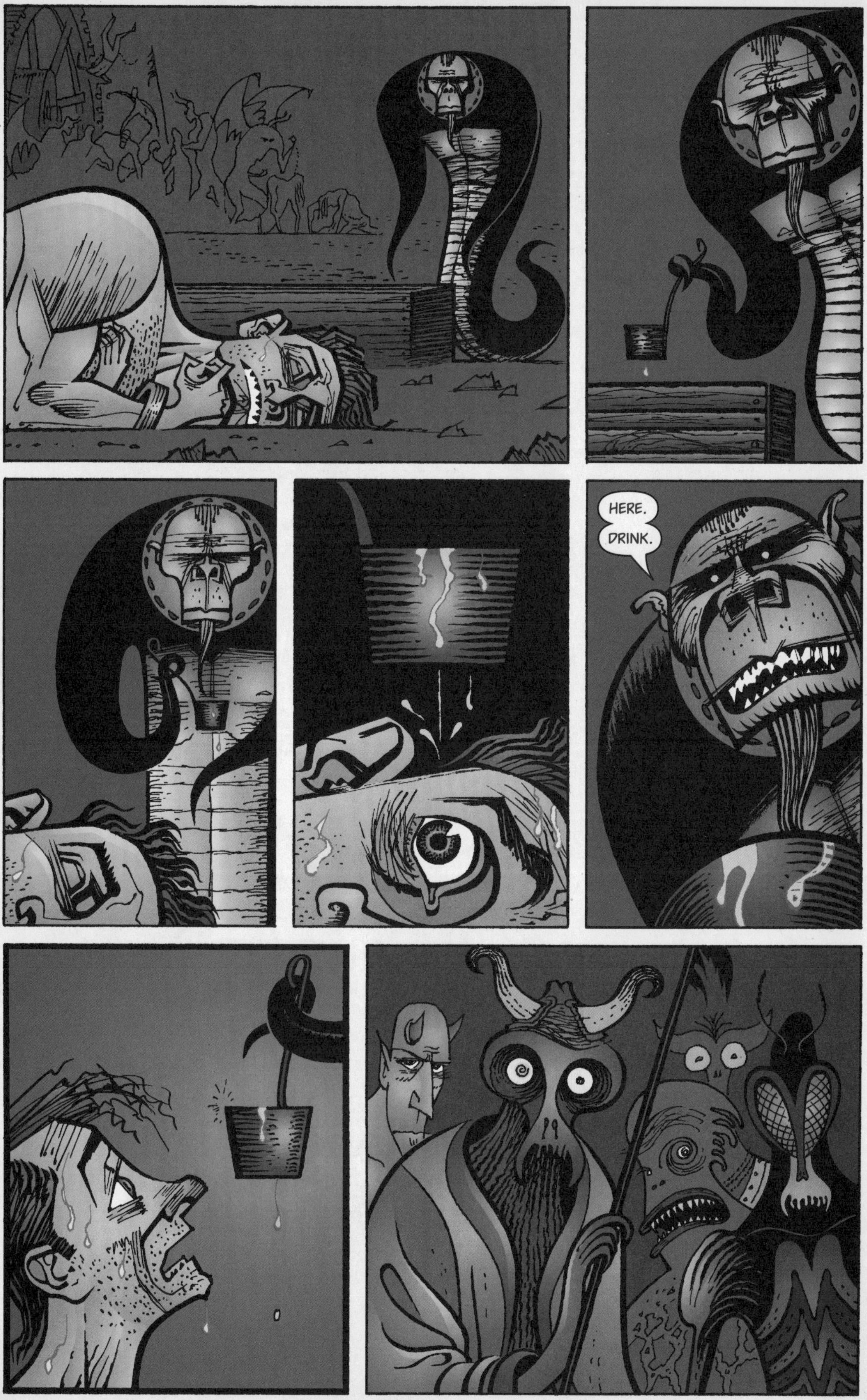
HERE.
DRINK.

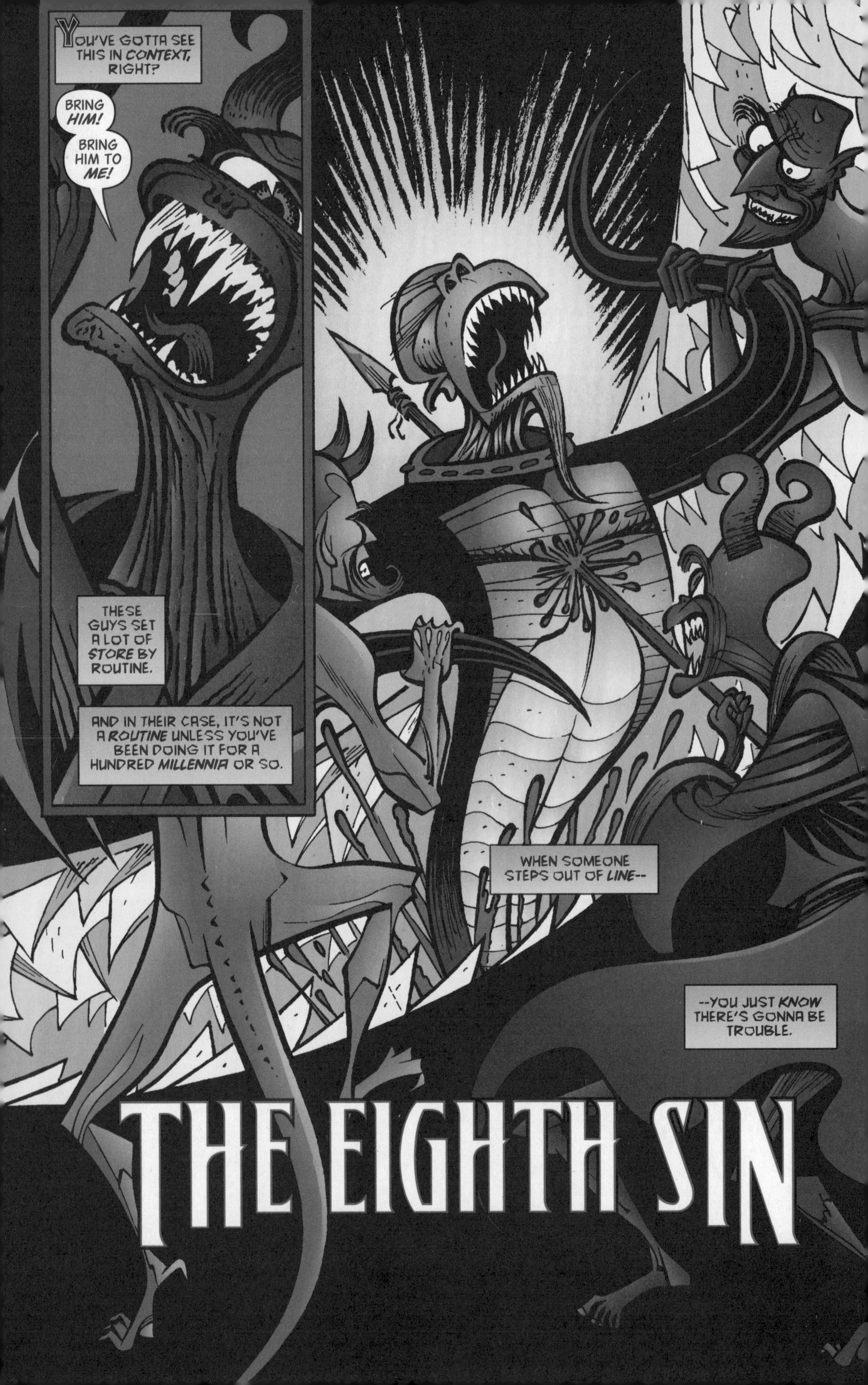
YOU'VE GOTTA SEE THIS IN CONTEXT, RIGHT?
BRING HIM!
BRING HIM TO ME!
THESE GUYS SET A LOT OF STORE BY ROUTINE.
AND IN THEIR CASE, IT'S NOT A ROUTINE UNLESS YOU'VE BEEN DOING IT FOR A HUNDRED MILLENNIA OR SO.
WHEN SOMEONE STEPS OUT OF LINE--
--YOU JUST KNOW THERE'S GONNA BE TROUBLE.
THE EIGHTH SIN

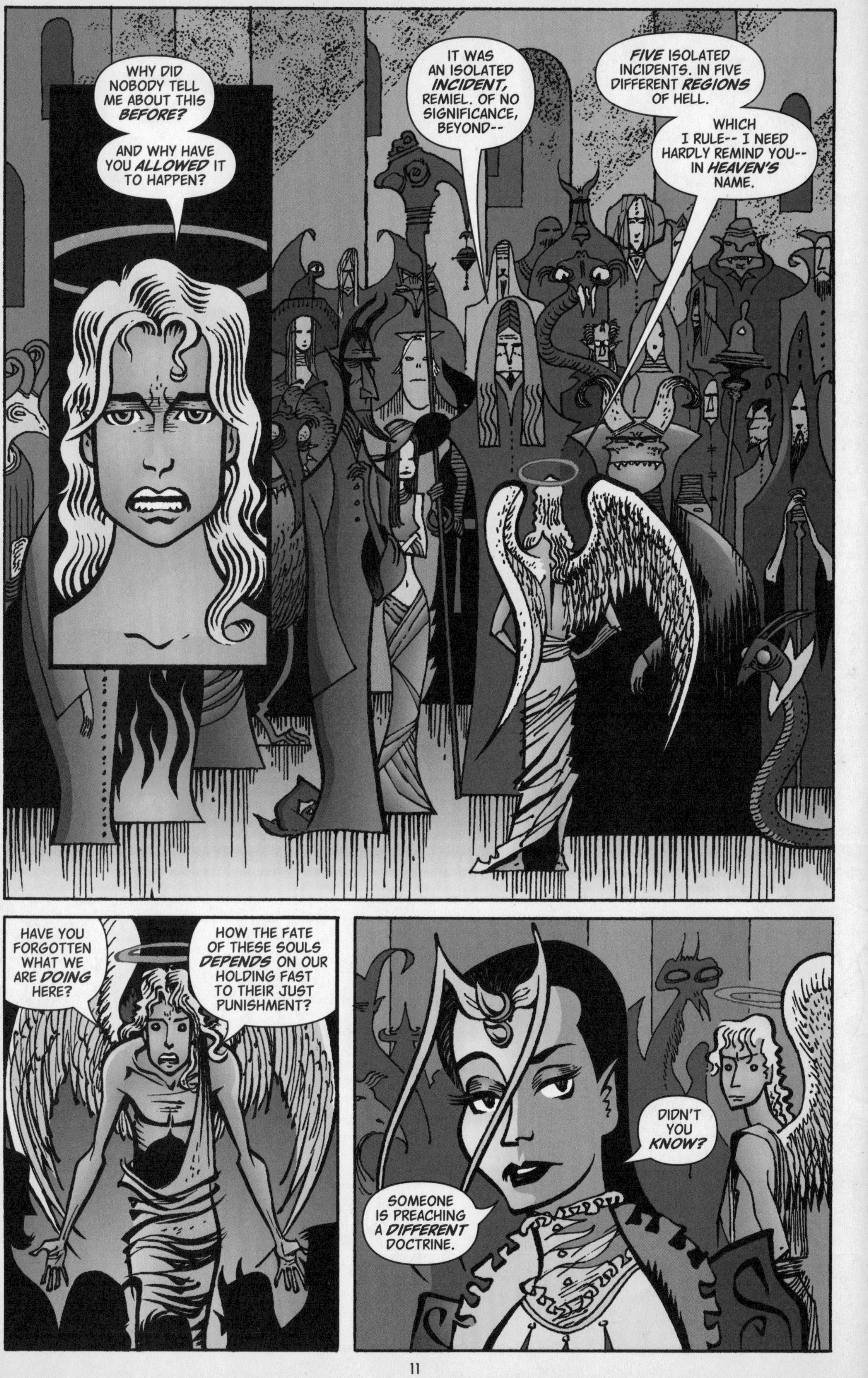

WHY DID NOBODY TELL ME ABOUT THIS *BEFORE?*
AND WHY HAVE YOU *ALLOWED* IT TO HAPPEN?
IT WAS AN ISOLATED *INCIDENT,* REMIEL. OF NO SIGNIFICANCE, BEYOND--
FIVE ISOLATED INCIDENTS. IN FIVE DIFFERENT *REGIONS* OF HELL.
WHICH I RULE-- I NEED HARDLY REMIND YOU-- IN *HEAVEN'S* NAME.
HAVE YOU FORGOTTEN WHAT WE ARE *DOING* HERE?
HOW THE FATE OF THESE SOULS *DEPENDS* ON OUR HOLDING FAST TO THEIR JUST PUNISHMENT?
DIDN'T YOU *KNOW?*
SOMEONE IS PREACHING A *DIFFERENT* DOCTRINE.

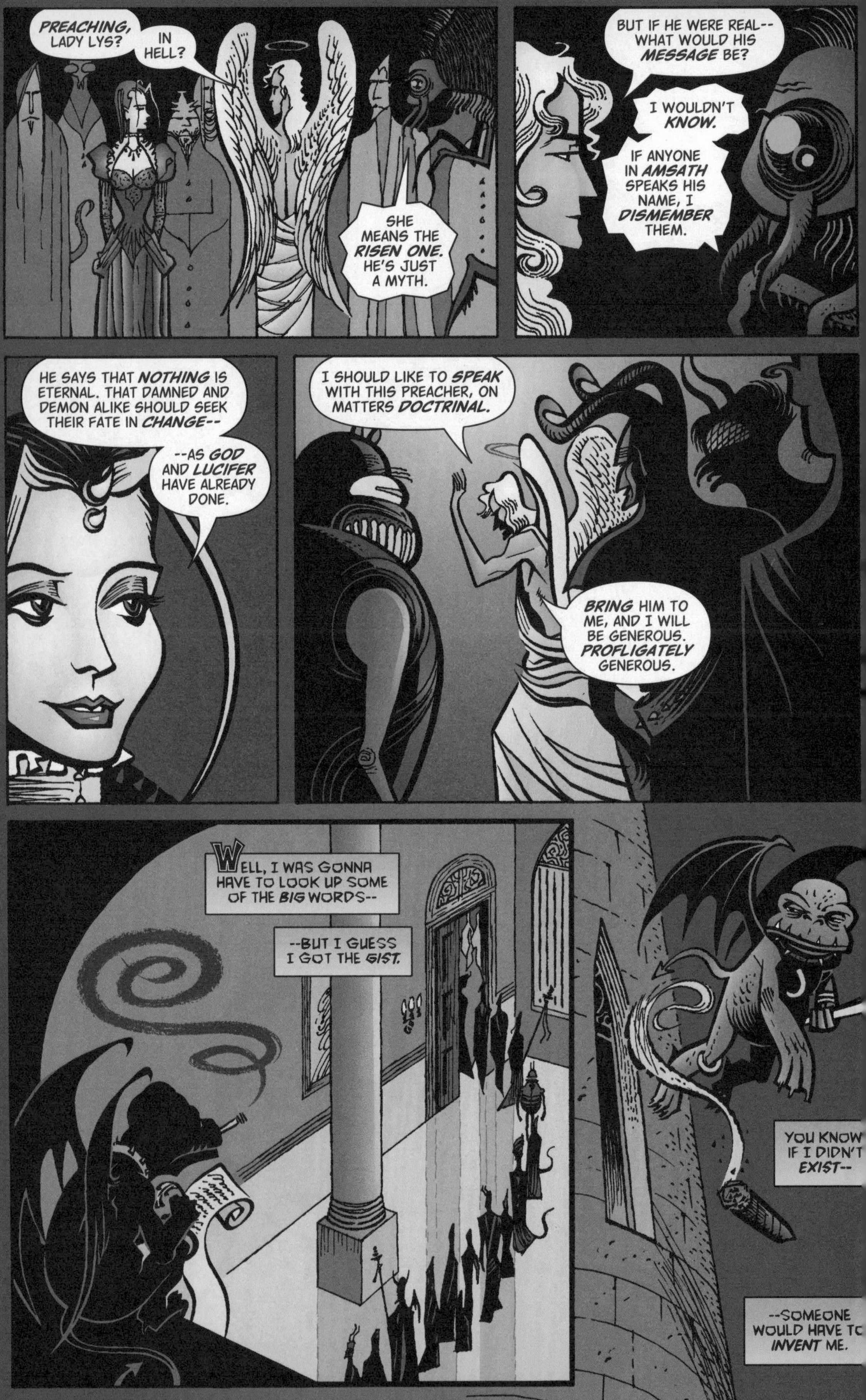

PREACHING, LADY LYS?
IN HELL?
SHE MEANS THE RISEN ONE. HE'S JUST A MYTH.
BUT IF HE WERE REAL--WHAT WOULD HIS MESSAGE BE?
I WOULDN'T KNOW.
IF ANYONE IN AMSATH SPEAKS HIS NAME, I DISMEMBER THEM.
HE SAYS THAT NOTHING IS ETERNAL. THAT DAMNED AND DEMON ALIKE SHOULD SEEK THEIR FATE IN CHANGE--
--AS GOD AND LUCIFER HAVE ALREADY DONE.
I SHOULD LIKE TO SPEAK WITH THIS PREACHER, ON MATTERS DOCTRINAL.
BRING HIM TO ME, AND I WILL BE GENEROUS. PROFLIGATELY GENEROUS.
WELL, I WAS GONNA HAVE TO LOOK UP SOME OF THE BIG WORDS--
--BUT I GUESS I GOT THE GIST.
YOU KNOW IF I DIDN'T EXIST--
--SOMEONE WOULD HAVE TO INVENT ME.

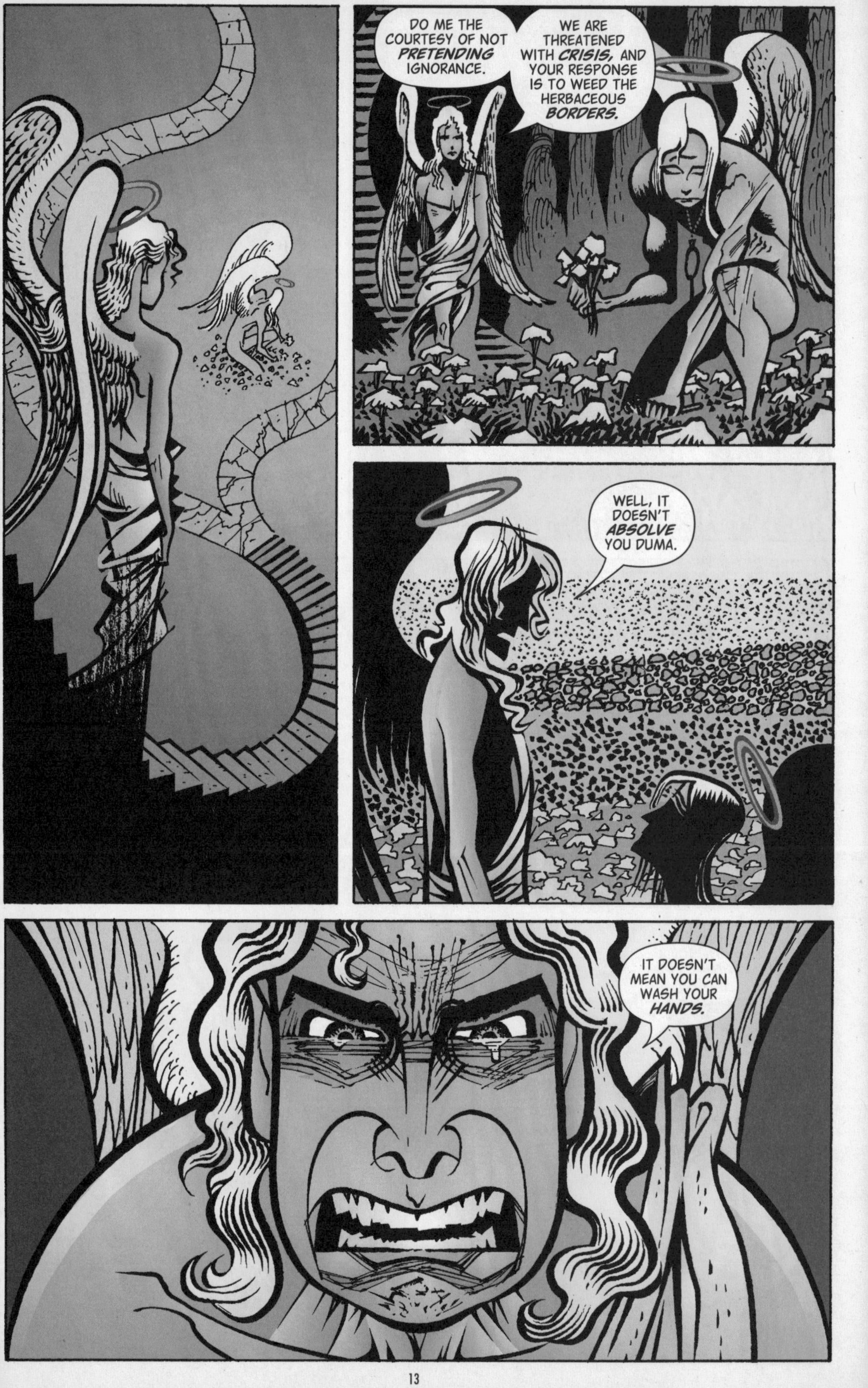
DO ME THE COURTESY OF NOT PRETENDING IGNORANCE.
WE ARE THREATENED WITH CRISIS, AND YOUR RESPONSE IS TO WEED THE HERBACEOUS BORDERS.
WELL, IT DOESN'T ABSOLVE YOU DUMA.
IT DOESN'T MEAN YOU CAN WASH YOUR HANDS.

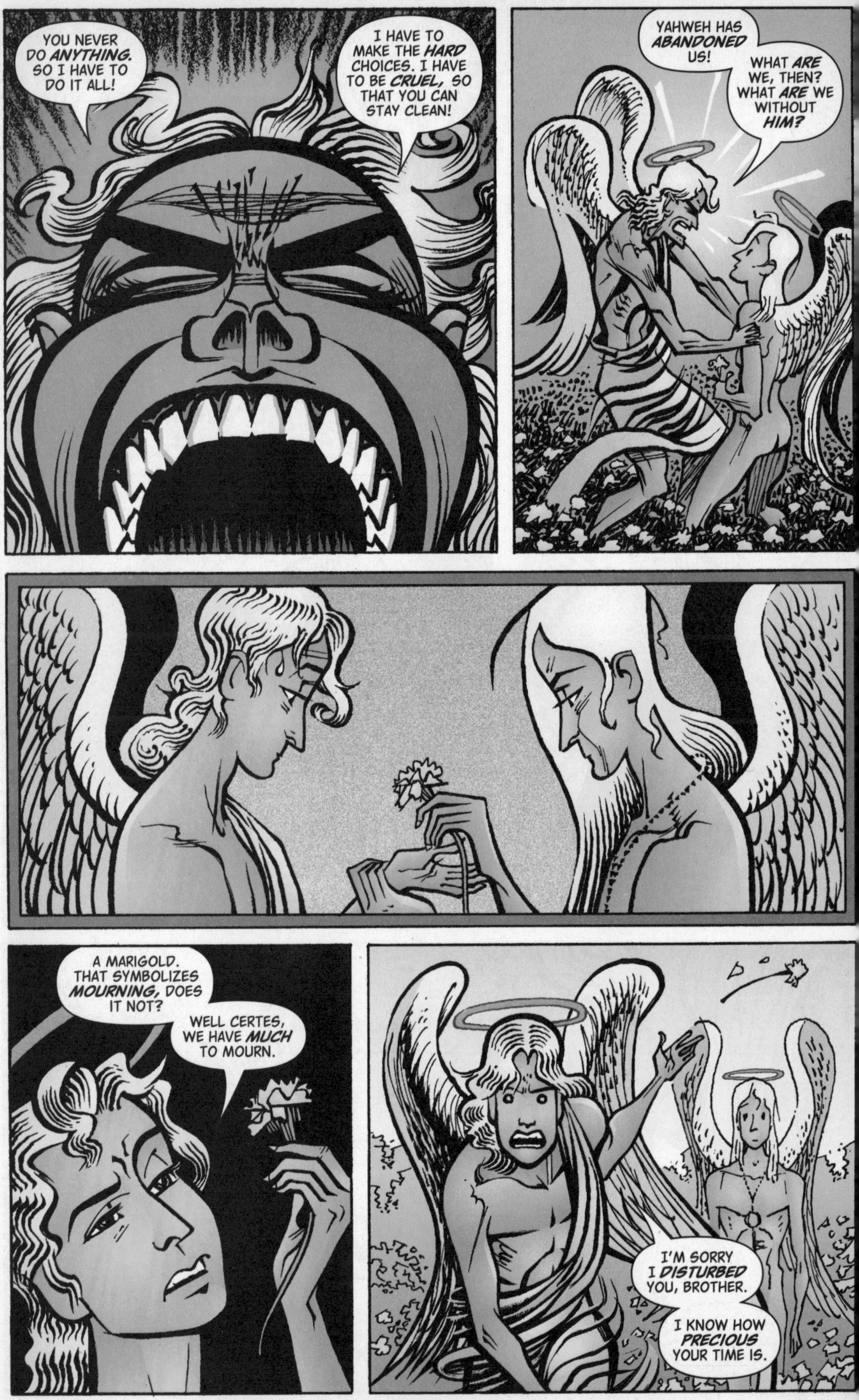
YOU NEVER DO *ANYTHING.* SO I HAVE TO DO IT ALL!
I HAVE TO MAKE THE *HARD* CHOICES. I HAVE TO BE *CRUEL,* SO THAT YOU CAN STAY CLEAN!
YAHWEH HAS *ABANDONED* US!
WHAT *ARE* WE, THEN? WHAT *ARE* WE WITHOUT *HIM?*
A MARIGOLD. THAT SYMBOLIZES *MOURNING,* DOES IT NOT?
WELL CERTES, WE HAVE *MUCH* TO MOURN.
I'M SORRY I *DISTURBED* YOU, BROTHER.
I KNOW HOW *PRECIOUS* YOUR TIME IS.

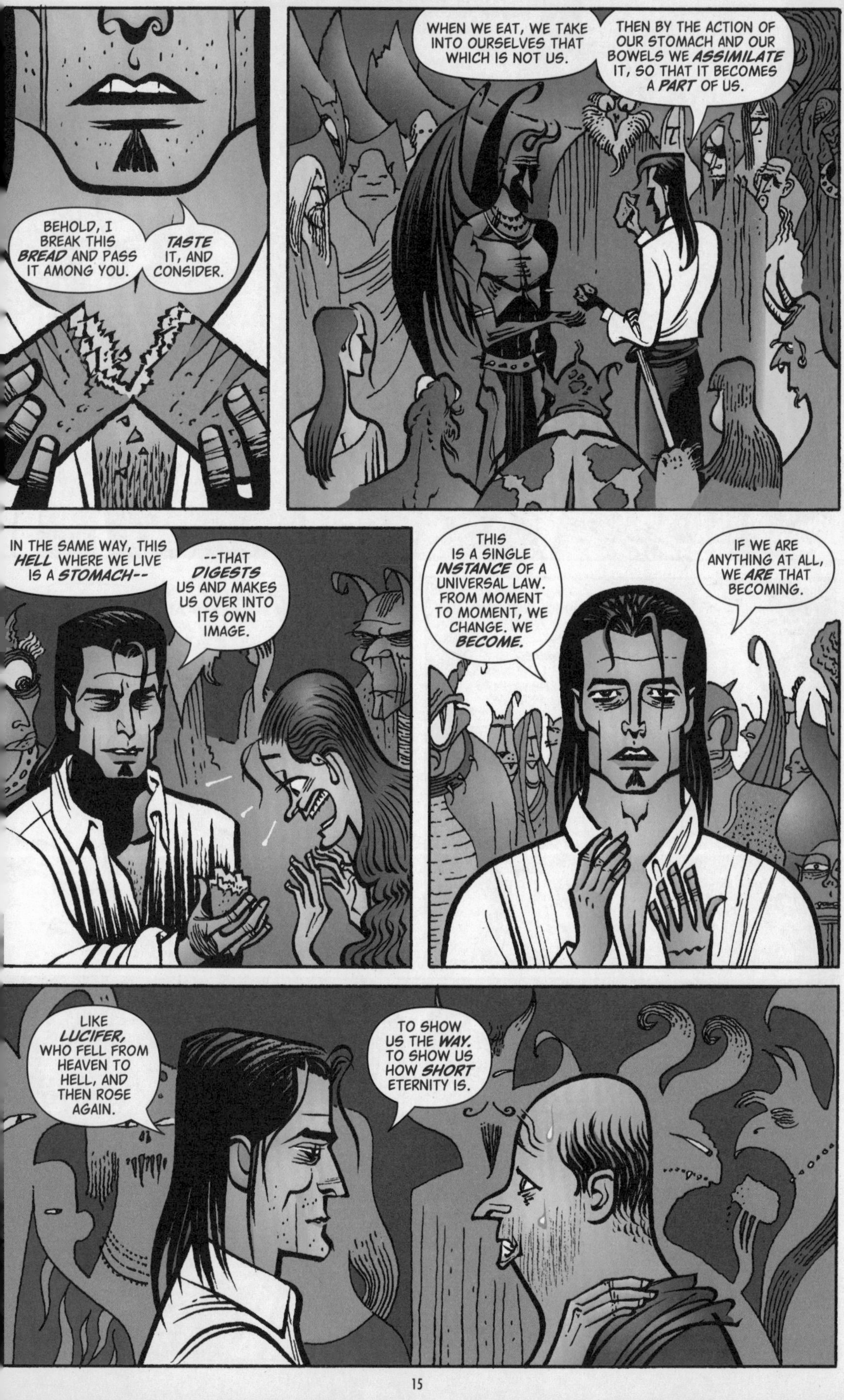
BEHOLD, I BREAK THIS BREAD AND PASS IT AMONG YOU.
TASTE IT, AND CONSIDER.
WHEN WE EAT, WE TAKE INTO OURSELVES THAT WHICH IS NOT US.
THEN BY THE ACTION OF OUR STOMACH AND OUR BOWELS WE ASSIMILATE IT, SO THAT IT BECOMES A PART OF US.
IN THE SAME WAY, THIS HELL WHERE WE LIVE IS A STOMACH--
--THAT DIGESTS US AND MAKES US OVER INTO ITS OWN IMAGE.
THIS IS A SINGLE INSTANCE OF A UNIVERSAL LAW. FROM MOMENT TO MOMENT, WE CHANGE. WE BECOME.
IF WE ARE ANYTHING AT ALL, WE ARE THAT BECOMING.
LIKE LUCIFER, WHO FELL FROM HEAVEN TO HELL, AND THEN ROSE AGAIN.
TO SHOW US THE WAY. TO SHOW US HOW SHORT ETERNITY IS.

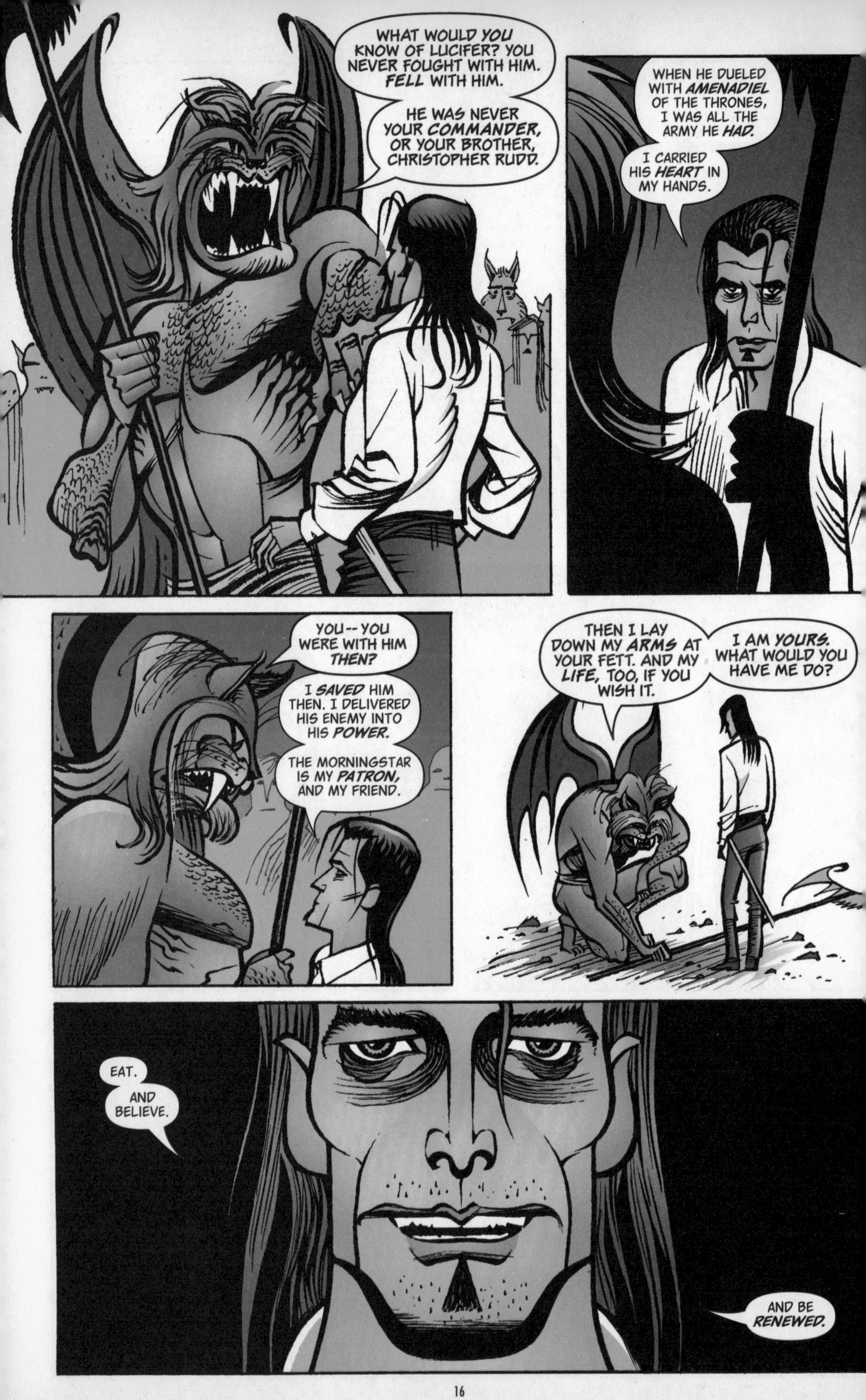
WHAT WOULD YOU KNOW OF LUCIFER? YOU NEVER FOUGHT WITH HIM. FELL WITH HIM.
HE WAS NEVER YOUR COMMANDER, OR YOUR BROTHER, CHRISTOPHER RUDD.
WHEN HE DUELED WITH AMENADIEL OF THE THRONES, I WAS ALL THE ARMY HE HAD.
I CARRIED HIS HEART IN MY HANDS.
YOU-- YOU WERE WITH HIM THEN?
I SAVED HIM THEN. I DELIVERED HIS ENEMY INTO HIS POWER.
THE MORNINGSTAR IS MY PATRON, AND MY FRIEND.
THEN I LAY DOWN MY ARMS AT YOUR FETT. AND MY LIFE, TOO, IF YOU WISH IT.
I AM YOURS. WHAT WOULD YOU HAVE ME DO?
EAT.
AND BELIEVE.
AND BE RENEWED.

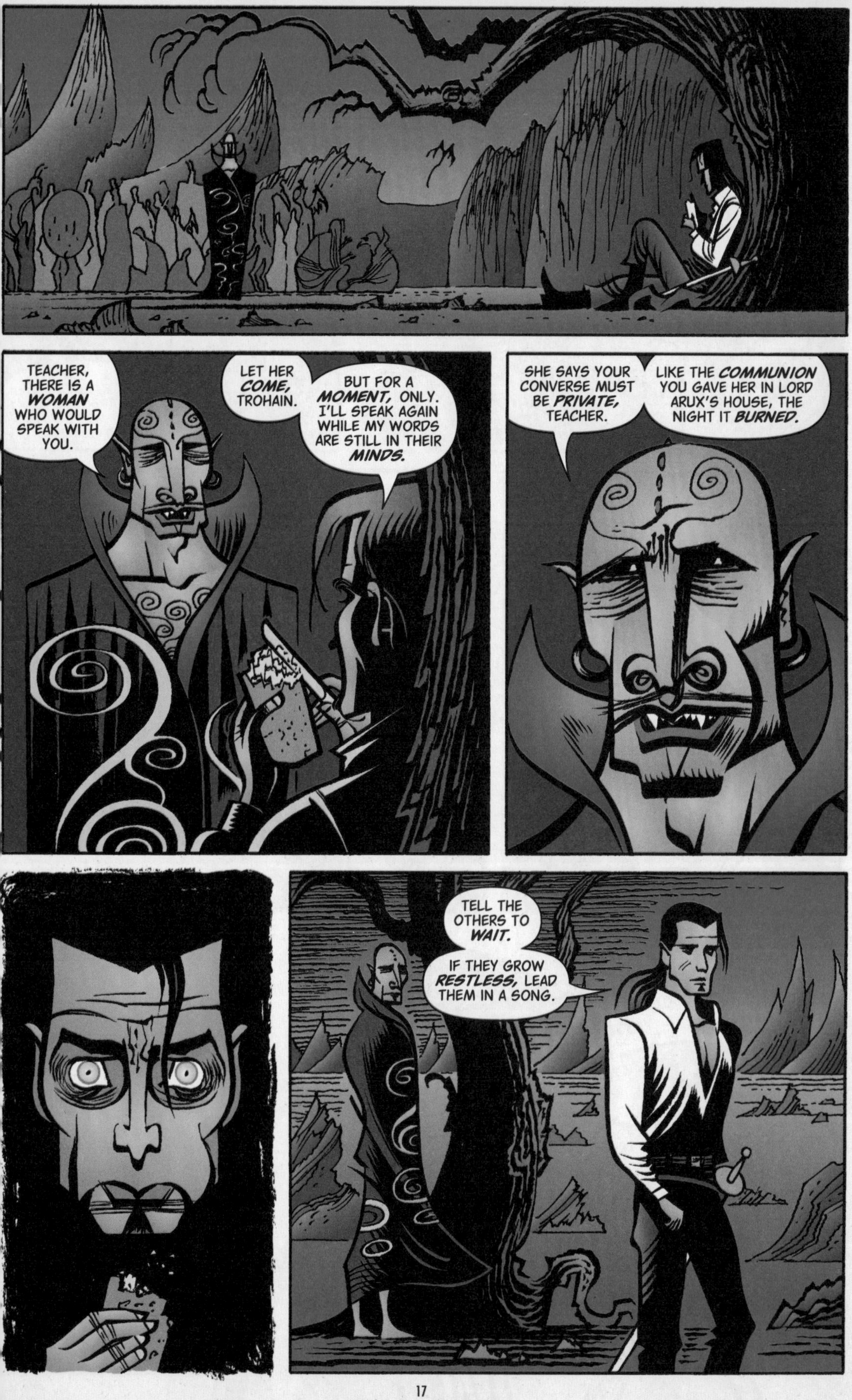
TEACHER, THERE IS A WOMAN WHO WOULD SPEAK WITH YOU.
LET HER COME, TROHAIN.
BUT FOR A MOMENT, ONLY. I'LL SPEAK AGAIN WHILE MY WORDS ARE STILL IN THEIR MINDS.
SHE SAYS YOUR CONVERSE MUST BE PRIVATE, TEACHER.
LIKE THE COMMUNION YOU GAVE HER IN LORD ARUX'S HOUSE, THE NIGHT IT BURNED.
TELL THE OTHERS TO WAIT.
IF THEY GROW RESTLESS, LEAD THEM IN A SONG.

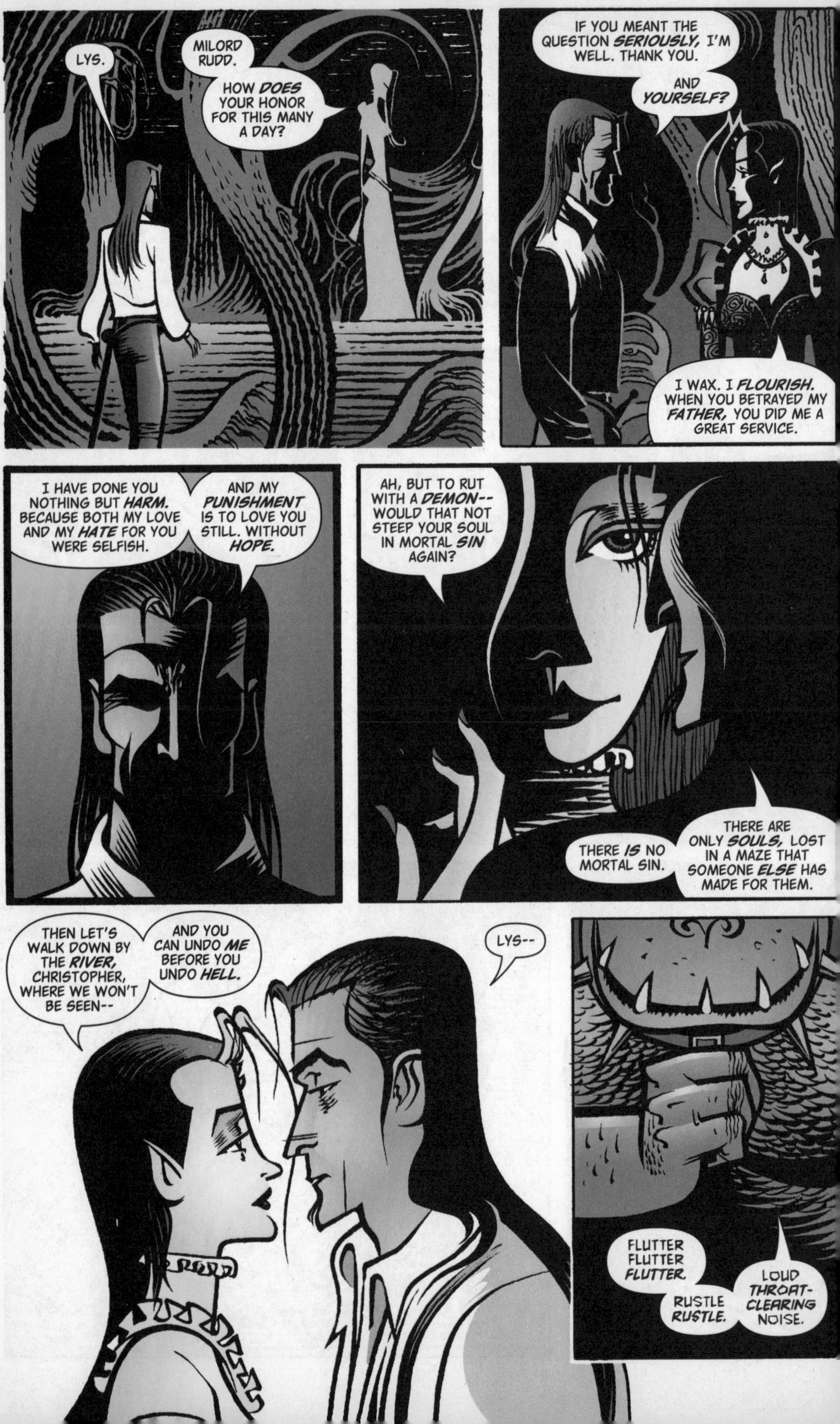
LYS.
MILORD RUDD.
HOW DOES YOUR HONOR FOR THIS MANY A DAY?
IF YOU MEANT THE QUESTION SERIOUSLY, I'M WELL. THANK YOU.
AND YOURSELF?
I WAX. I FLOURISH. WHEN YOU BETRAYED MY FATHER, YOU DID ME A GREAT SERVICE.
I HAVE DONE YOU NOTHING BUT HARM. BECAUSE BOTH MY LOVE AND MY HATE FOR YOU WERE SELFISH.
AND MY PUNISHMENT IS TO LOVE YOU STILL. WITHOUT HOPE.
AH, BUT TO RUT WITH A DEMON-- WOULD THAT NOT STEEP YOUR SOUL IN MORTAL SIN AGAIN?
THERE IS NO MORTAL SIN.
THERE ARE ONLY SOULS, LOST IN A MAZE THAT SOMEONE ELSE HAS MADE FOR THEM.
THEN LET'S WALK DOWN BY THE RIVER, CHRISTOPHER, WHERE WE WON'T BE SEEN--
AND YOU CAN UNDO ME BEFORE YOU UNDO HELL.
LYS--
FLUTTER FLUTTER FLUTTER.
RUSTLE RUSTLE.
LOUD THROAT-CLEARING NOISE.

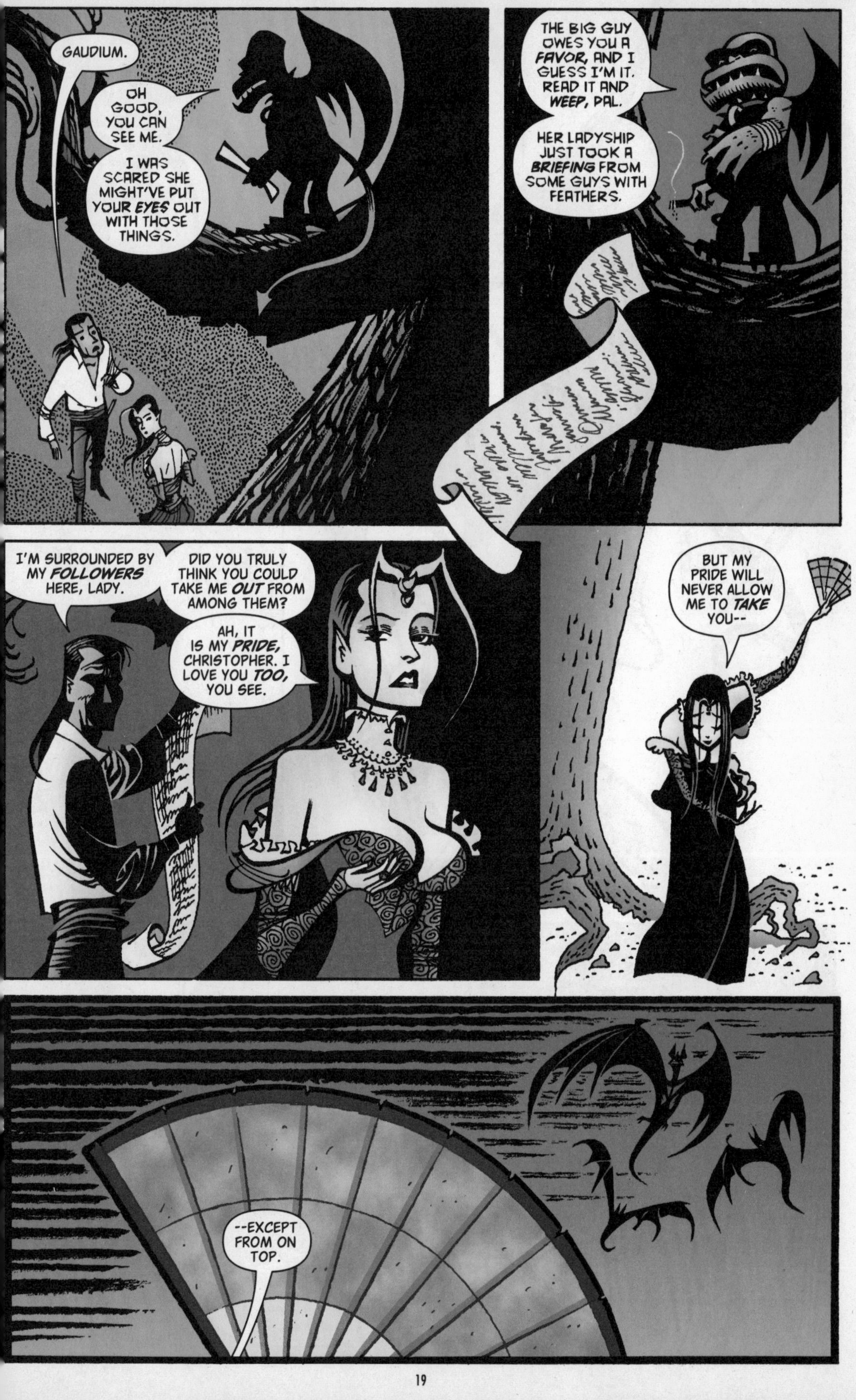
GAUDIUM.
OH GOOD, YOU CAN SEE ME.
I WAS SCARED SHE MIGHT'VE PUT YOUR EYES OUT WITH THOSE THINGS.
THE BIG GUY OWES YOU A FAVOR, AND I GUESS I'M IT. READ IT AND WEEP, PAL.
HER LADYSHIP JUST TOOK A BRIEFING FROM SOME GUYS WITH FEATHERS.
I'M SURROUNDED BY MY FOLLOWERS HERE, LADY.
DID YOU TRULY THINK YOU COULD TAKE ME OUT FROM AMONG THEM?
AH, IT IS MY PRIDE, CHRISTOPHER. I LOVE YOU TOO, YOU SEE.
BUT MY PRIDE WILL NEVER ALLOW ME TO TAKE YOU--
--EXCEPT FROM ON TOP.

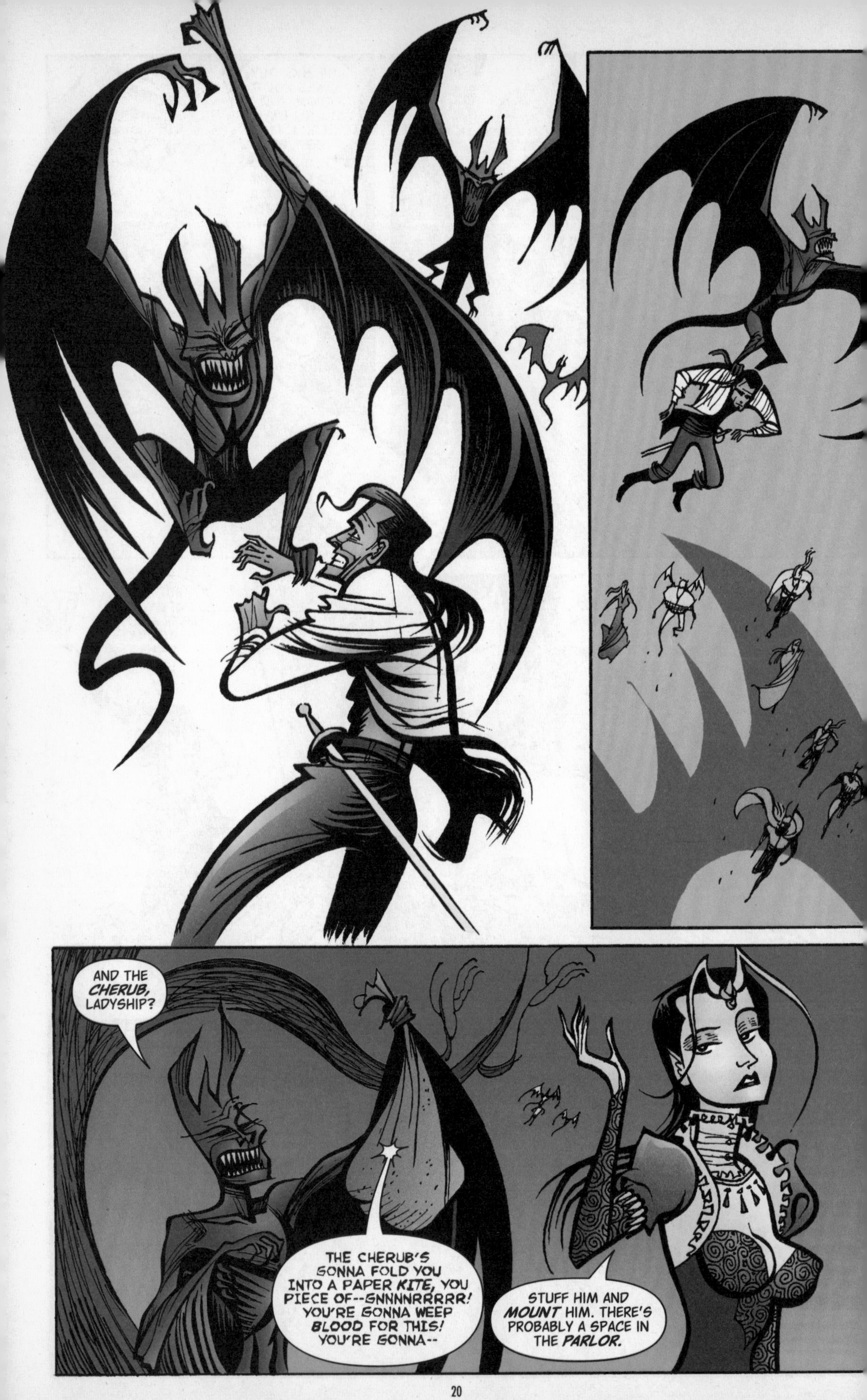
AND THE *CHERUB*, LADYSHIP?
THE CHERUB'S GONNA FOLD YOU INTO A PAPER *KITE*, YOU PIECE OF--GNNNNRRRRR! YOU'RE GONNA WEEP *BLOOD* FOR THIS! YOU'RE GONNA--
STUFF HIM AND *MOUNT* HIM. THERE'S PROBABLY A SPACE IN THE *PARLOR*.

"PAIN IS A *LADDER*, CHRISTOPHER RUDD, BY WHICH A PILGRIM SOUL MAY ASCEND TO *HEAVEN*."

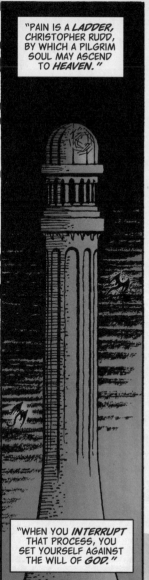

GOD IS *DEAD*.

A *COMMON* MISCONCEPTION. HE IS GONE, BUT HE WILL *RETURN*.

IN THE MEANTIME, WE EMBODY HIS *PLAN* AND HIS *AUTHORITY*.

THROUGH US, HIS GREAT *WORK* GOES ON.

THROUGH US, HIS *LOVE* ENFOLDS EVEN THOSE WHO TRY HARDEST TO REJECT IT.

NO. THE *TORTURE* YOU INFLICT HAS BECOME AN END IN ITSELF, REMIEL.

AND YOUR EXCESSES WILL BECOME *WORSE* AS YOUR FEAR GROWS. BECAUSE YOU'RE *ALONE* NOW, AND YOU'RE AFRAID THAT--

"WHEN YOU *INTERRUPT* THAT PROCESS, YOU SET YOURSELF AGAINST THE WILL OF *GOD*."

YOU ARE *MISTAKEN*.

YOU SPEAK ABOUT THINGS *FAR* BEYOND YOUR UNDER-STANDING.

SMACK

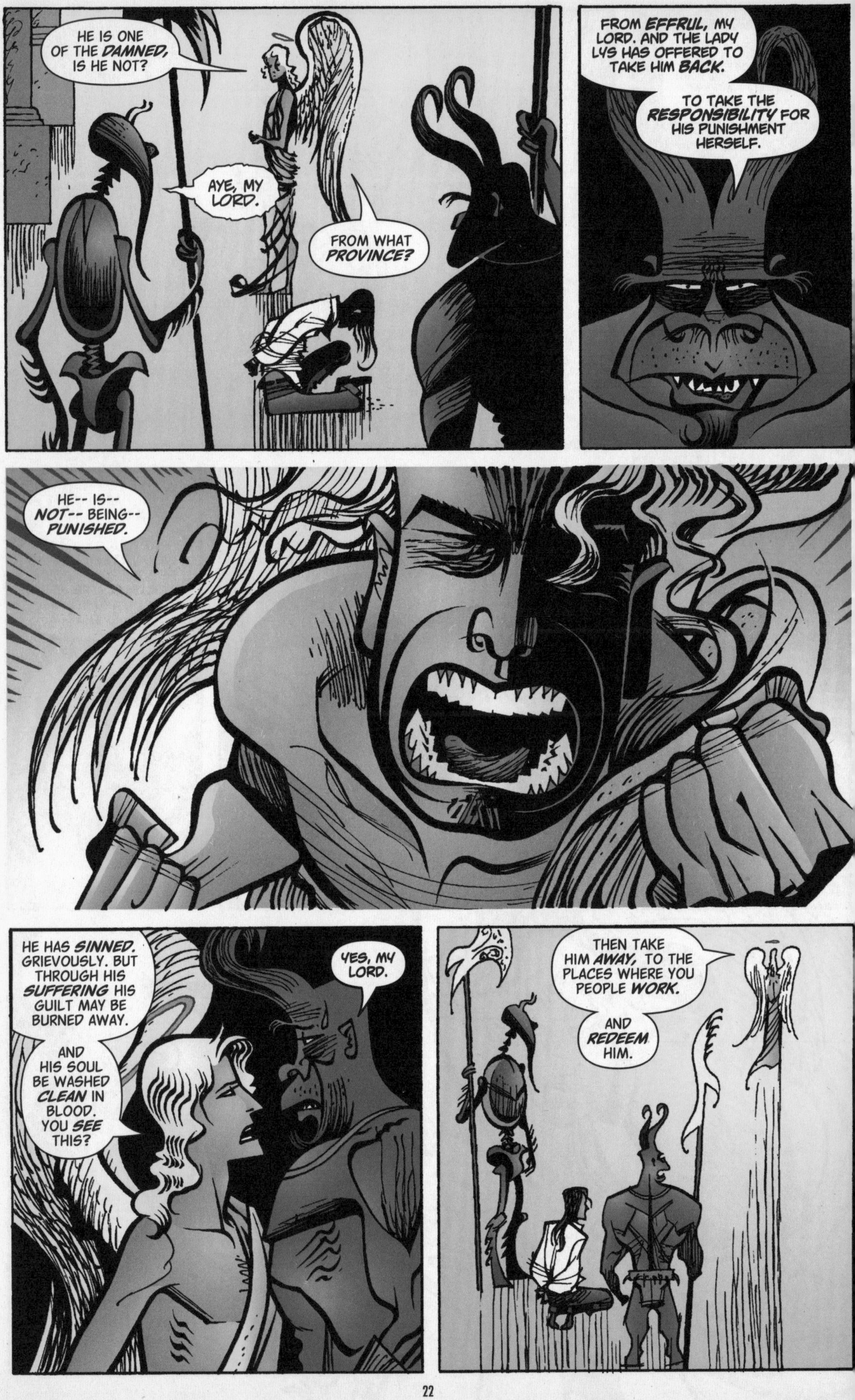
HE IS ONE OF THE DAMNED, IS HE NOT?
AYE, MY LORD.
FROM WHAT PROVINCE?
FROM EFFRUL, MY LORD. AND THE LADY LYS HAS OFFERED TO TAKE HIM BACK.
TO TAKE THE RESPONSIBILITY FOR HIS PUNISHMENT HERSELF.
HE-- IS-- NOT-- BEING-- PUNISHED.
HE HAS SINNED. GRIEVOUSLY. BUT THROUGH HIS SUFFERING HIS GUILT MAY BE BURNED AWAY.
YES, MY LORD.
AND HIS SOUL BE WASHED CLEAN IN BLOOD. YOU SEE THIS?
THEN TAKE HIM AWAY, TO THE PLACES WHERE YOU PEOPLE WORK.
AND REDEEM HIM.

IF THIS WERE A *MOVIE*, I THINK BY NOW WE'D HAVE REACHED THE END OF THE SECOND *ACT*.

HOW DO I *WHAT*?

I SAID, HOW DO YOU *STUFF* A CHERUB?

TAP TAP

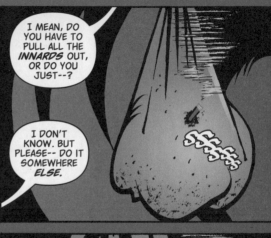

I MEAN, DO YOU HAVE TO PULL ALL THE *INNARDS* OUT, OR DO YOU JUST--?

I DON'T KNOW. BUT PLEASE-- DO IT SOMEWHERE *ELSE*.

THE PART WHERE EVERYTHING SEEMS *MAXIMALLY* FUCKED UP.

ONLY IT *ISN'T*. BECAUSE OUR CHARISMATIC *HERO* HAS GOT A PLAN.

WELL, COULD YOU LEND ME SOME *TOOLS*?

A *SPATULA*, OR--

...

SSSSSSSSS

AAAURGH!

BUT BECAUSE I'M MORE CHARISMATIC THAN *MOST*, I FIGURE IT'S OKAY IF I JUST MAKE IT *UP* AS I GO ALONG.

TO SWITCH METAPHORS, IT WAS THE BOTTOM OF THE *NINTH* AND THE BASES WERE TOWERING INFERNOS. WHO'S GONNA STEP UP TO THE *PLATE*?

WHO *ELSE*?

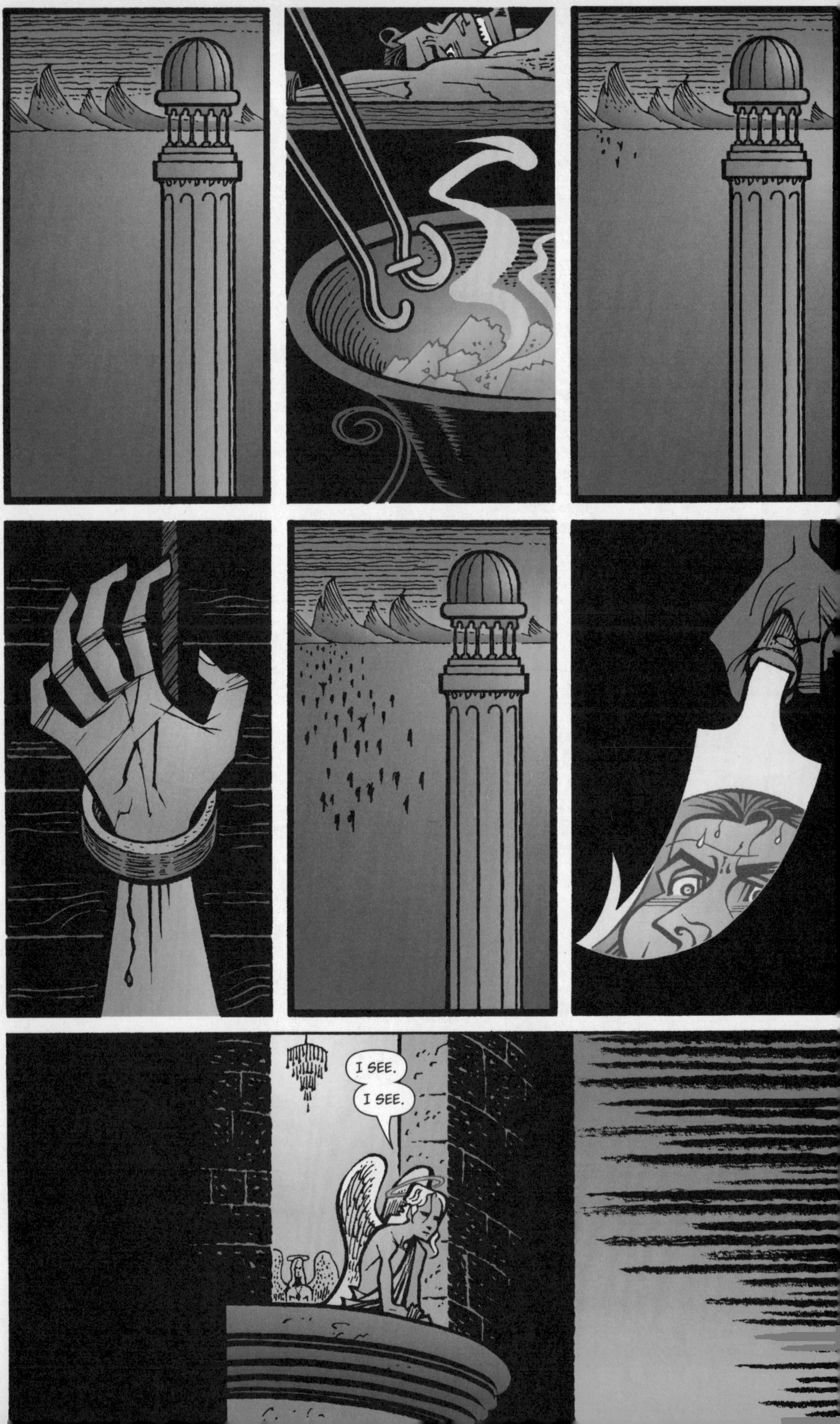
I SEE.
I SEE.

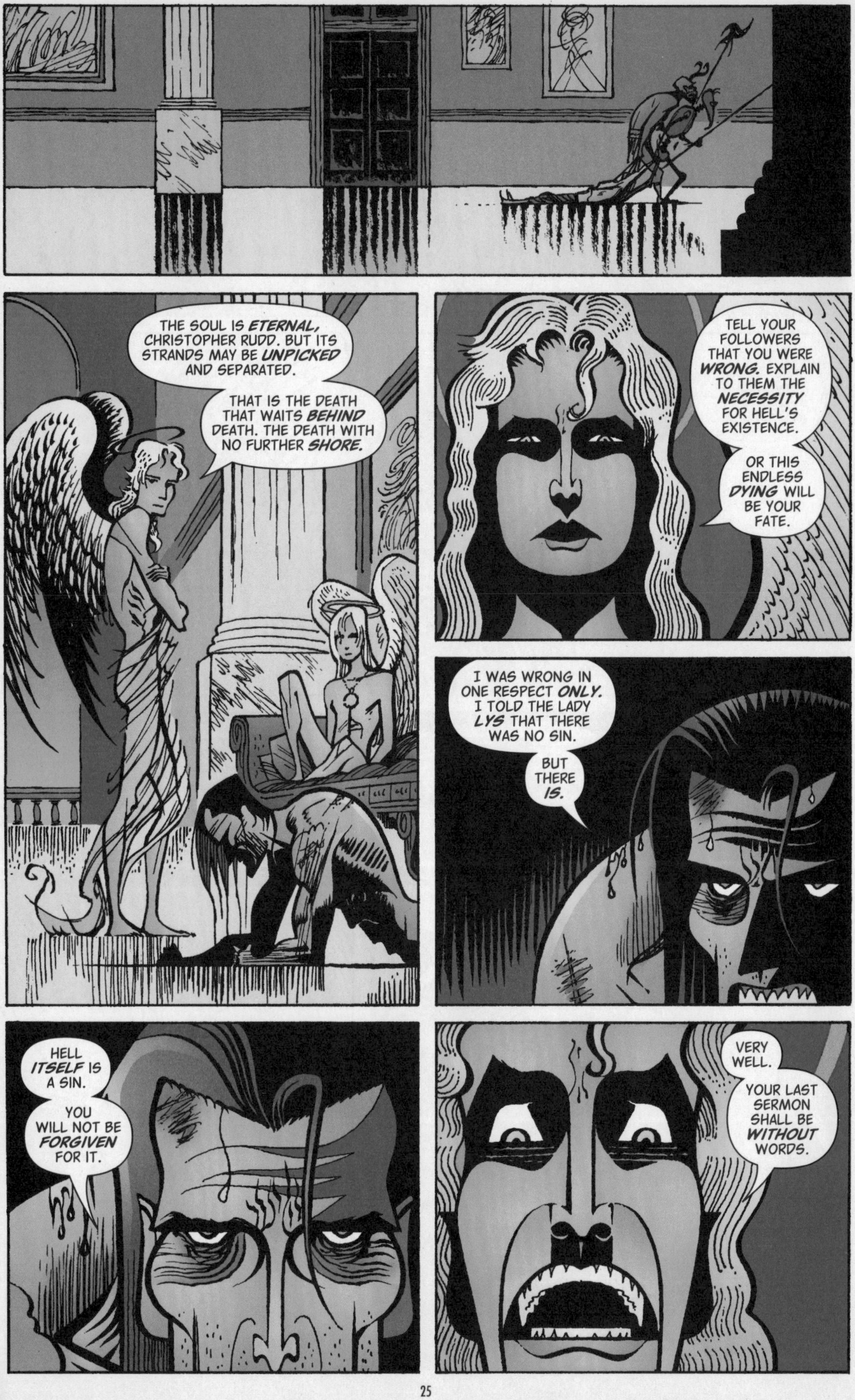
THE SOUL IS *ETERNAL,* CHRISTOPHER RUDD. BUT ITS STRANDS MAY BE *UNPICKED* AND SEPARATED.
THAT IS THE DEATH THAT WAITS *BEHIND* DEATH. THE DEATH WITH NO FURTHER *SHORE.*
TELL YOUR FOLLOWERS THAT YOU WERE *WRONG.* EXPLAIN TO THEM THE *NECESSITY* FOR HELL'S EXISTENCE.
OR THIS ENDLESS *DYING* WILL BE YOUR FATE.
I WAS WRONG IN ONE RESPECT *ONLY.* I TOLD THE LADY *LYS* THAT THERE WAS NO SIN.
BUT THERE *IS.*
HELL *ITSELF* IS A SIN.
YOU WILL NOT BE *FORGIVEN* FOR IT.
VERY WELL.
YOUR LAST SERMON SHALL BE *WITHOUT* WORDS.

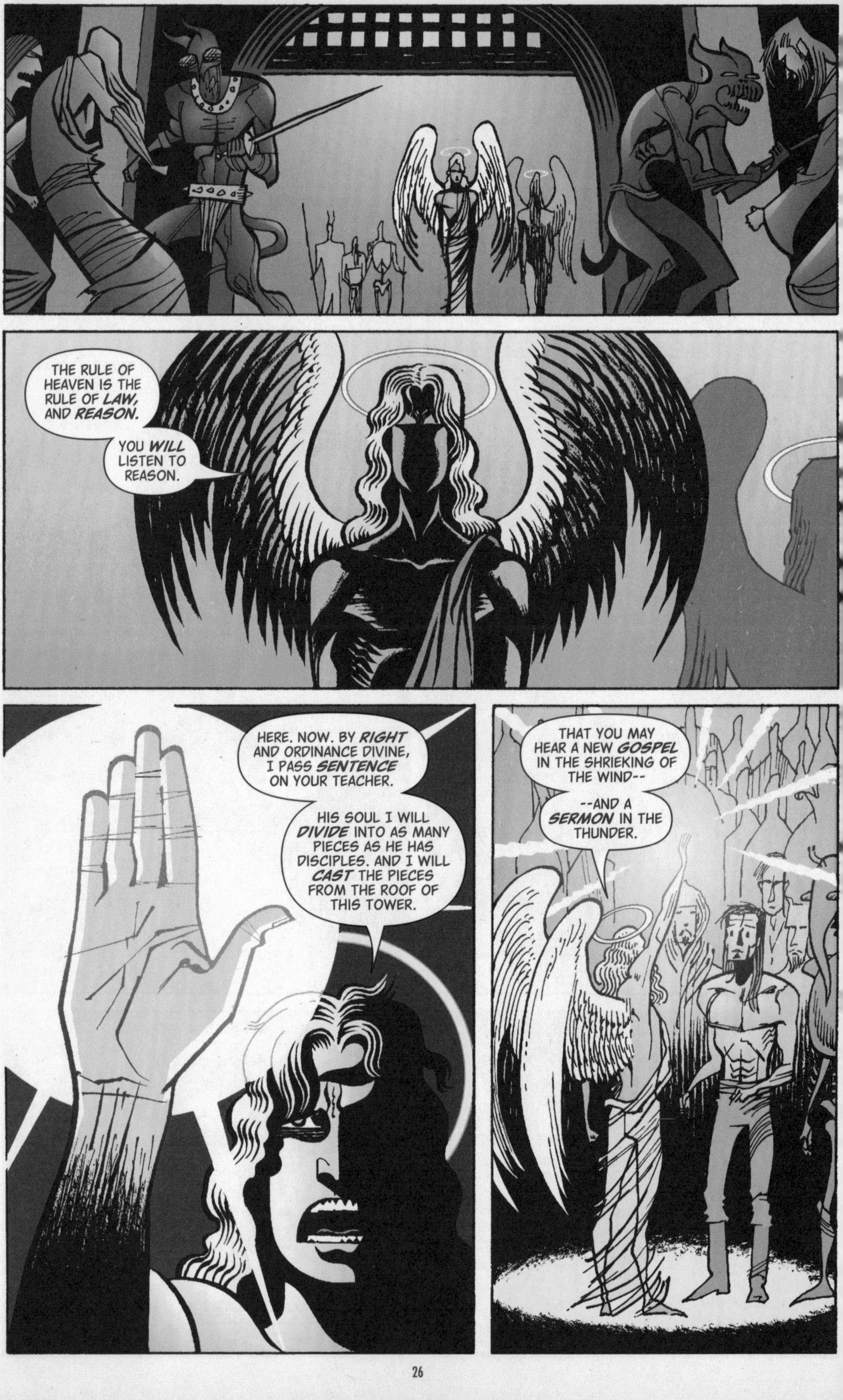
THE RULE OF HEAVEN IS THE RULE OF LAW, AND REASON.
YOU WILL LISTEN TO REASON.
HERE. NOW. BY RIGHT AND ORDINANCE DIVINE, I PASS SENTENCE ON YOUR TEACHER.
HIS SOUL I WILL DIVIDE INTO AS MANY PIECES AS HE HAS DISCIPLES. AND I WILL CAST THE PIECES FROM THE ROOF OF THIS TOWER.
THAT YOU MAY HEAR A NEW GOSPEL IN THE SHRIEKING OF THE WIND--
--AND A SERMON IN THE THUNDER.

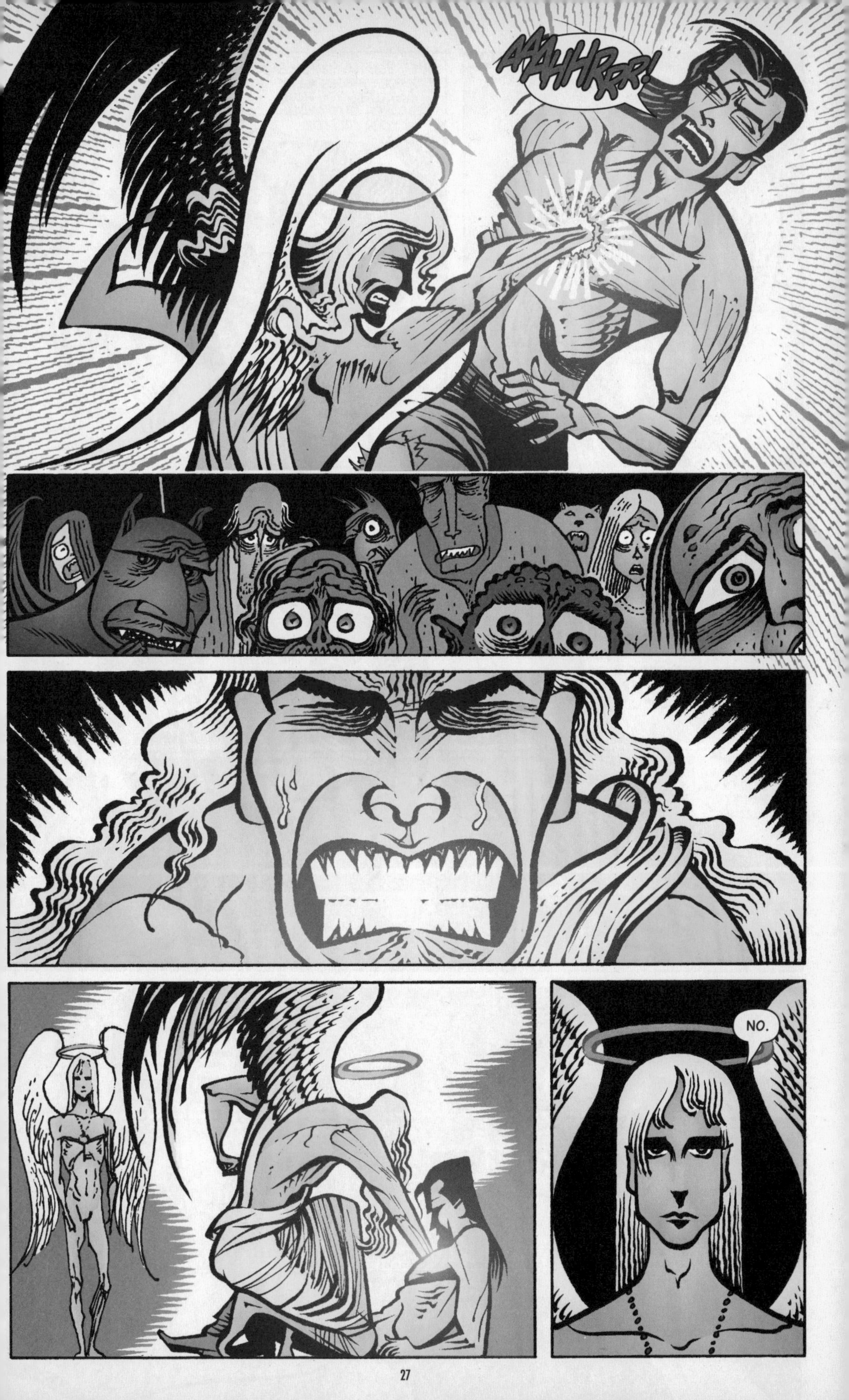
AAAHHRRRR!
NO.

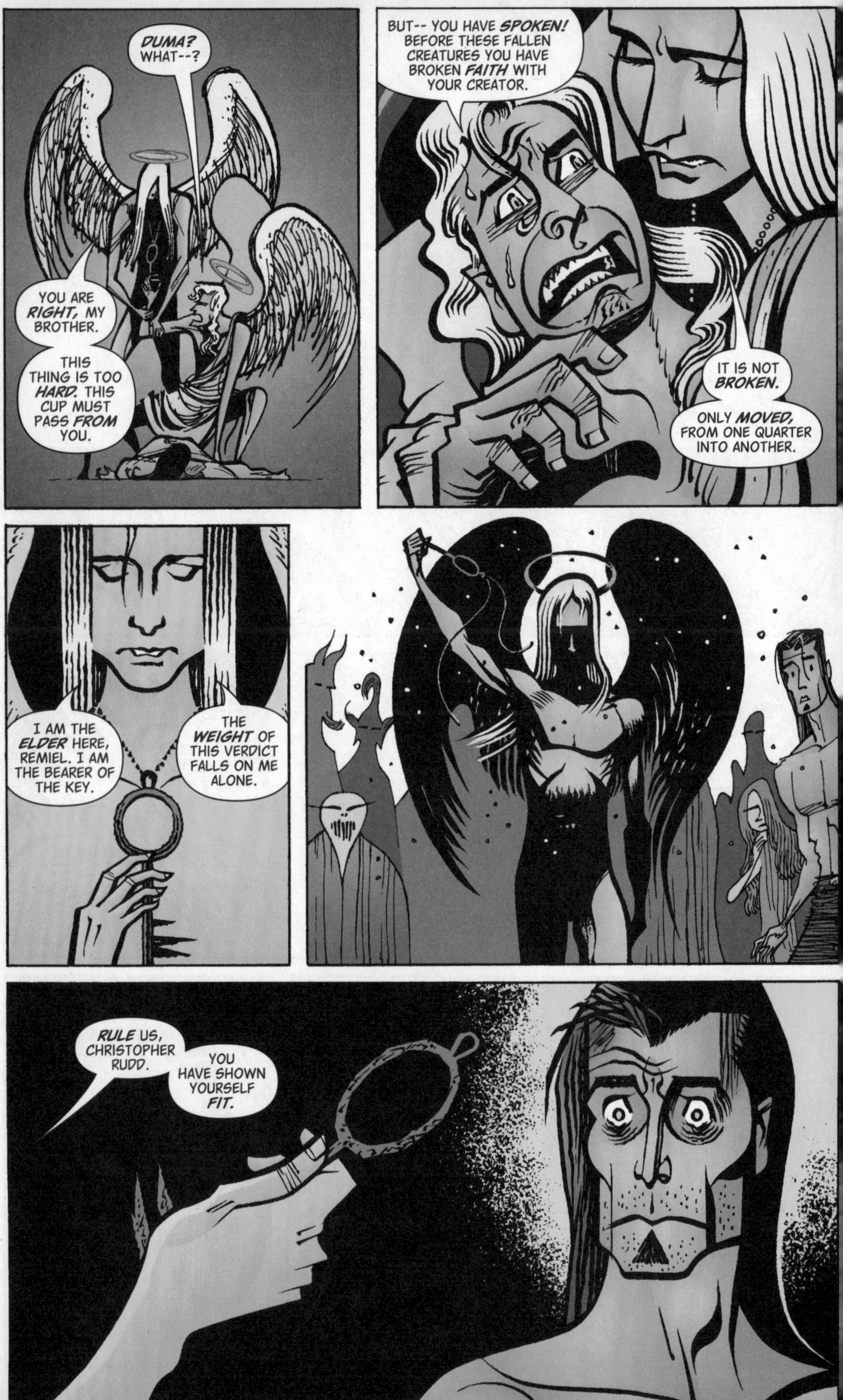
DUMA? WHAT--?
YOU ARE RIGHT, MY BROTHER.
THIS THING IS TOO HARD. THIS CUP MUST PASS FROM YOU.
BUT-- YOU HAVE SPOKEN! BEFORE THESE FALLEN CREATURES YOU HAVE BROKEN FAITH WITH YOUR CREATOR.
IT IS NOT BROKEN.
ONLY MOVED, FROM ONE QUARTER INTO ANOTHER.
I AM THE ELDER HERE, REMIEL. I AM THE BEARER OF THE KEY.
THE WEIGHT OF THIS VERDICT FALLS ON ME ALONE.
RULE US, CHRISTOPHER RUDD.
YOU HAVE SHOWN YOURSELF FIT.

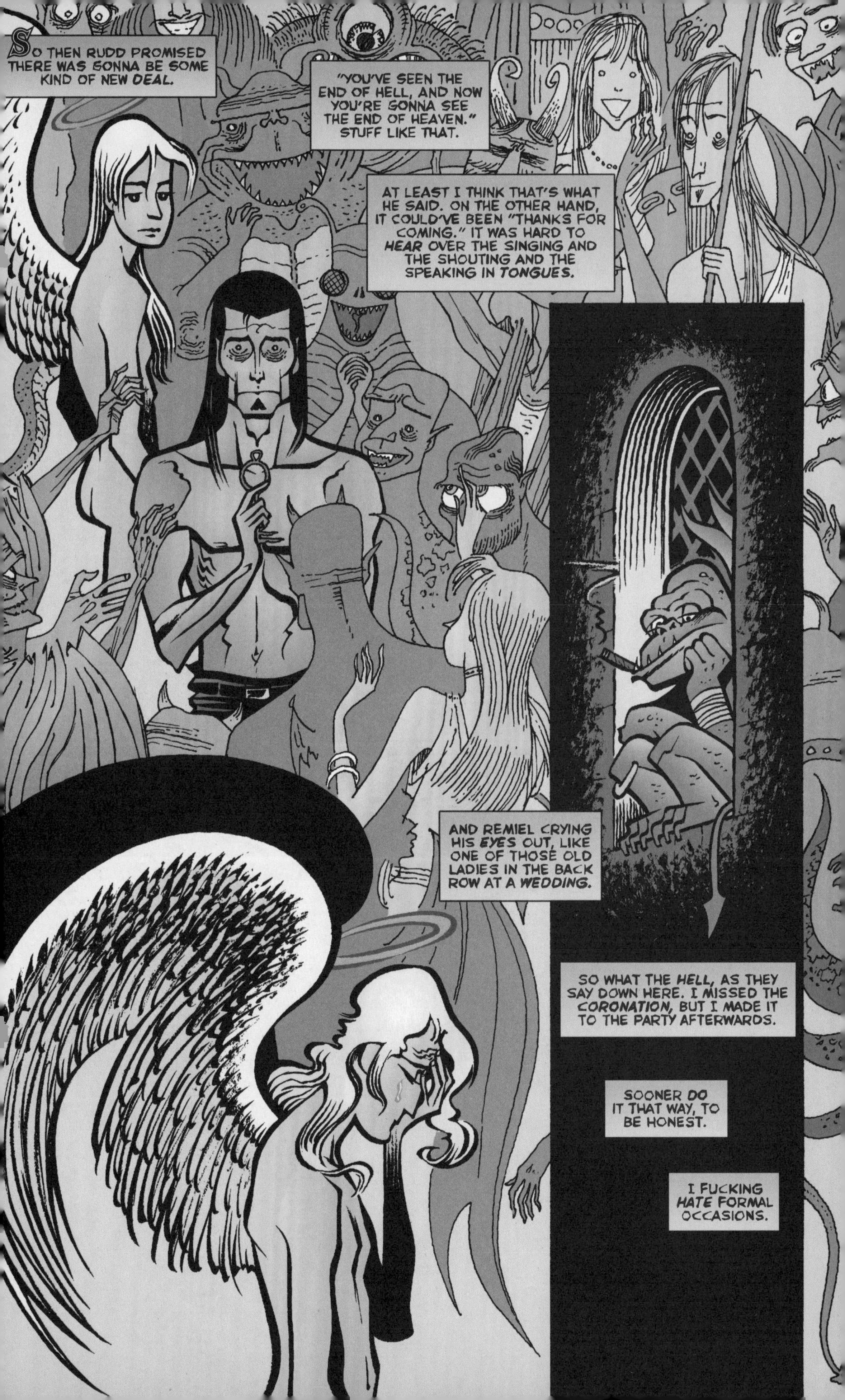
SO THEN RUDD PROMISED THERE WAS GONNA BE SOME KIND OF NEW DEAL.
"YOU'VE SEEN THE END OF HELL, AND NOW YOU'RE GONNA SEE THE END OF HEAVEN." STUFF LIKE THAT.
AT LEAST I THINK THAT'S WHAT HE SAID. ON THE OTHER HAND, IT COULD'VE BEEN "THANKS FOR COMING." IT WAS HARD TO HEAR OVER THE SINGING AND THE SHOUTING AND THE SPEAKING IN TONGUES.
AND REMIEL CRYING HIS EYES OUT, LIKE ONE OF THOSE OLD LADIES IN THE BACK ROW AT A WEDDING.
SO WHAT THE HELL, AS THEY SAY DOWN HERE. I MISSED THE CORONATION, BUT I MADE IT TO THE PARTY AFTERWARDS.
SOONER DO IT THAT WAY, TO BE HONEST.
I FUCKING HATE FORMAL OCCASIONS.

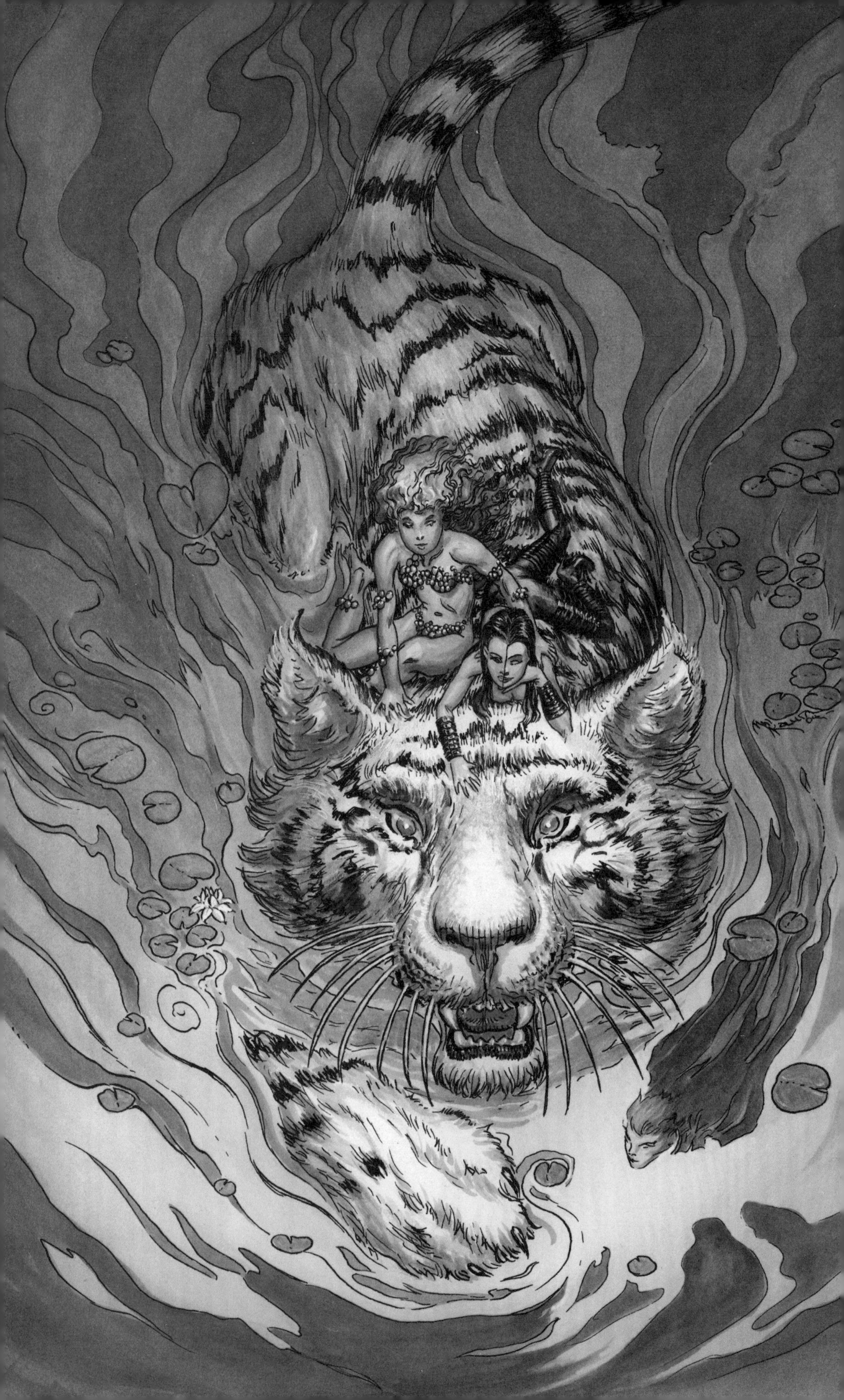

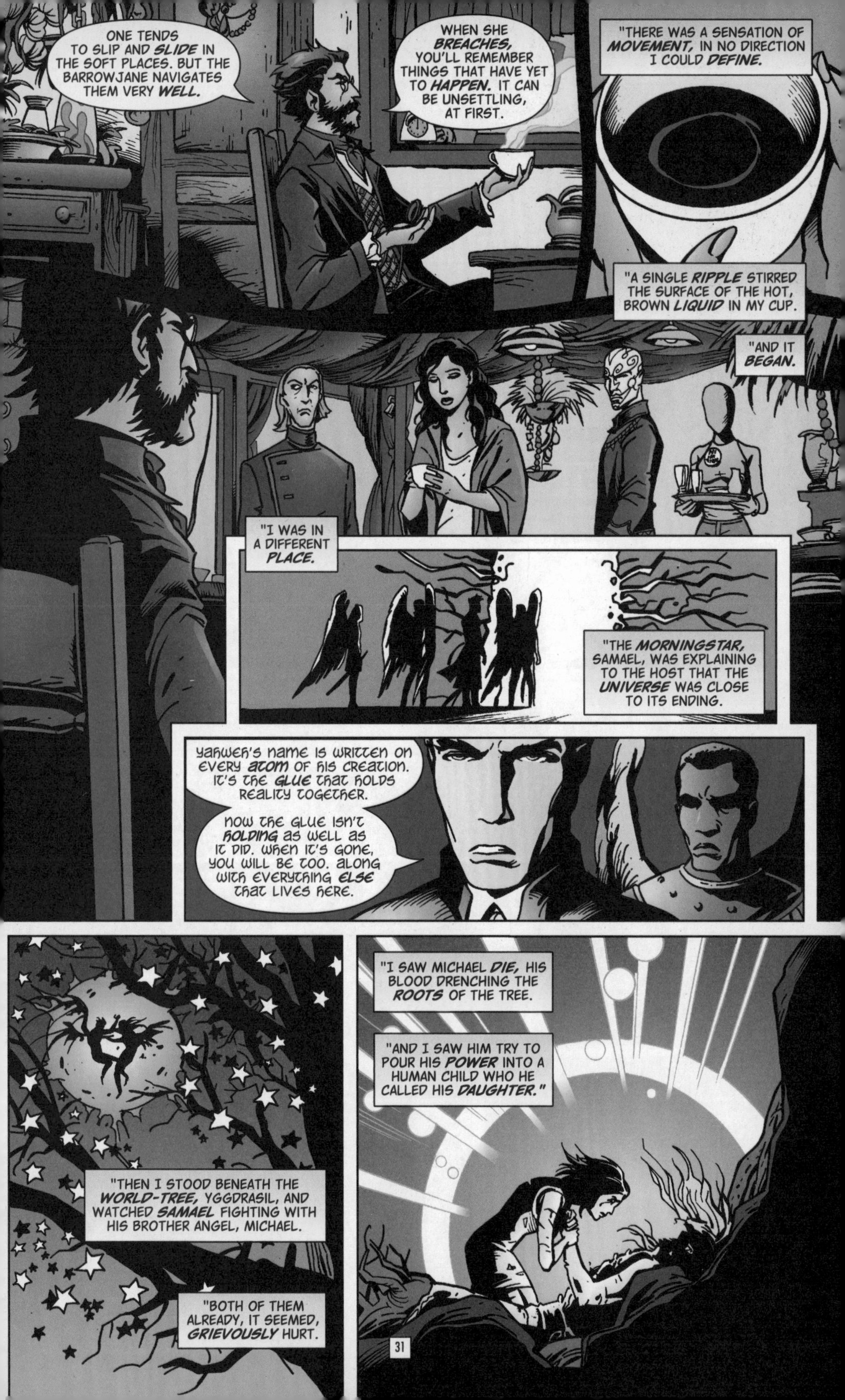
ONE TENDS TO SLIP AND SLIDE IN THE SOFT PLACES. BUT THE BARROWJANE NAVIGATES THEM VERY WELL.
WHEN SHE BREACHES, YOU'LL REMEMBER THINGS THAT HAVE YET TO HAPPEN. IT CAN BE UNSETTLING, AT FIRST.
"THERE WAS A SENSATION OF MOVEMENT, IN NO DIRECTION I COULD DEFINE.
"A SINGLE RIPPLE STIRRED THE SURFACE OF THE HOT, BROWN LIQUID IN MY CUP.
"AND IT BEGAN.
"I WAS IN A DIFFERENT PLACE.
"THE MORNINGSTAR, SAMAEL, WAS EXPLAINING TO THE HOST THAT THE UNIVERSE WAS CLOSE TO ITS ENDING.
YAHWEH'S NAME IS WRITTEN ON EVERY ATOM OF HIS CREATION. IT'S THE GLUE THAT HOLDS REALITY TOGETHER.
NOW THE GLUE ISN'T HOLDING AS WELL AS IT DID. WHEN IT'S GONE, YOU WILL BE TOO. ALONG WITH EVERYTHING ELSE THAT LIVES HERE.
"THEN I STOOD BENEATH THE WORLD-TREE, YGGDRASIL, AND WATCHED SAMAEL FIGHTING WITH HIS BROTHER ANGEL, MICHAEL.
"BOTH OF THEM ALREADY, IT SEEMED, GRIEVOUSLY HURT.
"I SAW MICHAEL DIE, HIS BLOOD DRENCHING THE ROOTS OF THE TREE.
"AND I SAW HIM TRY TO POUR HIS POWER INTO A HUMAN CHILD WHO HE CALLED HIS DAUGHTER."

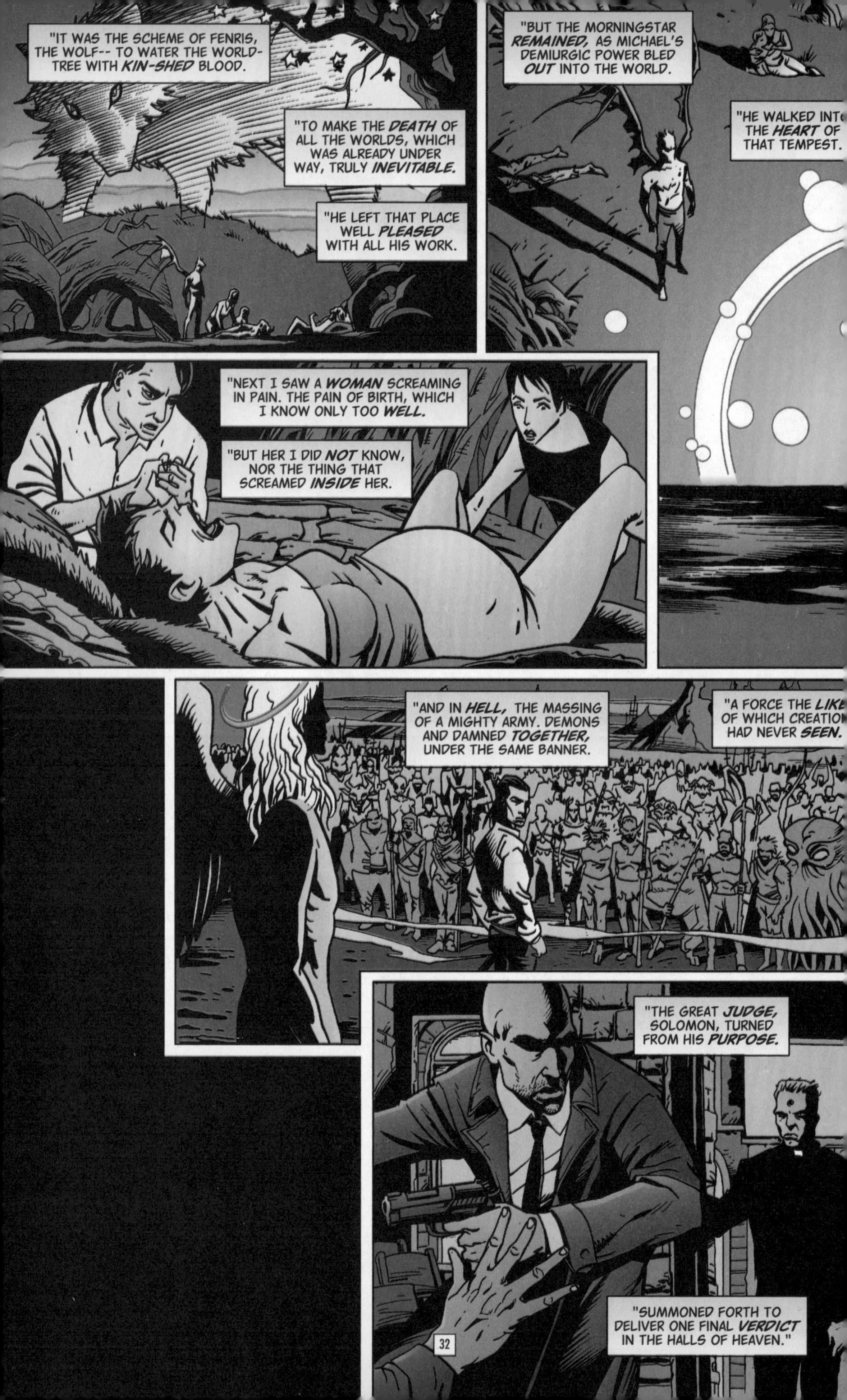

"IT WAS THE SCHEME OF FENRIS, THE WOLF-- TO WATER THE WORLD-TREE WITH KIN-SHED BLOOD.
"TO MAKE THE DEATH OF ALL THE WORLDS, WHICH WAS ALREADY UNDER WAY, TRULY INEVITABLE.
"HE LEFT THAT PLACE WELL PLEASED WITH ALL HIS WORK.
"BUT THE MORNINGSTAR REMAINED, AS MICHAEL'S DEMIURGIC POWER BLED OUT INTO THE WORLD.
"HE WALKED INT THE HEART OF THAT TEMPEST.
"NEXT I SAW A WOMAN SCREAMING IN PAIN. THE PAIN OF BIRTH, WHICH I KNOW ONLY TOO WELL.
"BUT HER I DID NOT KNOW, NOR THE THING THAT SCREAMED INSIDE HER.
"AND IN HELL, THE MASSING OF A MIGHTY ARMY. DEMONS AND DAMNED TOGETHER, UNDER THE SAME BANNER.
"A FORCE THE LIKE OF WHICH CREATIO HAD NEVER SEEN.
"THE GREAT JUDGE, SOLOMON, TURNED FROM HIS PURPOSE.
"SUMMONED FORTH TO DELIVER ONE FINAL VERDICT IN THE HALLS OF HEAVEN."

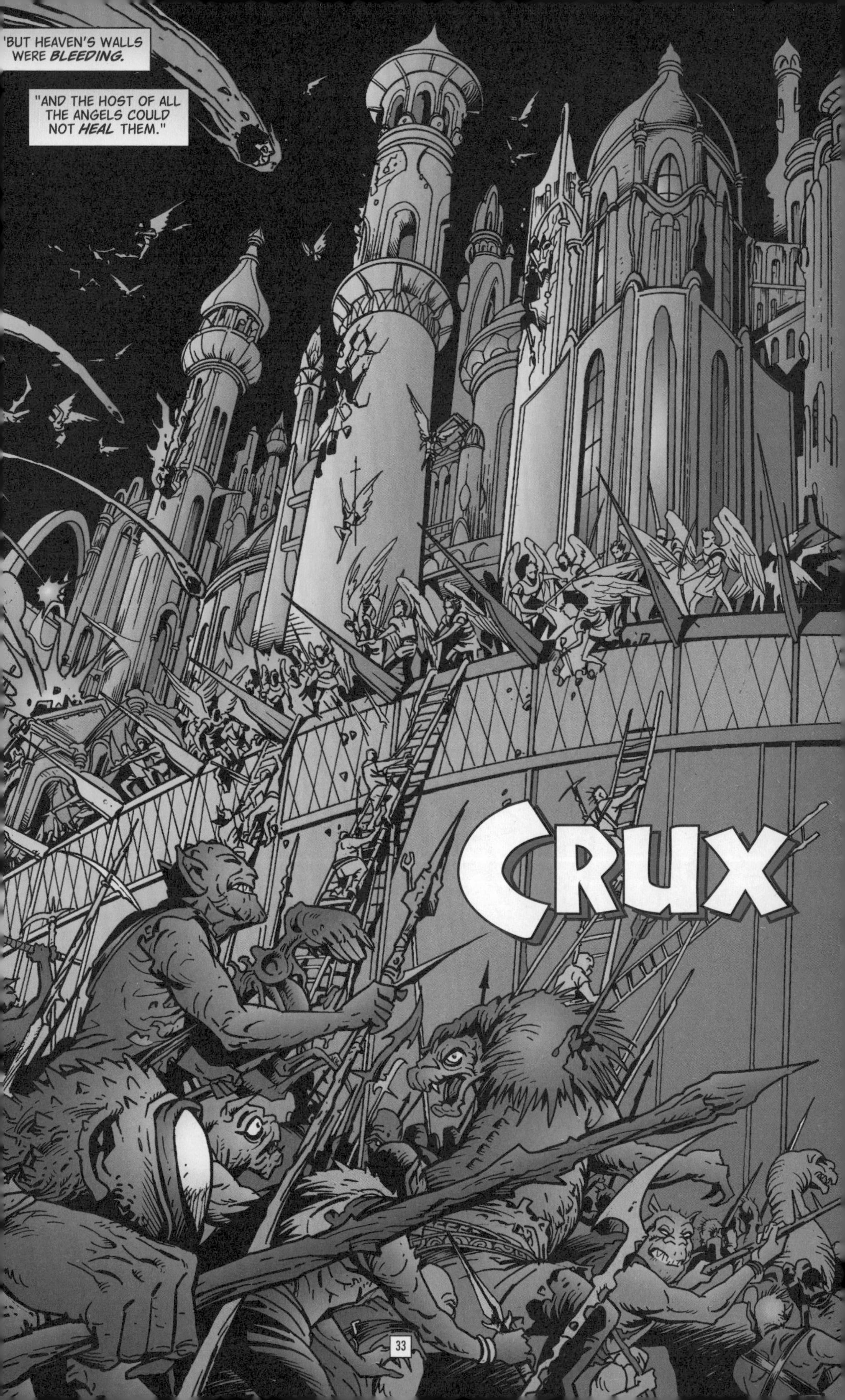
'BUT HEAVEN'S WALLS WERE BLEEDING.
"AND THE HOST OF ALL THE ANGELS COULD NOT HEAL THEM."
CRUX

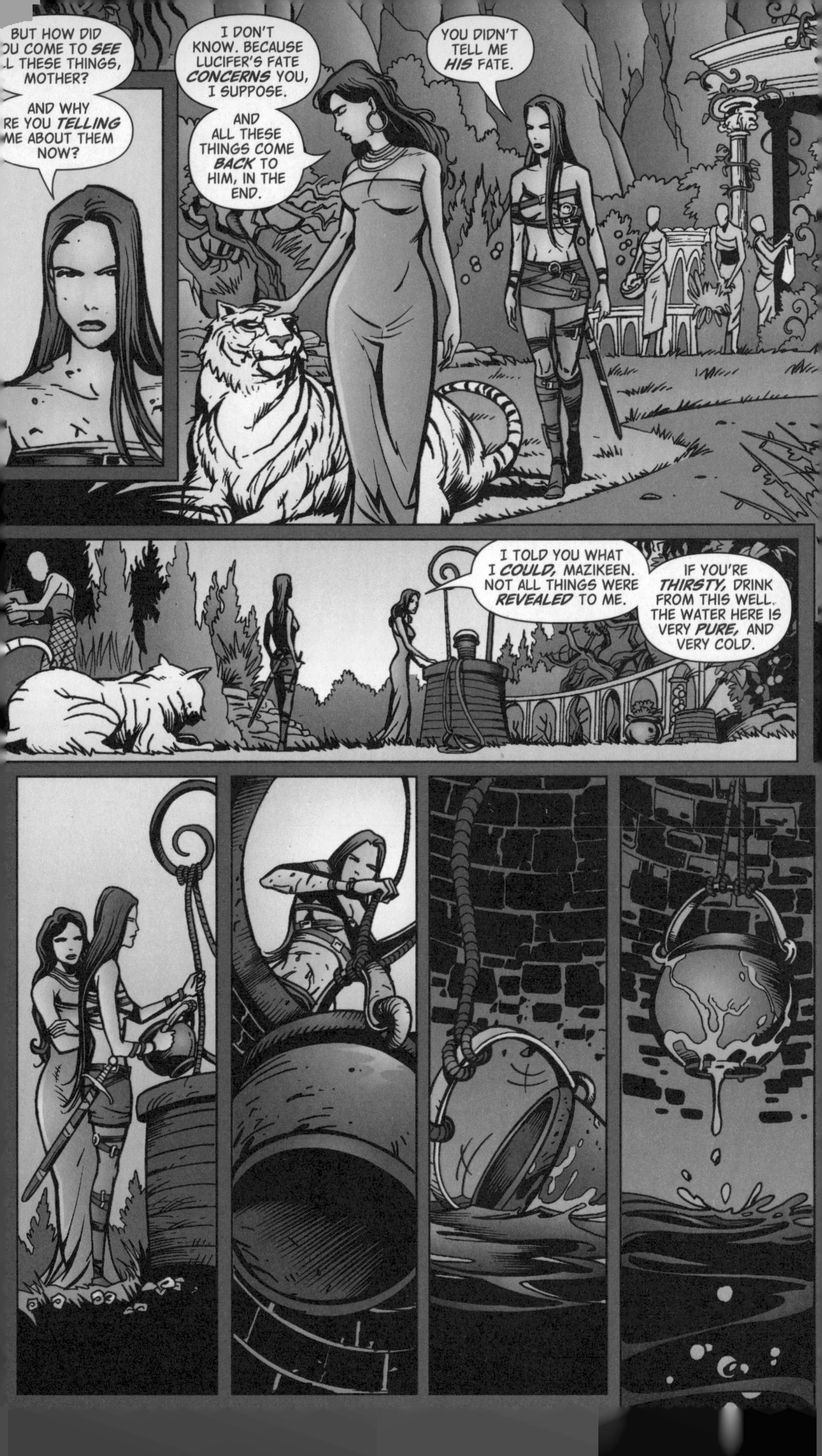
BUT HOW DID OU COME TO SEE L THESE THINGS, MOTHER?
AND WHY RE YOU TELLING ME ABOUT THEM NOW?
I DON'T KNOW. BECAUSE LUCIFER'S FATE CONCERNS YOU, I SUPPOSE.
AND ALL THESE THINGS COME BACK TO HIM, IN THE END.
YOU DIDN'T TELL ME HIS FATE.
I TOLD YOU WHAT I COULD, MAZIKEEN. NOT ALL THINGS WERE REVEALED TO ME.
IF YOU'RE THIRSTY, DRINK FROM THIS WELL. THE WATER HERE IS VERY PURE, AND VERY COLD.

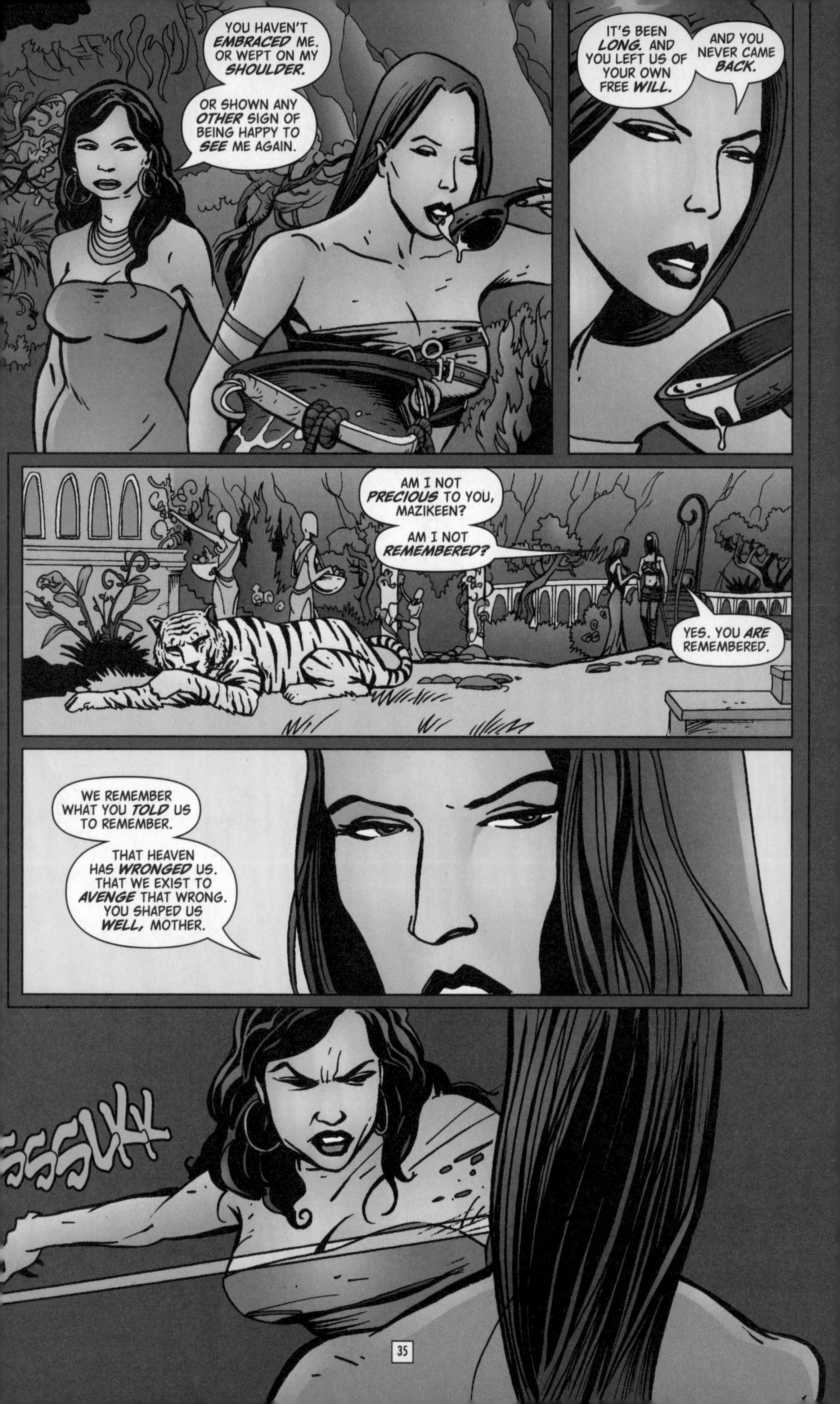

YOU HAVEN'T EMBRACED ME. OR WEPT ON MY SHOULDER.
OR SHOWN ANY OTHER SIGN OF BEING HAPPY TO SEE ME AGAIN.
IT'S BEEN LONG. AND YOU LEFT US OF YOUR OWN FREE WILL.
AND YOU NEVER CAME BACK.
AM I NOT PRECIOUS TO YOU, MAZIKEEN?
AM I NOT REMEMBERED?
YES. YOU ARE REMEMBERED.
WE REMEMBER WHAT YOU TOLD US TO REMEMBER.
THAT HEAVEN HAS WRONGED US. THAT WE EXIST TO AVENGE THAT WRONG. YOU SHAPED US WELL, MOTHER.

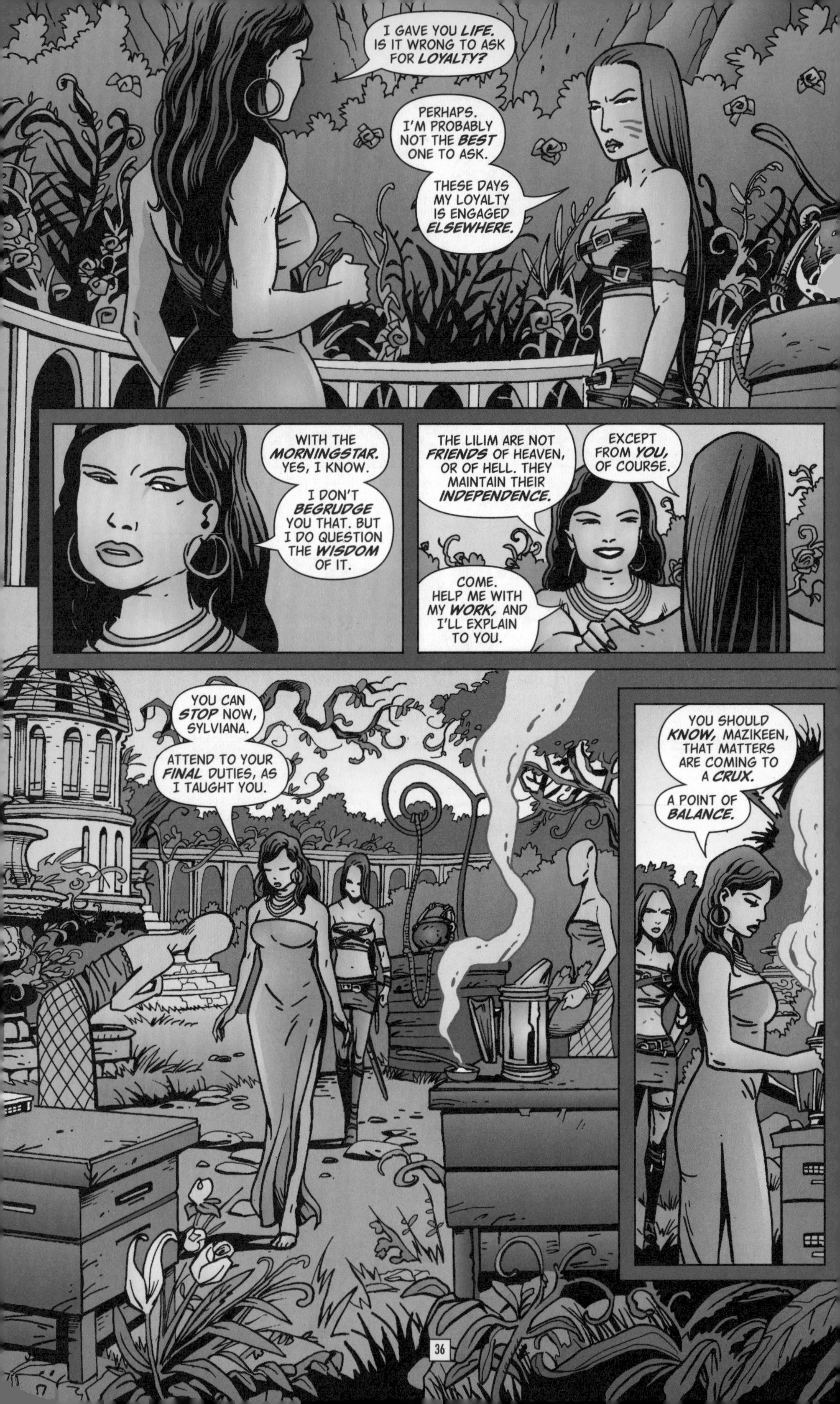

I GAVE YOU LIFE. IS IT WRONG TO ASK FOR LOYALTY?
PERHAPS. I'M PROBABLY NOT THE BEST ONE TO ASK.
THESE DAYS MY LOYALTY IS ENGAGED ELSEWHERE.
WITH THE MORNINGSTAR. YES, I KNOW.
I DON'T BEGRUDGE YOU THAT. BUT I DO QUESTION THE WISDOM OF IT.
THE LILIM ARE NOT FRIENDS OF HEAVEN, OR OF HELL. THEY MAINTAIN THEIR INDEPENDENCE.
EXCEPT FROM YOU, OF COURSE.
COME. HELP ME WITH MY WORK, AND I'LL EXPLAIN TO YOU.
YOU CAN STOP NOW, SYLVIANA.
ATTEND TO YOUR FINAL DUTIES, AS I TAUGHT YOU.
YOU SHOULD KNOW, MAZIKEEN, THAT MATTERS ARE COMING TO A CRUX.
A POINT OF BALANCE.

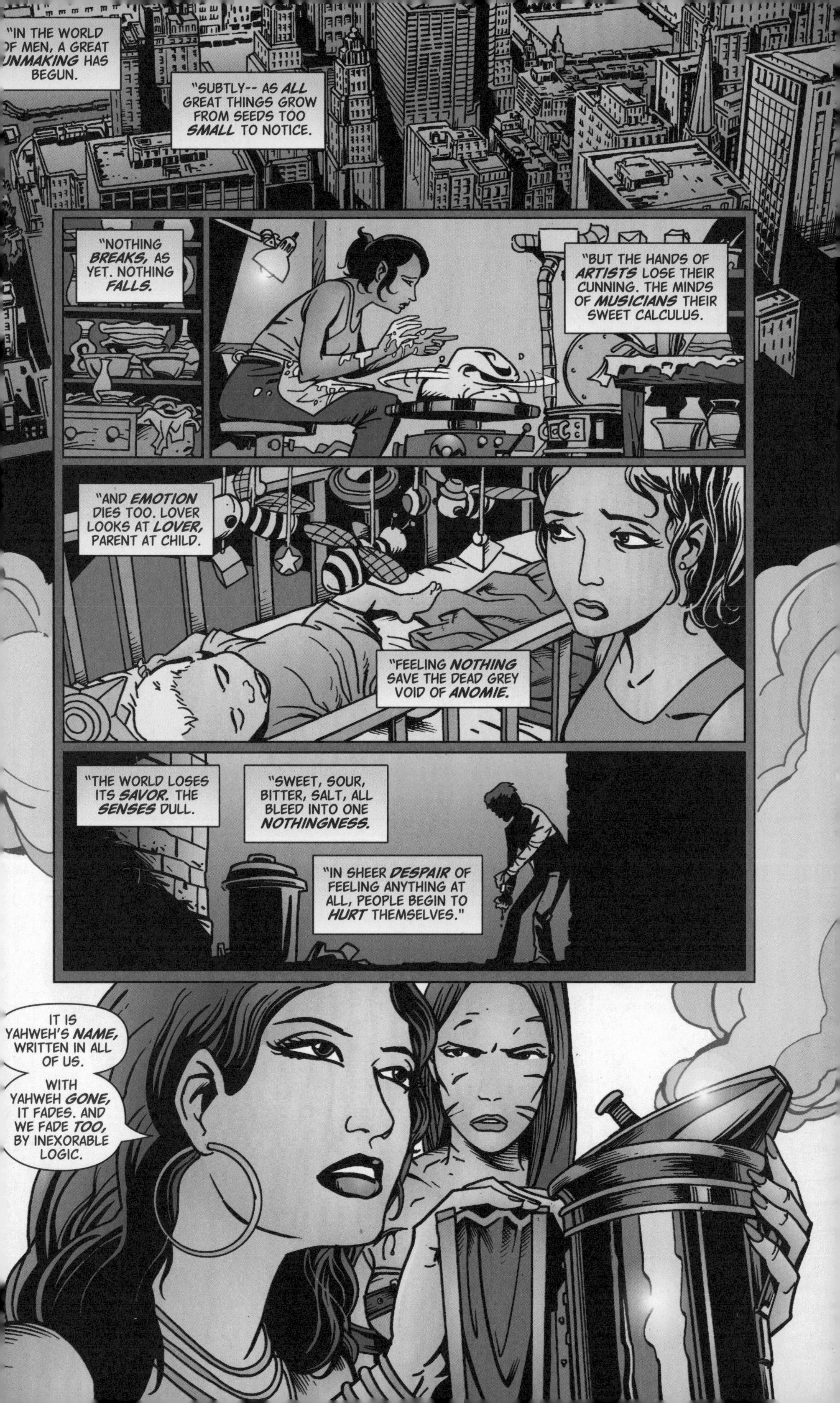
"IN THE WORLD OF MEN, A GREAT UNMAKING HAS BEGUN.
"SUBTLY-- AS ALL GREAT THINGS GROW FROM SEEDS TOO SMALL TO NOTICE.
"NOTHING BREAKS, AS YET. NOTHING FALLS.
"BUT THE HANDS OF ARTISTS LOSE THEIR CUNNING. THE MINDS OF MUSICIANS THEIR SWEET CALCULUS.
"AND EMOTION DIES TOO. LOVER LOOKS AT LOVER, PARENT AT CHILD.
"FEELING NOTHING SAVE THE DEAD GREY VOID OF ANOMIE.
"THE WORLD LOSES ITS SAVOR. THE SENSES DULL.
"SWEET, SOUR, BITTER, SALT, ALL BLEED INTO ONE NOTHINGNESS.
"IN SHEER DESPAIR OF FEELING ANYTHING AT ALL, PEOPLE BEGIN TO HURT THEMSELVES."
IT IS YAHWEH'S NAME, WRITTEN IN ALL OF US.
WITH YAHWEH GONE, IT FADES. AND WE FADE TOO, BY INEXORABLE LOGIC.

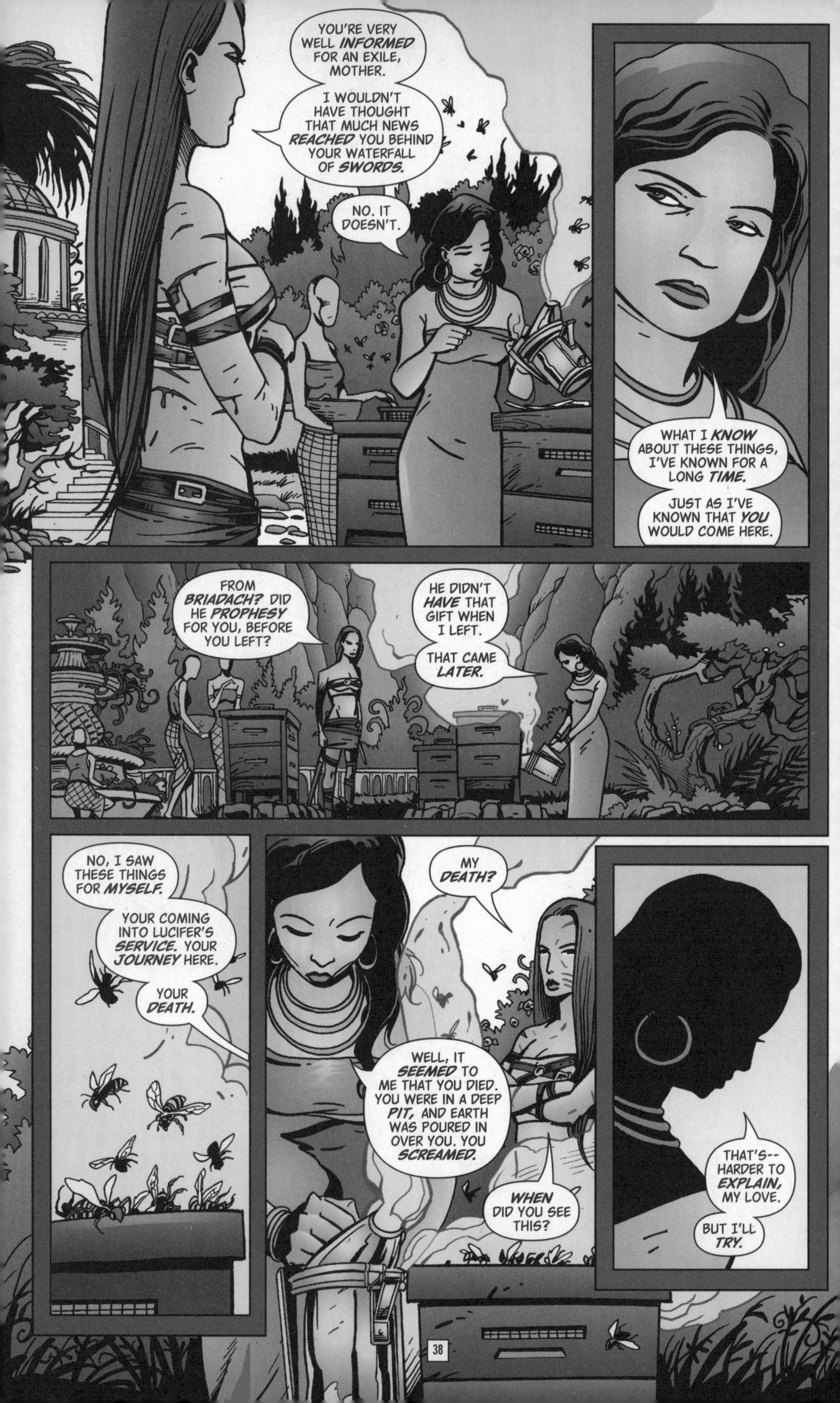

YOU'RE VERY WELL INFORMED FOR AN EXILE, MOTHER.
I WOULDN'T HAVE THOUGHT THAT MUCH NEWS REACHED YOU BEHIND YOUR WATERFALL OF SWORDS.
NO. IT DOESN'T.
WHAT I KNOW ABOUT THESE THINGS, I'VE KNOWN FOR A LONG TIME.
JUST AS I'VE KNOWN THAT YOU WOULD COME HERE.
FROM BRIADACH? DID HE PROPHESY FOR YOU, BEFORE YOU LEFT?
HE DIDN'T HAVE THAT GIFT WHEN I LEFT.
THAT CAME LATER.
NO, I SAW THESE THINGS FOR MYSELF.
YOUR COMING INTO LUCIFER'S SERVICE. YOUR JOURNEY HERE.
YOUR DEATH.
MY DEATH?
WELL, IT SEEMED TO ME THAT YOU DIED. YOU WERE IN A DEEP PIT, AND EARTH WAS POURED IN OVER YOU. YOU SCREAMED.
WHEN DID YOU SEE THIS?
THAT'S-- HARDER TO EXPLAIN, MY LOVE.
BUT I'LL TRY.

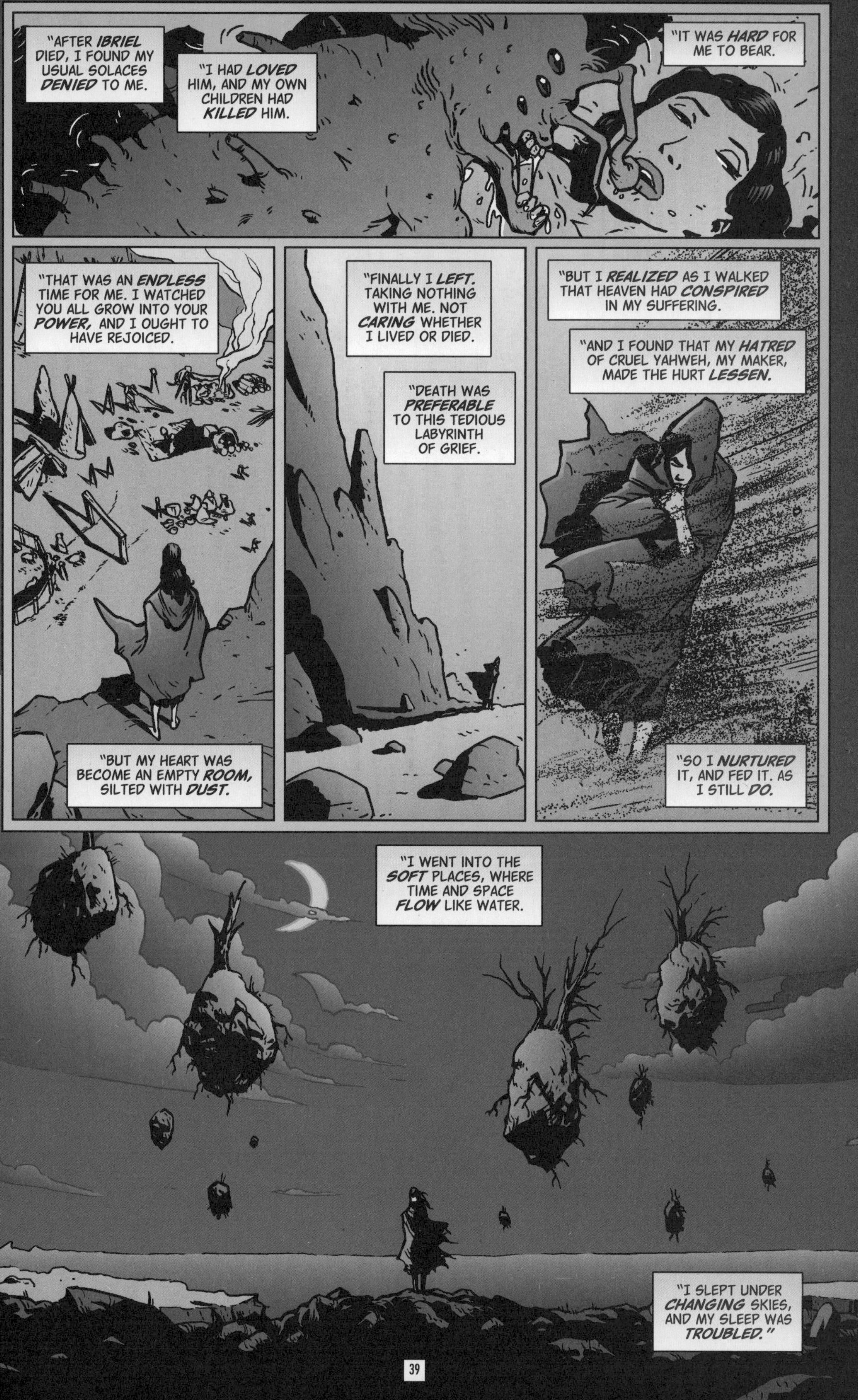
"AFTER IBRIEL DIED, I FOUND MY USUAL SOLACES DENIED TO ME.
"I HAD LOVED HIM, AND MY OWN CHILDREN HAD KILLED HIM.
"IT WAS HARD FOR ME TO BEAR.
"THAT WAS AN ENDLESS TIME FOR ME. I WATCHED YOU ALL GROW INTO YOUR POWER, AND I OUGHT TO HAVE REJOICED.
"BUT MY HEART WAS BECOME AN EMPTY ROOM, SILTED WITH DUST.
"FINALLY I LEFT. TAKING NOTHING WITH ME. NOT CARING WHETHER I LIVED OR DIED.
"DEATH WAS PREFERABLE TO THIS TEDIOUS LABYRINTH OF GRIEF.
"BUT I REALIZED AS I WALKED THAT HEAVEN HAD CONSPIRED IN MY SUFFERING.
"AND I FOUND THAT MY HATRED OF CRUEL YAHWEH, MY MAKER, MADE THE HURT LESSEN.
"SO I NURTURED IT, AND FED IT. AS I STILL DO.
"I WENT INTO THE SOFT PLACES, WHERE TIME AND SPACE FLOW LIKE WATER.
"I SLEPT UNDER CHANGING SKIES, AND MY SLEEP WAS TROUBLED."

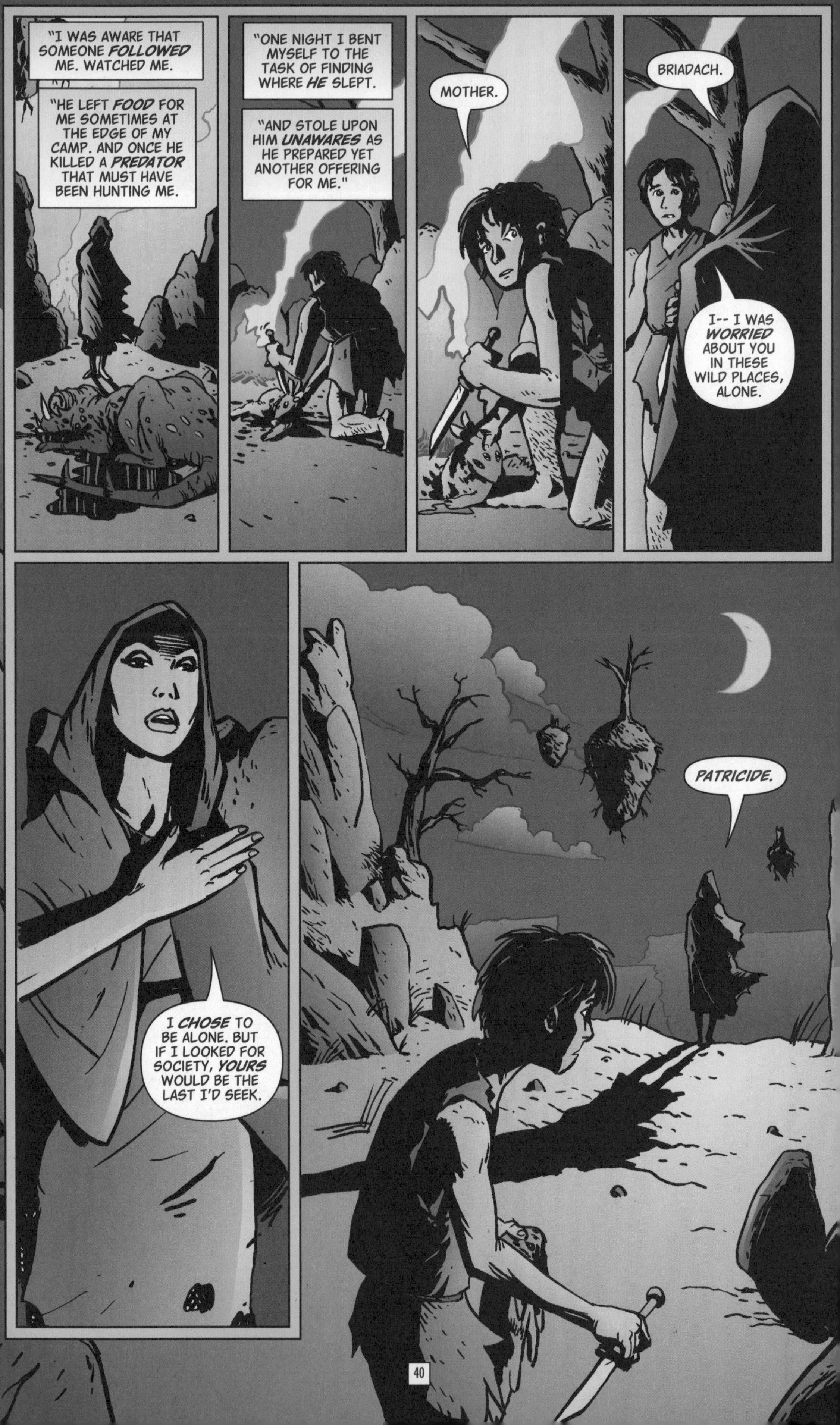
"I WAS AWARE THAT SOMEONE FOLLOWED ME. WATCHED ME.
"HE LEFT FOOD FOR ME SOMETIMES AT THE EDGE OF MY CAMP. AND ONCE HE KILLED A PREDATOR THAT MUST HAVE BEEN HUNTING ME.
"ONE NIGHT I BENT MYSELF TO THE TASK OF FINDING WHERE HE SLEPT.
"AND STOLE UPON HIM UNAWARES AS HE PREPARED YET ANOTHER OFFERING FOR ME."
MOTHER.
BRIADACH.
I-- I WAS WORRIED ABOUT YOU IN THESE WILD PLACES, ALONE.
I CHOSE TO BE ALONE. BUT IF I LOOKED FOR SOCIETY, YOURS WOULD BE THE LAST I'D SEEK.
PATRICIDE.

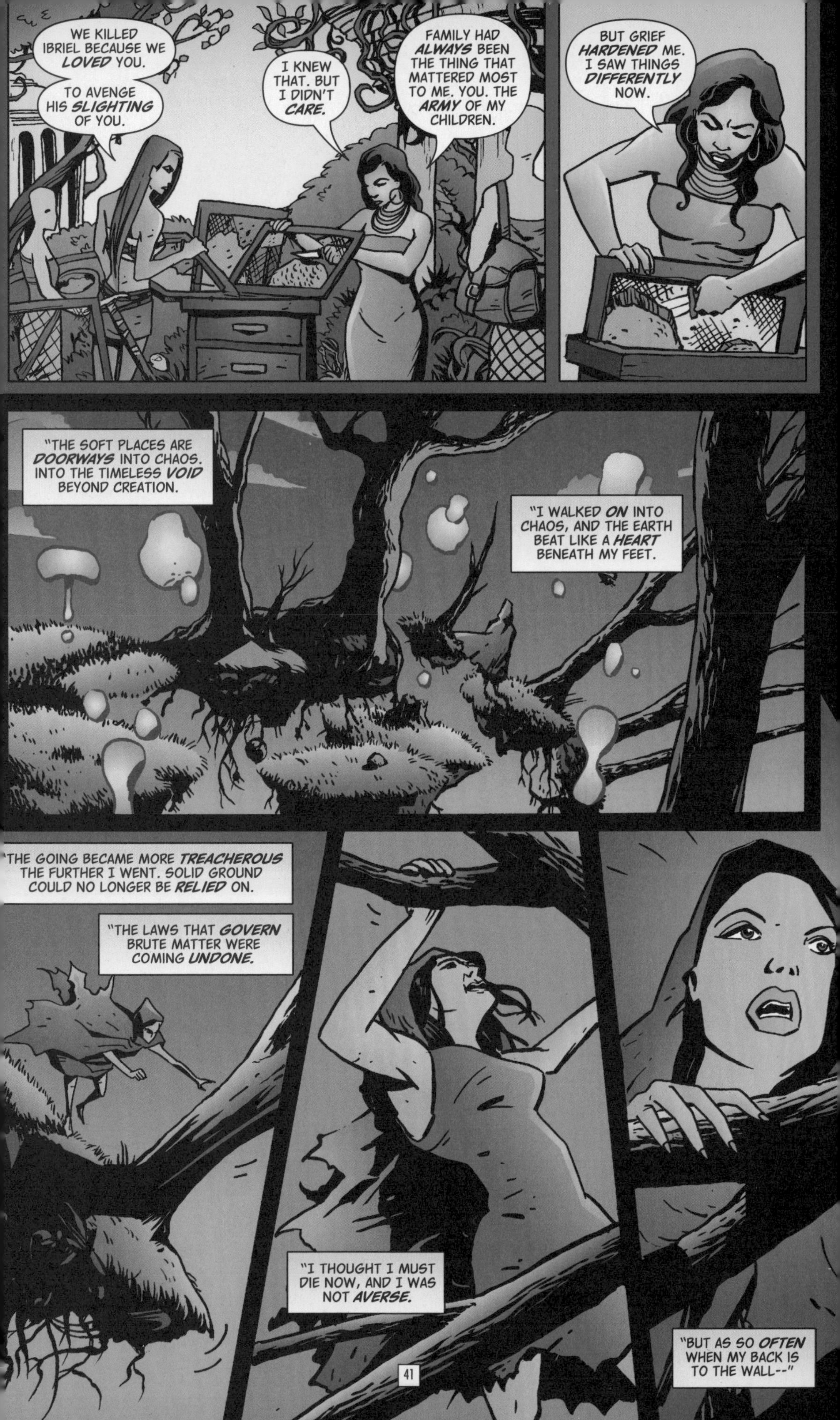
WE KILLED IBRIEL BECAUSE WE LOVED YOU.
TO AVENGE HIS SLIGHTING OF YOU.
I KNEW THAT. BUT I DIDN'T CARE.
FAMILY HAD ALWAYS BEEN THE THING THAT MATTERED MOST TO ME. YOU. THE ARMY OF MY CHILDREN.
BUT GRIEF HARDENED ME. I SAW THINGS DIFFERENTLY NOW.
"THE SOFT PLACES ARE DOORWAYS INTO CHAOS. INTO THE TIMELESS VOID BEYOND CREATION.
"I WALKED ON INTO CHAOS, AND THE EARTH BEAT LIKE A HEART BENEATH MY FEET.
"THE GOING BECAME MORE TREACHEROUS THE FURTHER I WENT. SOLID GROUND COULD NO LONGER BE RELIED ON.
"THE LAWS THAT GOVERN BRUTE MATTER WERE COMING UNDONE.
"I THOUGHT I MUST DIE NOW, AND I WAS NOT AVERSE.
"BUT AS SO OFTEN WHEN MY BACK IS TO THE WALL--"

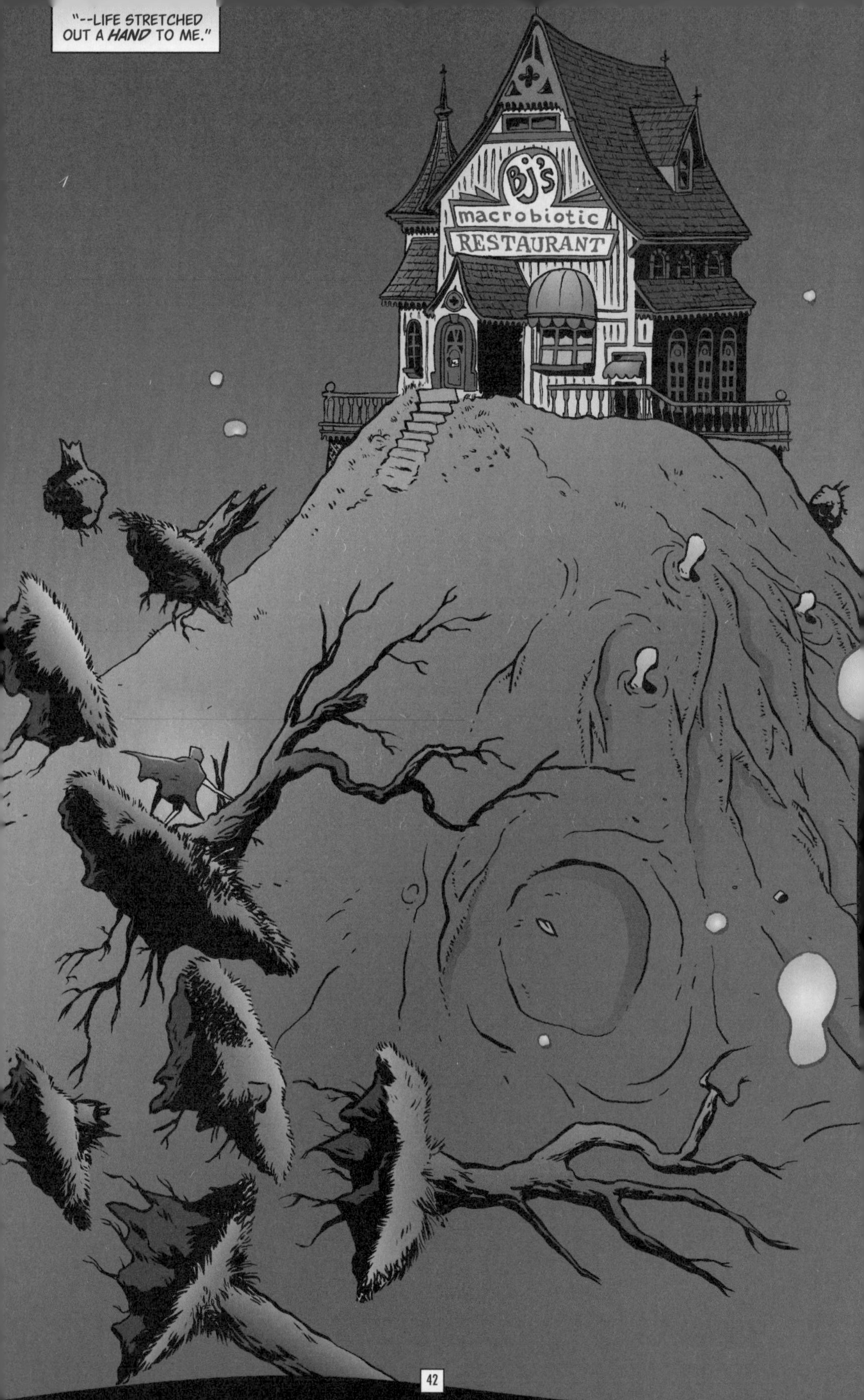
"--LIFE STRETCHED OUT A *HAND* TO ME."
BJ's
macrobiotic
RESTAURANT

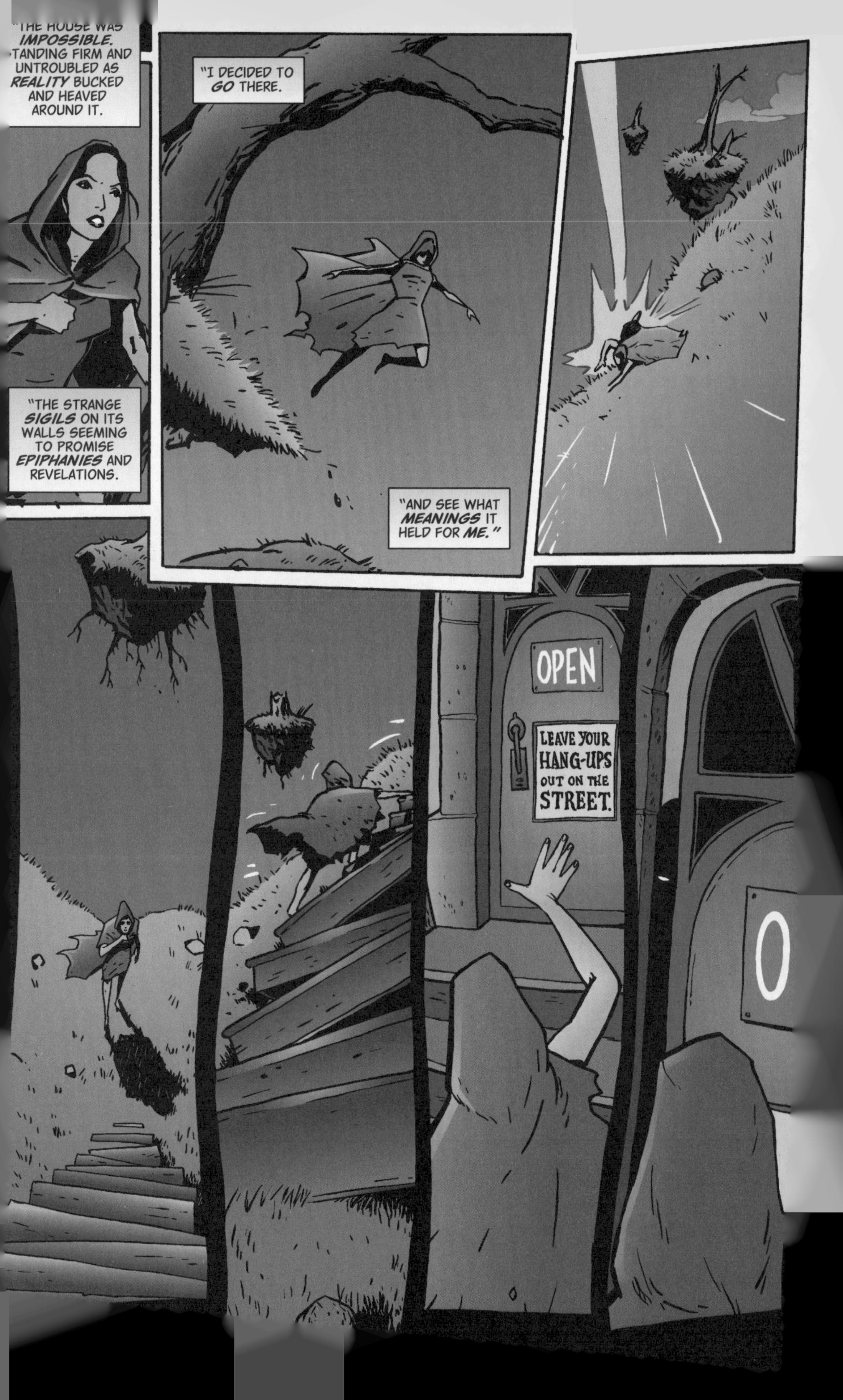
"THE HOUSE WAS IMPOSSIBLE. STANDING FIRM AND UNTROUBLED AS REALITY BUCKED AND HEAVED AROUND IT.
"THE STRANGE SIGILS ON ITS WALLS SEEMING TO PROMISE EPIPHANIES AND REVELATIONS.
"I DECIDED TO GO THERE.
"AND SEE WHAT MEANINGS IT HELD FOR ME."
OPEN
LEAVE YOUR HANG-UPS OUT ON THE STREET.

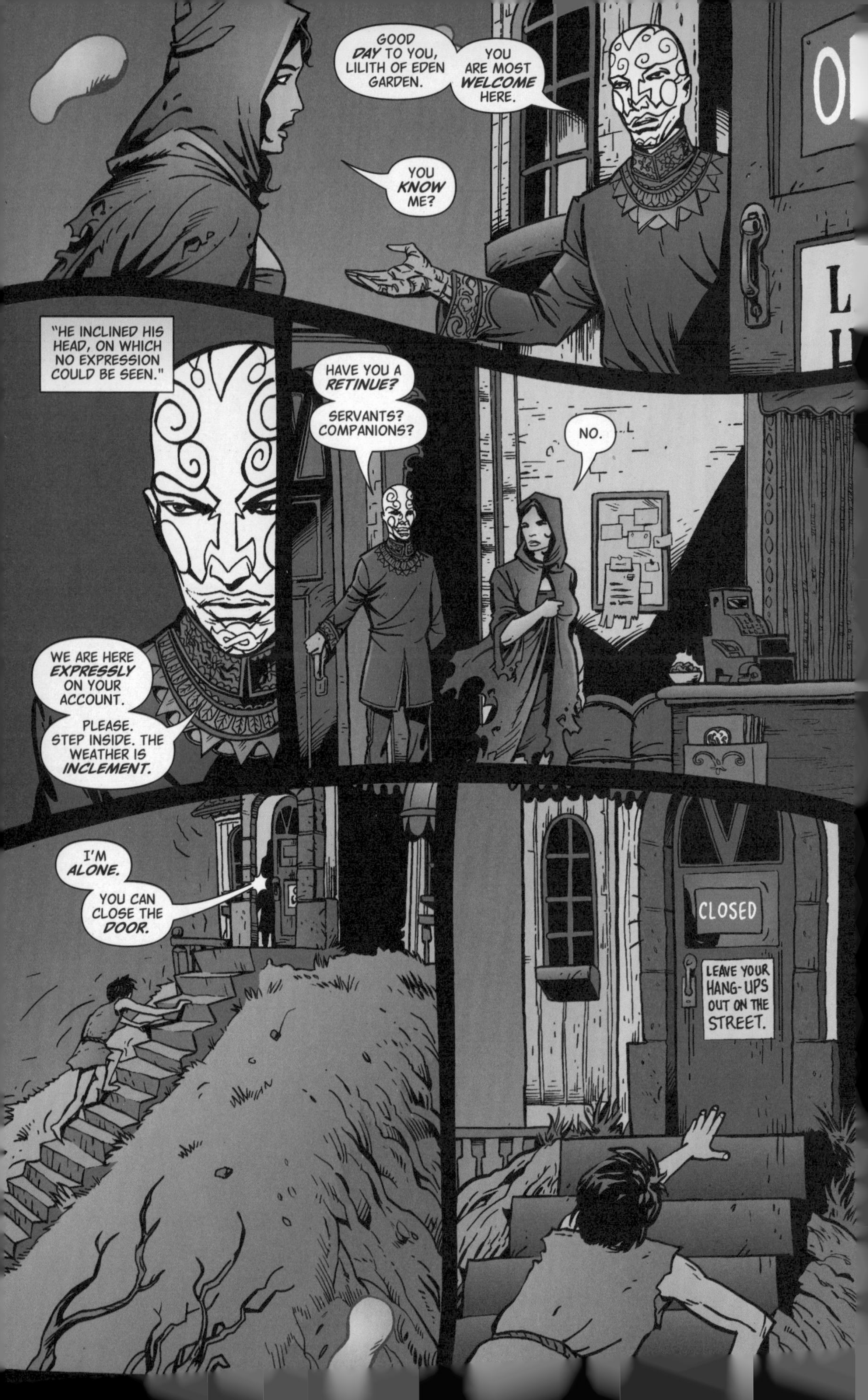
GOOD DAY TO YOU, LILITH OF EDEN GARDEN.
YOU ARE MOST WELCOME HERE.
YOU KNOW ME?
"HE INCLINED HIS HEAD, ON WHICH NO EXPRESSION COULD BE SEEN."
WE ARE HERE EXPRESSLY ON YOUR ACCOUNT.
PLEASE. STEP INSIDE. THE WEATHER IS INCLEMENT.
HAVE YOU A RETINUE?
SERVANTS? COMPANIONS?
NO.
I'M ALONE.
YOU CAN CLOSE THE DOOR.
CLOSED
LEAVE YOUR HANG-UPS OUT ON THE STREET.

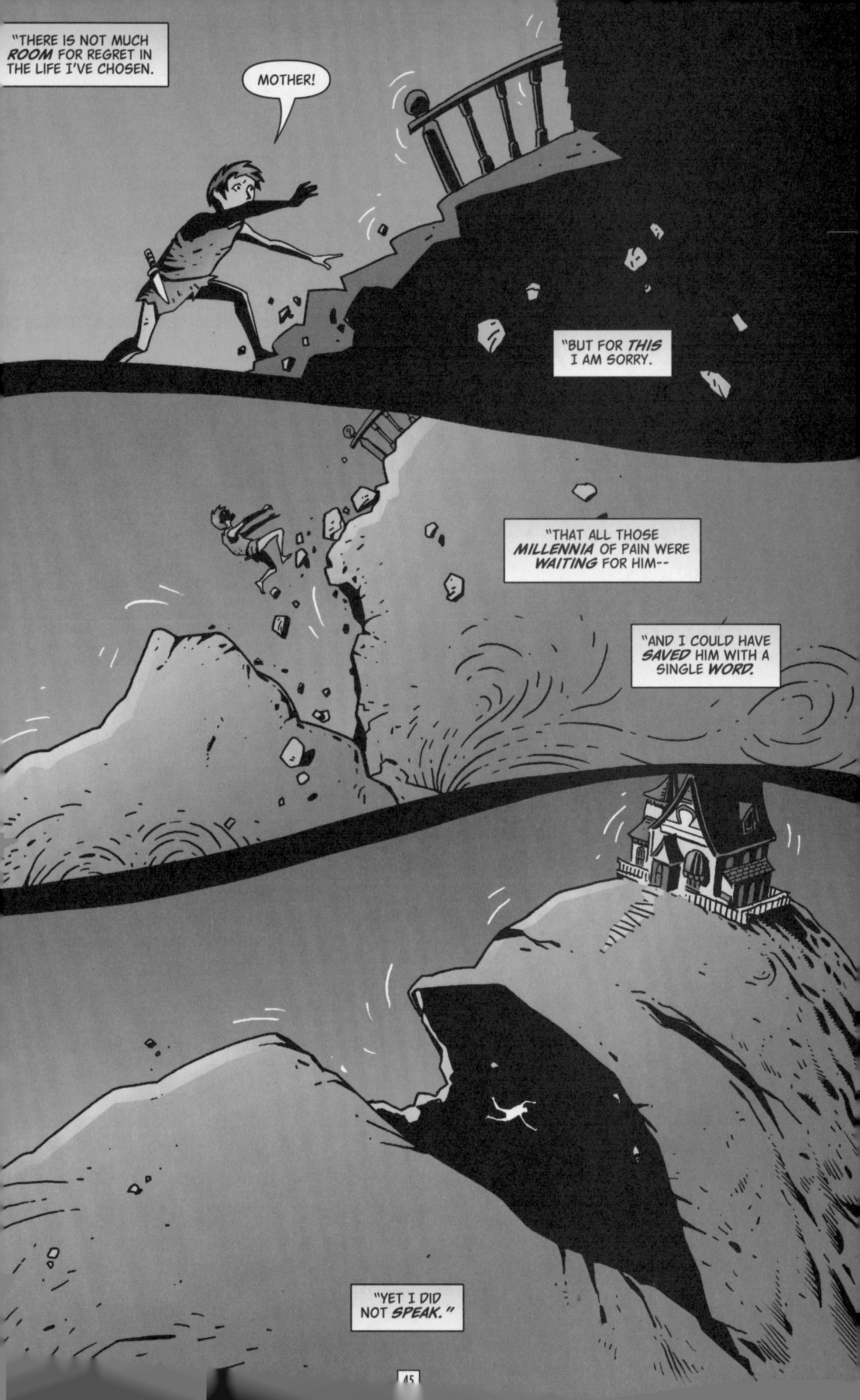
"THERE IS NOT MUCH ROOM FOR REGRET IN THE LIFE I'VE CHOSEN.
MOTHER!
"BUT FOR THIS I AM SORRY.
"THAT ALL THOSE MILLENNIA OF PAIN WERE WAITING FOR HIM--
"AND I COULD HAVE SAVED HIM WITH A SINGLE WORD.
"YET I DID NOT SPEAK."

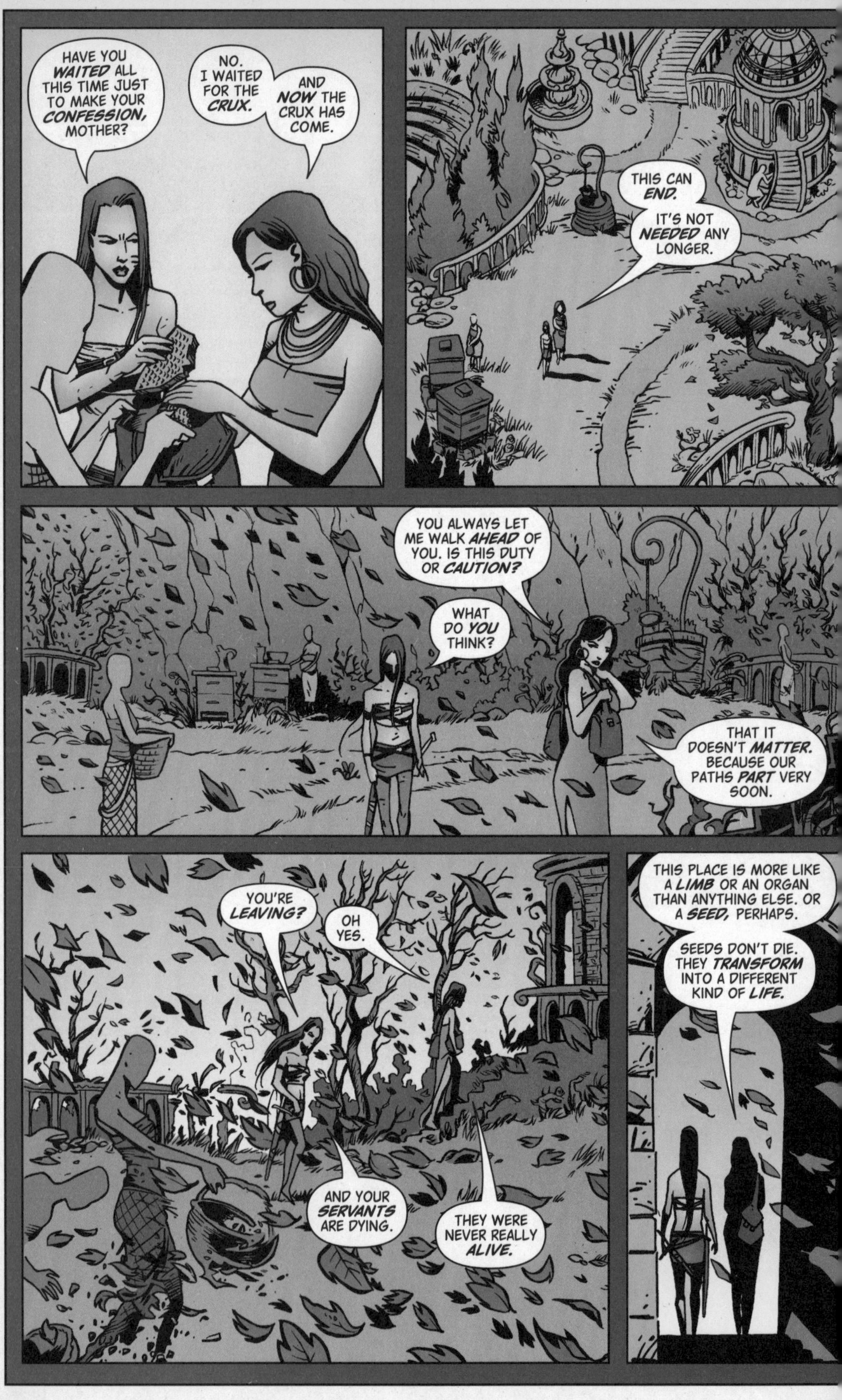

HAVE YOU WAITED ALL THIS TIME JUST TO MAKE YOUR CONFESSION, MOTHER?
NO. I WAITED FOR THE CRUX.
AND NOW THE CRUX HAS COME.
THIS CAN END.
IT'S NOT NEEDED ANY LONGER.
YOU ALWAYS LET ME WALK AHEAD OF YOU. IS THIS DUTY OR CAUTION?
WHAT DO YOU THINK?
THAT IT DOESN'T MATTER. BECAUSE OUR PATHS PART VERY SOON.
YOU'RE LEAVING?
OH YES.
AND YOUR SERVANTS ARE DYING.
THEY WERE NEVER REALLY ALIVE.
THIS PLACE IS MORE LIKE A LIMB OR AN ORGAN THAN ANYTHING ELSE. OR A SEED, PERHAPS.
SEEDS DON'T DIE. THEY TRANSFORM INTO A DIFFERENT KIND OF LIFE.

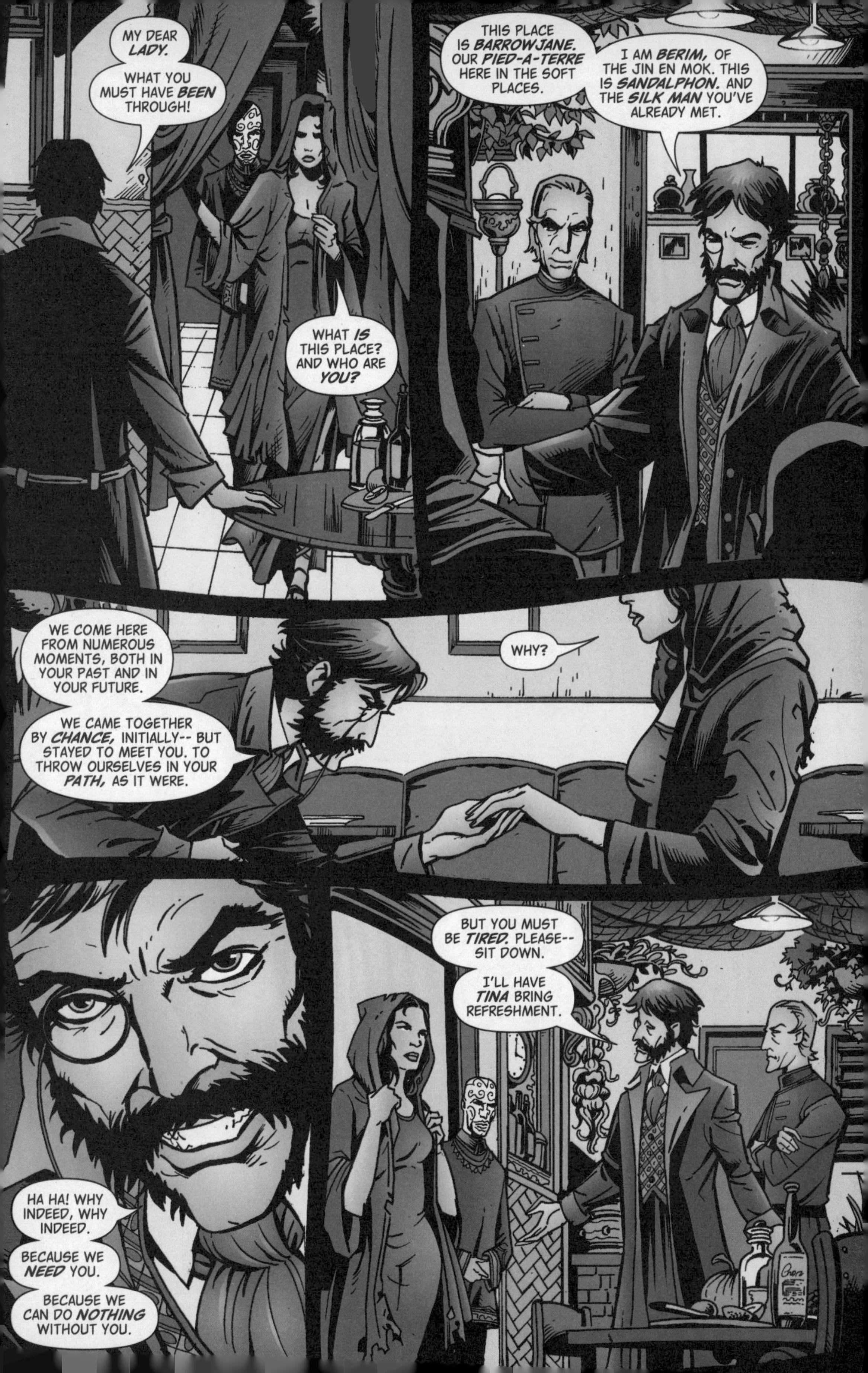
MY DEAR LADY.
WHAT YOU MUST HAVE BEEN THROUGH!
WHAT IS THIS PLACE? AND WHO ARE YOU?
THIS PLACE IS BARROWJANE. OUR PIED-A-TERRE HERE IN THE SOFT PLACES.
I AM BERIM, OF THE JIN EN MOK. THIS IS SANDALPHON. AND THE SILK MAN YOU'VE ALREADY MET.
WE COME HERE FROM NUMEROUS MOMENTS, BOTH IN YOUR PAST AND IN YOUR FUTURE.
WE CAME TOGETHER BY CHANCE, INITIALLY-- BUT STAYED TO MEET YOU. TO THROW OURSELVES IN YOUR PATH, AS IT WERE.
WHY?
HA HA! WHY INDEED, WHY INDEED.
BECAUSE WE NEED YOU.
BECAUSE WE CAN DO NOTHING WITHOUT YOU.
BUT YOU MUST BE TIRED. PLEASE-- SIT DOWN.
I'LL HAVE TINA BRING REFRESHMENT.

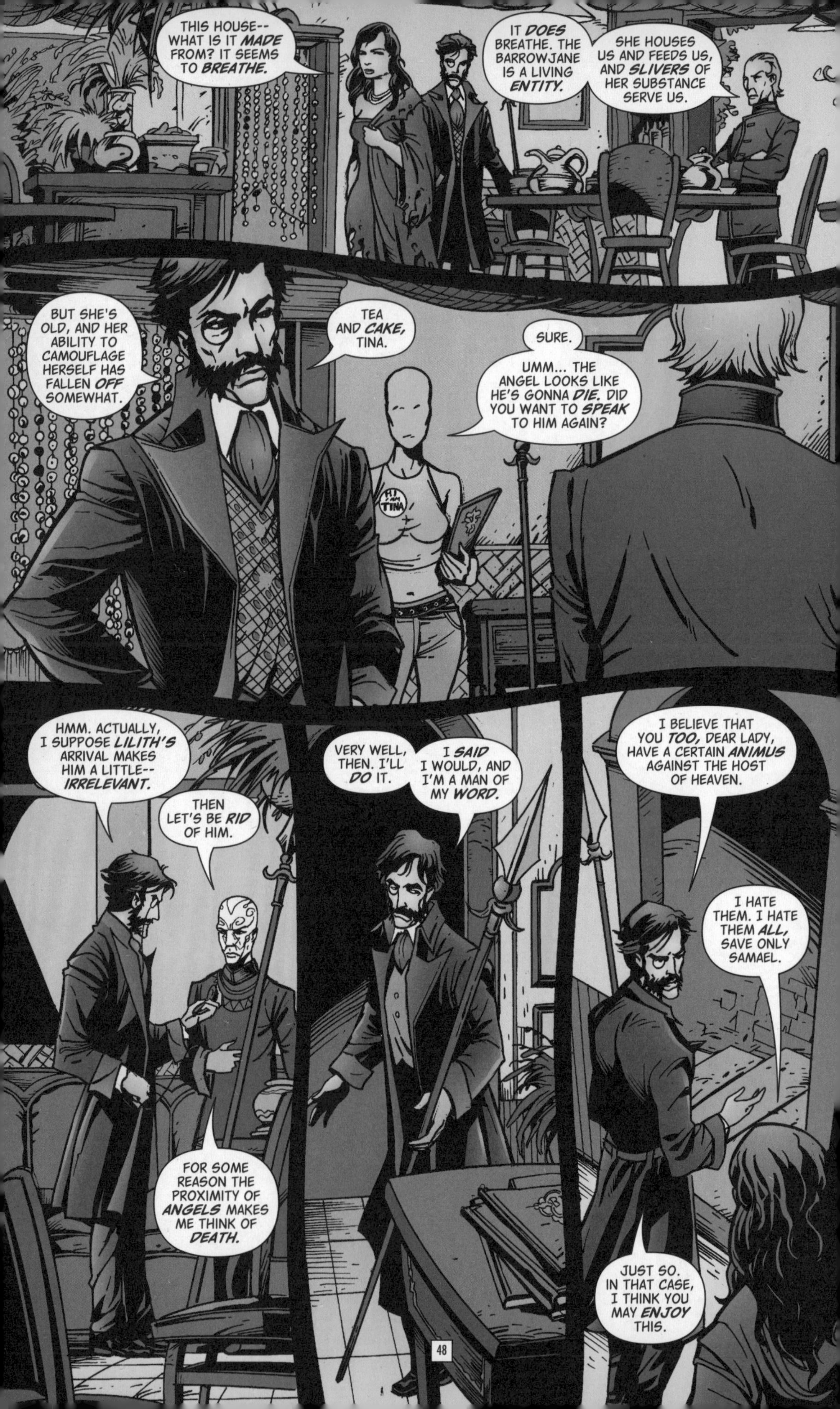
THIS HOUSE-- WHAT IS IT MADE FROM? IT SEEMS TO BREATHE.
IT DOES BREATHE. THE BARROWJANE IS A LIVING ENTITY.
SHE HOUSES US AND FEEDS US, AND SLIVERS OF HER SUBSTANCE SERVE US.
BUT SHE'S OLD, AND HER ABILITY TO CAMOUFLAGE HERSELF HAS FALLEN OFF SOMEWHAT.
TEA AND CAKE, TINA.
SURE.
UMM... THE ANGEL LOOKS LIKE HE'S GONNA DIE. DID YOU WANT TO SPEAK TO HIM AGAIN?
HI I AM TINA
HMM. ACTUALLY, I SUPPOSE LILITH'S ARRIVAL MAKES HIM A LITTLE-- IRRELEVANT.
THEN LET'S BE RID OF HIM.
FOR SOME REASON THE PROXIMITY OF ANGELS MAKES ME THINK OF DEATH.
VERY WELL, THEN. I'LL DO IT.
I SAID I WOULD, AND I'M A MAN OF MY WORD.
I BELIEVE THAT YOU TOO, DEAR LADY, HAVE A CERTAIN ANIMUS AGAINST THE HOST OF HEAVEN.
I HATE THEM. I HATE THEM ALL, SAVE ONLY SAMAEL.
JUST SO. IN THAT CASE, I THINK YOU MAY ENJOY THIS.

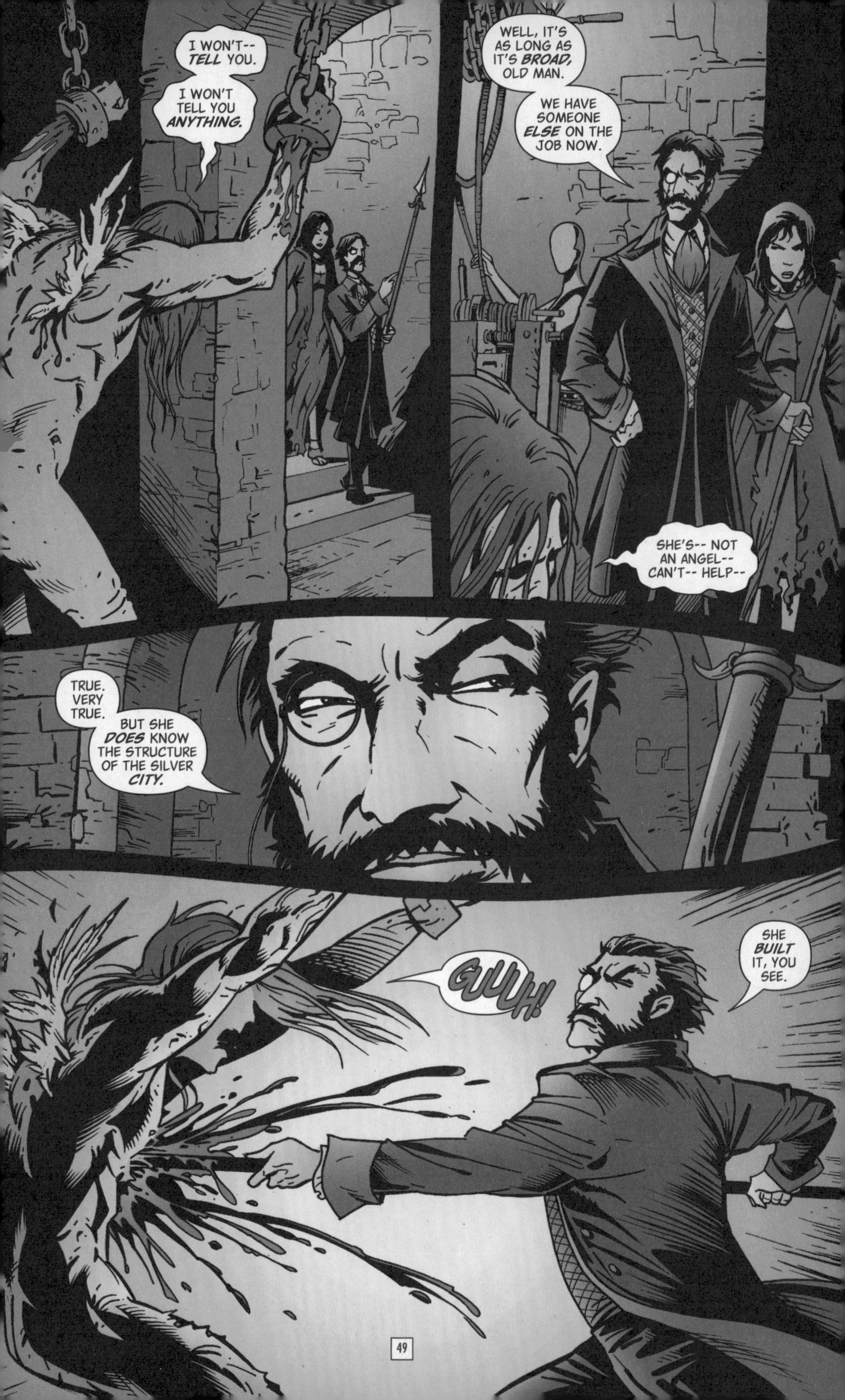
I WON'T-- TELL YOU.
I WON'T TELL YOU ANYTHING.
WELL, IT'S AS LONG AS IT'S BROAD, OLD MAN.
WE HAVE SOMEONE ELSE ON THE JOB NOW.
SHE'S-- NOT AN ANGEL-- CAN'T-- HELP--
TRUE. VERY TRUE.
BUT SHE DOES KNOW THE STRUCTURE OF THE SILVER CITY.
GUUUH!
SHE BUILT IT, YOU SEE.

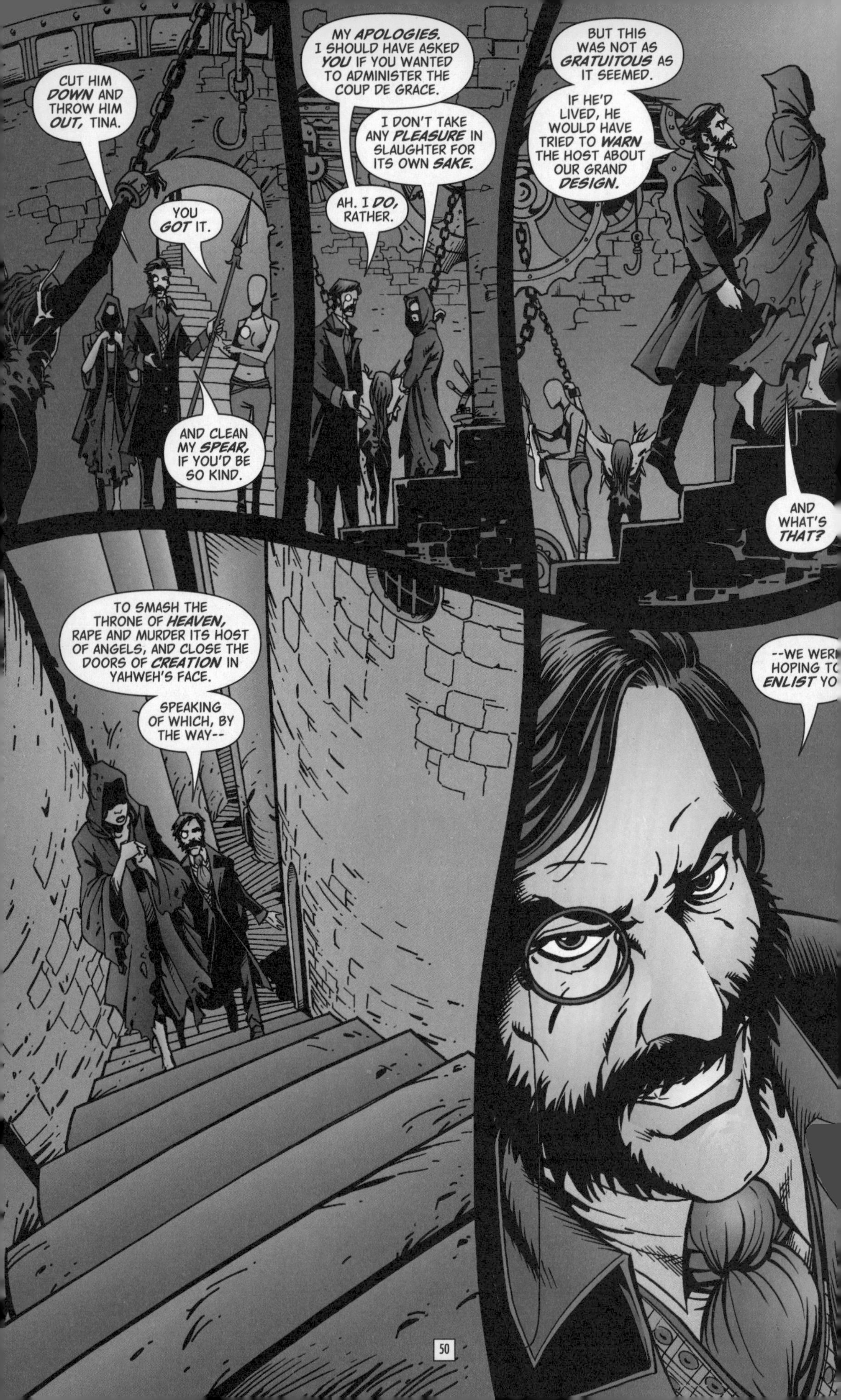

CUT HIM DOWN AND THROW HIM OUT, TINA.
YOU GOT IT.
AND CLEAN MY SPEAR, IF YOU'D BE SO KIND.
MY APOLOGIES. I SHOULD HAVE ASKED YOU IF YOU WANTED TO ADMINISTER THE COUP DE GRACE.
I DON'T TAKE ANY PLEASURE IN SLAUGHTER FOR ITS OWN SAKE.
AH. I DO, RATHER.
BUT THIS WAS NOT AS GRATUITOUS AS IT SEEMED.
IF HE'D LIVED, HE WOULD HAVE TRIED TO WARN THE HOST ABOUT OUR GRAND DESIGN.
AND WHAT'S THAT?
TO SMASH THE THRONE OF HEAVEN, RAPE AND MURDER ITS HOST OF ANGELS, AND CLOSE THE DOORS OF CREATION IN YAHWEH'S FACE.
SPEAKING OF WHICH, BY THE WAY--

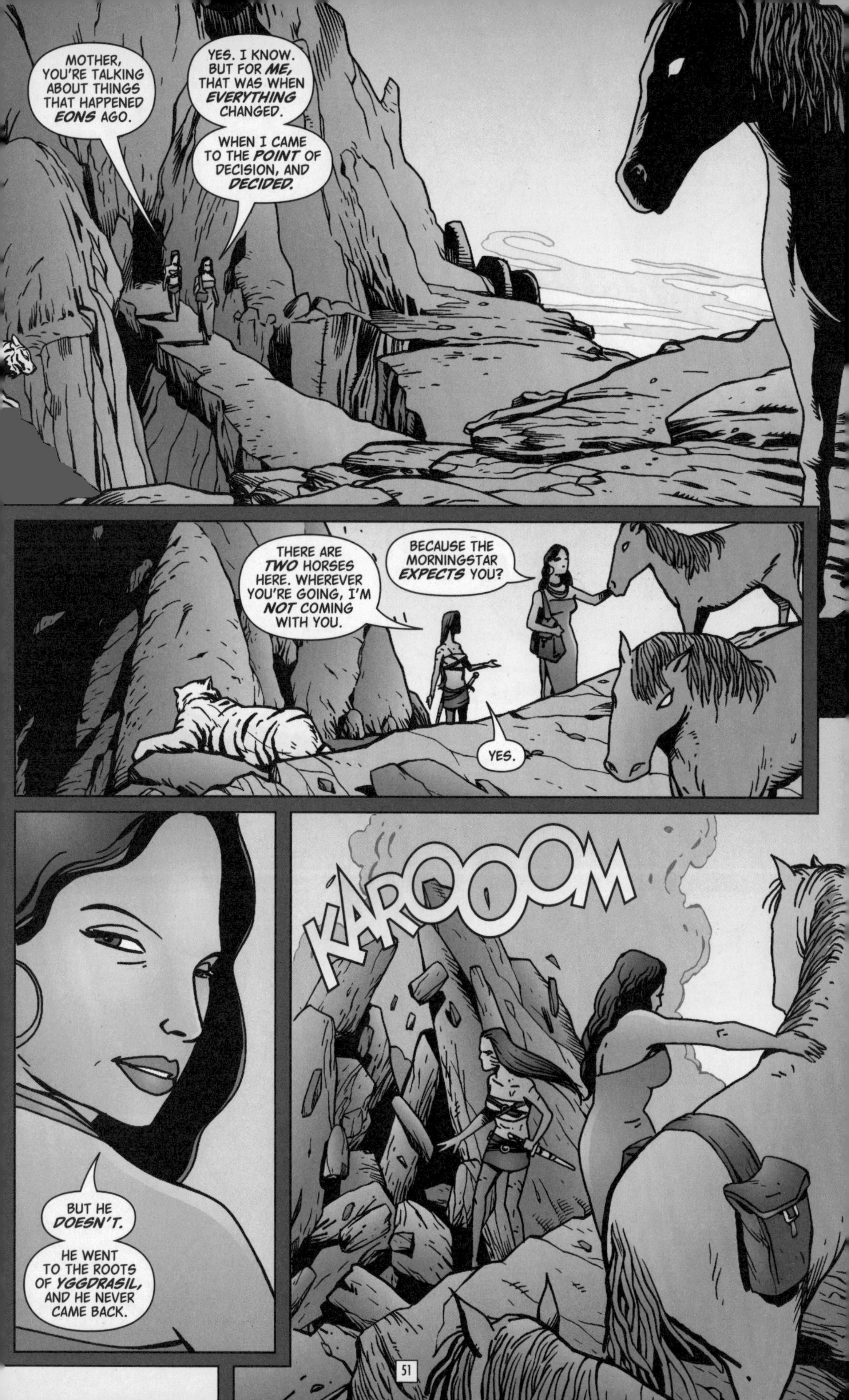

MOTHER, YOU'RE TALKING ABOUT THINGS THAT HAPPENED EONS AGO.
YES. I KNOW. BUT FOR ME, THAT WAS WHEN EVERYTHING CHANGED.
WHEN I CAME TO THE POINT OF DECISION, AND DECIDED.
THERE ARE TWO HORSES HERE. WHEREVER YOU'RE GOING, I'M NOT COMING WITH YOU.
BECAUSE THE MORNINGSTAR EXPECTS YOU?
YES.
BUT HE DOESN'T.
HE WENT TO THE ROOTS OF YGGDRASIL, AND HE NEVER CAME BACK.
KAROOOM

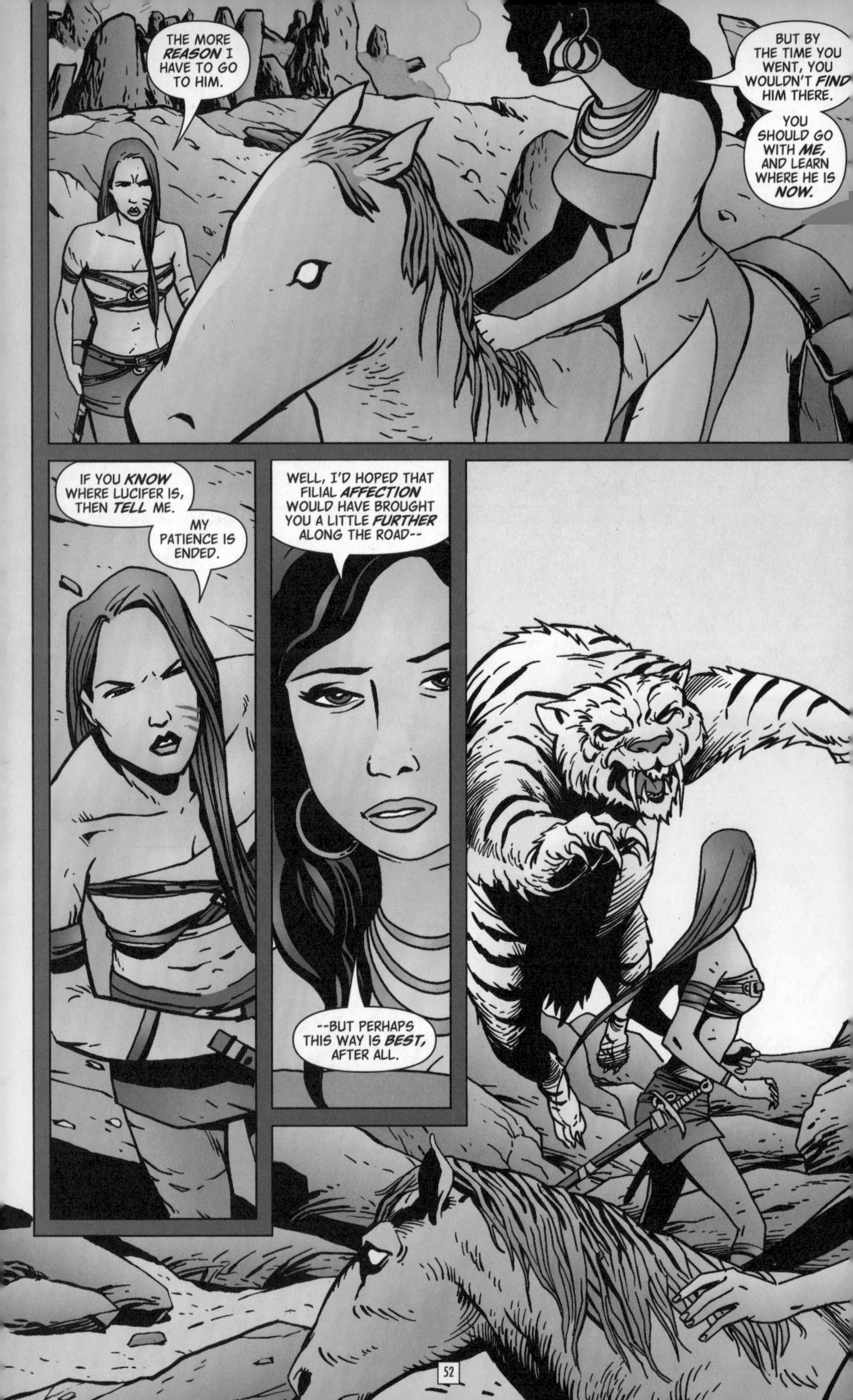
THE MORE REASON I HAVE TO GO TO HIM.
BUT BY THE TIME YOU WENT, YOU WOULDN'T FIND HIM THERE.
YOU SHOULD GO WITH ME, AND LEARN WHERE HE IS NOW.
IF YOU KNOW WHERE LUCIFER IS, THEN TELL ME.
MY PATIENCE IS ENDED.
WELL, I'D HOPED THAT FILIAL AFFECTION WOULD HAVE BROUGHT YOU A LITTLE FURTHER ALONG THE ROAD--
--BUT PERHAPS THIS WAY IS BEST, AFTER ALL.

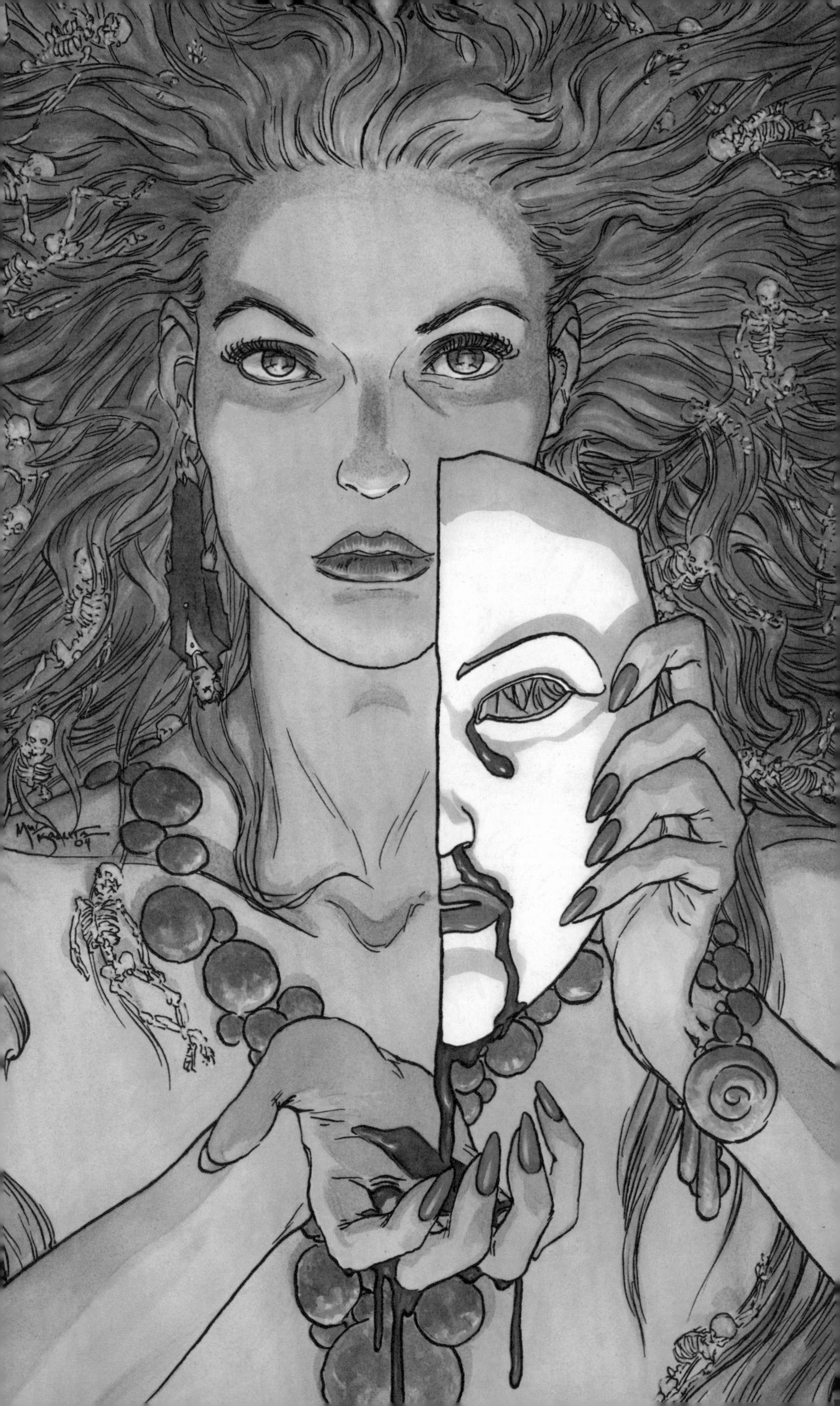

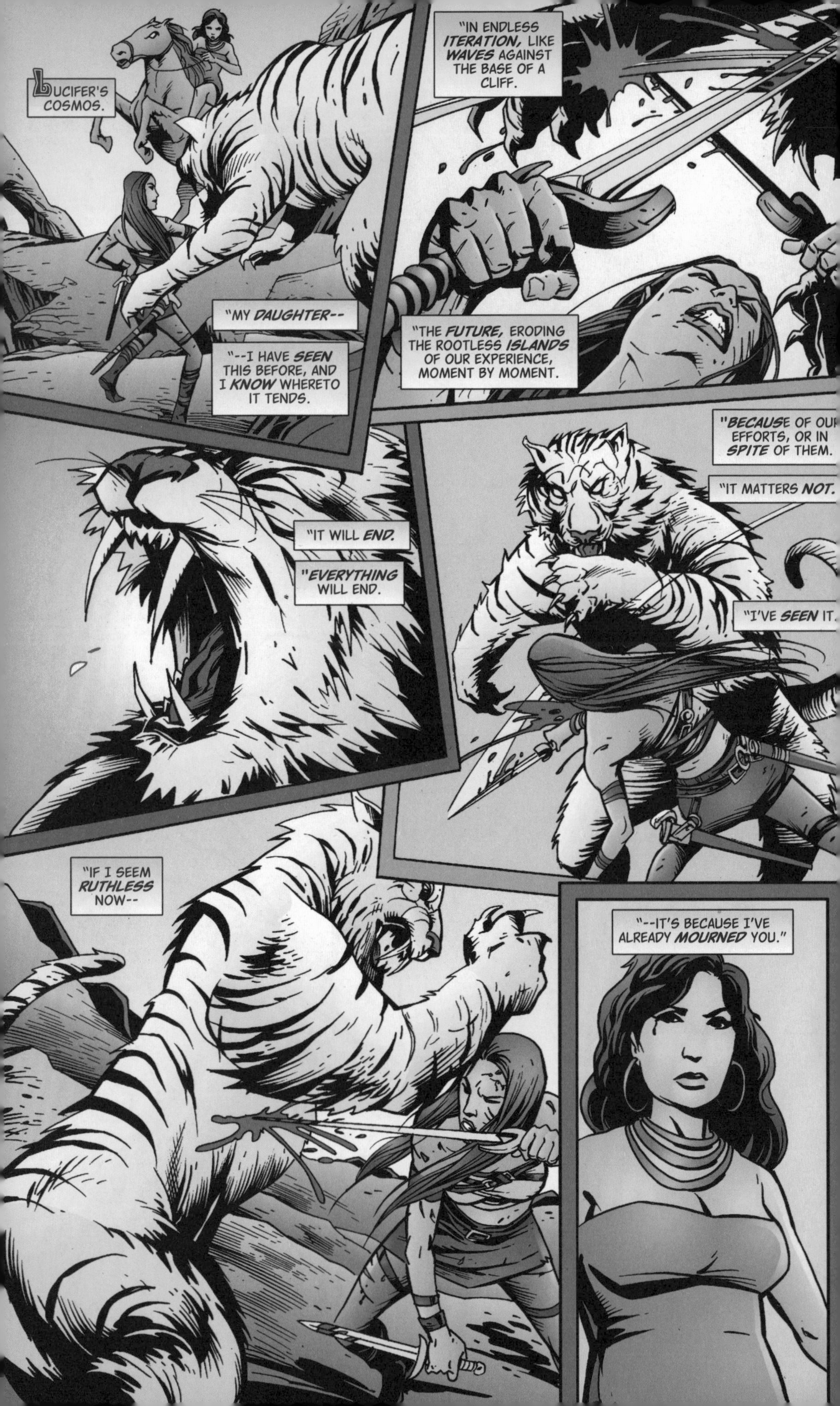
LUCIFER'S COSMOS.
"MY DAUGHTER--
"--I HAVE SEEN THIS BEFORE, AND I KNOW WHERETO IT TENDS.
"IN ENDLESS ITERATION, LIKE WAVES AGAINST THE BASE OF A CLIFF.
"THE FUTURE, ERODING THE ROOTLESS ISLANDS OF OUR EXPERIENCE, MOMENT BY MOMENT.
"IT WILL END.
"EVERYTHING WILL END.
"BECAUSE OF OUR EFFORTS, OR IN SPITE OF THEM.
"IT MATTERS NOT.
"I'VE SEEN IT.
"IF I SEEM RUTHLESS NOW--
"--IT'S BECAUSE I'VE ALREADY MOURNED YOU."

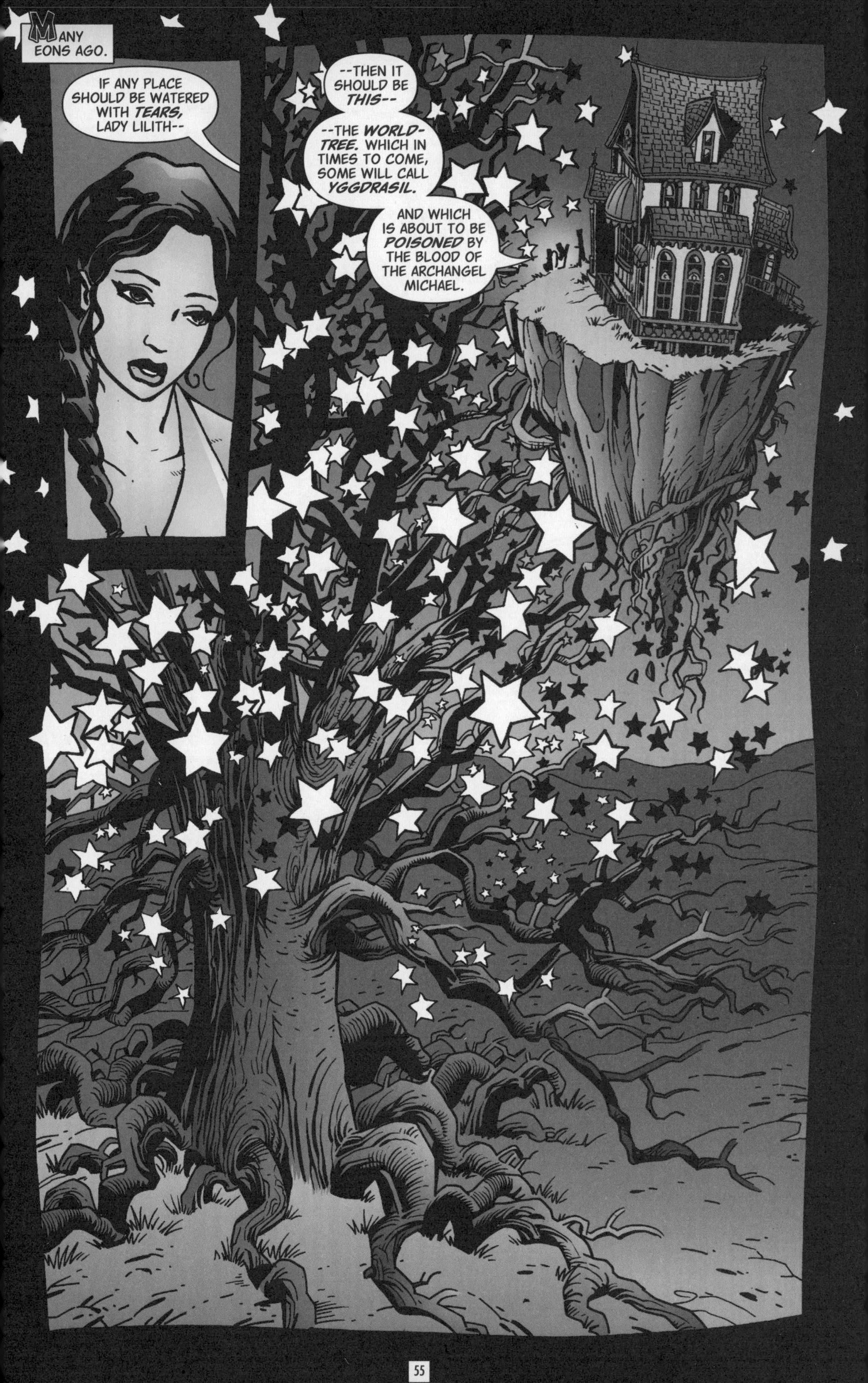
MANY EONS AGO.
IF ANY PLACE SHOULD BE WATERED WITH TEARS, LADY LILITH--
--THEN IT SHOULD BE THIS--
--THE WORLD-TREE. WHICH IN TIMES TO COME, SOME WILL CALL YGGDRASIL.
AND WHICH IS ABOUT TO BE POISONED BY THE BLOOD OF THE ARCHANGEL MICHAEL.

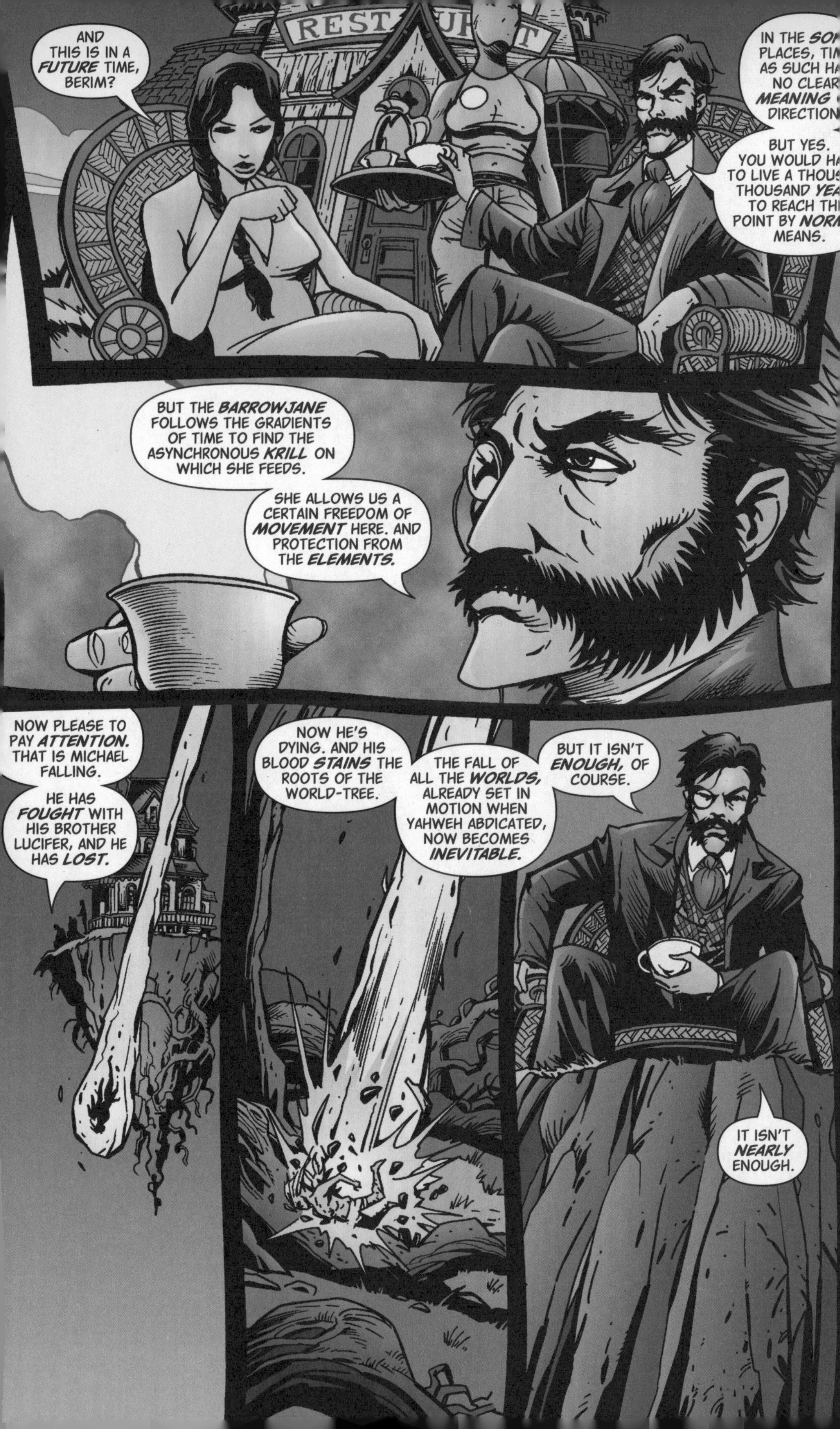
AND THIS IS IN A FUTURE TIME, BERIM?
IN THE SO PLACES, TIM AS SUCH HA NO CLEAR MEANING DIRECTION
BUT YES. YOU WOULD HA TO LIVE A THOUS THOUSAND YEA TO REACH TH POINT BY NOR MEANS.
BUT THE BARROWJANE FOLLOWS THE GRADIENTS OF TIME TO FIND THE ASYNCHRONOUS KRILL ON WHICH SHE FEEDS.
SHE ALLOWS US A CERTAIN FREEDOM OF MOVEMENT HERE. AND PROTECTION FROM THE ELEMENTS.
NOW PLEASE TO PAY ATTENTION. THAT IS MICHAEL FALLING.
HE HAS FOUGHT WITH HIS BROTHER LUCIFER, AND HE HAS LOST.
NOW HE'S DYING. AND HIS BLOOD STAINS THE ROOTS OF THE WORLD-TREE.
THE FALL OF ALL THE WORLDS, ALREADY SET IN MOTION WHEN YAHWEH ABDICATED, NOW BECOMES INEVITABLE.
BUT IT ISN'T ENOUGH, OF COURSE.
IT ISN'T NEARLY ENOUGH.

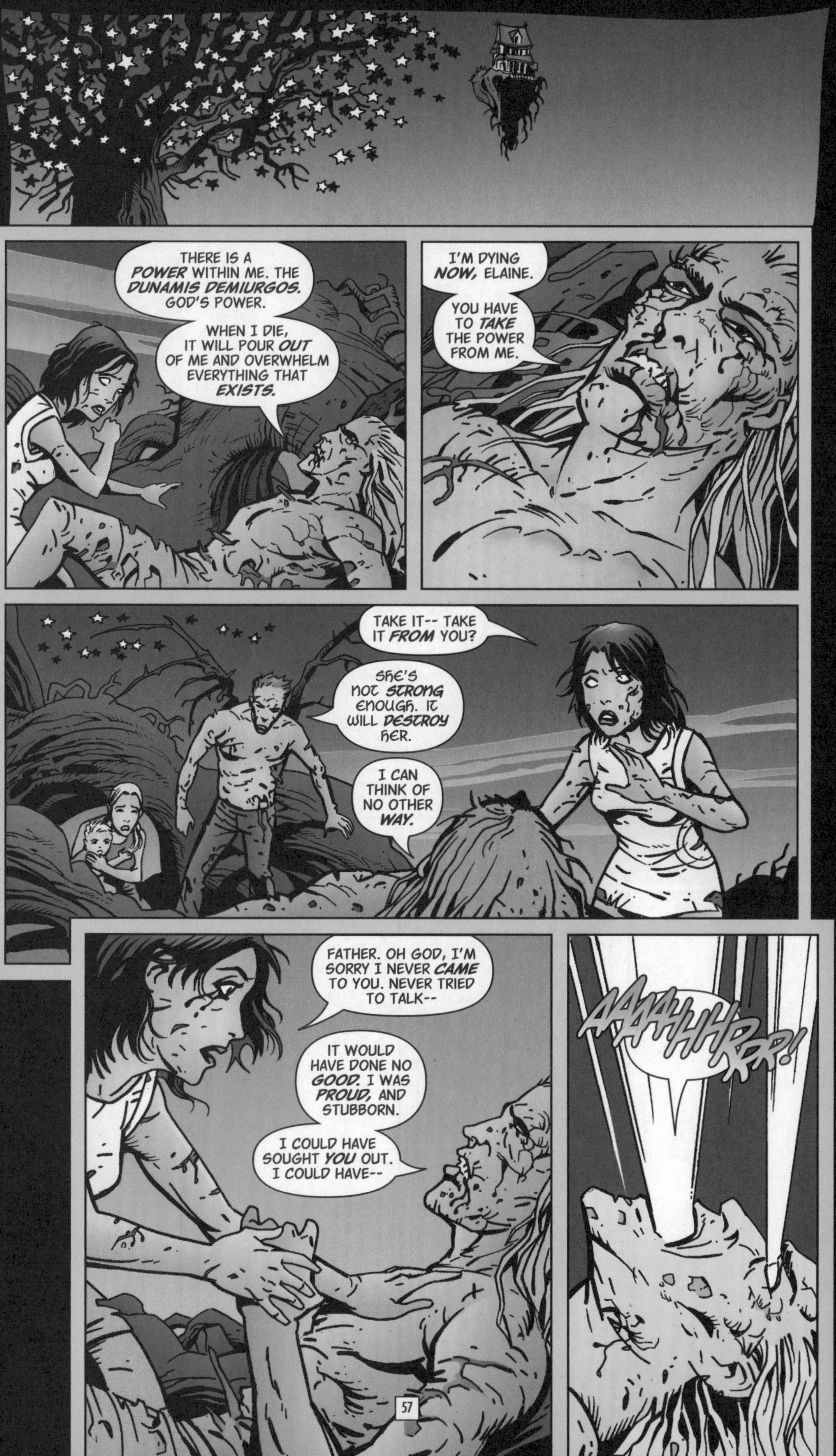
THERE IS A POWER WITHIN ME. THE DUNAMIS DEMIURGOS. GOD'S POWER.
WHEN I DIE, IT WILL POUR OUT OF ME AND OVERWHELM EVERYTHING THAT EXISTS.
I'M DYING NOW, ELAINE.
YOU HAVE TO TAKE THE POWER FROM ME.
TAKE IT-- TAKE IT FROM YOU?
SHE'S NOT STRONG ENOUGH. IT WILL DESTROY HER.
I CAN THINK OF NO OTHER WAY.
FATHER. OH GOD, I'M SORRY I NEVER CAME TO YOU. NEVER TRIED TO TALK--
IT WOULD HAVE DONE NO GOOD. I WAS PROUD, AND STUBBORN.
I COULD HAVE SOUGHT YOU OUT. I COULD HAVE--
AAAAHHHRRR!

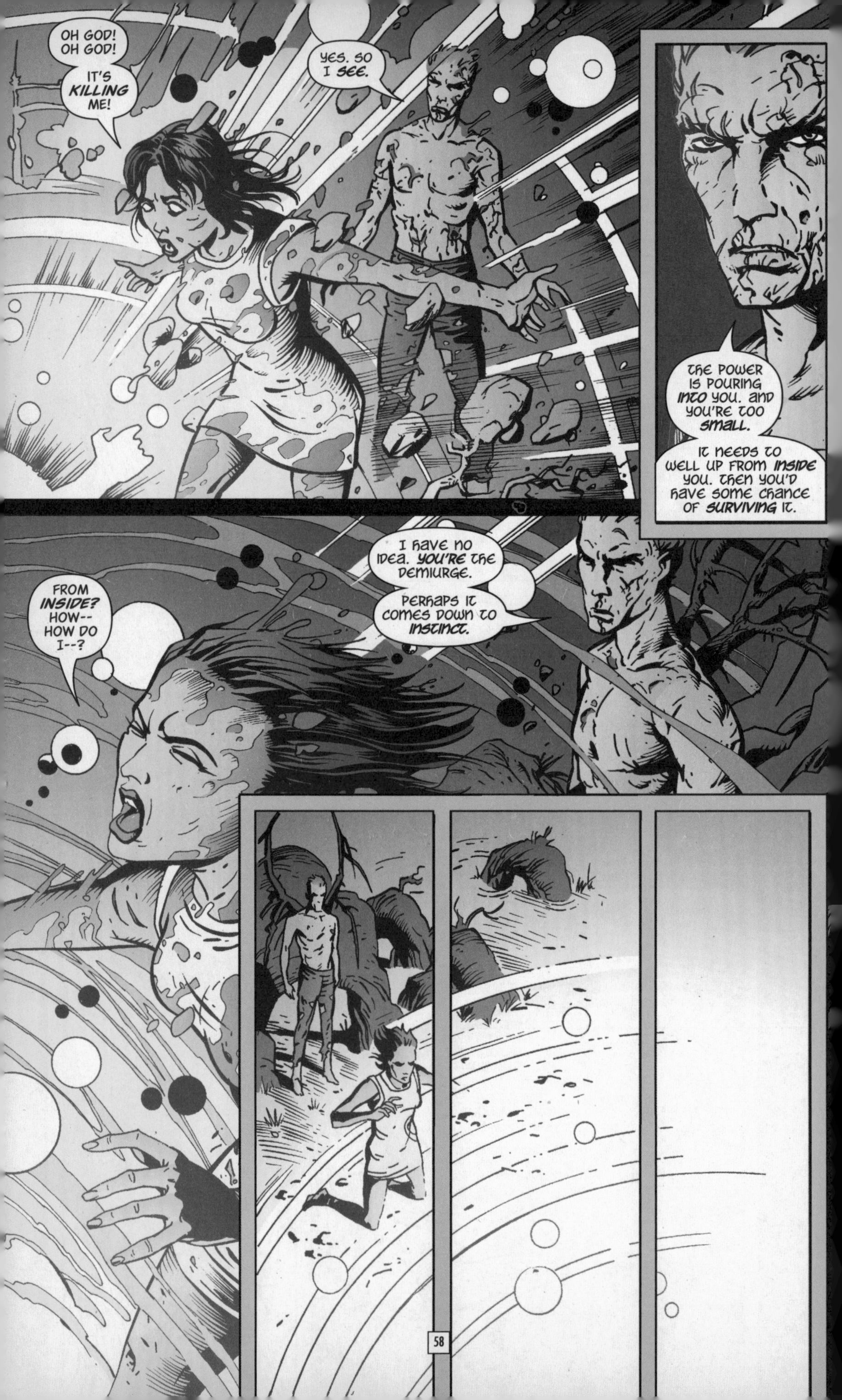
OH GOD! OH GOD!
IT'S KILLING ME!
YES. SO I SEE.
THE POWER IS POURING INTO YOU. AND YOU'RE TOO SMALL.
IT NEEDS TO WELL UP FROM INSIDE YOU. THEN YOU'D HAVE SOME CHANCE OF SURVIVING IT.
FROM INSIDE? HOW-- HOW DO I--?
I HAVE NO IDEA. YOU'RE THE DEMIURGE.
PERHAPS IT COMES DOWN TO INSTINCT.

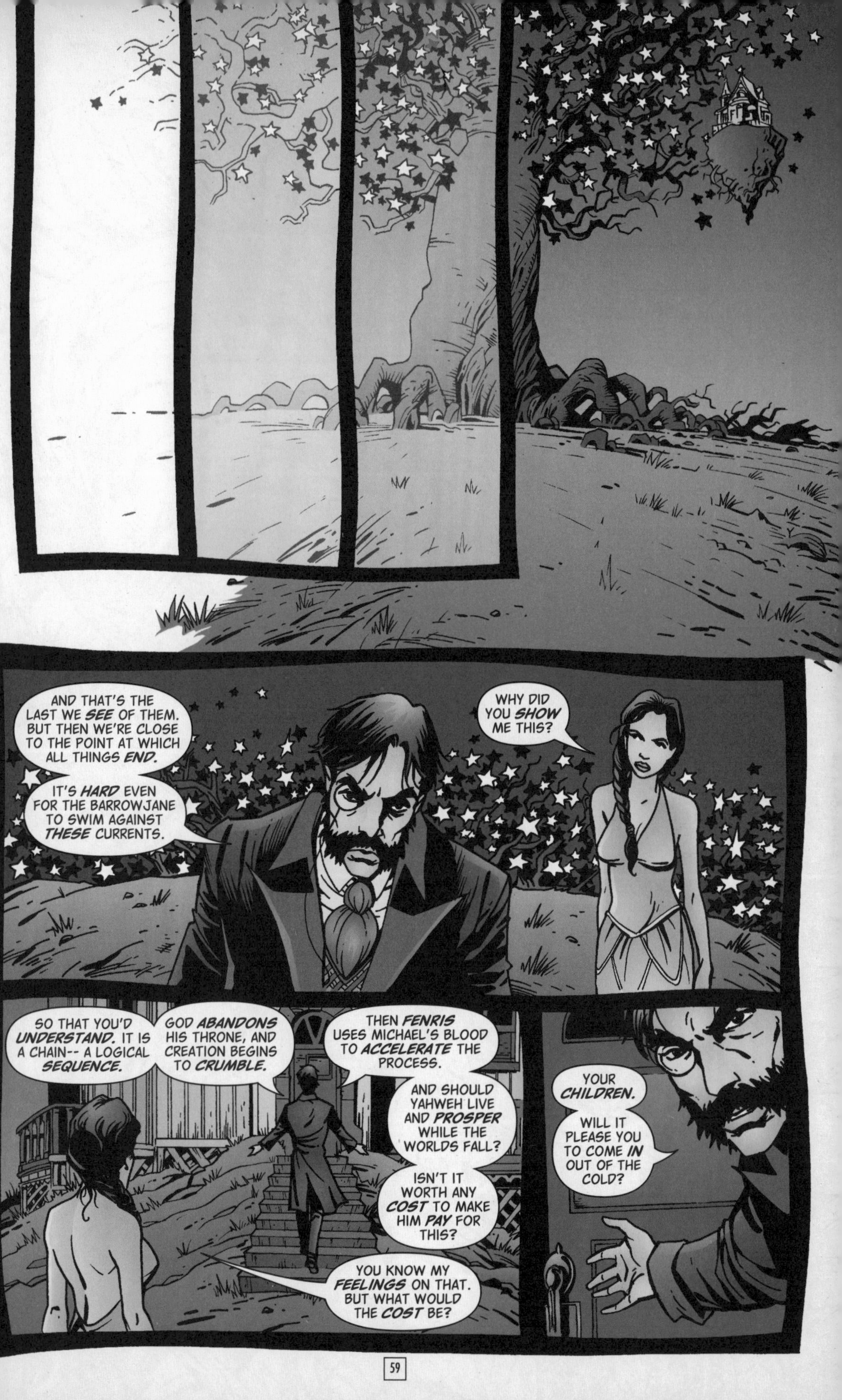
AND THAT'S THE LAST WE SEE OF THEM. BUT THEN WE'RE CLOSE TO THE POINT AT WHICH ALL THINGS END.
IT'S HARD EVEN FOR THE BARROWJANE TO SWIM AGAINST THESE CURRENTS.
WHY DID YOU SHOW ME THIS?
SO THAT YOU'D UNDERSTAND. IT IS A CHAIN-- A LOGICAL SEQUENCE.
GOD ABANDONS HIS THRONE, AND CREATION BEGINS TO CRUMBLE.
THEN FENRIS USES MICHAEL'S BLOOD TO ACCELERATE THE PROCESS.
AND SHOULD YAHWEH LIVE AND PROSPER WHILE THE WORLDS FALL?
ISN'T IT WORTH ANY COST TO MAKE HIM PAY FOR THIS?
YOU KNOW MY FEELINGS ON THAT. BUT WHAT WOULD THE COST BE?
YOUR CHILDREN.
WILL IT PLEASE YOU TO COME IN OUT OF THE COLD?

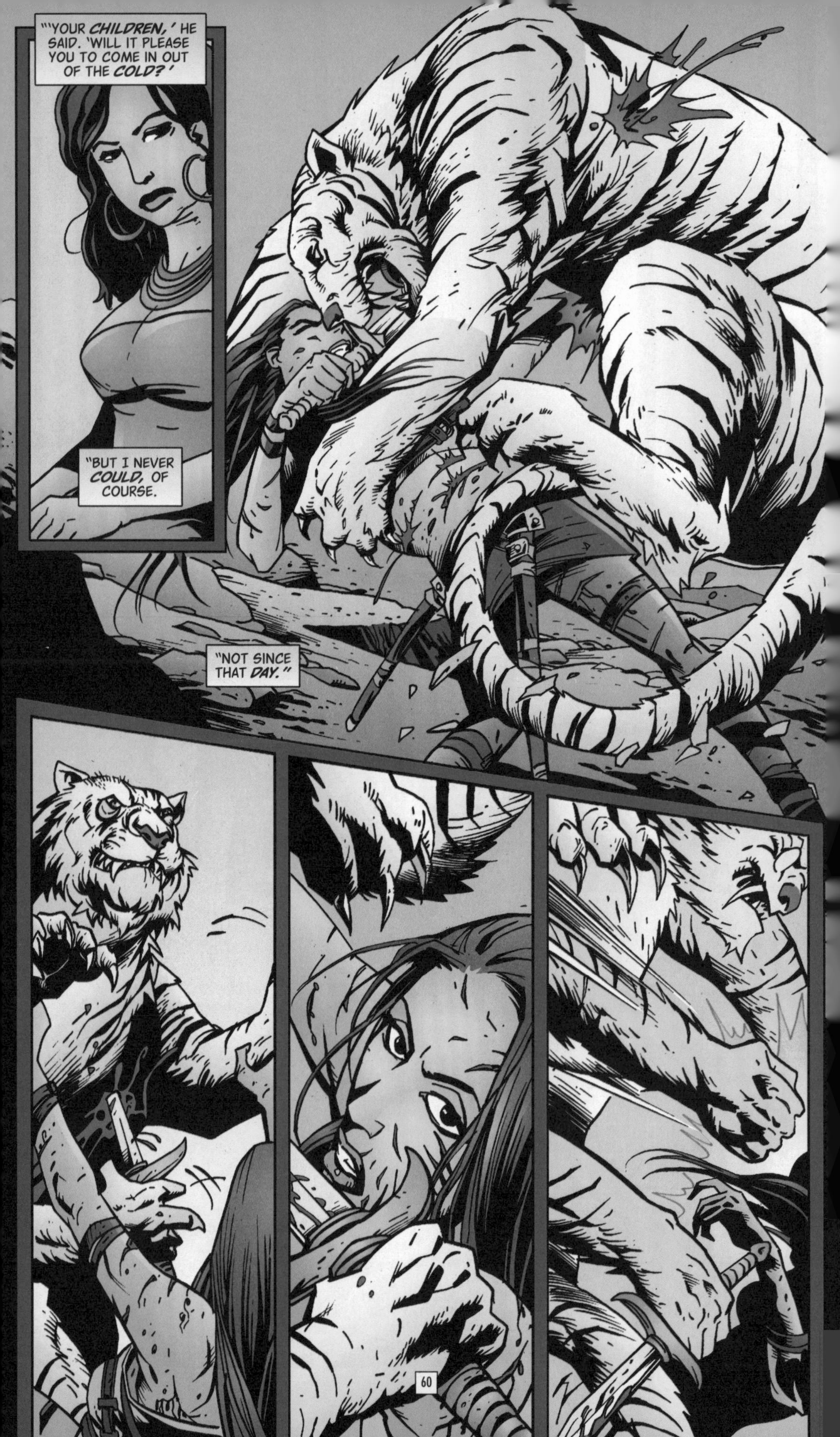
"'YOUR CHILDREN,' HE SAID. 'WILL IT PLEASE YOU TO COME IN OUT OF THE COLD?'
"BUT I NEVER COULD, OF COURSE.
"NOT SINCE THAT DAY."

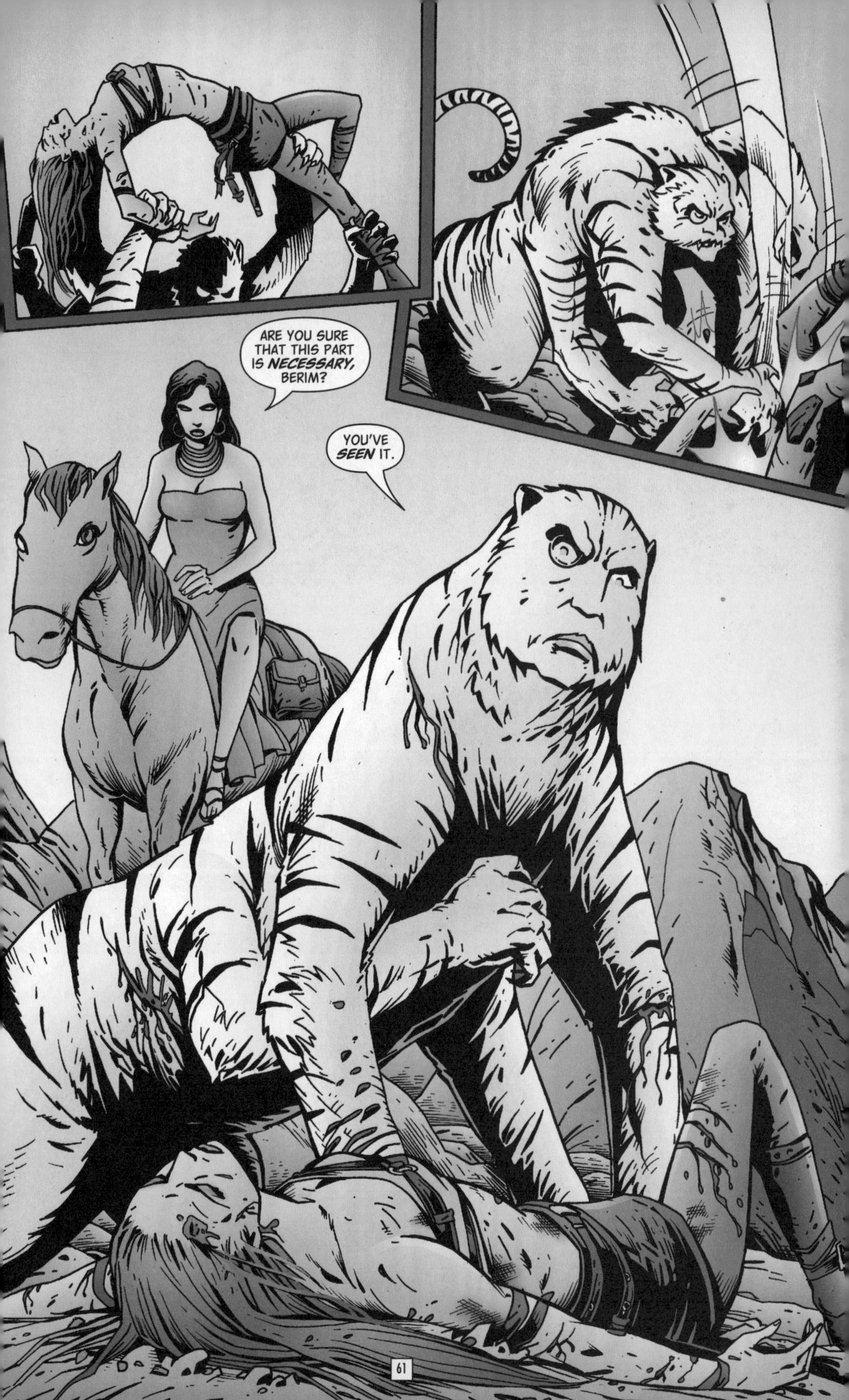
ARE YOU SURE THAT THIS PART IS NECESSARY, BERIM?
YOU'VE SEEN IT.

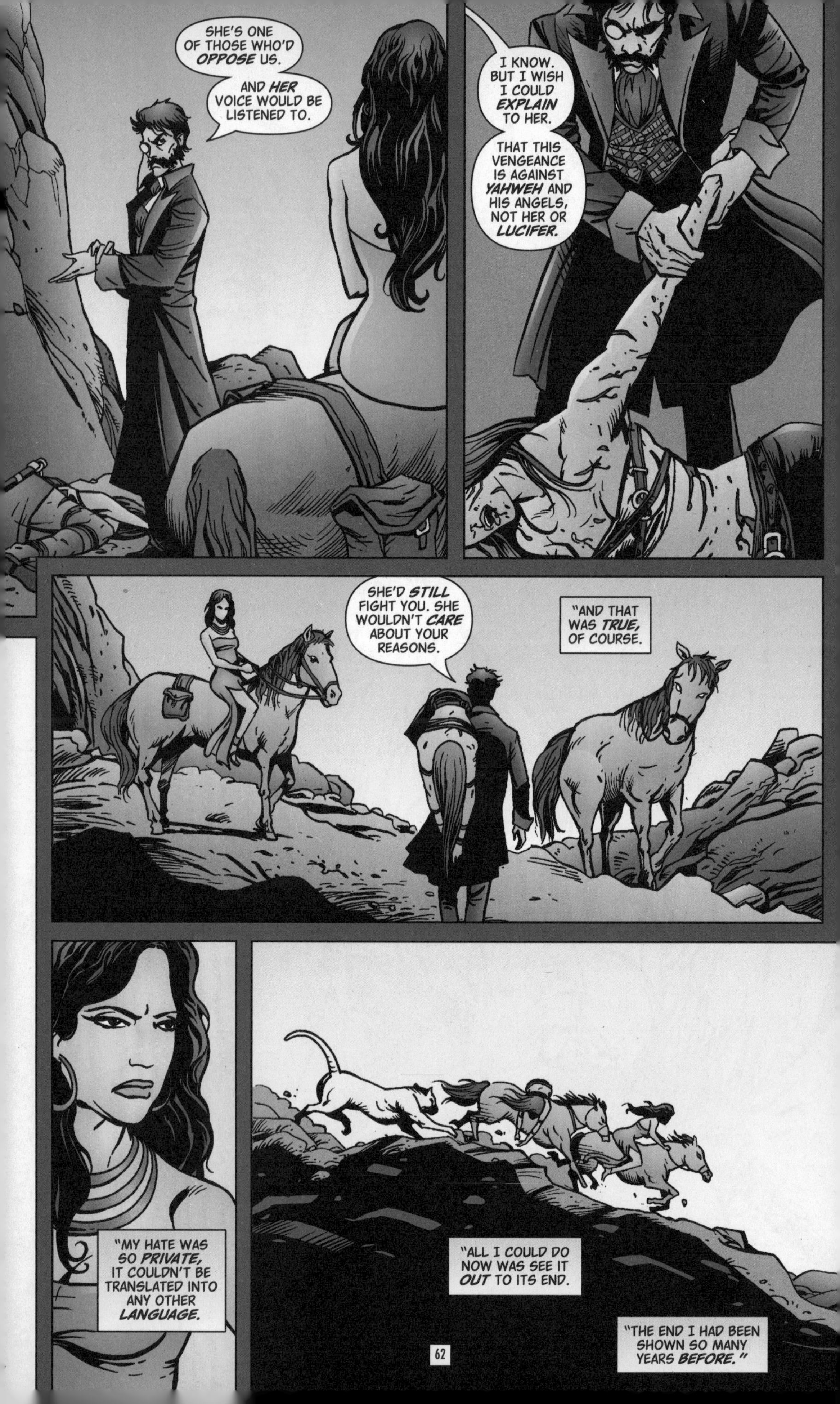
SHE'S ONE OF THOSE WHO'D OPPOSE US.
AND HER VOICE WOULD BE LISTENED TO.
I KNOW. BUT I WISH I COULD EXPLAIN TO HER.
THAT THIS VENGEANCE IS AGAINST YAHWEH AND HIS ANGELS, NOT HER OR LUCIFER.
SHE'D STILL FIGHT YOU. SHE WOULDN'T CARE ABOUT YOUR REASONS.
"AND THAT WAS TRUE, OF COURSE.
"MY HATE WAS SO PRIVATE, IT COULDN'T BE TRANSLATED INTO ANY OTHER LANGUAGE.
"ALL I COULD DO NOW WAS SEE IT OUT TO ITS END.
"THE END I HAD BEEN SHOWN SO MANY YEARS BEFORE."

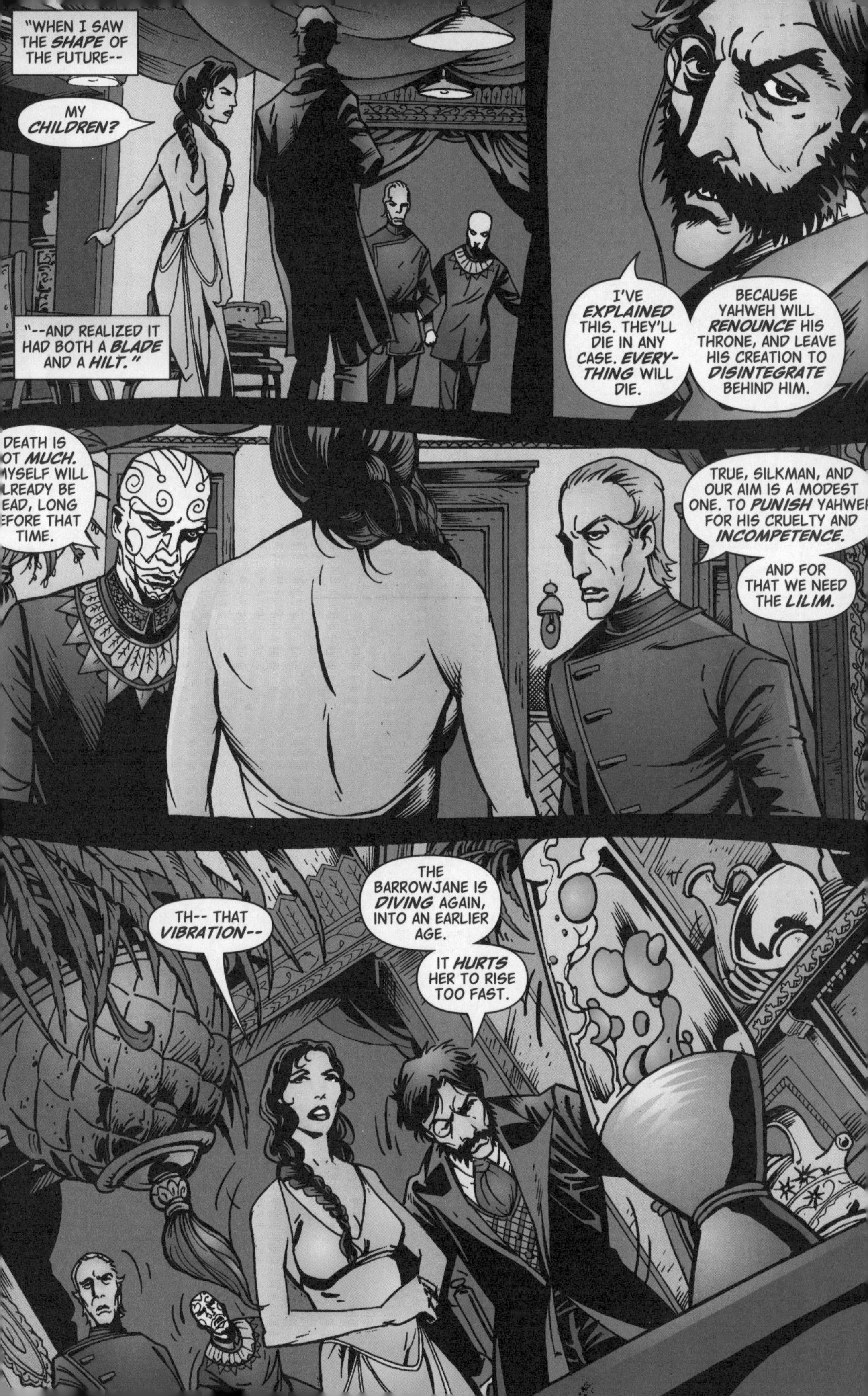
"WHEN I SAW THE SHAPE OF THE FUTURE--
MY CHILDREN?
"--AND REALIZED IT HAD BOTH A BLADE AND A HILT."
I'VE EXPLAINED THIS. THEY'LL DIE IN ANY CASE. EVERY-THING WILL DIE.
BECAUSE YAHWEH WILL RENOUNCE HIS THRONE, AND LEAVE HIS CREATION TO DISINTEGRATE BEHIND HIM.
DEATH IS OT MUCH. MYSELF WILL LREADY BE EAD, LONG EFORE THAT TIME.
TRUE, SILKMAN, AND OUR AIM IS A MODEST ONE. TO PUNISH YAHWE FOR HIS CRUELTY AND INCOMPETENCE.
AND FOR THAT WE NEED THE LILIM.
TH-- THAT VIBRATION--
THE BARROWJANE IS DIVING AGAIN, INTO AN EARLIER AGE.
IT HURTS HER TO RISE TOO FAST.

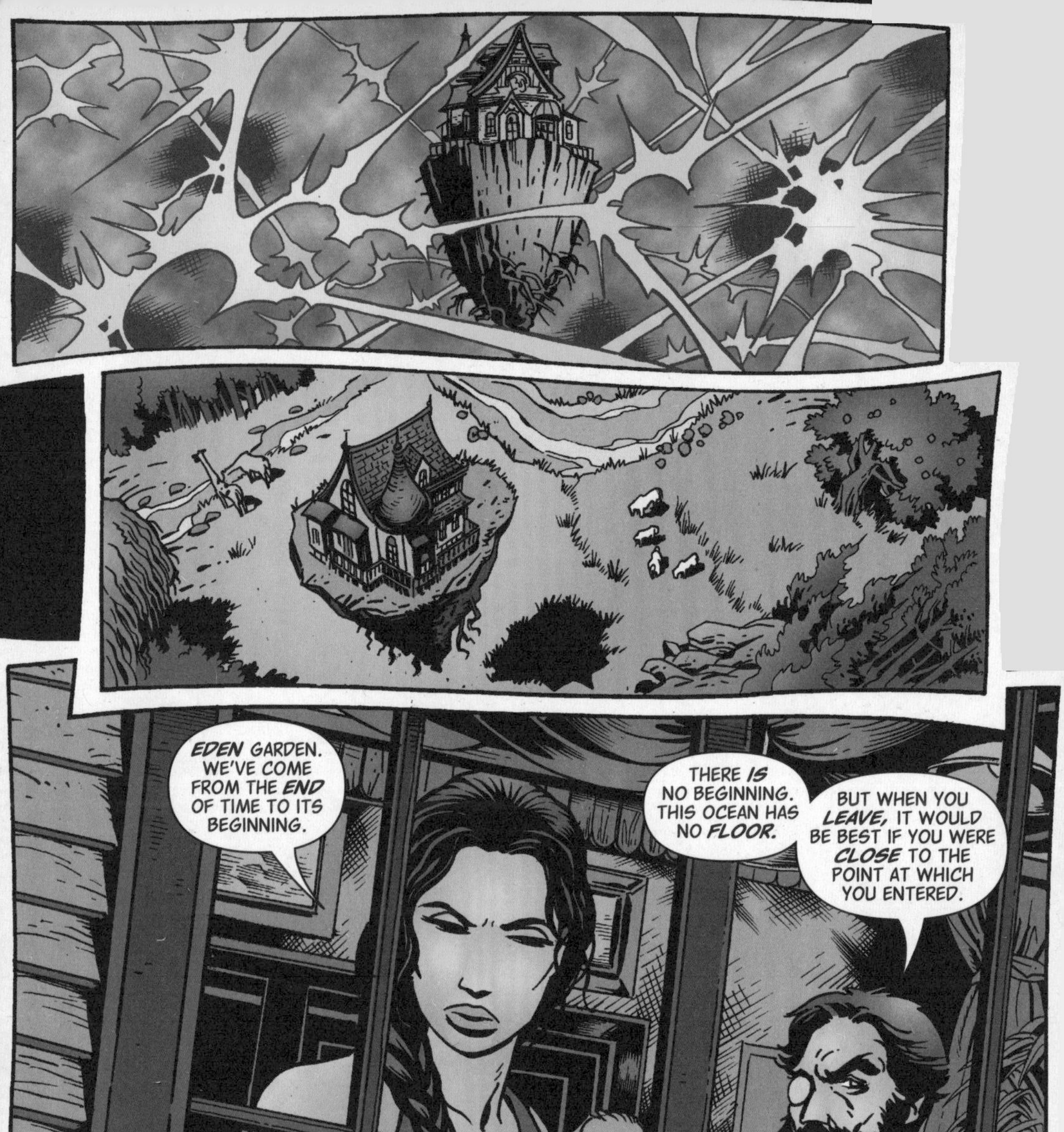
EDEN GARDEN. WE'VE COME FROM THE END OF TIME TO ITS BEGINNING.
THERE IS NO BEGINNING. THIS OCEAN HAS NO FLOOR.
BUT WHEN YOU LEAVE, IT WOULD BE BEST IF YOU WERE CLOSE TO THE POINT AT WHICH YOU ENTERED.

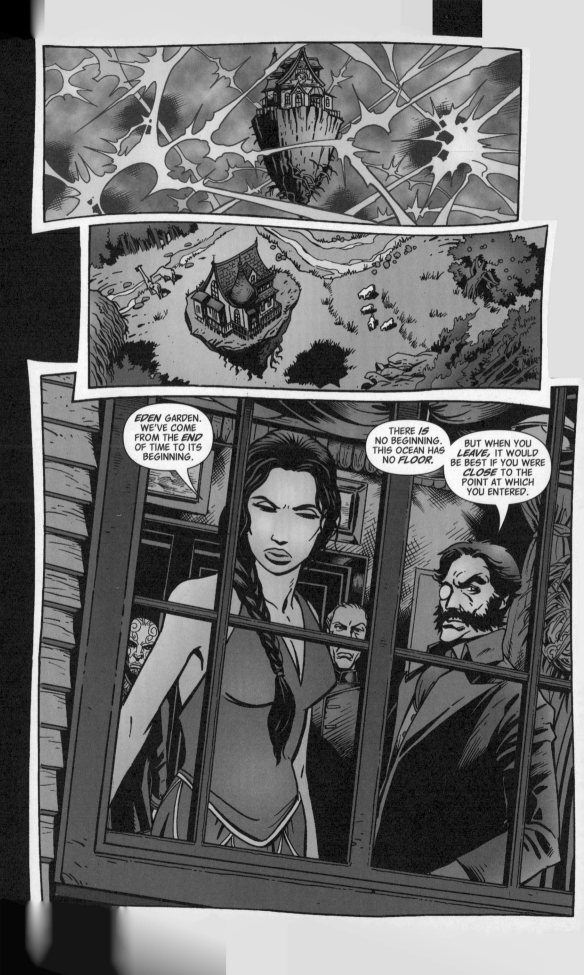

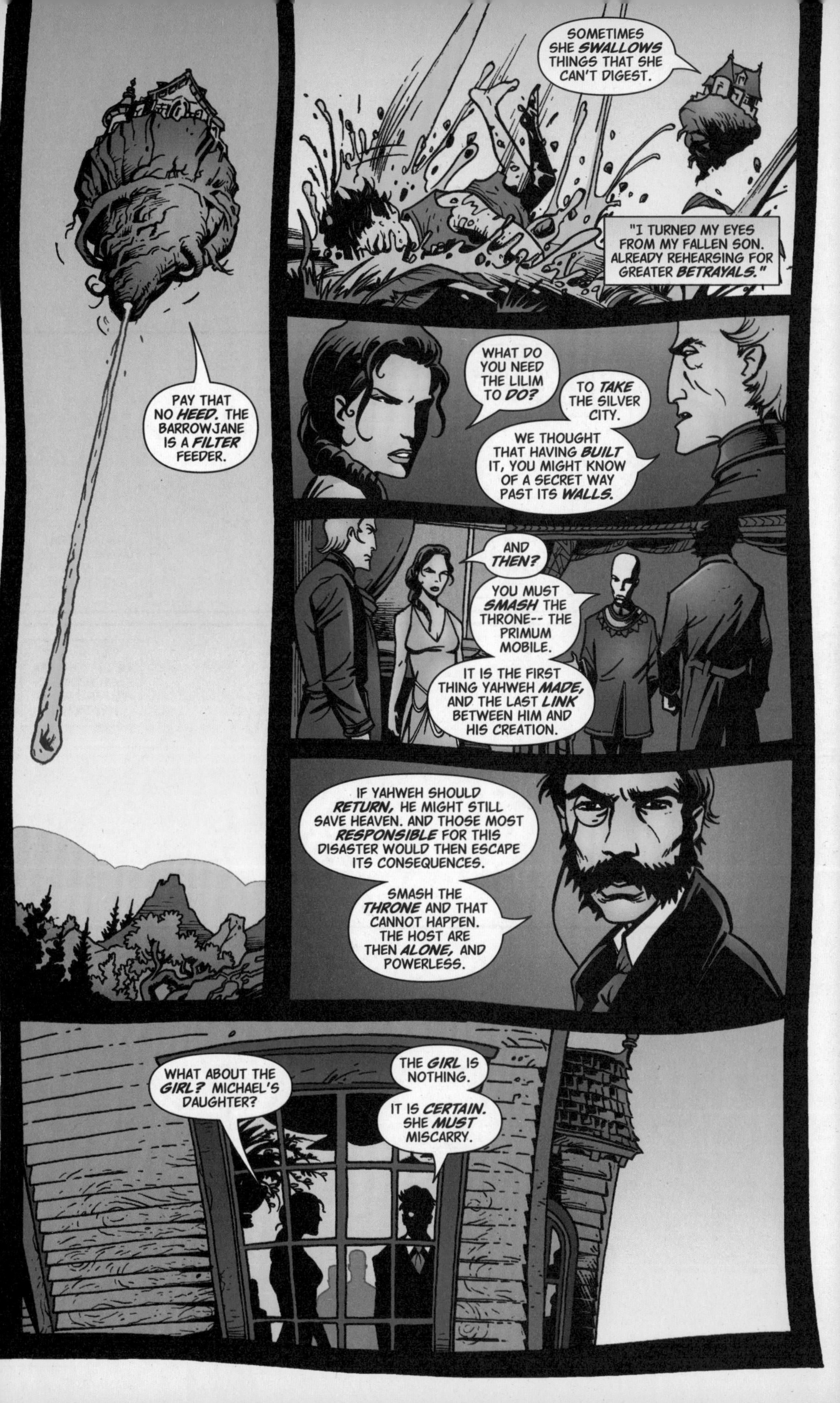

SOMETIMES SHE SWALLOWS THINGS THAT SHE CAN'T DIGEST.
"I TURNED MY EYES FROM MY FALLEN SON. ALREADY REHEARSING FOR GREATER BETRAYALS."
PAY THAT NO HEED. THE BARROWJANE IS A FILTER FEEDER.
WHAT DO YOU NEED THE LILIM TO DO?
TO TAKE THE SILVER CITY.
WE THOUGHT THAT HAVING BUILT IT, YOU MIGHT KNOW OF A SECRET WAY PAST ITS WALLS.
AND THEN?
YOU MUST SMASH THE THRONE-- THE PRIMUM MOBILE.
IT IS THE FIRST THING YAHWEH MADE, AND THE LAST LINK BETWEEN HIM AND HIS CREATION.
IF YAHWEH SHOULD RETURN, HE MIGHT STILL SAVE HEAVEN. AND THOSE MOST RESPONSIBLE FOR THIS DISASTER WOULD THEN ESCAPE ITS CONSEQUENCES.
SMASH THE THRONE AND THAT CANNOT HAPPEN. THE HOST ARE THEN ALONE, AND POWERLESS.
WHAT ABOUT THE GIRL? MICHAEL'S DAUGHTER?
THE GIRL IS NOTHING.
IT IS CERTAIN. SHE MUST MISCARRY.

"THE POWER IS TOO *FIERCE* AND CORROSIVE.

"AND SHE IS TOO *FRAIL* A VESSEL.

"AS I SAID, WE HAVE NOT *FOUND* HER ON TIME'S FURTHER SHORE.

"SHE IS *SWALLOWED* BY THE POWER, AND SHE DOES NOT *EMERGE* AGAIN.

"WE BELIEVE SHE IS *DISMANTLED* BY IT.

"SHE *IS*, AFTER ALL, PARTLY OF *HUMAN* FLESH.

"AND IN THAT *FURNACE*, FLESH IS LIKE *CHAFF* IN A HURRICANE.

"WHAT COULD SHE *HAVE* TO SET AGAINST THAT WIND OF FIRE?

"HER *WILL?* HER HOPE? HER SMATTERING OF HALF-GLIMPSED *WISDOM?*

"NOTHING.

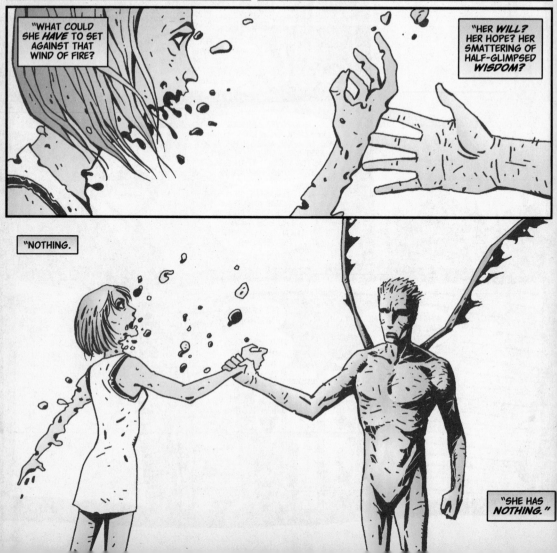

"SHE HAS *NOTHING.*"

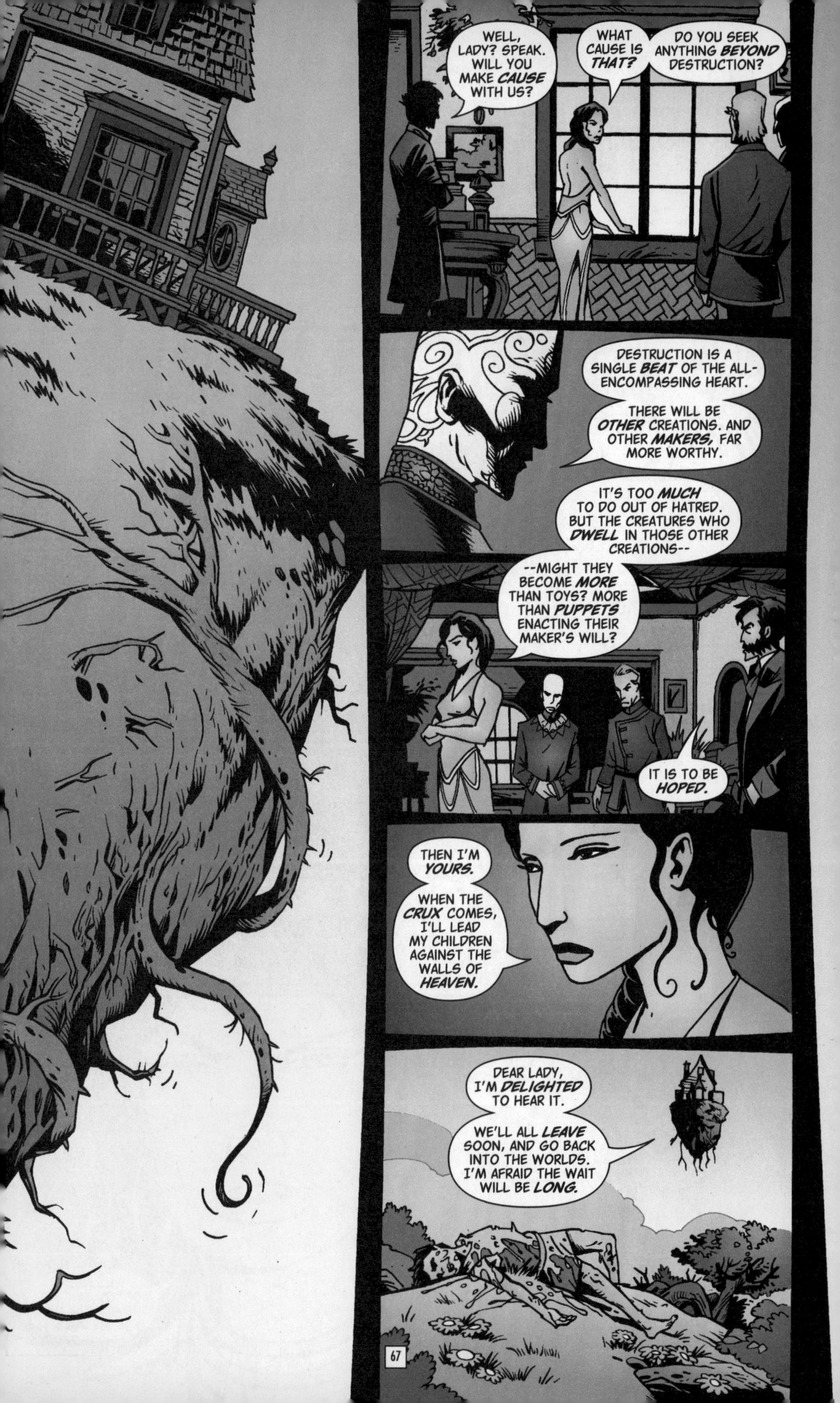
WELL, LADY? SPEAK. WILL YOU MAKE CAUSE WITH US?
WHAT CAUSE IS THAT?
DO YOU SEEK ANYTHING BEYOND DESTRUCTION?
DESTRUCTION IS A SINGLE BEAT OF THE ALL-ENCOMPASSING HEART.
THERE WILL BE OTHER CREATIONS. AND OTHER MAKERS, FAR MORE WORTHY.
IT'S TOO MUCH TO DO OUT OF HATRED. BUT THE CREATURES WHO DWELL IN THOSE OTHER CREATIONS--
--MIGHT THEY BECOME MORE THAN TOYS? MORE THAN PUPPETS ENACTING THEIR MAKER'S WILL?
IT IS TO BE HOPED.
THEN I'M YOURS.
WHEN THE CRUX COMES, I'LL LEAD MY CHILDREN AGAINST THE WALLS OF HEAVEN.
DEAR LADY, I'M DELIGHTED TO HEAR IT.
WE'LL ALL LEAVE SOON, AND GO BACK INTO THE WORLDS. I'M AFRAID THE WAIT WILL BE LONG.

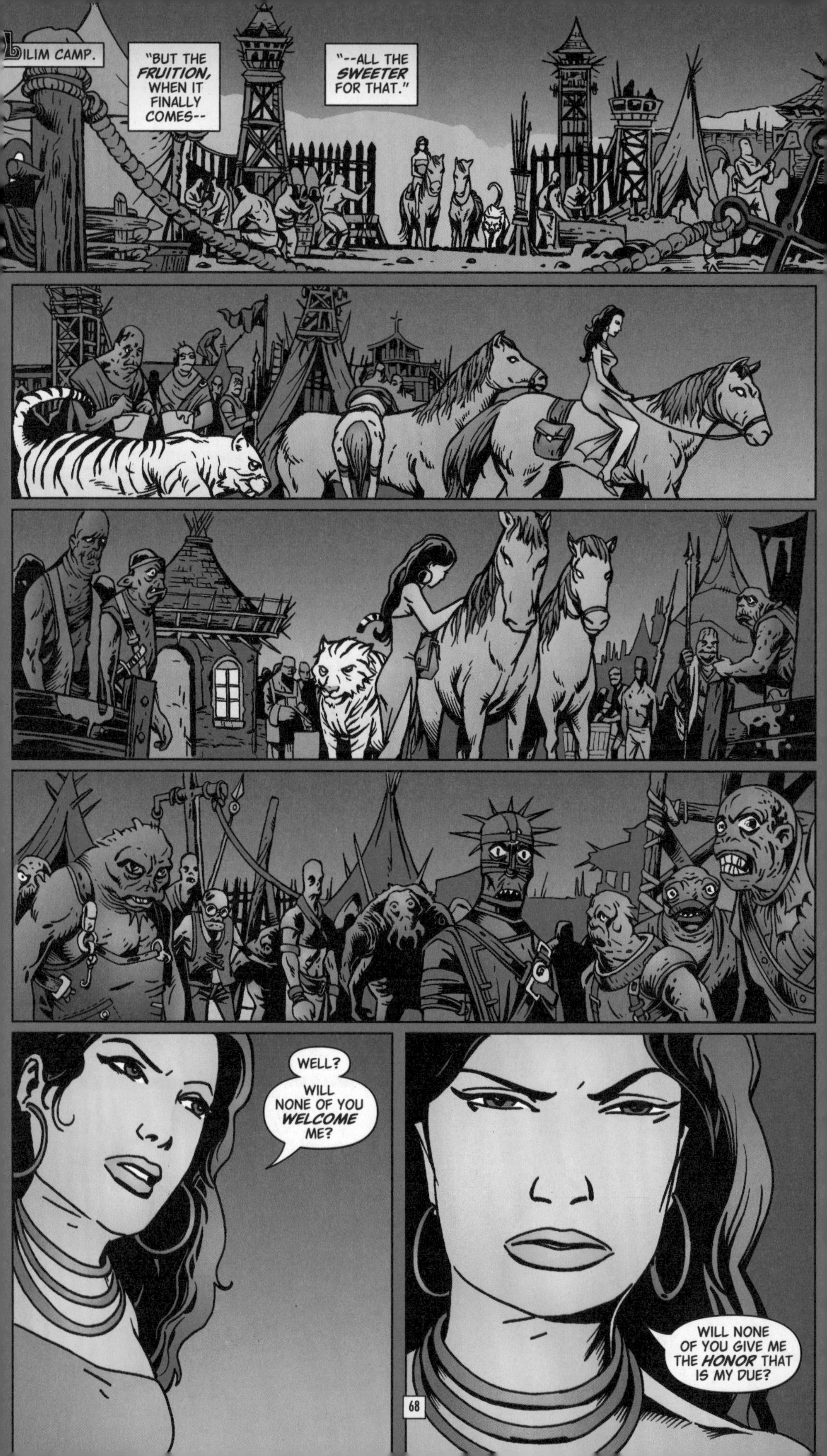

LILIM CAMP.
"BUT THE FRUITION, WHEN IT FINALLY COMES--
"--ALL THE SWEETER FOR THAT."
WELL?
WILL NONE OF YOU WELCOME ME?
WILL NONE OF YOU GIVE ME THE HONOR THAT IS MY DUE?

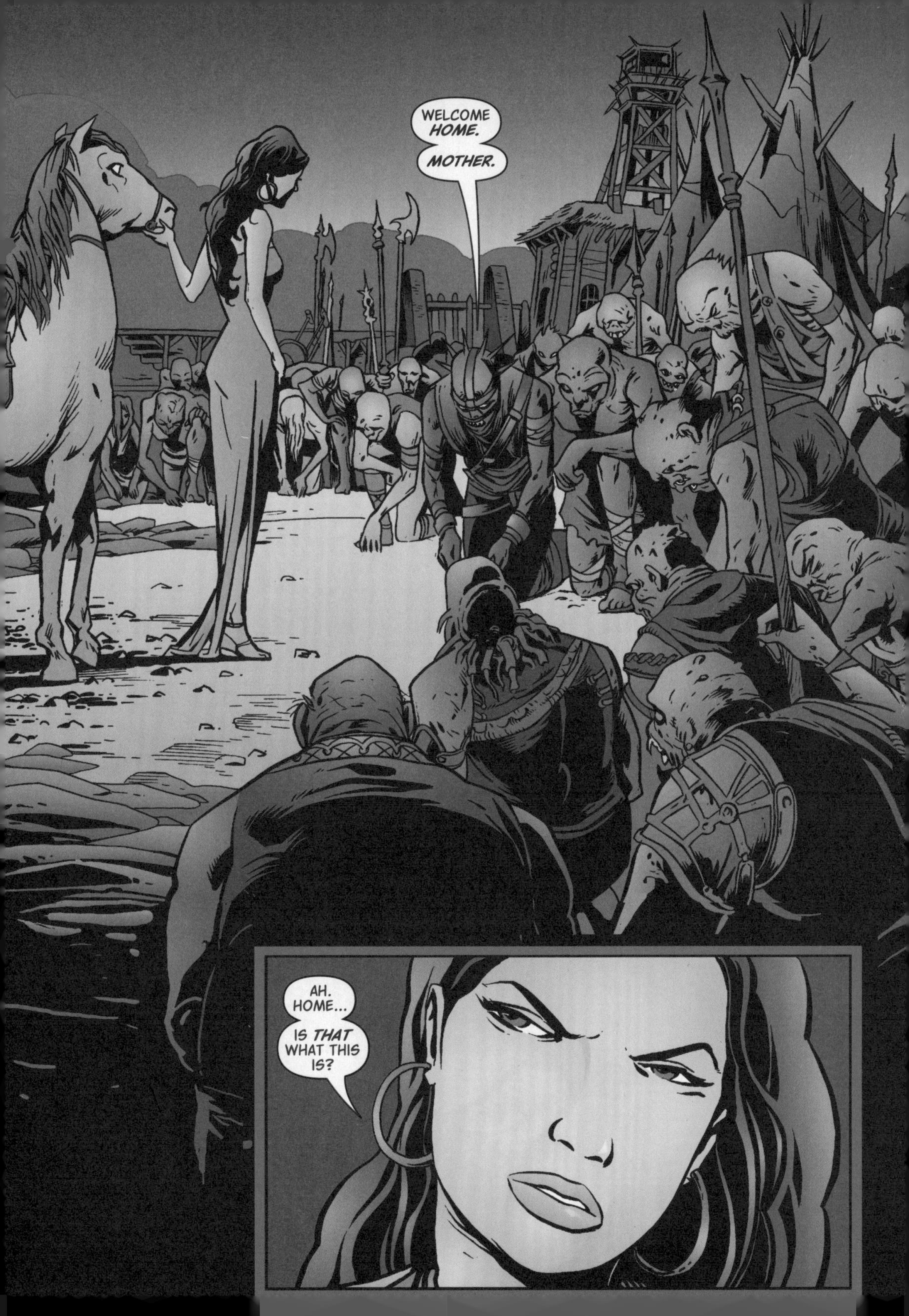
WELCOME HOME.
MOTHER.
AH. HOME...
IS THAT WHAT THIS IS?

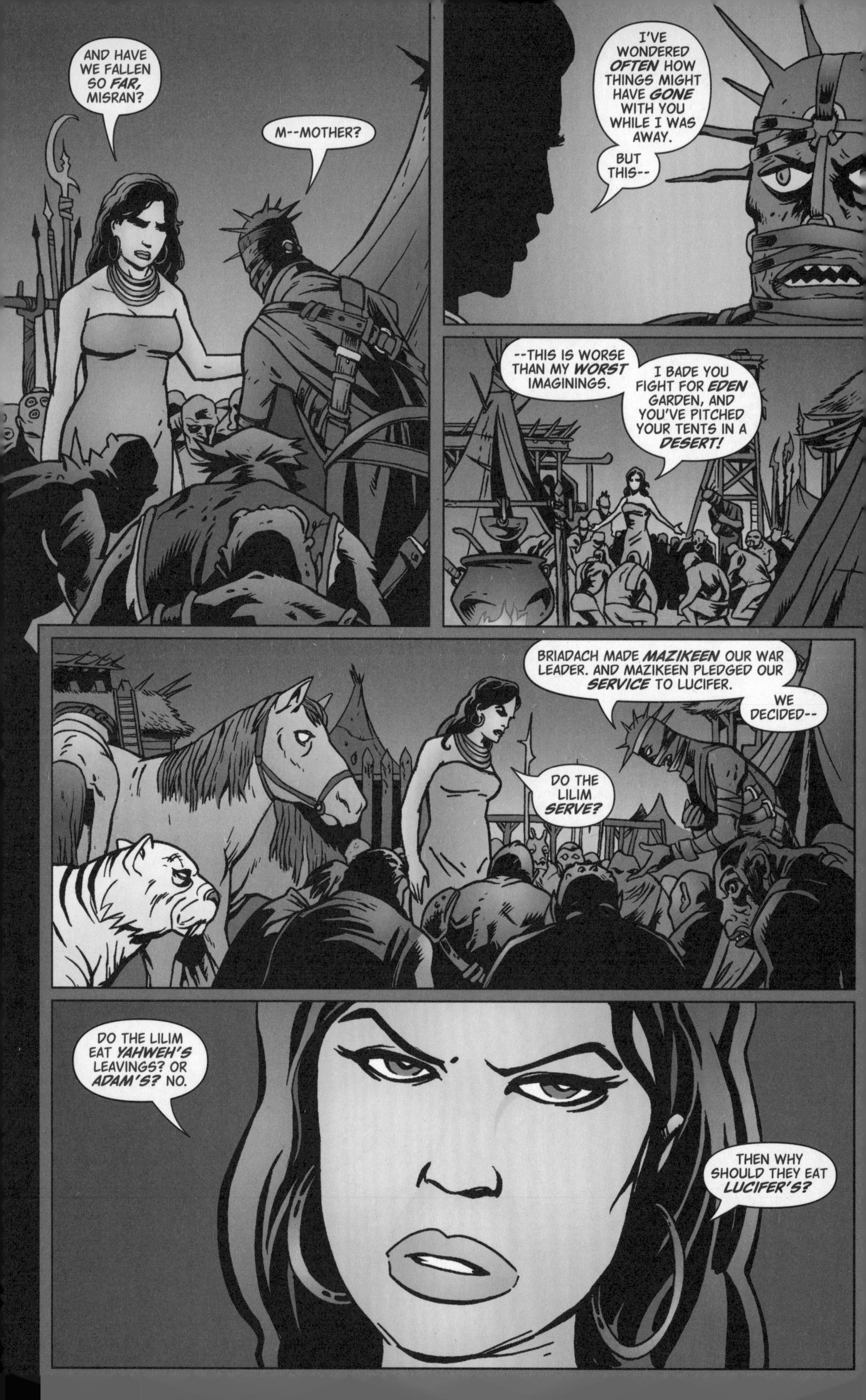
AND HAVE WE FALLEN SO FAR, MISRAN?
M--MOTHER?
I'VE WONDERED OFTEN HOW THINGS MIGHT HAVE GONE WITH YOU WHILE I WAS AWAY.
BUT THIS--
--THIS IS WORSE THAN MY WORST IMAGININGS.
I BADE YOU FIGHT FOR EDEN GARDEN, AND YOU'VE PITCHED YOUR TENTS IN A DESERT!
BRIADACH MADE MAZIKEEN OUR WAR LEADER. AND MAZIKEEN PLEDGED OUR SERVICE TO LUCIFER.
WE DECIDED--
DO THE LILIM SERVE?
DO THE LILIM EAT YAHWEH'S LEAVINGS? OR ADAM'S? NO.
THEN WHY SHOULD THEY EAT LUCIFER'S?

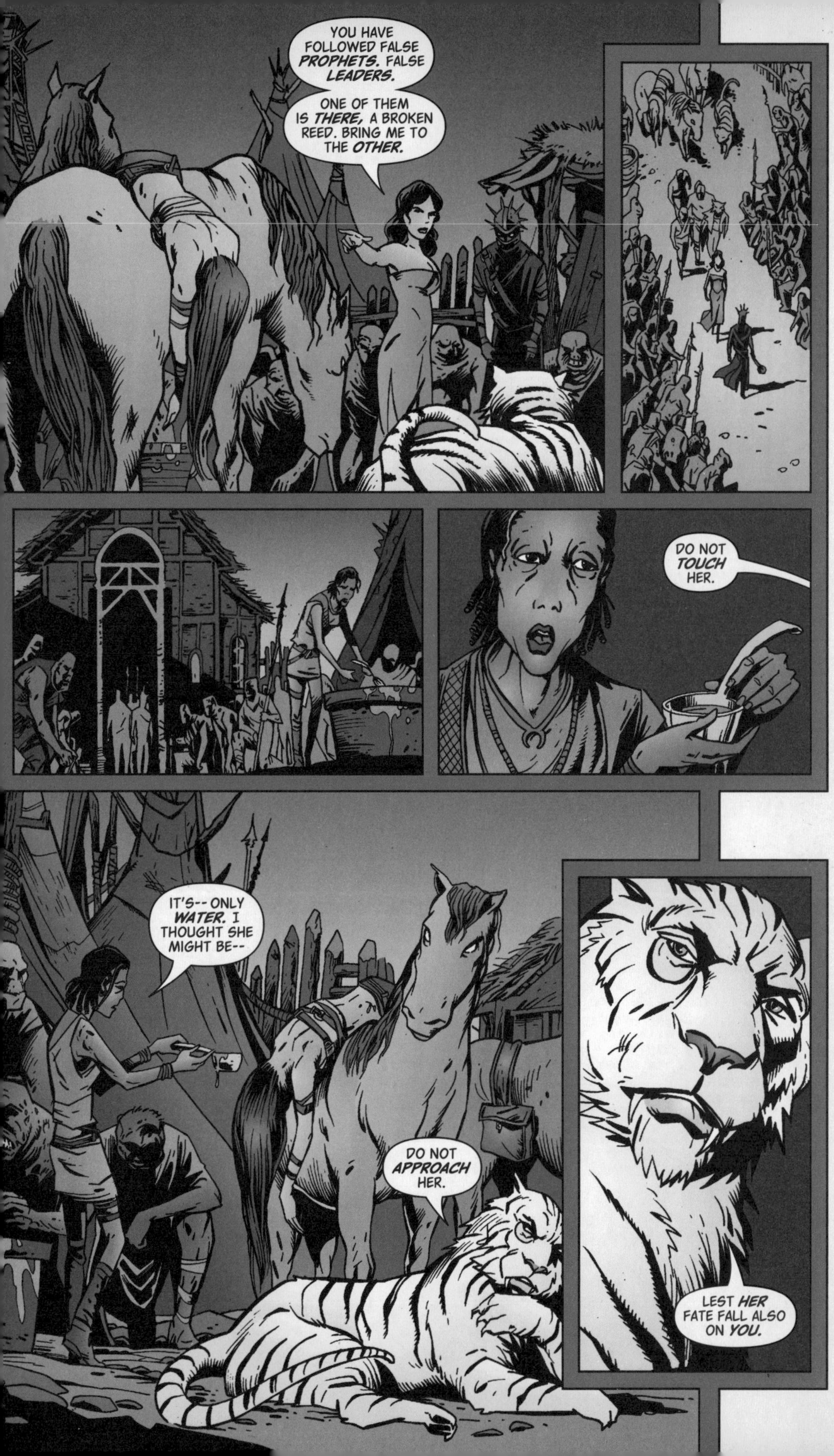

YOU HAVE FOLLOWED FALSE PROPHETS. FALSE LEADERS.
ONE OF THEM IS THERE, A BROKEN REED. BRING ME TO THE OTHER.
DO NOT TOUCH HER.
IT'S-- ONLY WATER. I THOUGHT SHE MIGHT BE--
DO NOT APPROACH HER.
LEST HER FATE FALL ALSO ON YOU.

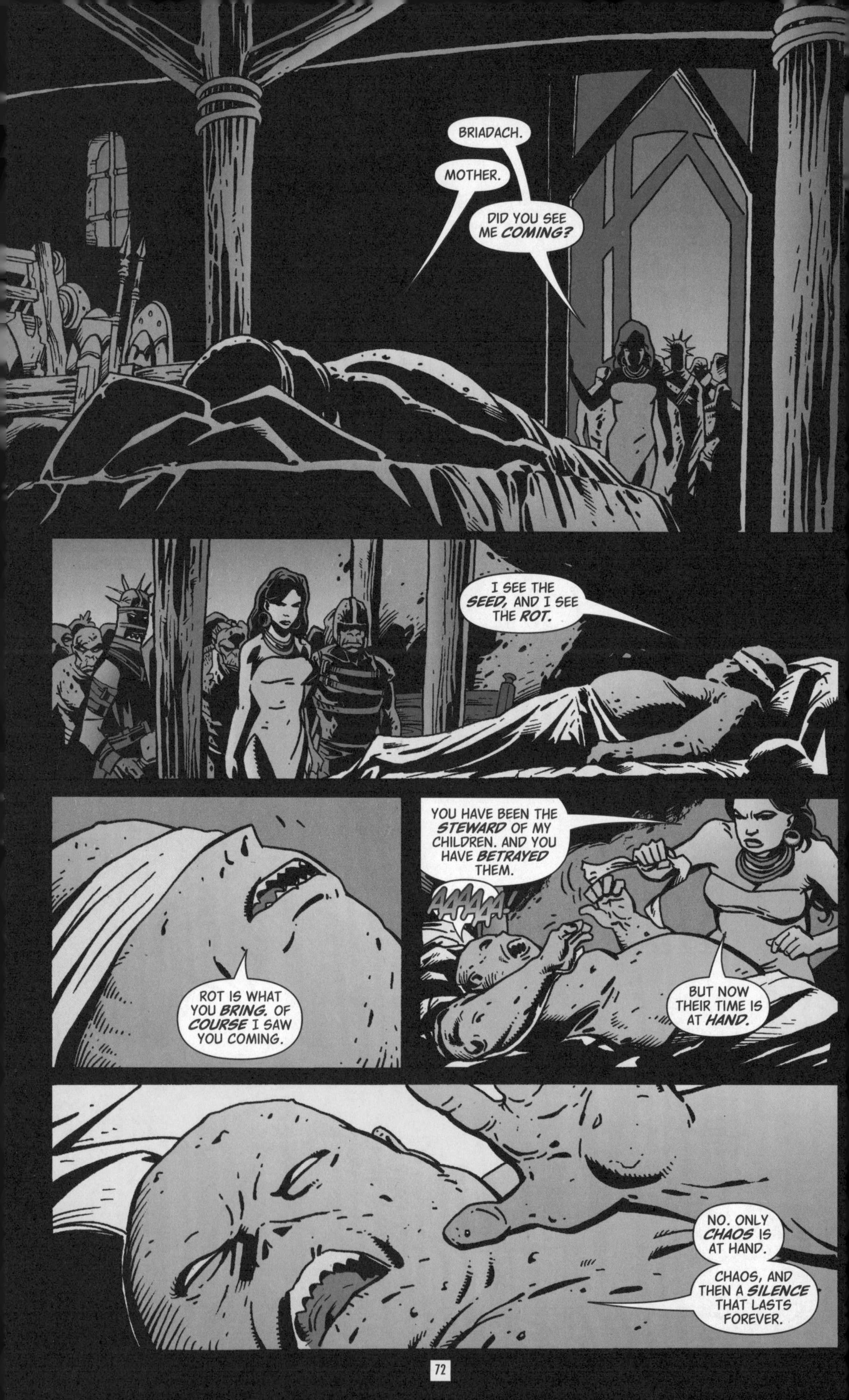
BRIADACH.
MOTHER.
DID YOU SEE ME *COMING?*
I SEE THE *SEED,* AND I SEE THE *ROT.*
ROT IS WHAT YOU *BRING.* OF *COURSE* I SAW YOU COMING.
YOU HAVE BEEN THE *STEWARD* OF MY CHILDREN. AND YOU HAVE *BETRAYED* THEM.
AAAAAA!
BUT NOW THEIR TIME IS AT *HAND.*
NO. ONLY *CHAOS* IS AT HAND.
CHAOS, AND THEN A *SILENCE* THAT LASTS FOREVER.

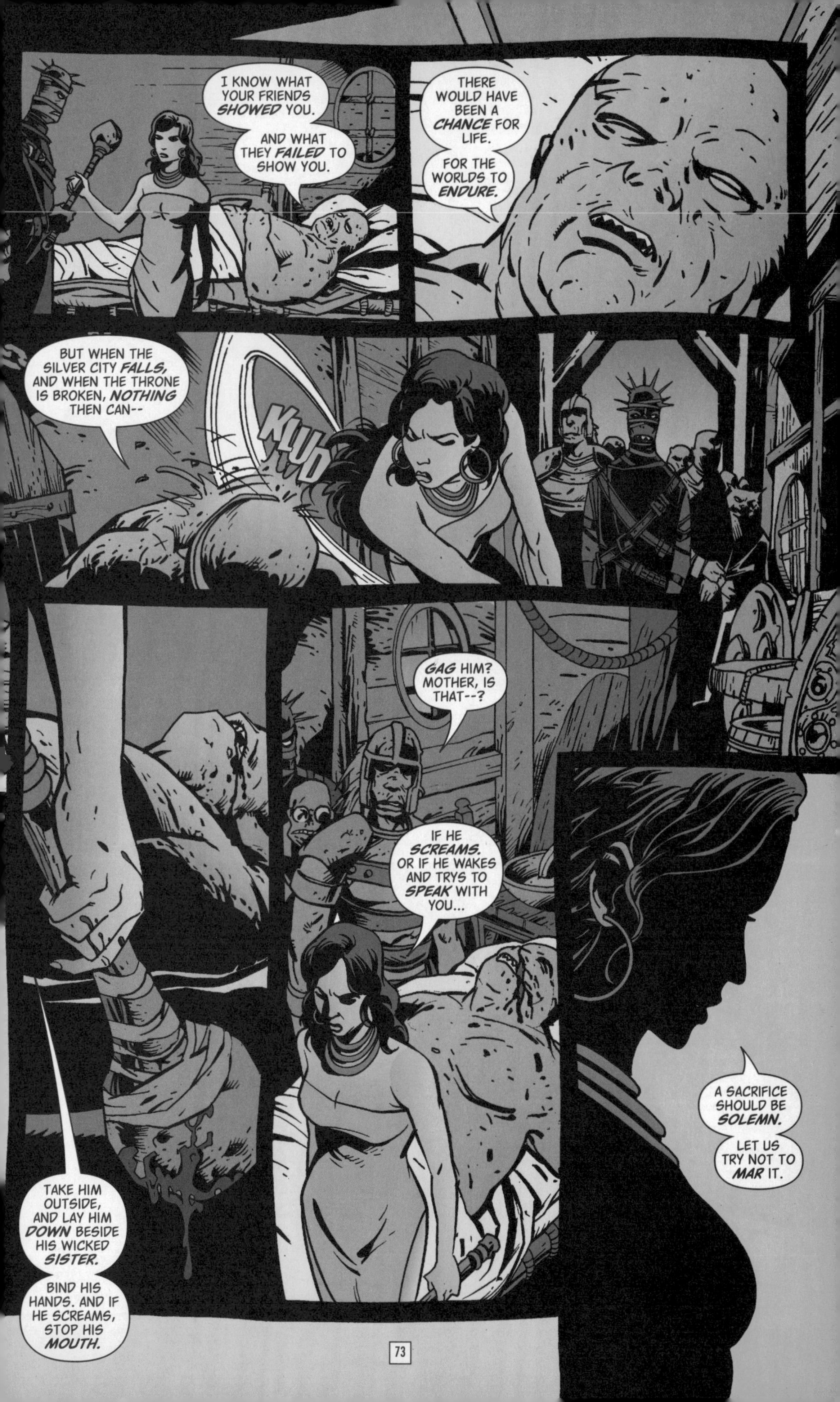

I KNOW WHAT YOUR FRIENDS SHOWED YOU.
AND WHAT THEY FAILED TO SHOW YOU.
THERE WOULD HAVE BEEN A CHANCE FOR LIFE.
FOR THE WORLDS TO ENDURE.
BUT WHEN THE SILVER CITY FALLS, AND WHEN THE THRONE IS BROKEN, NOTHING THEN CAN--
KLUD
TAKE HIM OUTSIDE, AND LAY HIM DOWN BESIDE HIS WICKED SISTER.
BIND HIS HANDS. AND IF HE SCREAMS, STOP HIS MOUTH.
GAG HIM? MOTHER, IS THAT--?
IF HE SCREAMS. OR IF HE WAKES AND TRYS TO SPEAK WITH YOU...
A SACRIFICE SHOULD BE SOLEMN.
LET US TRY NOT TO MAR IT.

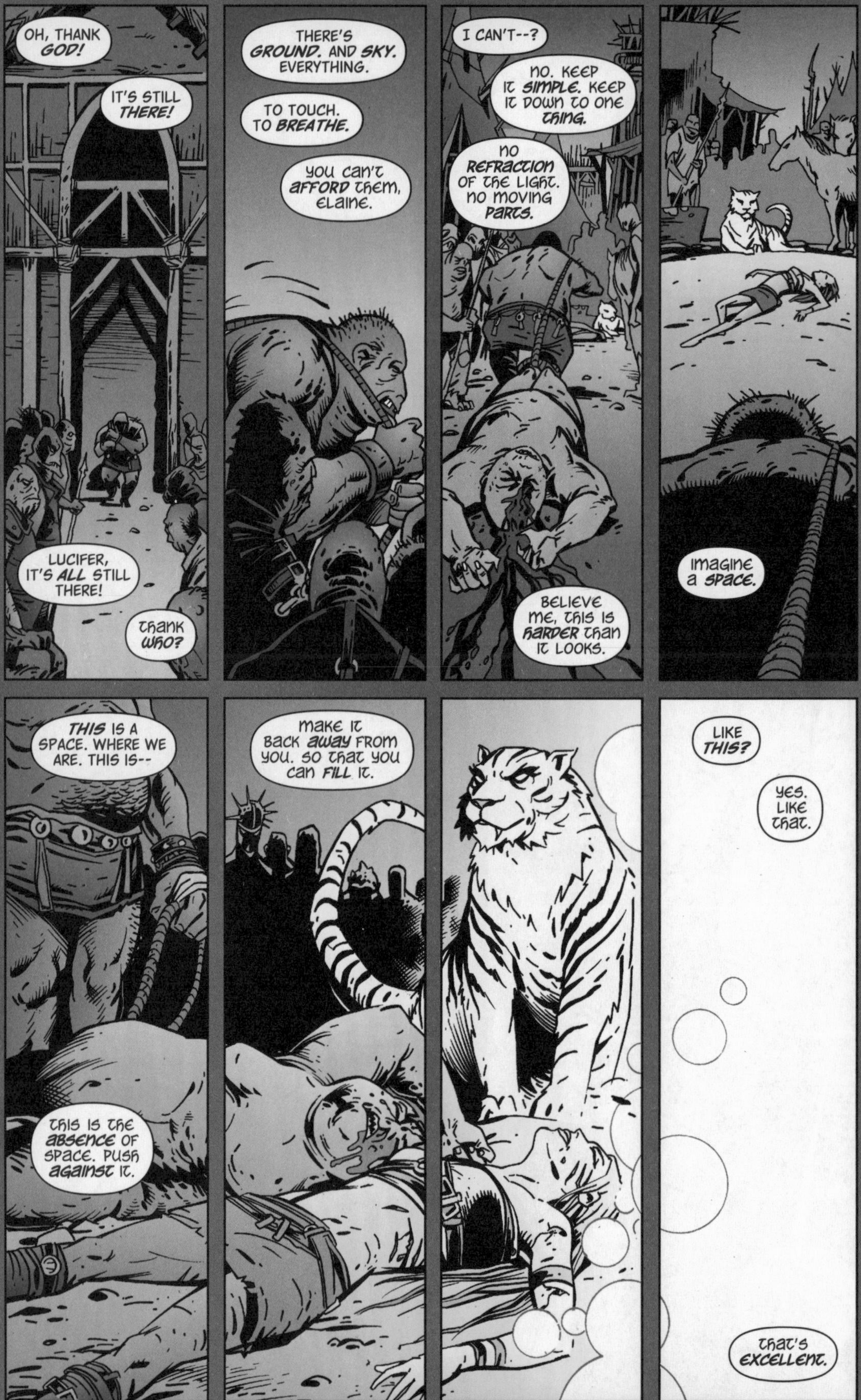

OH, THANK GOD!
IT'S STILL THERE!
LUCIFER, IT'S ALL STILL THERE!
THANK WHO?
THERE'S GROUND. AND SKY. EVERYTHING.
TO TOUCH. TO BREATHE.
YOU CAN'T AFFORD THEM, ELAINE.
I CAN'T--?
NO. KEEP IT SIMPLE. KEEP IT DOWN TO ONE THING.
NO REFRACTION OF THE LIGHT. NO MOVING PARTS.
BELIEVE ME, THIS IS HARDER THAN IT LOOKS.
IMAGINE A SPACE.
THIS IS A SPACE. WHERE WE ARE. THIS IS--
THIS IS THE ABSENCE OF SPACE. PUSH AGAINST IT.
MAKE IT BACK AWAY FROM YOU. SO THAT YOU CAN FILL IT.
LIKE THIS?
YES. LIKE THAT.
THAT'S EXCELLENT.

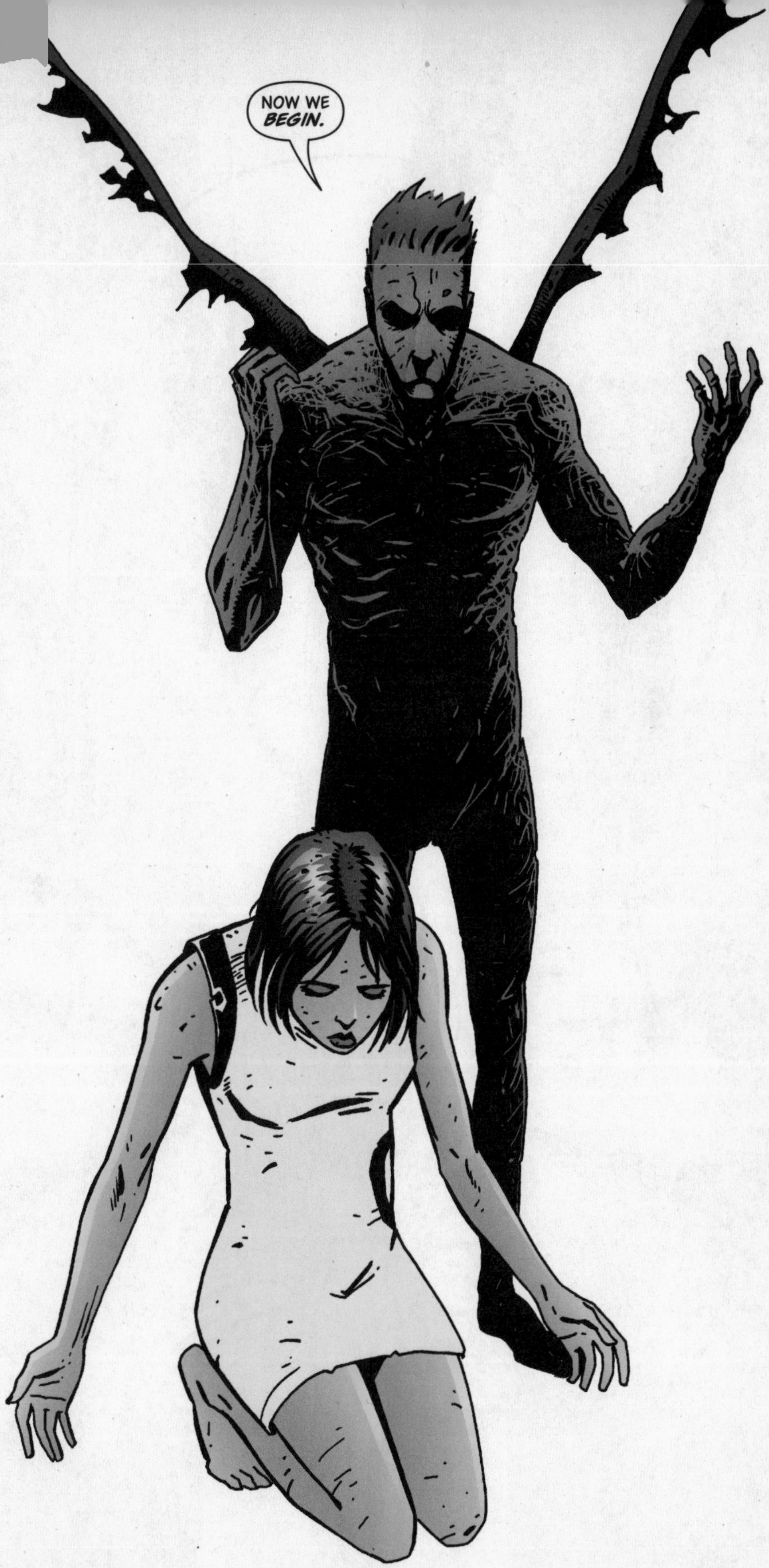
NOW WE BEGIN.

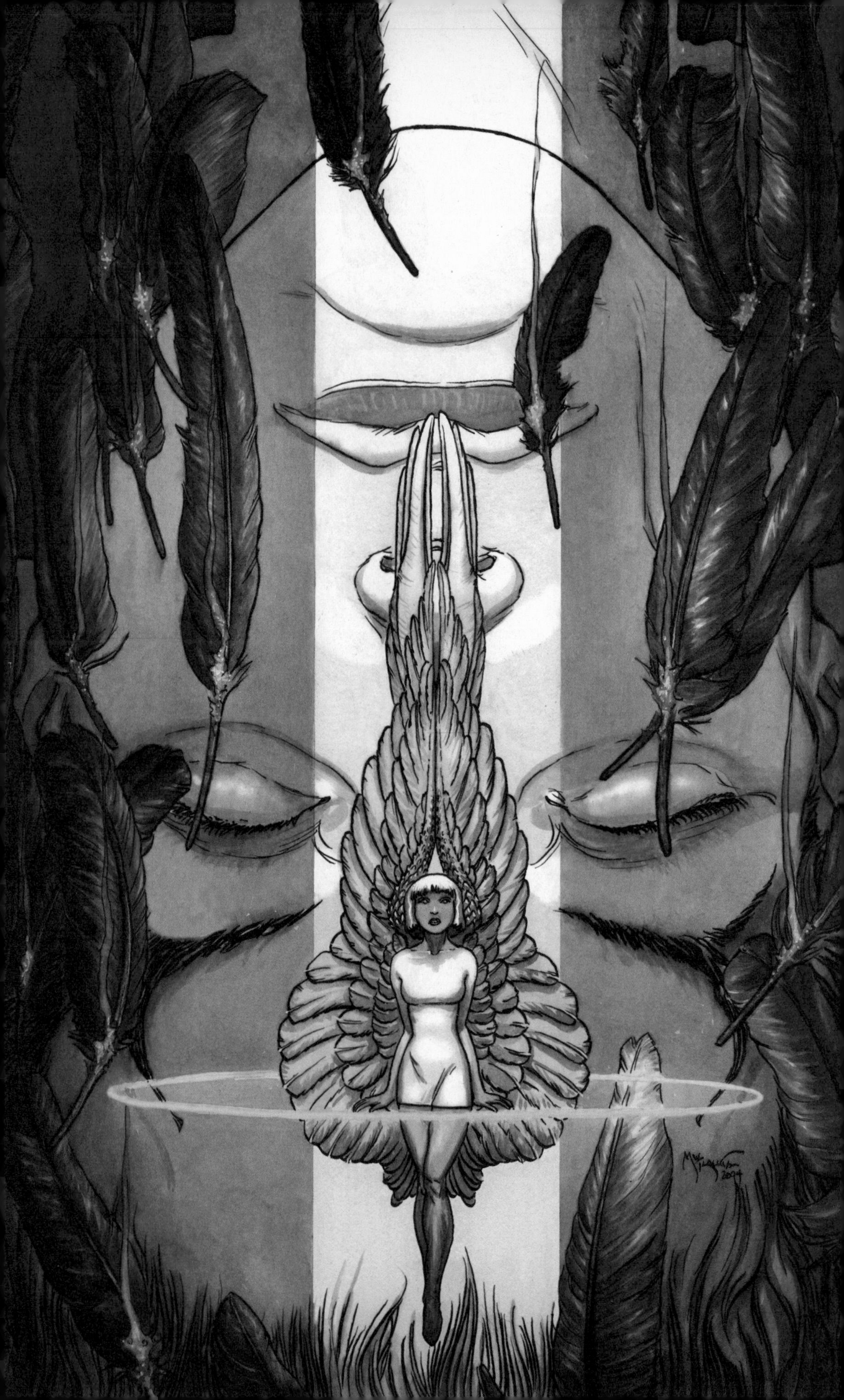

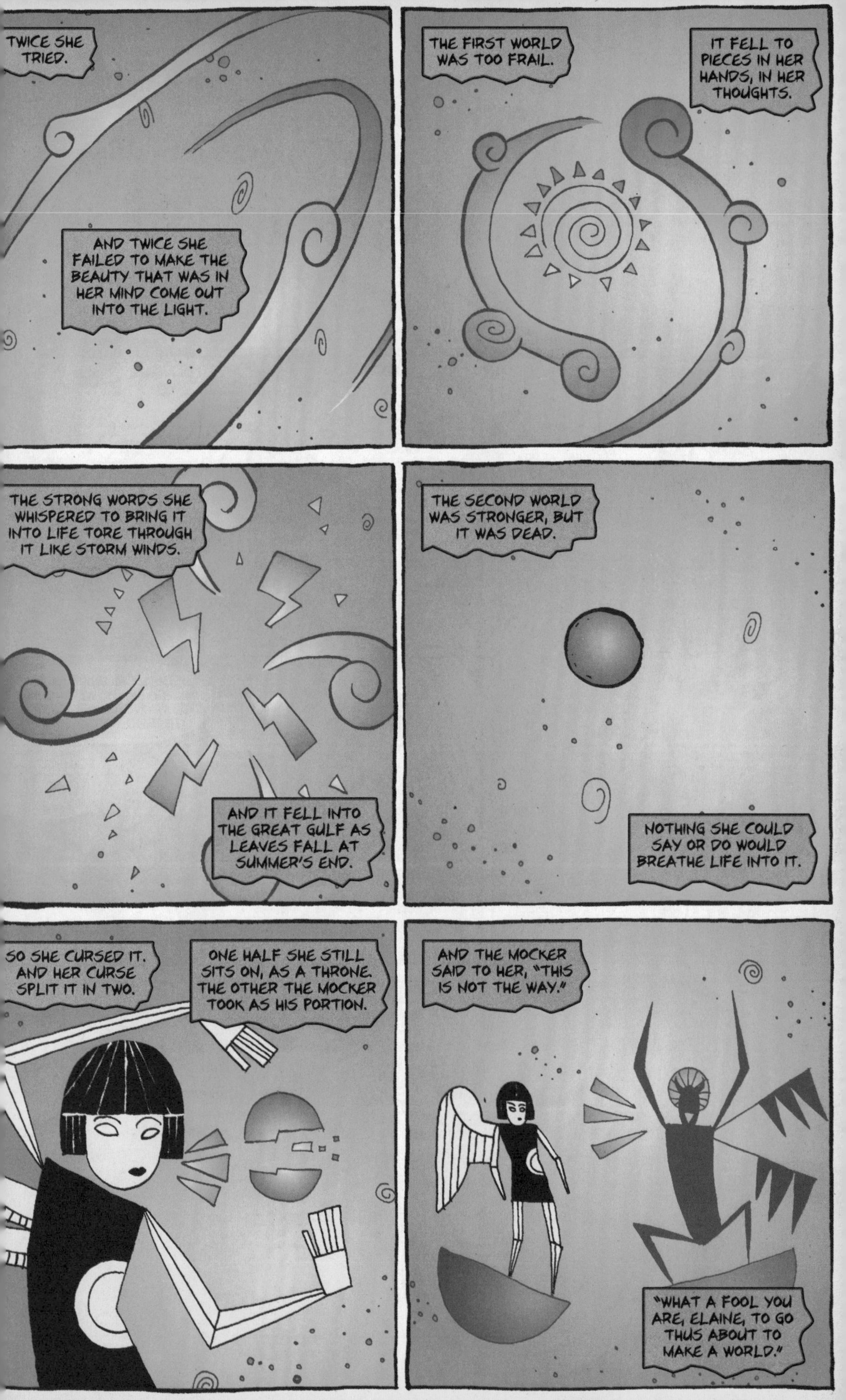
TWICE SHE TRIED.
AND TWICE SHE FAILED TO MAKE THE BEAUTY THAT WAS IN HER MIND COME OUT INTO THE LIGHT.
THE FIRST WORLD WAS TOO FRAIL.
IT FELL TO PIECES IN HER HANDS, IN HER THOUGHTS.
THE STRONG WORDS SHE WHISPERED TO BRING IT INTO LIFE TORE THROUGH IT LIKE STORM WINDS.
AND IT FELL INTO THE GREAT GULF AS LEAVES FALL AT SUMMER'S END.
THE SECOND WORLD WAS STRONGER, BUT IT WAS DEAD.
NOTHING SHE COULD SAY OR DO WOULD BREATHE LIFE INTO IT.
SO SHE CURSED IT. AND HER CURSE SPLIT IT IN TWO.
ONE HALF SHE STILL SITS ON, AS A THRONE. THE OTHER THE MOCKER TOOK AS HIS PORTION.
AND THE MOCKER SAID TO HER, "THIS IS NOT THE WAY."
"WHAT A FOOL YOU ARE, ELAINE, TO GO THUS ABOUT TO MAKE A WORLD."

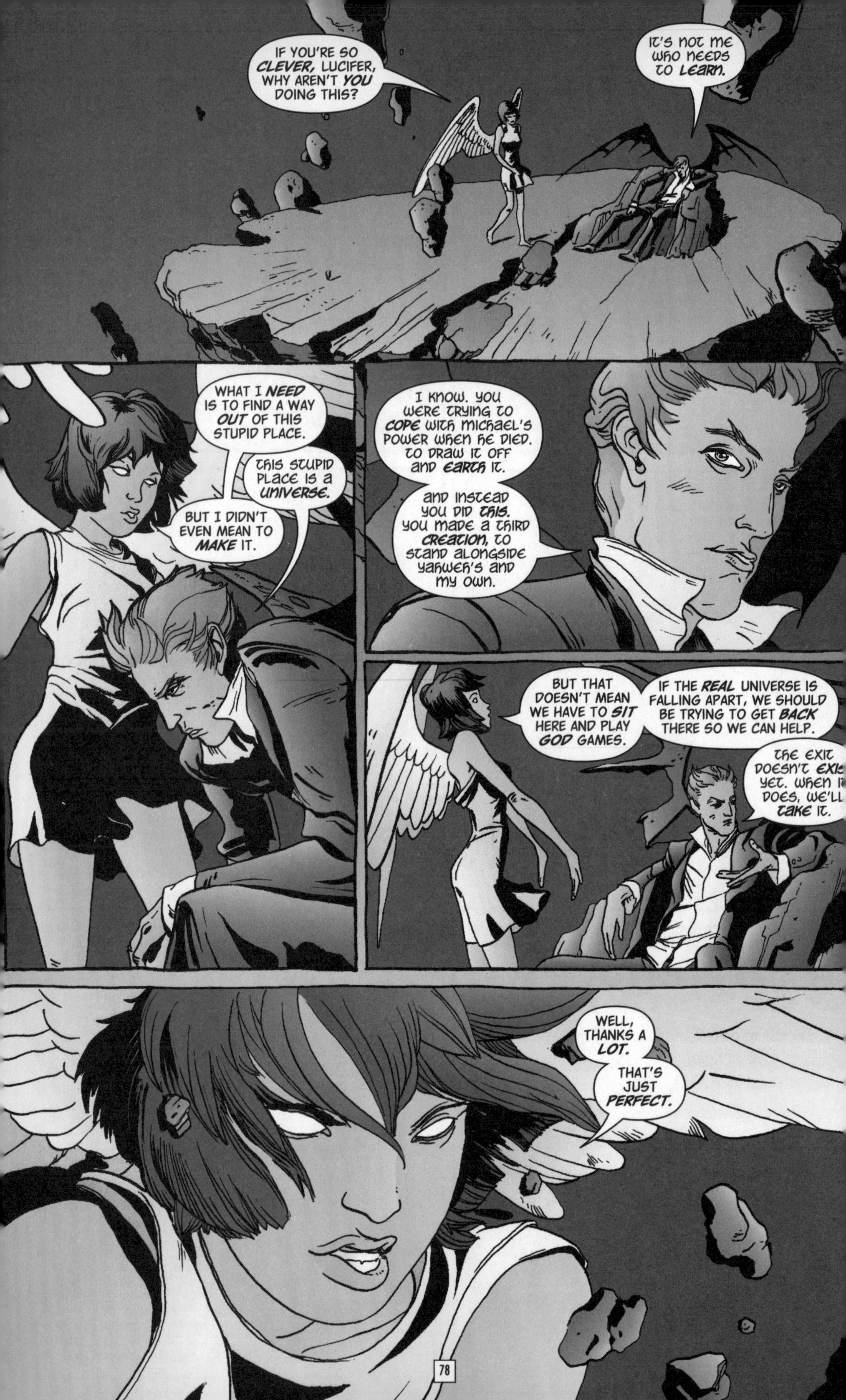
IF YOU'RE SO CLEVER, LUCIFER, WHY AREN'T YOU DOING THIS?
IT'S NOT ME WHO NEEDS TO LEARN.
WHAT I NEED IS TO FIND A WAY OUT OF THIS STUPID PLACE.
THIS STUPID PLACE IS A UNIVERSE.
BUT I DIDN'T EVEN MEAN TO MAKE IT.
I KNOW. YOU WERE TRYING TO COPE WITH MICHAEL'S POWER WHEN HE DIED. TO DRAW IT OFF AND EARTH IT.
AND INSTEAD YOU DID THIS. YOU MADE A THIRD CREATION, TO STAND ALONGSIDE YAHWEH'S AND MY OWN.
BUT THAT DOESN'T MEAN WE HAVE TO SIT HERE AND PLAY GOD GAMES.
IF THE REAL UNIVERSE IS FALLING APART, WE SHOULD BE TRYING TO GET BACK THERE SO WE CAN HELP.
THE EXIT DOESN'T EXIS YET. WHEN IT DOES, WE'LL TAKE IT.
WELL, THANKS A LOT.
THAT'S JUST PERFECT.

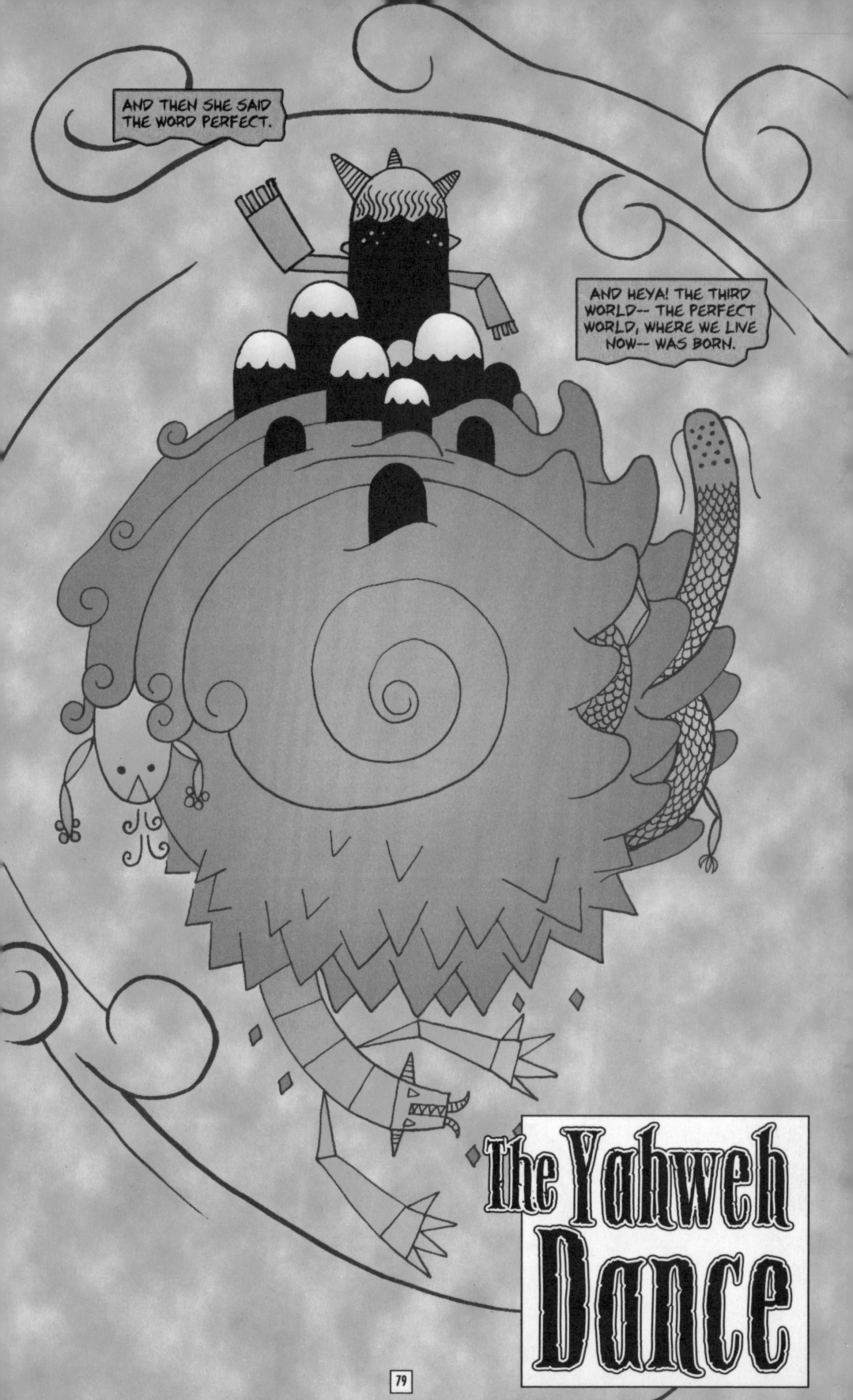
AND THEN SHE SAID THE WORD PERFECT.
AND HEYA! THE THIRD WORLD-- THE PERFECT WORLD, WHERE WE LIVE NOW-- WAS BORN.
The Yahweh Dance

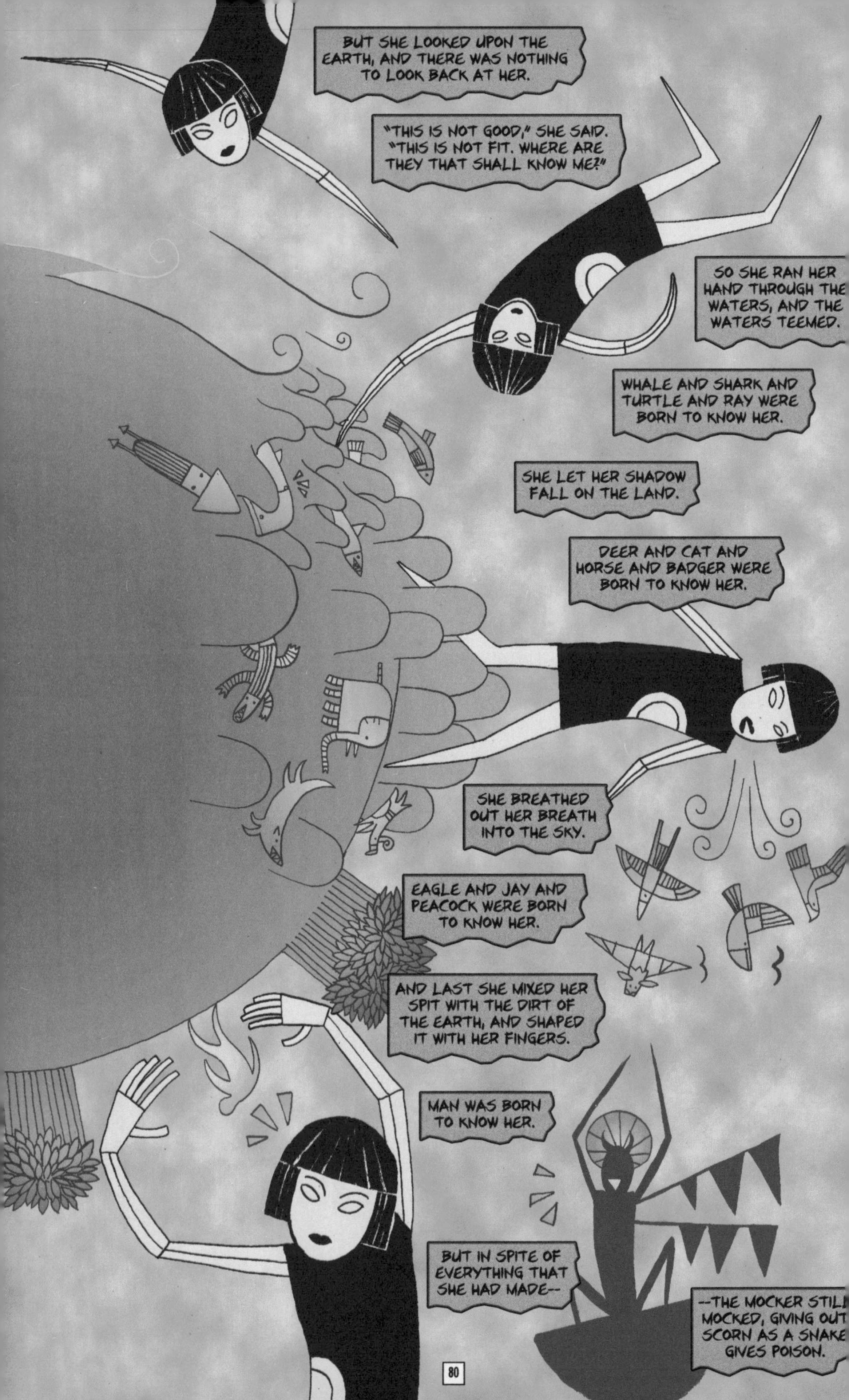

BUT SHE LOOKED UPON THE EARTH, AND THERE WAS NOTHING TO LOOK BACK AT HER.
"THIS IS NOT GOOD," SHE SAID. "THIS IS NOT FIT. WHERE ARE THEY THAT SHALL KNOW ME?"
SO SHE RAN HER HAND THROUGH THE WATERS, AND THE WATERS TEEMED.
WHALE AND SHARK AND TURTLE AND RAY WERE BORN TO KNOW HER.
SHE LET HER SHADOW FALL ON THE LAND.
DEER AND CAT AND HORSE AND BADGER WERE BORN TO KNOW HER.
SHE BREATHED OUT HER BREATH INTO THE SKY.
EAGLE AND JAY AND PEACOCK WERE BORN TO KNOW HER.
AND LAST SHE MIXED HER SPIT WITH THE DIRT OF THE EARTH, AND SHAPED IT WITH HER FINGERS.
MAN WAS BORN TO KNOW HER.
BUT IN SPITE OF EVERYTHING THAT SHE HAD MADE--
--THE MOCKER STILL MOCKED, GIVING OUT SCORN AS A SNAKE GIVES POISON.

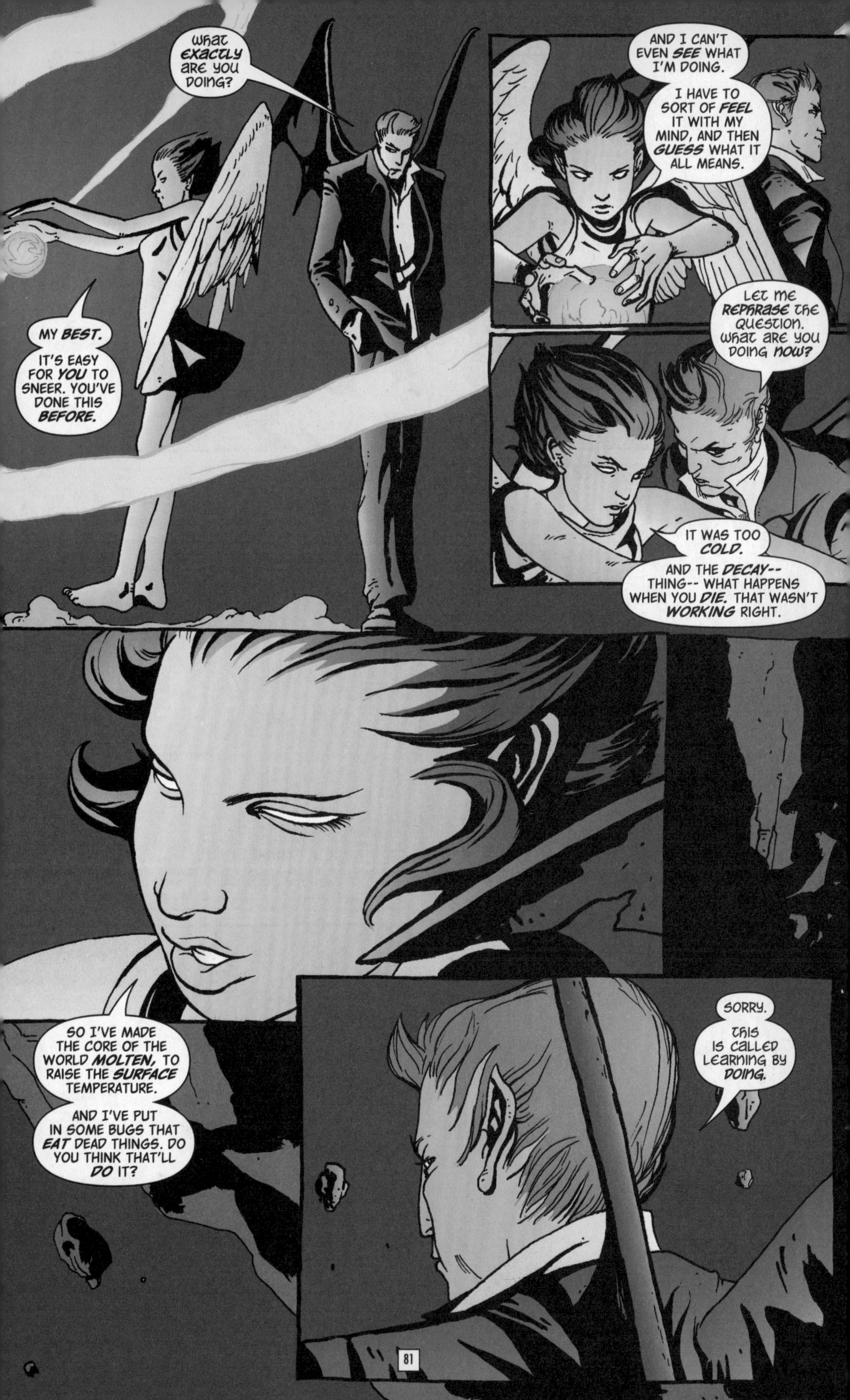
WHAT EXACTLY ARE YOU DOING?
MY BEST.
IT'S EASY FOR YOU TO SNEER. YOU'VE DONE THIS BEFORE.
AND I CAN'T EVEN SEE WHAT I'M DOING.
I HAVE TO SORT OF FEEL IT WITH MY MIND, AND THEN GUESS WHAT IT ALL MEANS.
LET ME REPHRASE THE QUESTION. WHAT ARE YOU DOING NOW?
IT WAS TOO COLD.
AND THE DECAY-- THING-- WHAT HAPPENS WHEN YOU DIE. THAT WASN'T WORKING RIGHT.
SO I'VE MADE THE CORE OF THE WORLD MOLTEN, TO RAISE THE SURFACE TEMPERATURE.
AND I'VE PUT IN SOME BUGS THAT EAT DEAD THINGS. DO YOU THINK THAT'LL DO IT?
SORRY.
THIS IS CALLED LEARNING BY DOING.

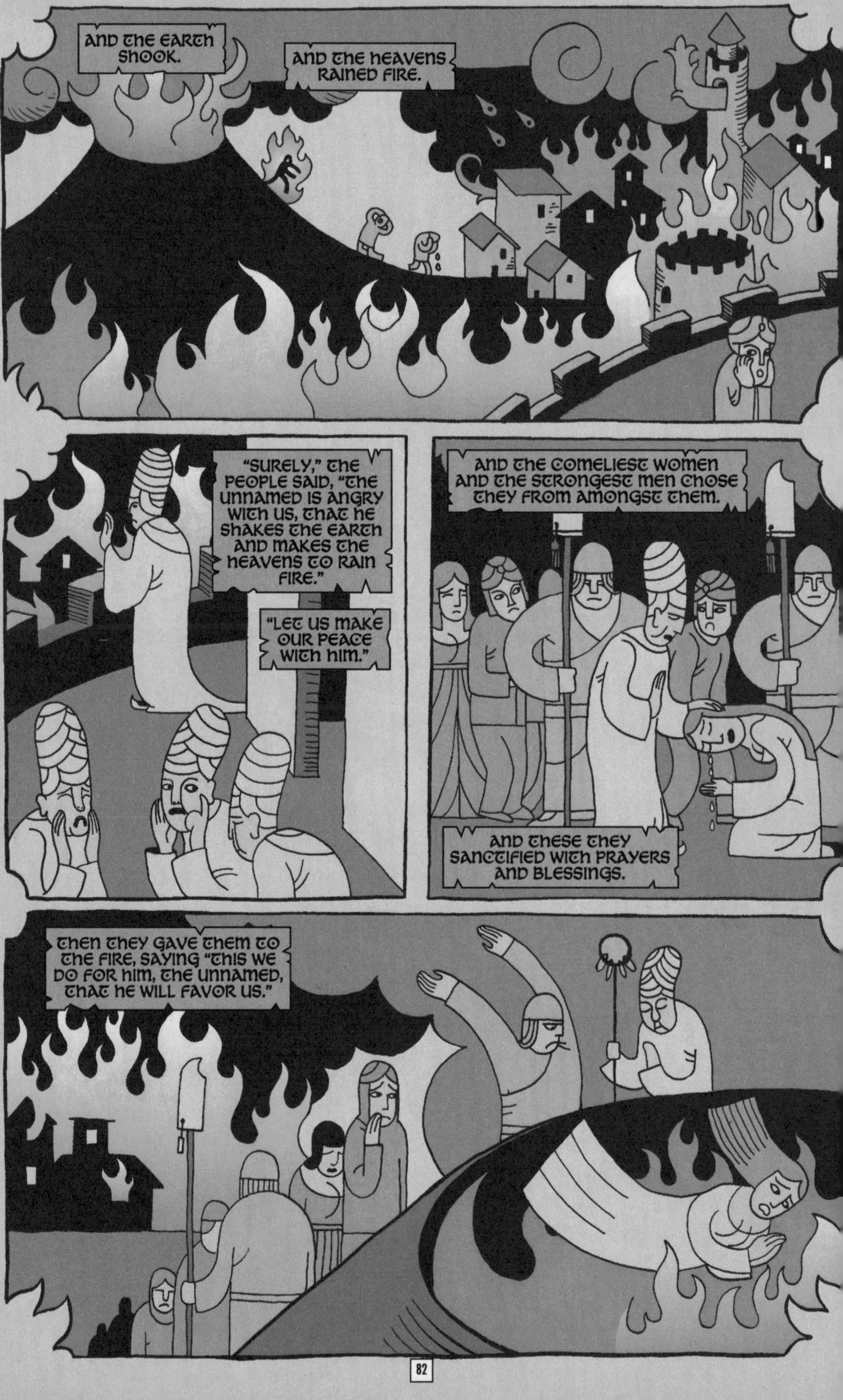
AND THE EARTH SHOOK.
AND THE HEAVENS RAINED FIRE.
"SURELY," THE PEOPLE SAID, "THE UNNAMED IS ANGRY WITH US, THAT HE SHAKES THE EARTH AND MAKES THE HEAVENS TO RAIN FIRE."
"LET US MAKE OUR PEACE WITH HIM."
AND THE COMELIEST WOMEN AND THE STRONGEST MEN CHOSE THEY FROM AMONGST THEM.
AND THESE THEY SANCTIFIED WITH PRAYERS AND BLESSINGS.
THEN THEY GAVE THEM TO THE FIRE, SAYING "THIS WE DO FOR HIM, THE UNNAMED, THAT HE WILL FAVOR US."

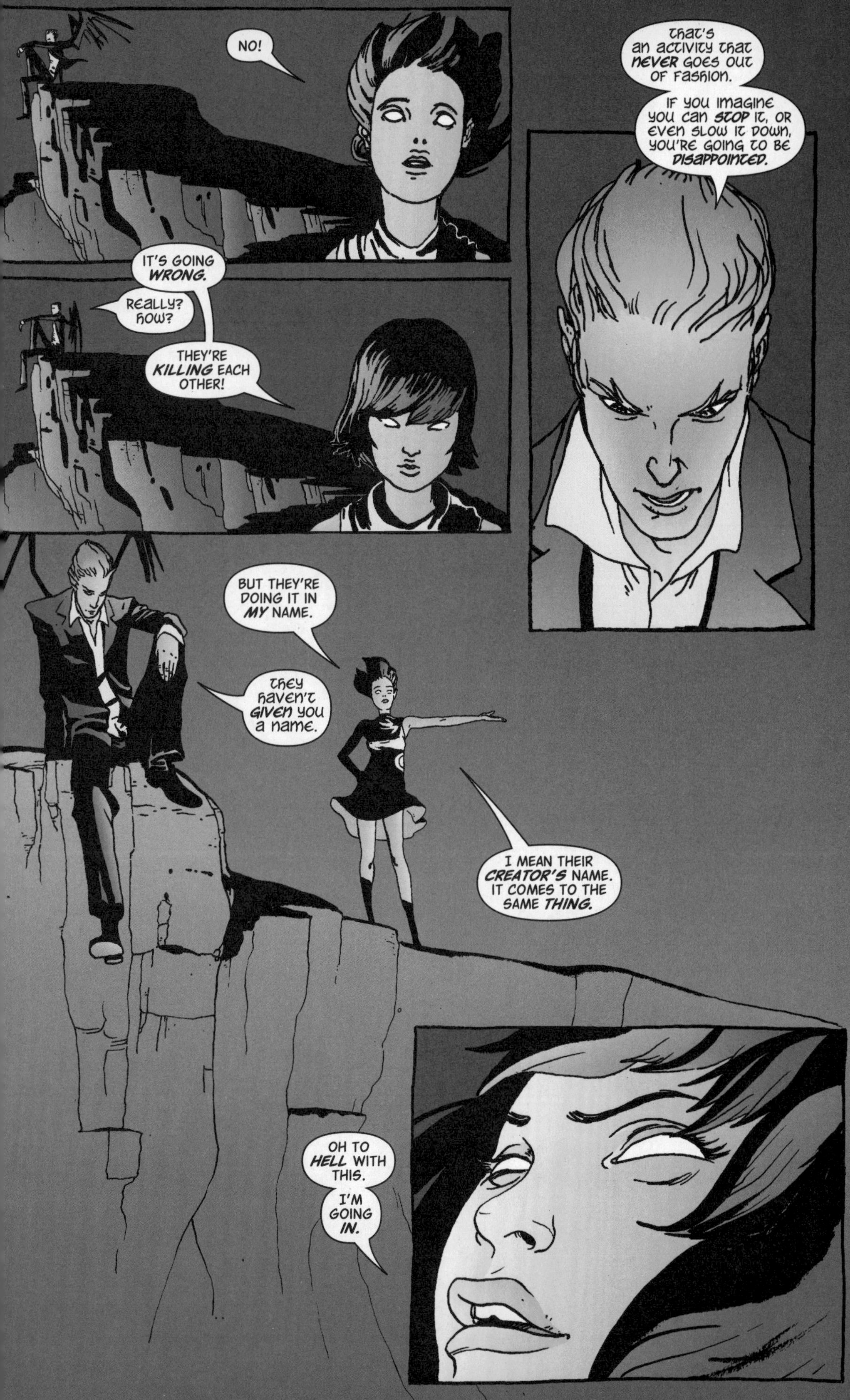
NO!
THAT'S AN ACTIVITY THAT NEVER GOES OUT OF FASHION.
IF YOU IMAGINE YOU CAN STOP IT, OR EVEN SLOW IT DOWN, YOU'RE GOING TO BE DISAPPOINTED.
IT'S GOING WRONG.
REALLY? HOW?
THEY'RE KILLING EACH OTHER!
BUT THEY'RE DOING IT IN MY NAME.
THEY HAVEN'T GIVEN YOU A NAME.
I MEAN THEIR CREATOR'S NAME. IT COMES TO THE SAME THING.
OH TO HELL WITH THIS.
I'M GOING IN.

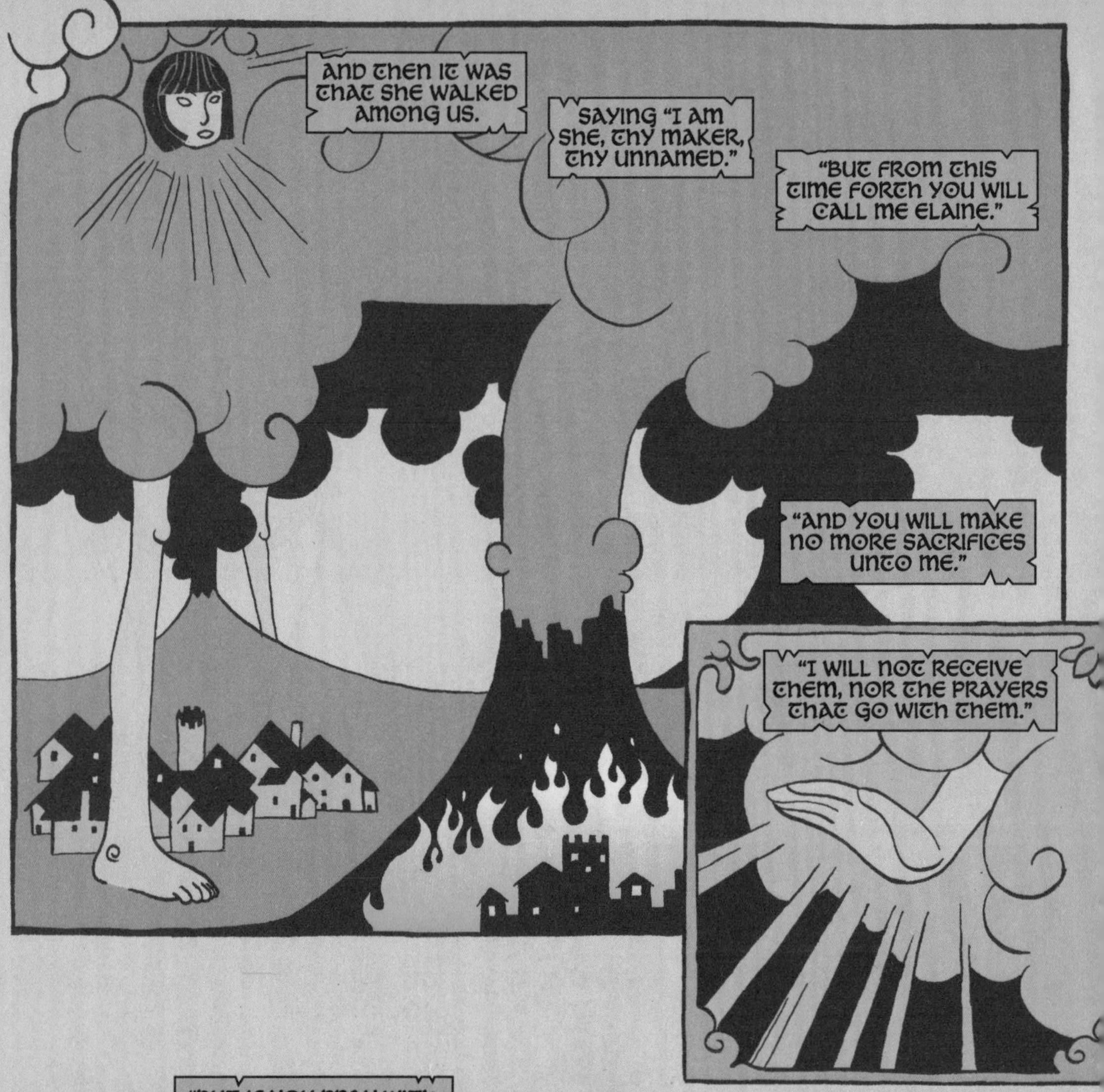
AND THEN IT WAS THAT SHE WALKED AMONG US.
SAYING "I AM SHE, THY MAKER, THY UNNAMED."
"BUT FROM THIS TIME FORTH YOU WILL CALL ME ELAINE."
"AND YOU WILL MAKE NO MORE SACRIFICES UNTO ME."
"I WILL NOT RECEIVE THEM, NOR THE PRAYERS THAT GO WITH THEM."

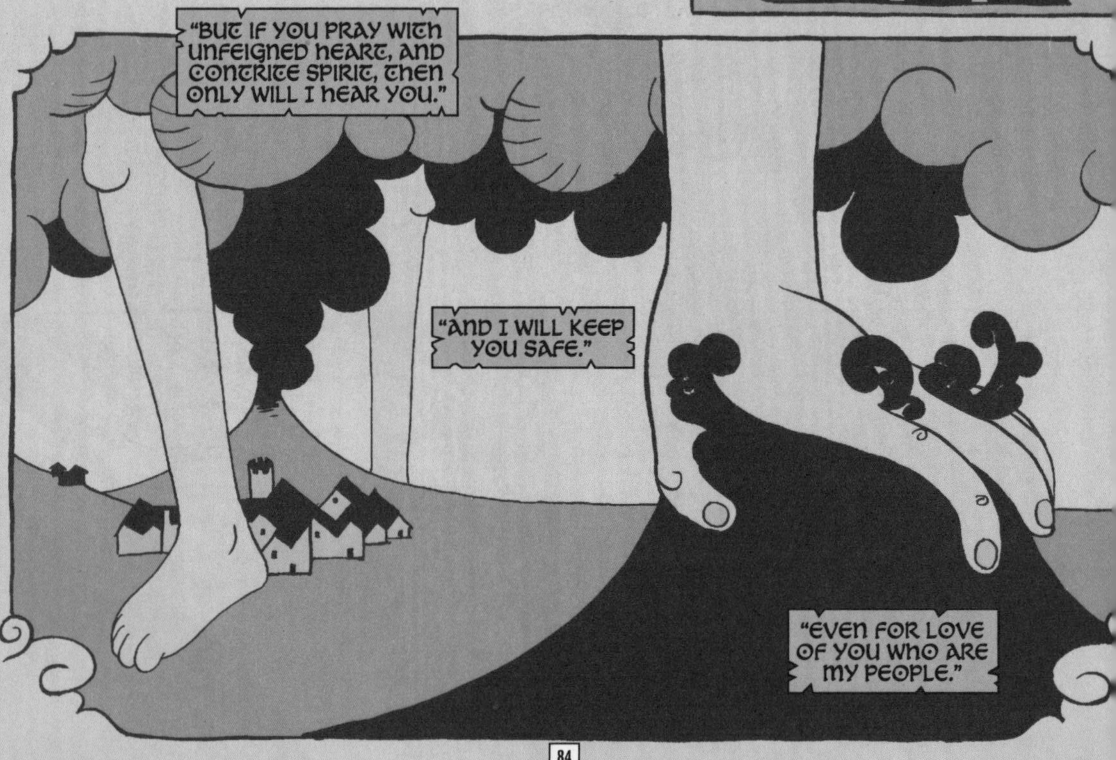
"BUT IF YOU PRAY WITH UNFEIGNED HEART, AND CONTRITE SPIRIT, THEN ONLY WILL I HEAR YOU."
"AND I WILL KEEP YOU SAFE."
"EVEN FOR LOVE OF YOU WHO ARE MY PEOPLE."

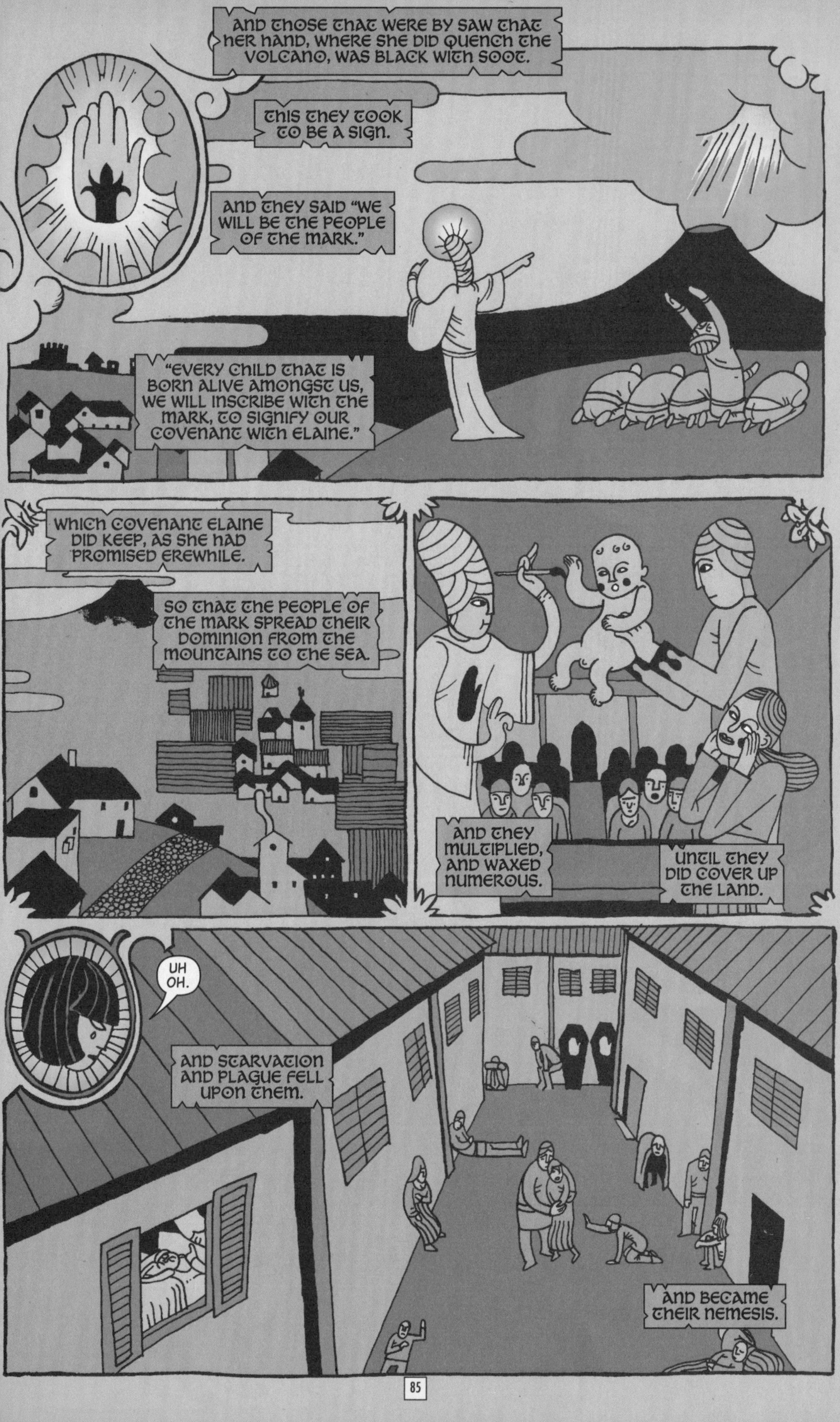
AND THOSE THAT WERE BY SAW THAT HER HAND, WHERE SHE DID QUENCH THE VOLCANO, WAS BLACK WITH SOOT.
THIS THEY TOOK TO BE A SIGN.
AND THEY SAID "WE WILL BE THE PEOPLE OF THE MARK."
"EVERY CHILD THAT IS BORN ALIVE AMONGST US, WE WILL INSCRIBE WITH THE MARK, TO SIGNIFY OUR COVENANT WITH ELAINE."
WHICH COVENANT ELAINE DID KEEP, AS SHE HAD PROMISED EREWHILE.
SO THAT THE PEOPLE OF THE MARK SPREAD THEIR DOMINION FROM THE MOUNTAINS TO THE SEA.
AND THEY MULTIPLIED, AND WAXED NUMEROUS.
UNTIL THEY DID COVER UP THE LAND.
UH OH.
AND STARVATION AND PLAGUE FELL UPON THEM.
AND BECAME THEIR NEMESIS.

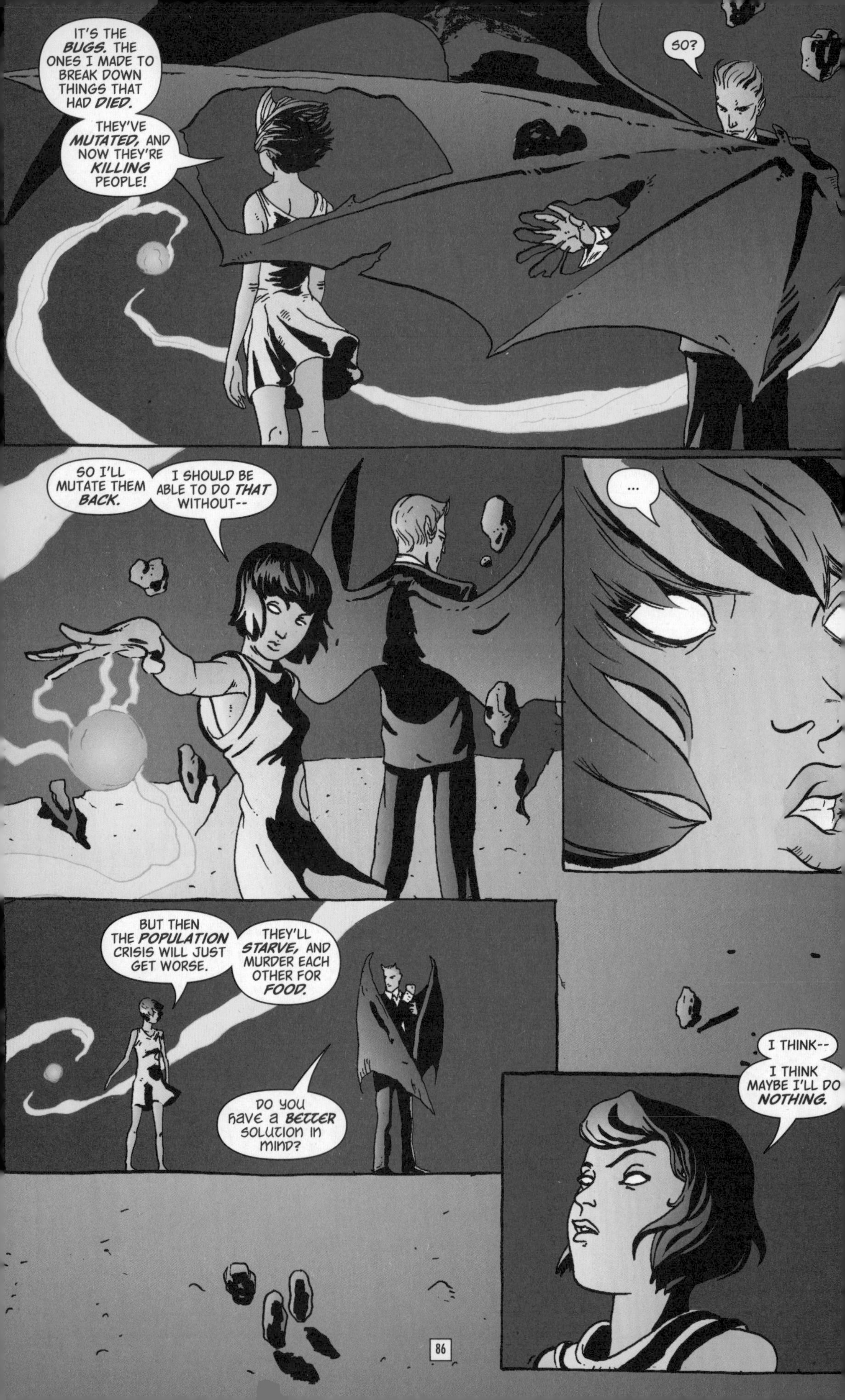
IT'S THE BUGS. THE ONES I MADE TO BREAK DOWN THINGS THAT HAD DIED.
THEY'VE MUTATED, AND NOW THEY'RE KILLING PEOPLE!
SO?
SO I'LL MUTATE THEM BACK.
I SHOULD BE ABLE TO DO THAT WITHOUT--
...
BUT THEN THE POPULATION CRISIS WILL JUST GET WORSE.
THEY'LL STARVE, AND MURDER EACH OTHER FOR FOOD.
DO YOU HAVE A BETTER SOLUTION IN MIND?
I THINK--
I THINK MAYBE I'LL DO NOTHING.

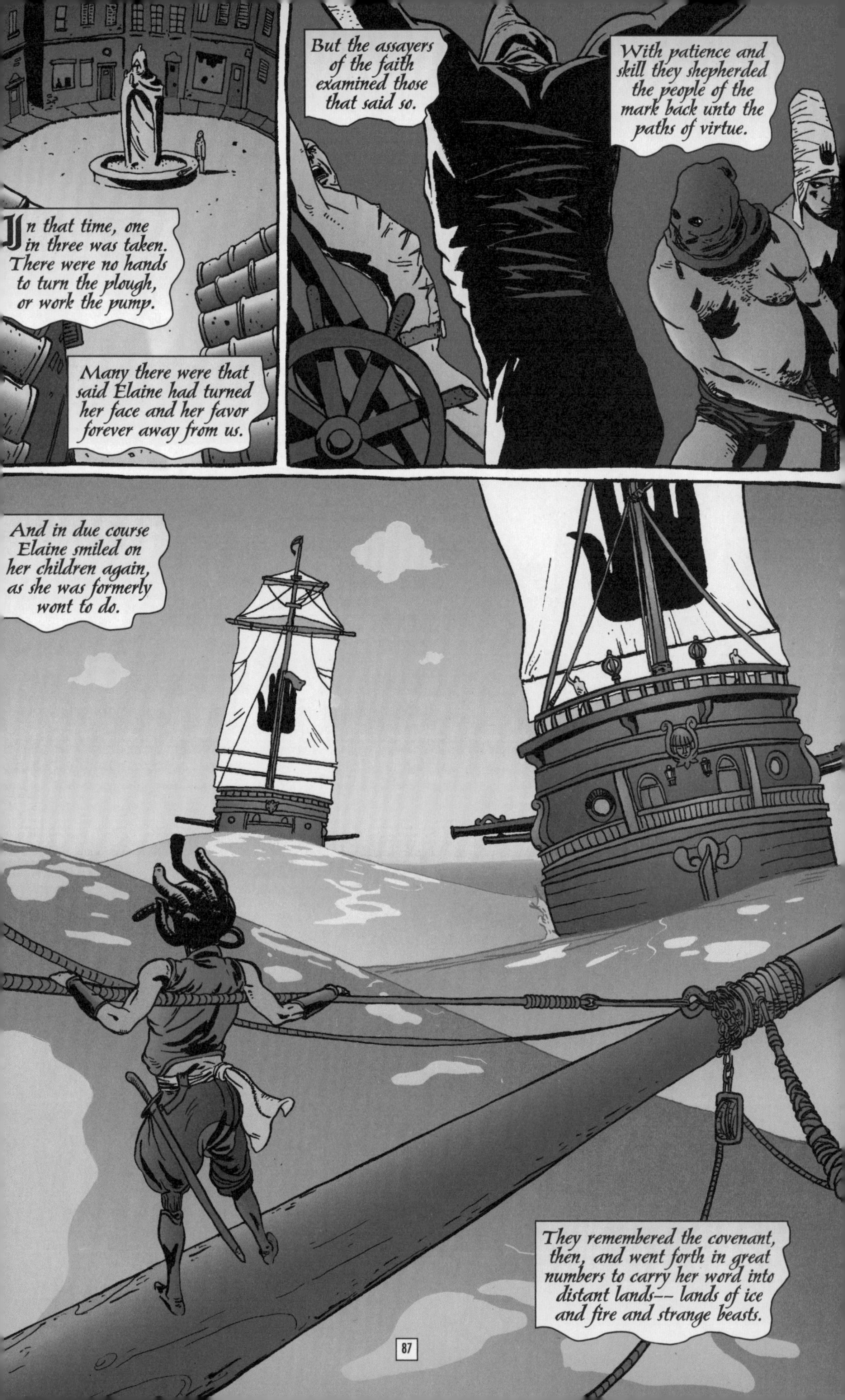
In that time, one in three was taken. There were no hands to turn the plough, or work the pump.
Many there were that said Elaine had turned her face and her favor forever away from us.
But the assayers of the faith examined those that said so.
With patience and skill they shepherded the people of the mark back unto the paths of virtue.
And in due course Elaine smiled on her children again, as she was formerly wont to do.
They remembered the covenant, then, and went forth in great numbers to carry her word into distant lands-- lands of ice and fire and strange beasts.

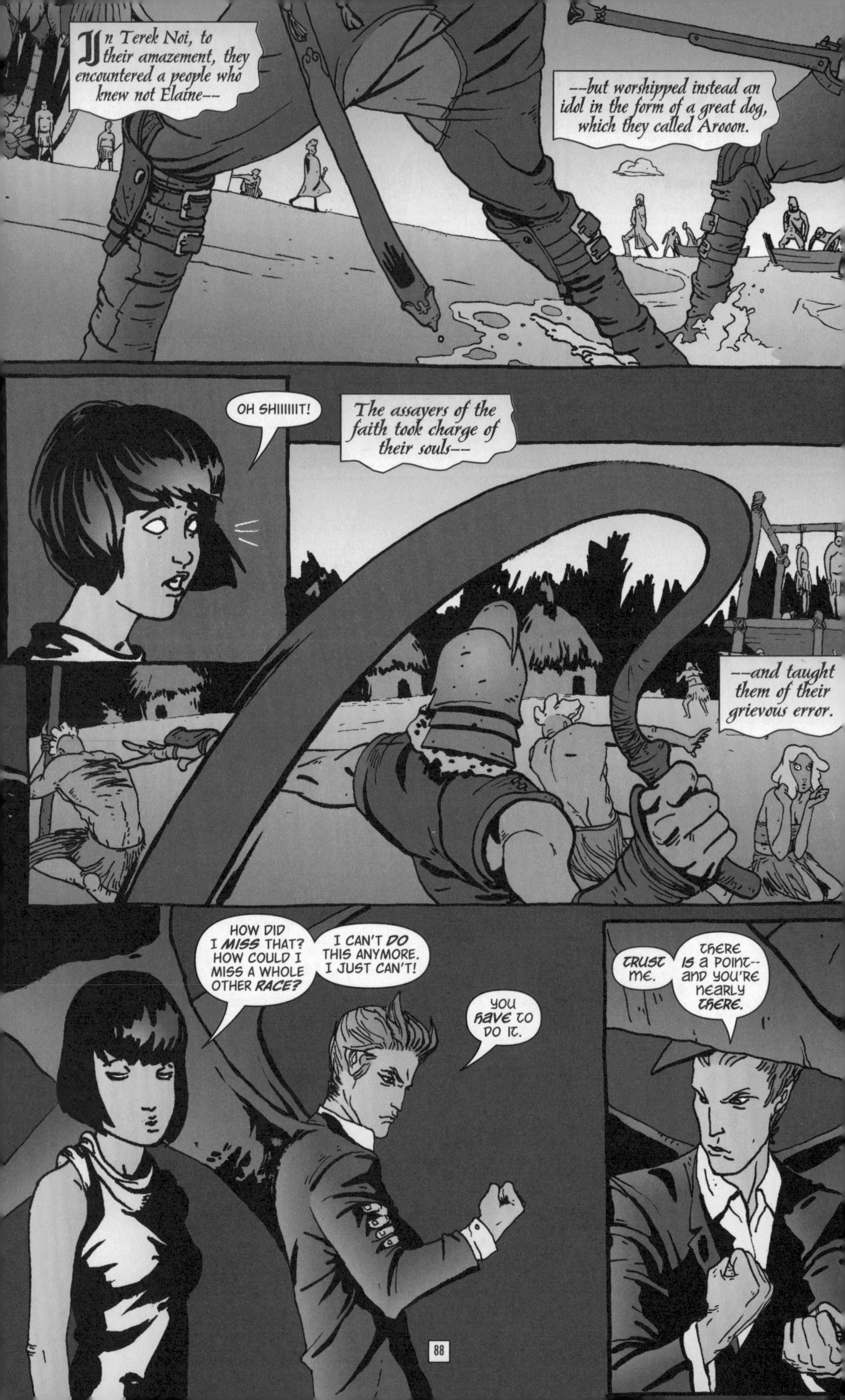
In Terek Noi, to their amazement, they encountered a people who knew not Elaine--
--but worshipped instead an idol in the form of a great dog, which they called Arooon.
OH SHIIIIIIT!
The assayers of the faith took charge of their souls--
--and taught them of their grievous error.
HOW DID I MISS THAT? HOW COULD I MISS A WHOLE OTHER RACE?
I CAN'T DO THIS ANYMORE. I JUST CAN'T!
YOU HAVE TO DO IT.
TRUST ME.
THERE IS A POINT-- AND YOU'RE NEARLY THERE.

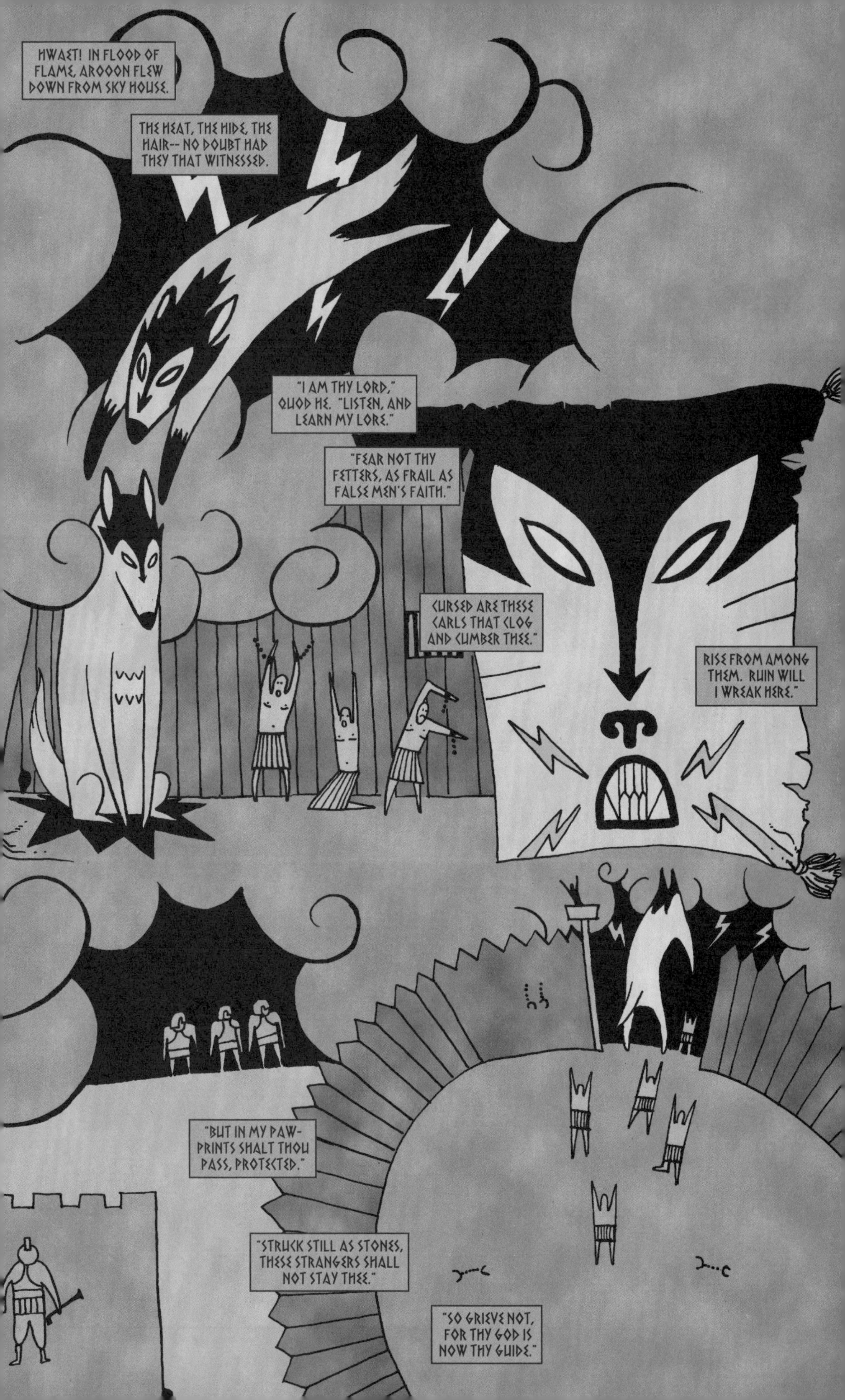
HWÆT! IN FLOOD OF FLAME, AROOON FLEW DOWN FROM SKY HOUSE.
THE HEAT, THE HIDE, THE HAIR-- NO DOUBT HAD THEY THAT WITNESSED.
"I AM THY LORD," QUOD HE. "LISTEN, AND LEARN MY LORE."
"FEAR NOT THY FETTERS, AS FRAIL AS FALSE MEN'S FAITH."
CURSED ARE THESE CARLS THAT CLOG AND CUMBER THEE."
RISE FROM AMONG THEM. RUIN WILL I WREAK HERE."
"BUT IN MY PAW-PRINTS SHALT THOU PASS, PROTECTED."
"STRUCK STILL AS STONES, THESE STRANGERS SHALL NOT STAY THEE."
"SO GRIEVE NOT, FOR THY GOD IS NOW THY GUIDE."

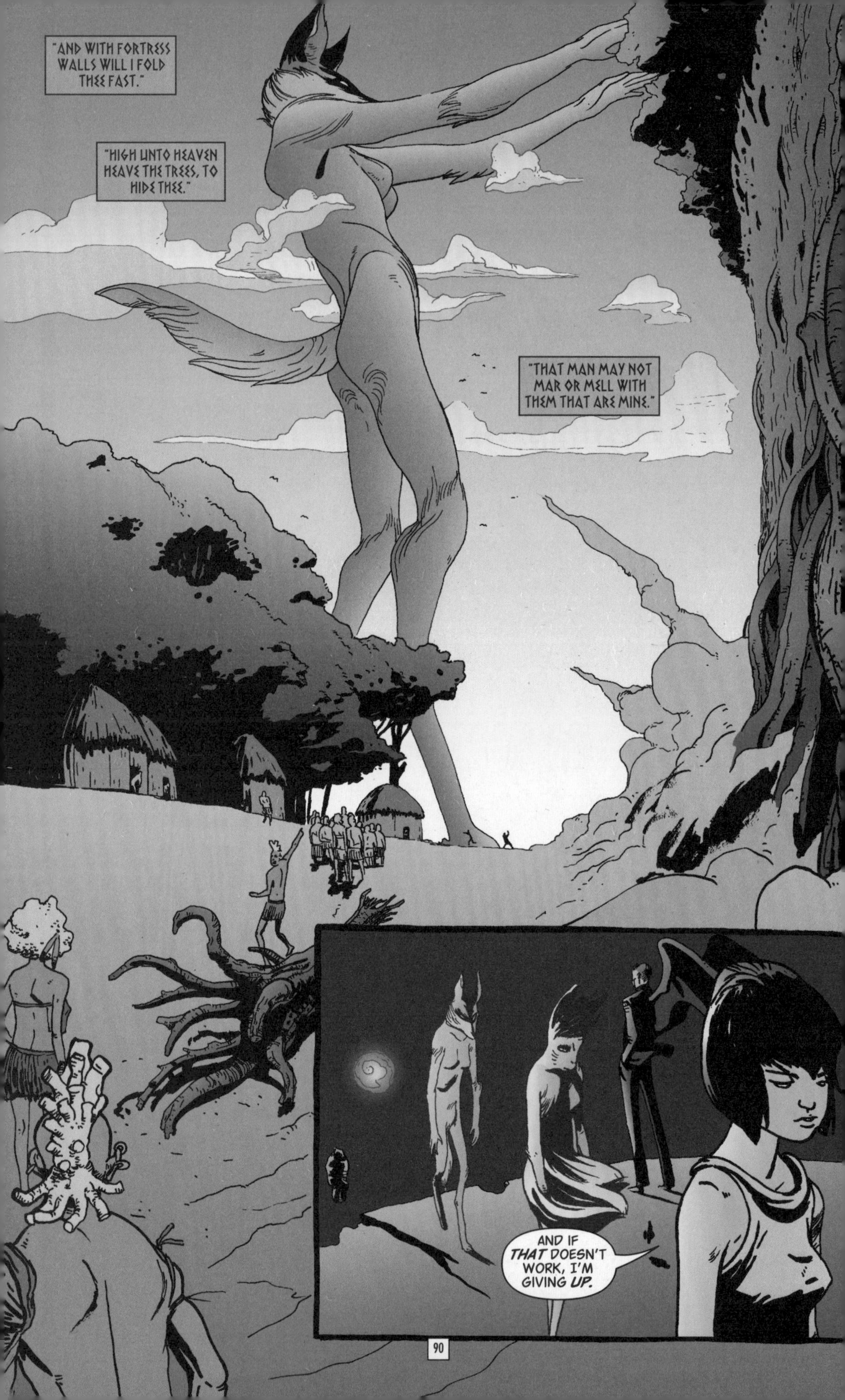
"AND WITH FORTRESS WALLS WILL I FOLD THEE FAST."
"HIGH UNTO HEAVEN HEAVE THE TREES, TO HIDE THEE."
"THAT MAN MAY NOT MAR OR MELL WITH THEM THAT ARE MINE."
AND IF *THAT* DOESN'T WORK, I'M GIVING *UP*.

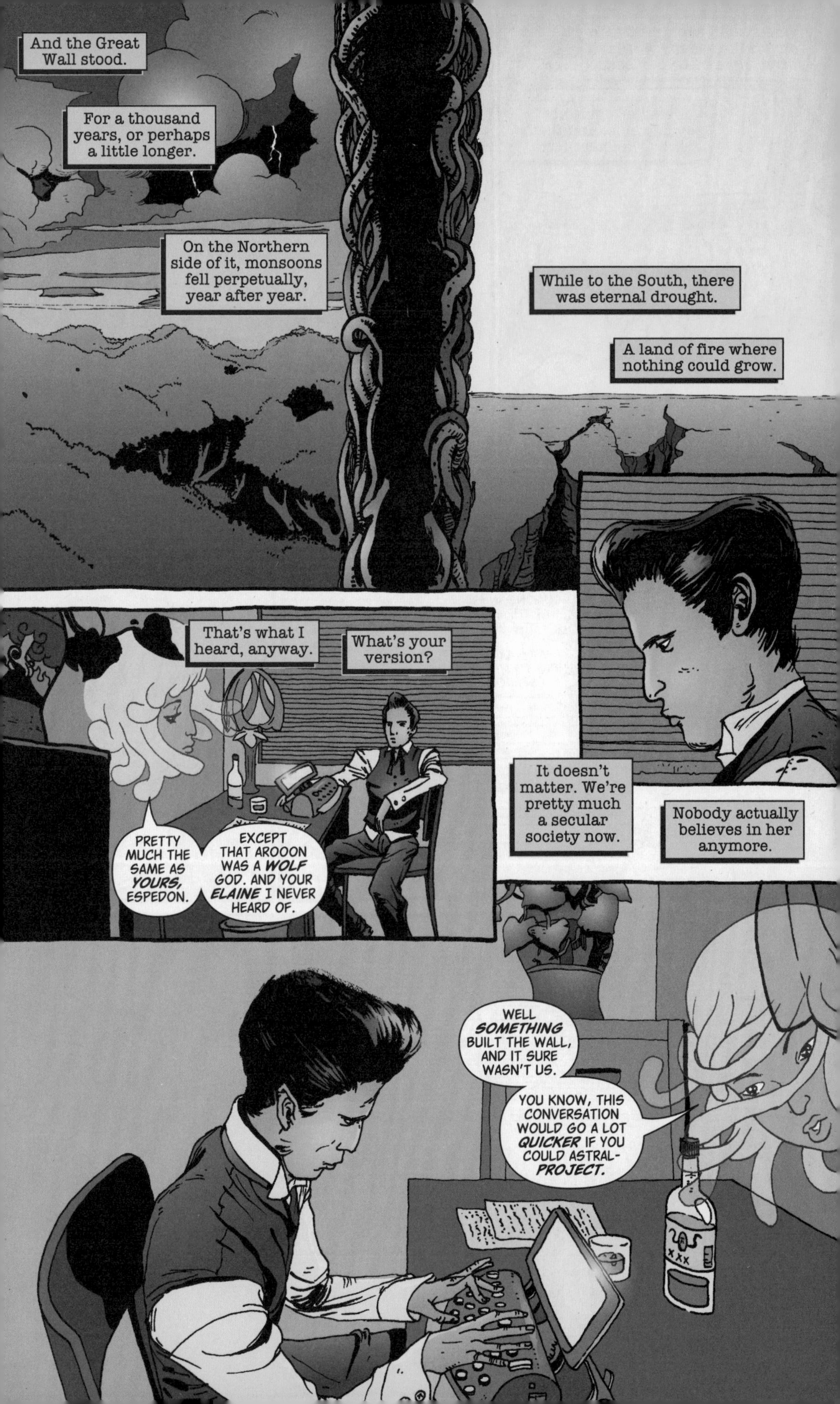
And the Great Wall stood.
For a thousand years, or perhaps a little longer.
On the Northern side of it, monsoons fell perpetually, year after year.
While to the South, there was eternal drought.
A land of fire where nothing could grow.
That's what I heard, anyway.
What's your version?
PRETTY MUCH THE SAME AS *YOURS,* ESPEDON.
EXCEPT THAT AROOON WAS A *WOLF* GOD. AND YOUR *ELAINE* I NEVER HEARD OF.
It doesn't matter. We're pretty much a secular society now.
Nobody actually believes in her anymore.
WELL *SOMETHING* BUILT THE WALL, AND IT SURE WASN'T US.
YOU KNOW, THIS CONVERSATION WOULD GO A LOT *QUICKER* IF YOU COULD ASTRAL-*PROJECT.*

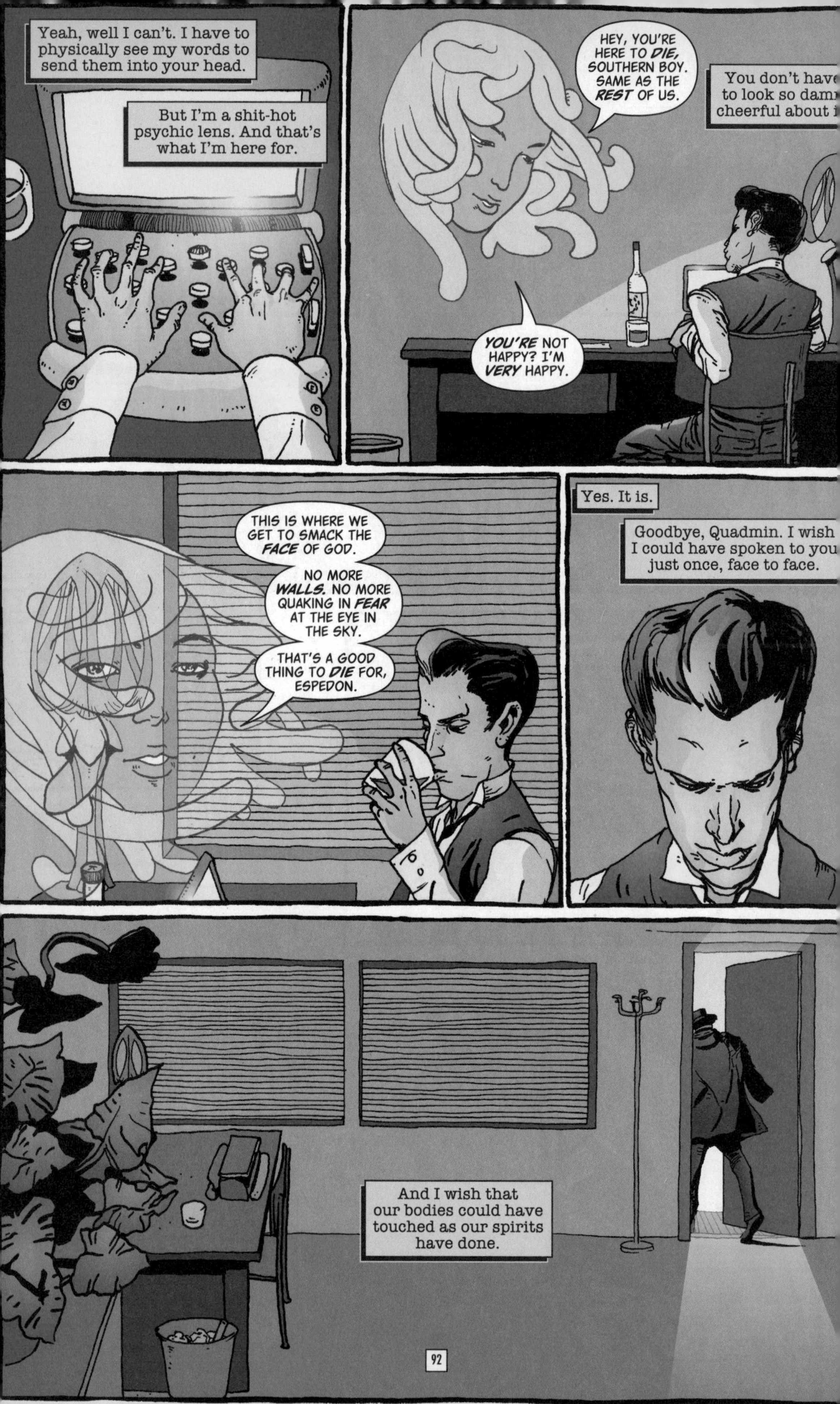

Yeah, well I can't. I have to physically see my words to send them into your head.
But I'm a shit-hot psychic lens. And that's what I'm here for.
HEY, YOU'RE HERE TO *DIE*, SOUTHERN BOY. SAME AS THE *REST* OF US.
You don't have to look so damn cheerful about it
YOU'RE NOT HAPPY? I'M *VERY* HAPPY.
THIS IS WHERE WE GET TO SMACK THE *FACE* OF GOD.
NO MORE *WALLS.* NO MORE QUAKING IN *FEAR* AT THE EYE IN THE SKY.
THAT'S A GOOD THING TO *DIE* FOR, ESPEDON.
Yes. It is.
Goodbye, Quadmin. I wish I could have spoken to you just once, face to face.
And I wish that our bodies could have touched as our spirits have done.

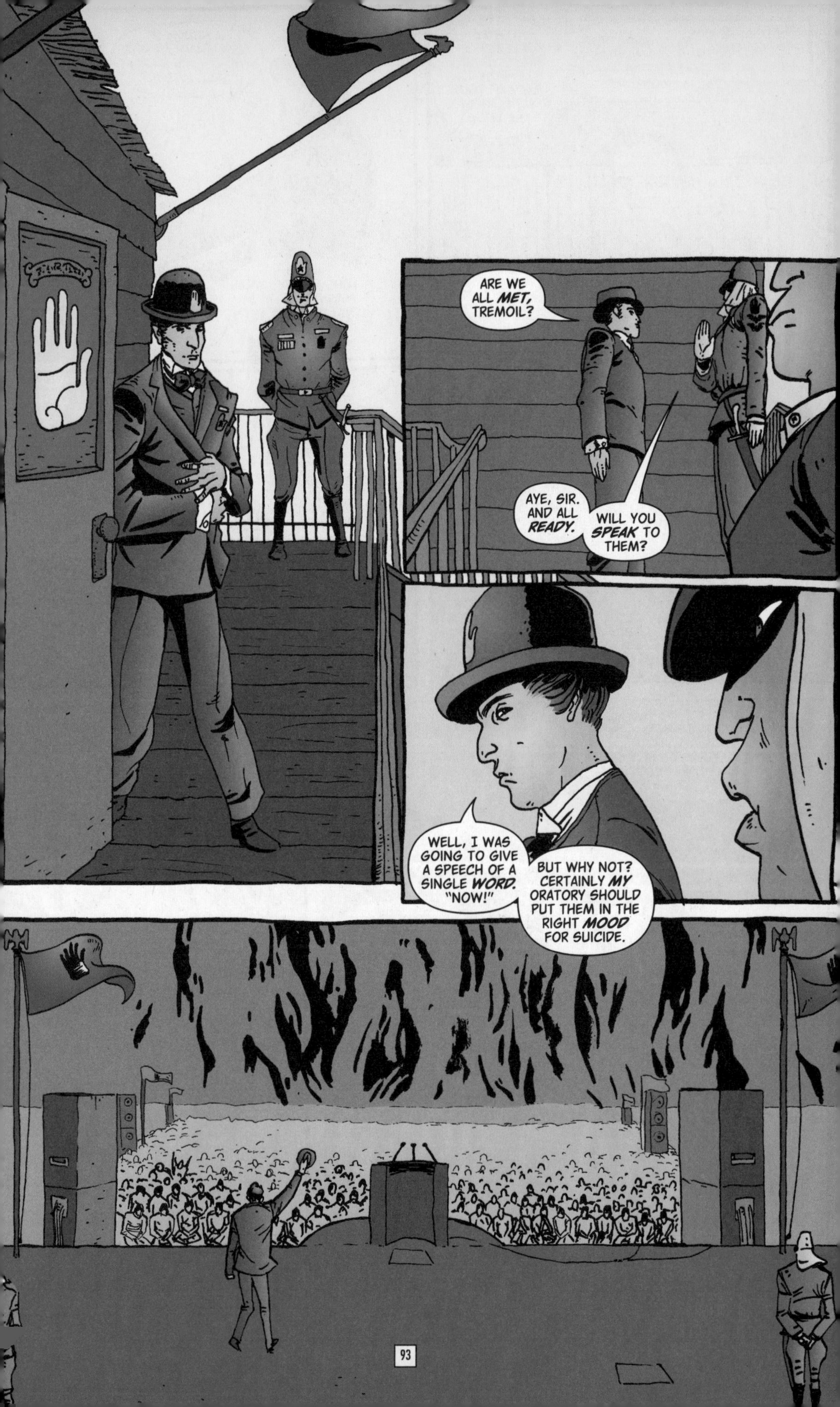

ARE WE ALL MET, TREMOIL?
AYE, SIR. AND ALL READY.
WILL YOU SPEAK TO THEM?
WELL, I WAS GOING TO GIVE A SPEECH OF A SINGLE WORD. "NOW!"
BUT WHY NOT? CERTAINLY MY ORATORY SHOULD PUT THEM IN THE RIGHT MOOD FOR SUICIDE.

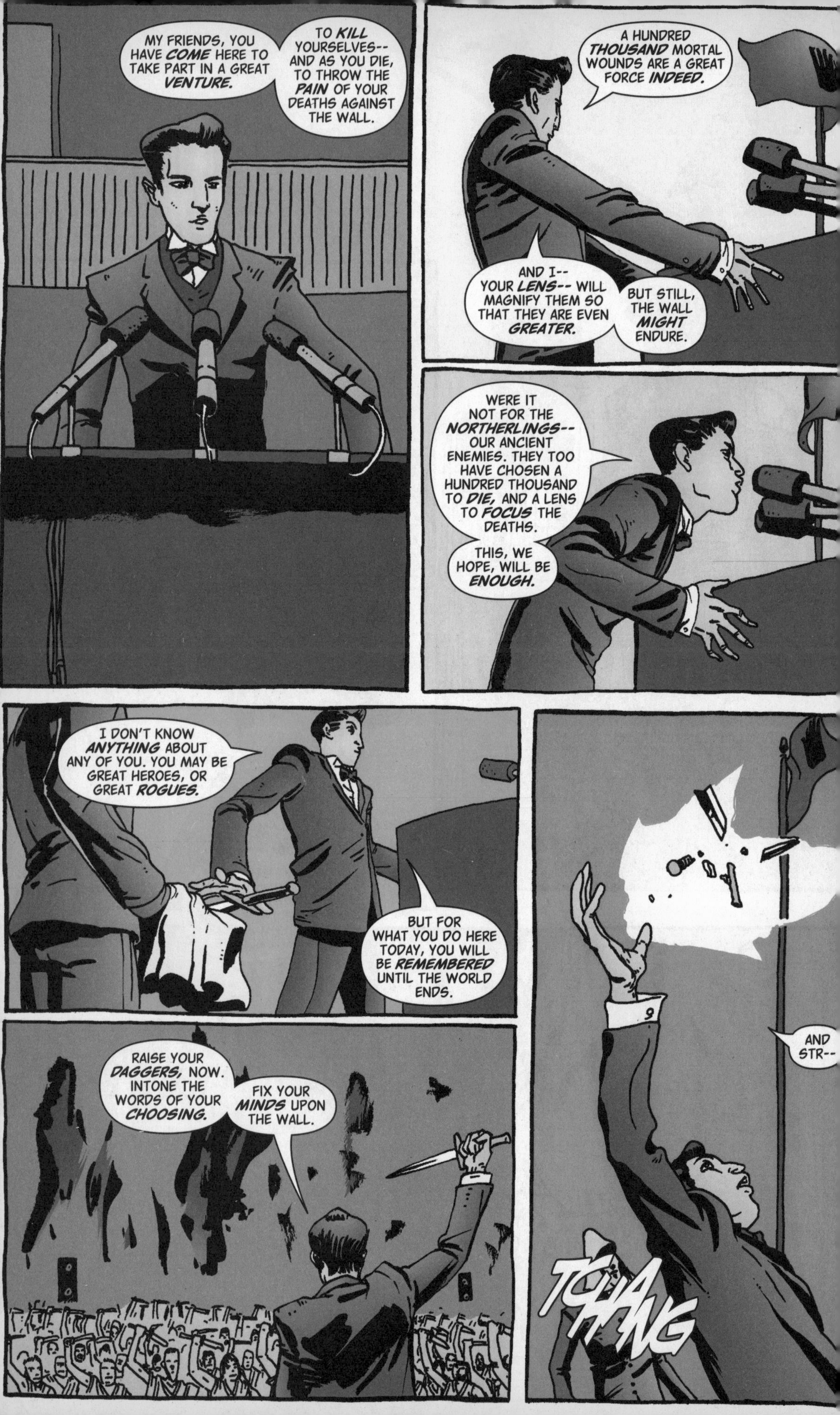

MY FRIENDS, YOU HAVE COME HERE TO TAKE PART IN A GREAT VENTURE.
TO KILL YOURSELVES-- AND AS YOU DIE, TO THROW THE PAIN OF YOUR DEATHS AGAINST THE WALL.
A HUNDRED THOUSAND MORTAL WOUNDS ARE A GREAT FORCE INDEED.
AND I-- YOUR LENS-- WILL MAGNIFY THEM SO THAT THEY ARE EVEN GREATER.
BUT STILL, THE WALL MIGHT ENDURE.
WERE IT NOT FOR THE NORTHERLINGS-- OUR ANCIENT ENEMIES. THEY TOO HAVE CHOSEN A HUNDRED THOUSAND TO DIE, AND A LENS TO FOCUS THE DEATHS.
THIS, WE HOPE, WILL BE ENOUGH.
I DON'T KNOW ANYTHING ABOUT ANY OF YOU. YOU MAY BE GREAT HEROES, OR GREAT ROGUES.
BUT FOR WHAT YOU DO HERE TODAY, YOU WILL BE REMEMBERED UNTIL THE WORLD ENDS.
RAISE YOUR DAGGERS, NOW. INTONE THE WORDS OF YOUR CHOOSING.
FIX YOUR MINDS UPON THE WALL.
AND STR--
TCHANG

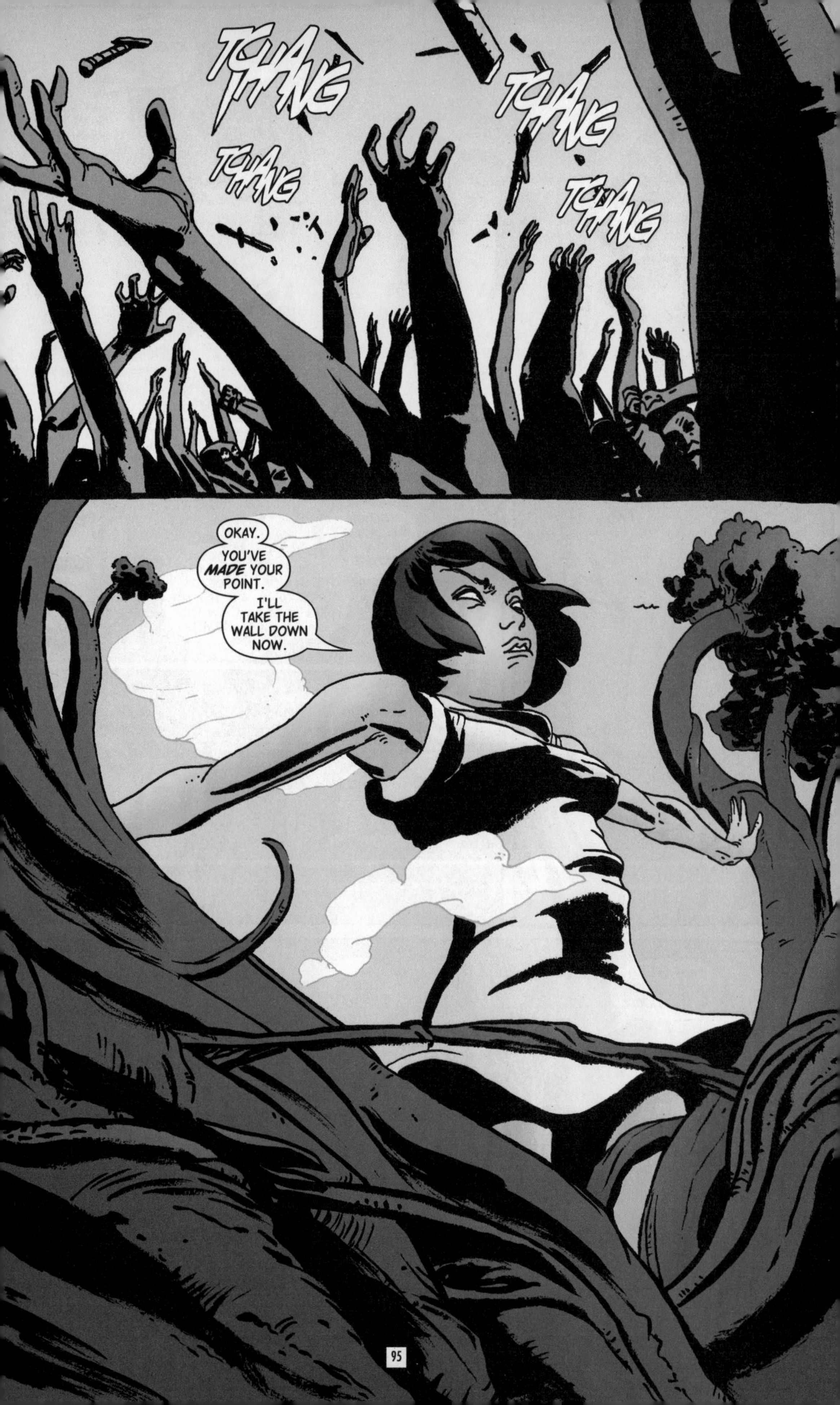
TCHANG
TCHANG
TCHANG
TCHANG
OKAY.
YOU'VE *MADE* YOUR POINT.
I'LL TAKE THE WALL DOWN NOW.

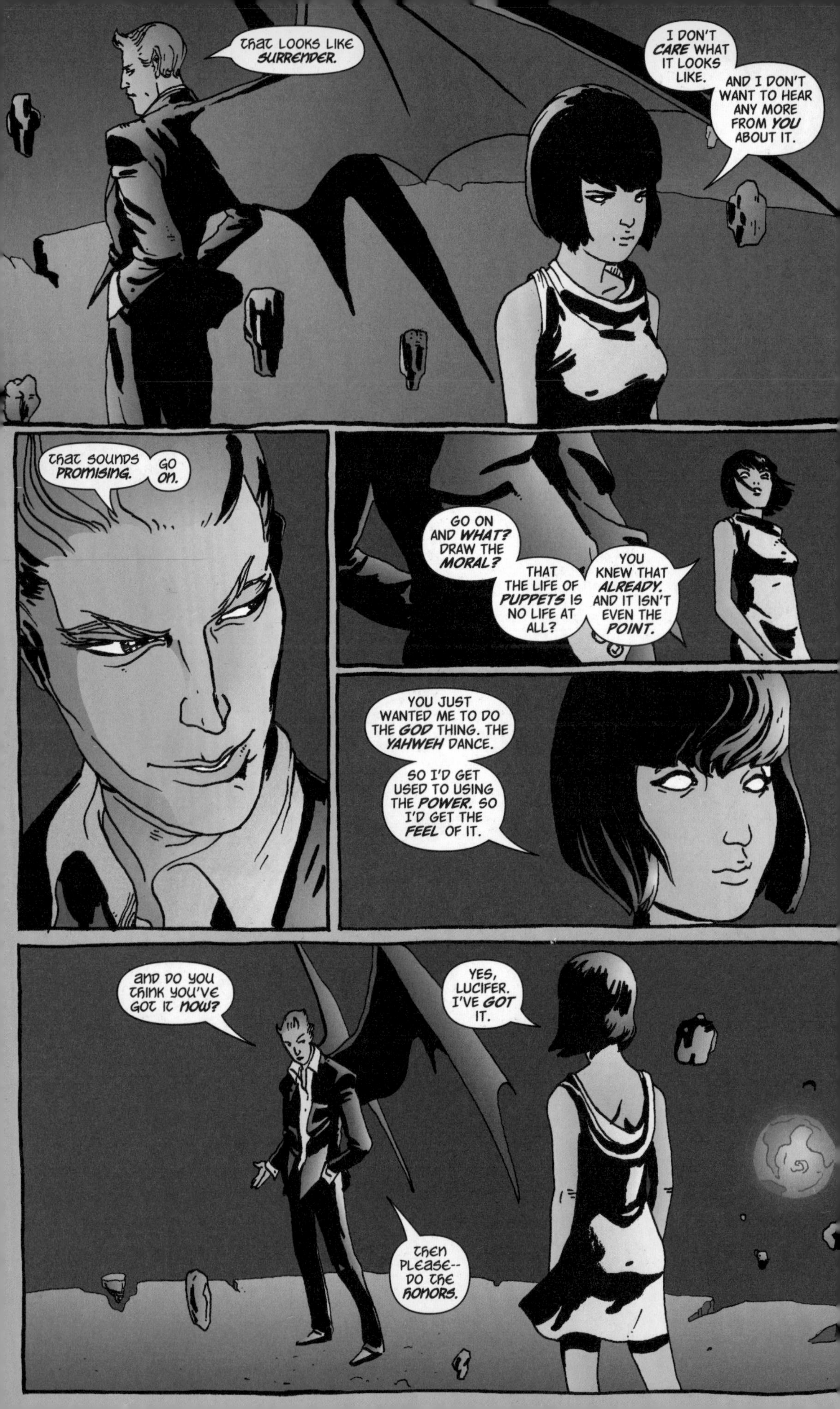
THAT LOOKS LIKE SURRENDER.
I DON'T CARE WHAT IT LOOKS LIKE.
AND I DON'T WANT TO HEAR ANY MORE FROM YOU ABOUT IT.
THAT SOUNDS PROMISING.
GO ON.
GO ON AND WHAT? DRAW THE MORAL?
THAT THE LIFE OF PUPPETS IS NO LIFE AT ALL?
YOU KNEW THAT ALREADY. AND IT ISN'T EVEN THE POINT.
YOU JUST WANTED ME TO DO THE GOD THING. THE YAHWEH DANCE.
SO I'D GET USED TO USING THE POWER. SO I'D GET THE FEEL OF IT.
AND DO YOU THINK YOU'VE GOT IT NOW?
YES, LUCIFER. I'VE GOT IT.
THEN PLEASE-- DO THE HONORS.

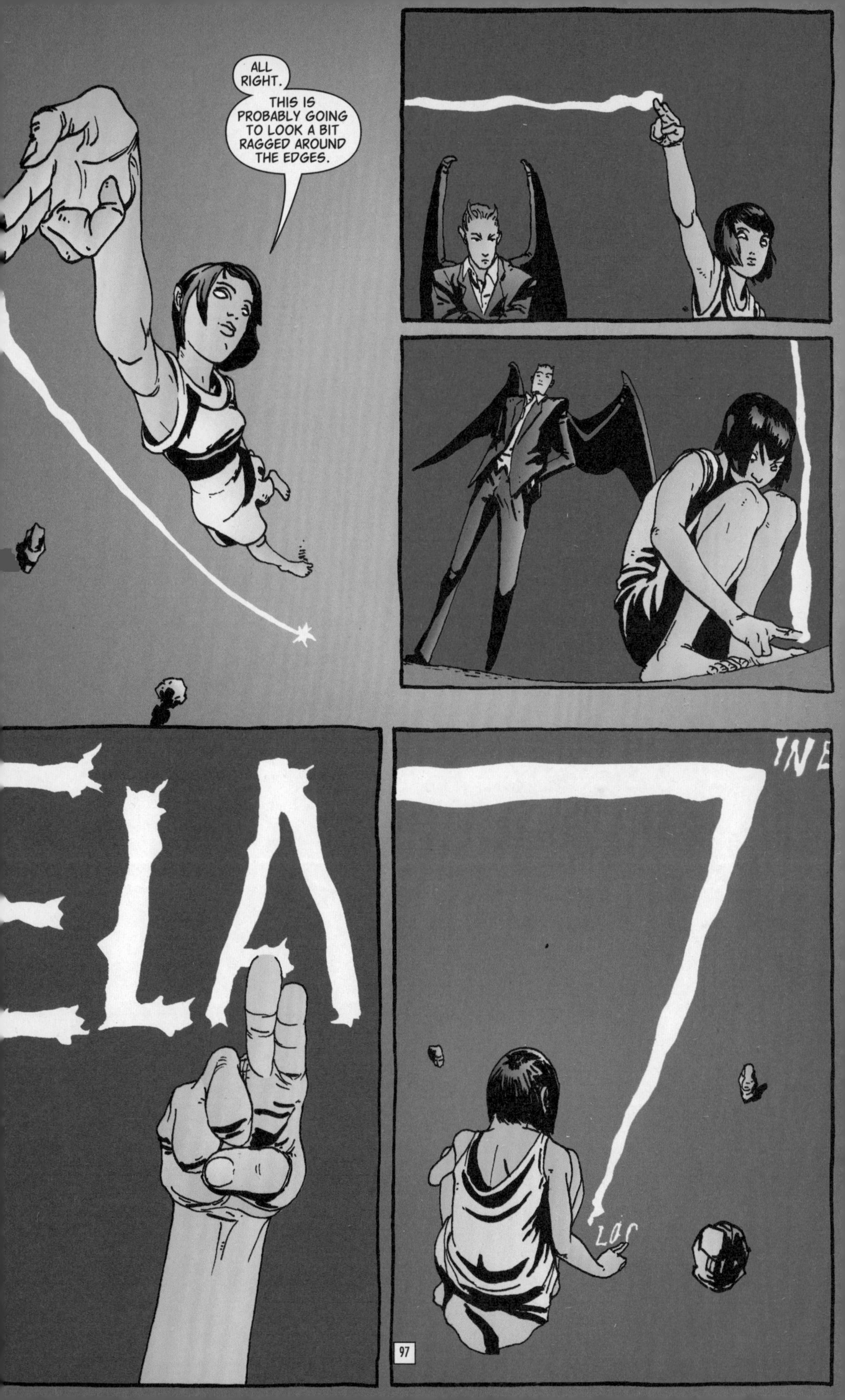
ALL RIGHT.
THIS IS PROBABLY GOING TO LOOK A BIT RAGGED AROUND THE EDGES.

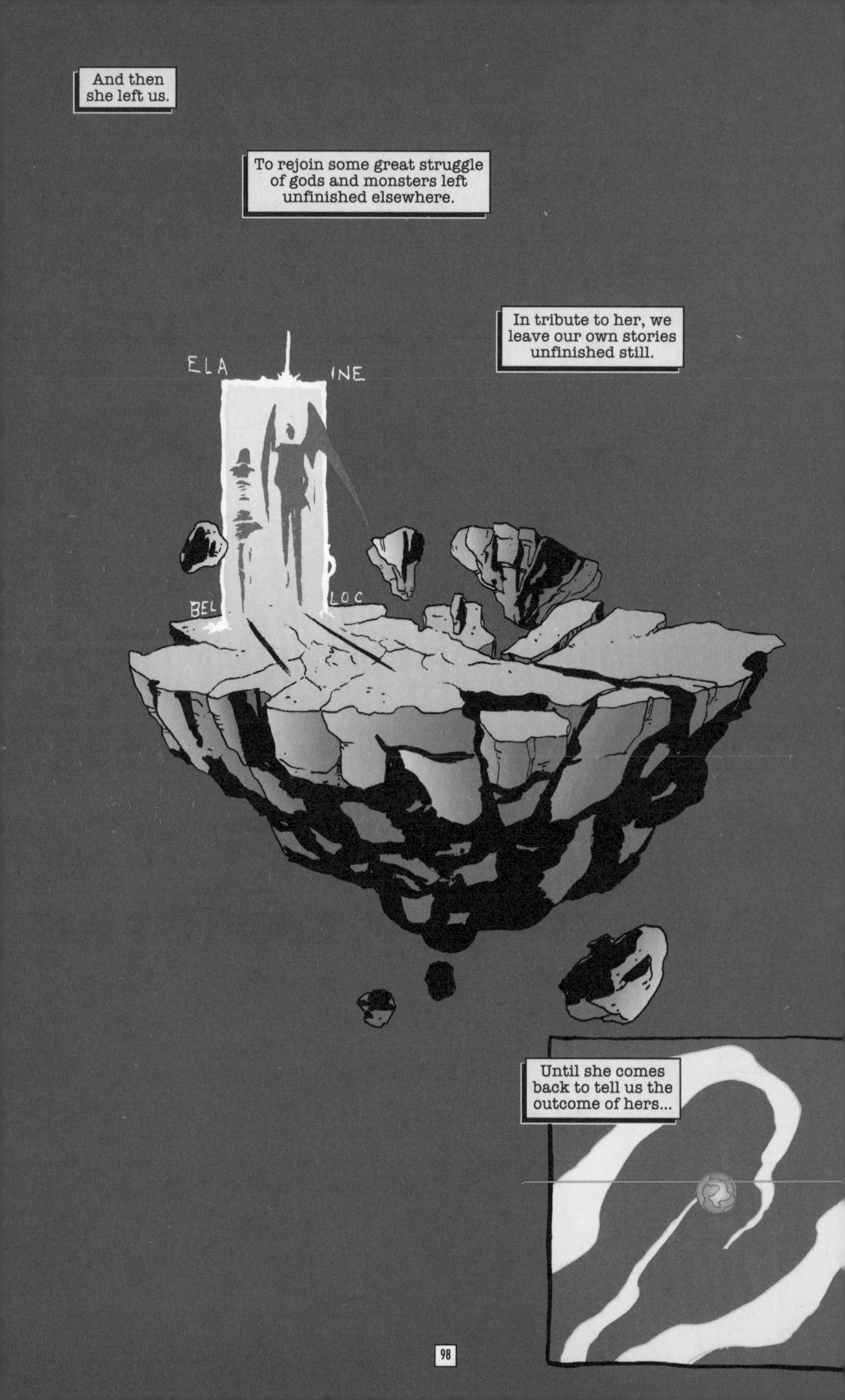
And then she left us.
To rejoin some great struggle of gods and monsters left unfinished elsewhere.
In tribute to her, we leave our own stories unfinished still.
ELA
INE
BEL
LOC
Until she comes back to tell us the outcome of hers...

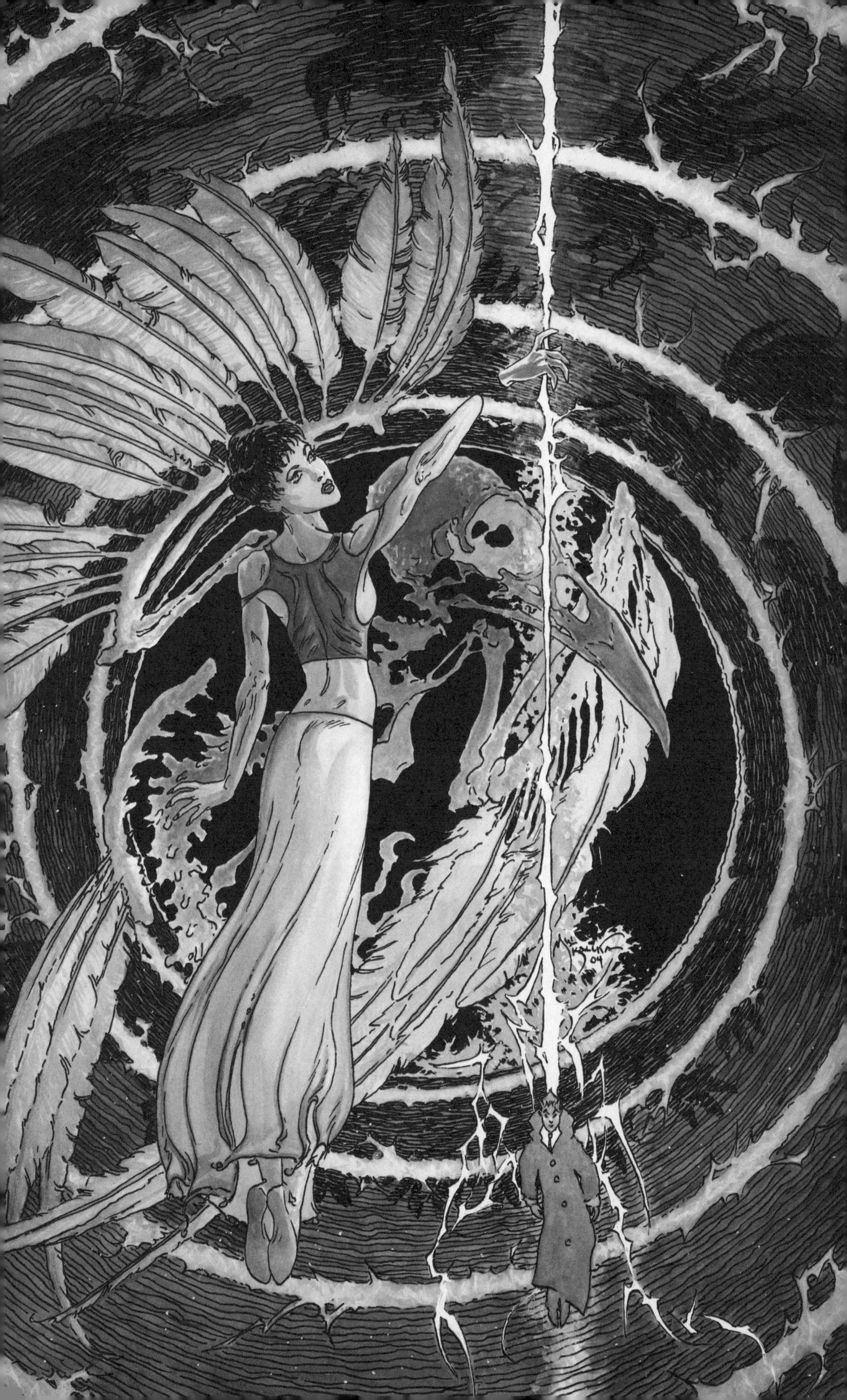

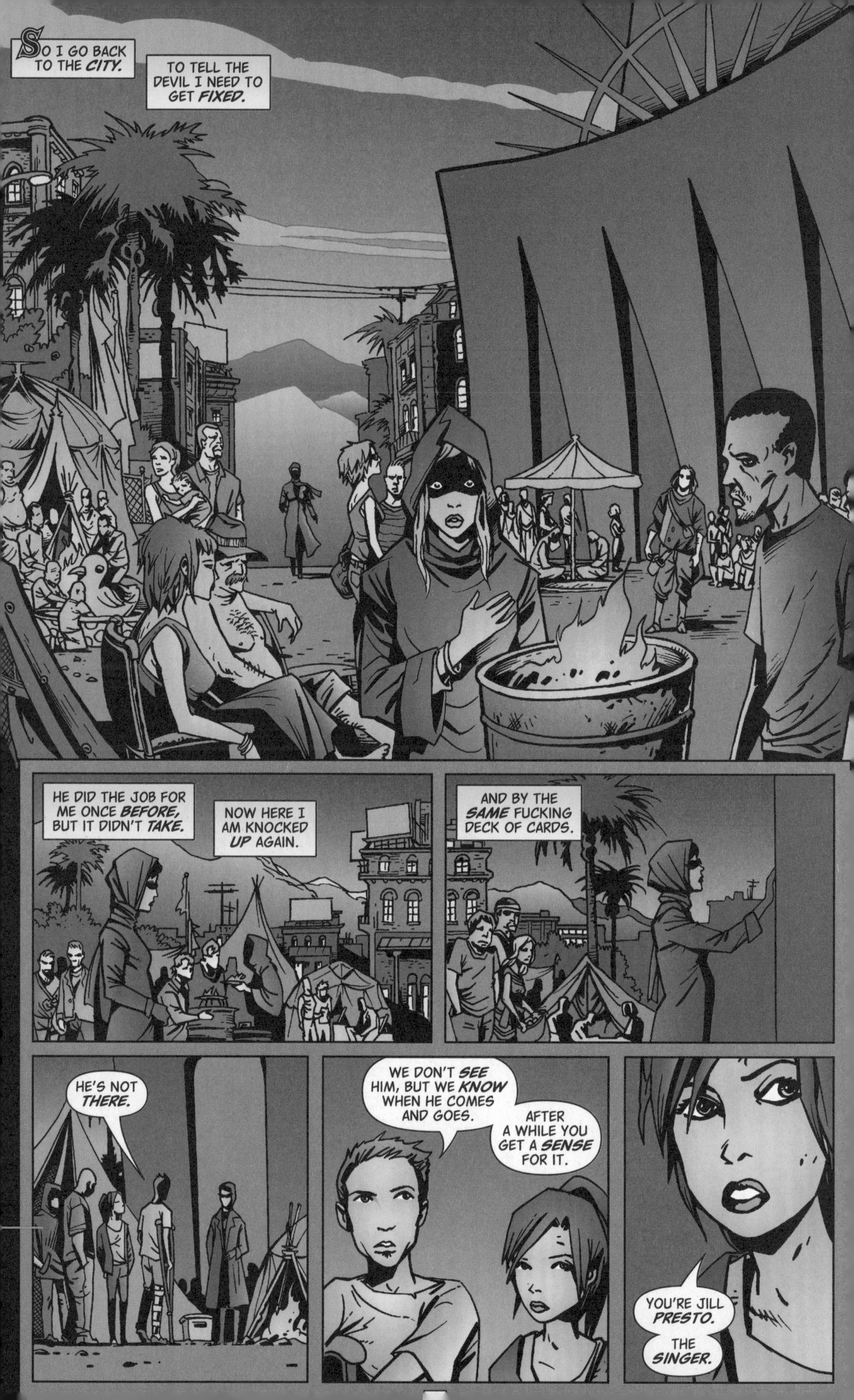

SO I GO BACK TO THE CITY.
TO TELL THE DEVIL I NEED TO GET FIXED.
HE DID THE JOB FOR ME ONCE BEFORE, BUT IT DIDN'T TAKE.
NOW HERE I AM KNOCKED UP AGAIN.
AND BY THE SAME FUCKING DECK OF CARDS.
HE'S NOT THERE.
WE DON'T SEE HIM, BUT WE KNOW WHEN HE COMES AND GOES.
AFTER A WHILE YOU GET A SENSE FOR IT.
YOU'RE JILL PRESTO.
THE SINGER.

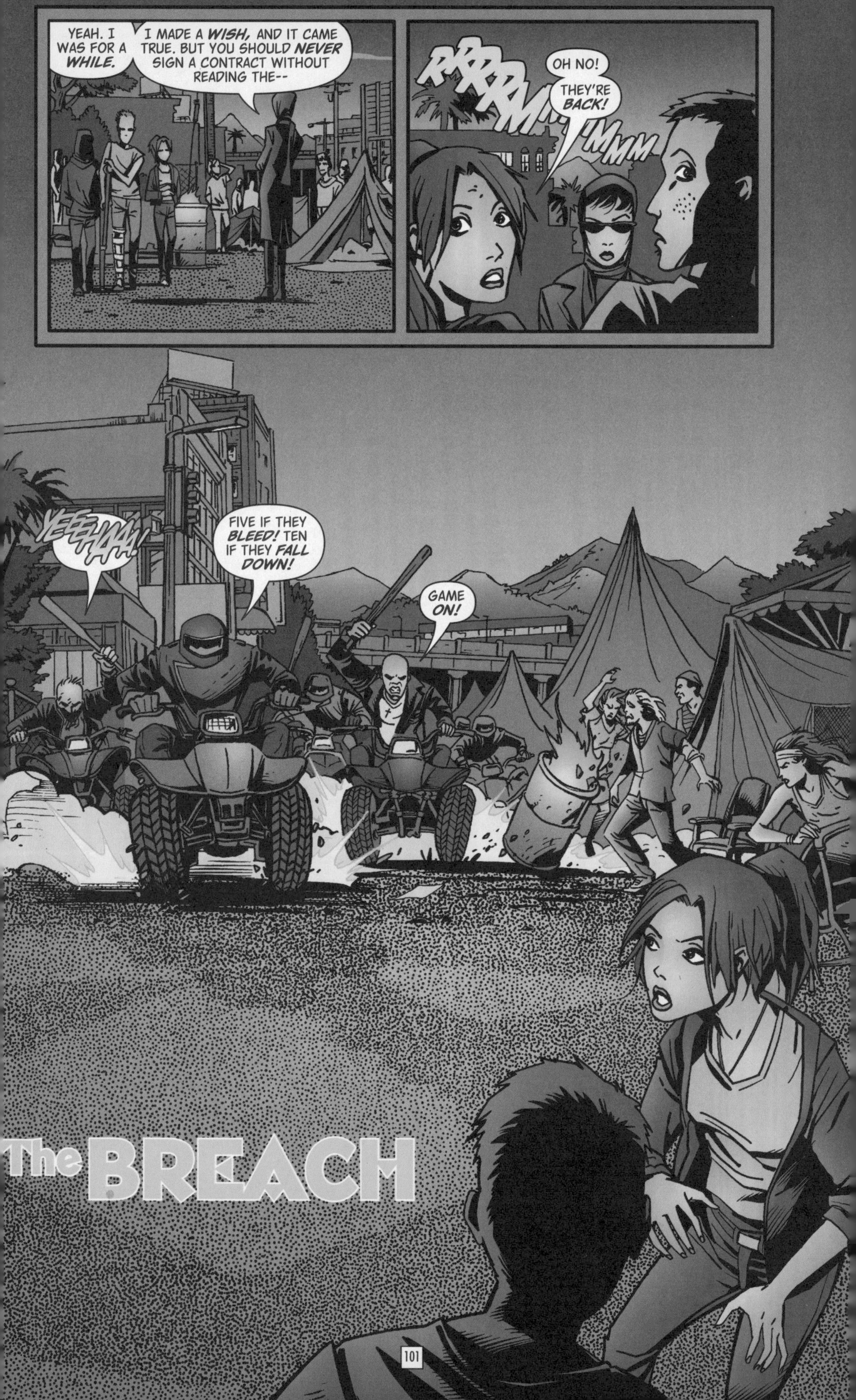
YEAH. I WAS FOR A WHILE.
I MADE A WISH, AND IT CAME TRUE. BUT YOU SHOULD NEVER SIGN A CONTRACT WITHOUT READING THE--
RRRRMMMMMM
OH NO!
THEY'RE BACK!
YEEEHAAA!
FIVE IF THEY BLEED! TEN IF THEY FALL DOWN!
GAME ON!
The BREACH

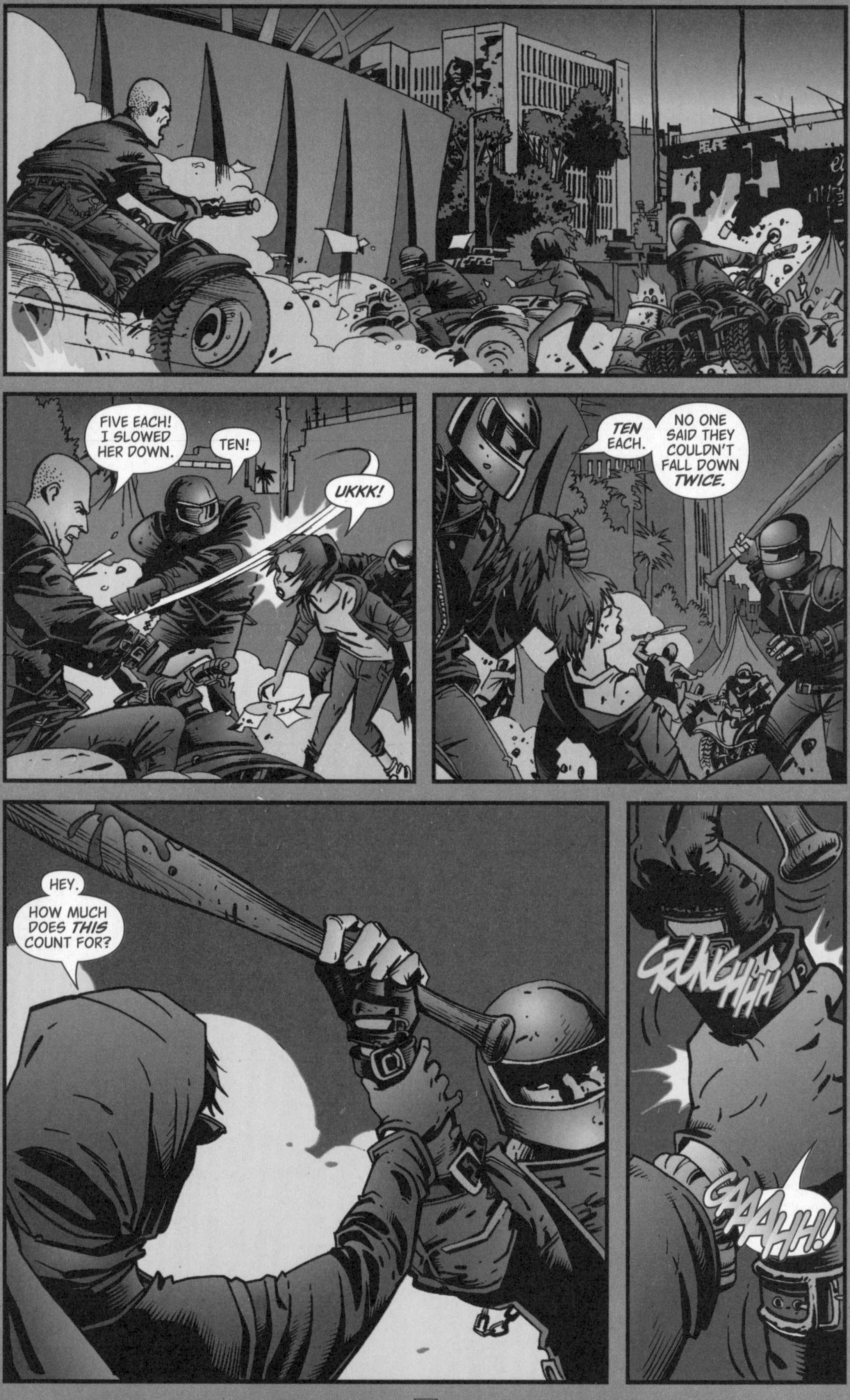

FIVE EACH! I SLOWED HER DOWN.
TEN!
UKKK!
TEN EACH.
NO ONE SAID THEY COULDN'T FALL DOWN TWICE.
HEY. HOW MUCH DOES THIS COUNT FOR?
CRUNCHHHH
GAAAHH!

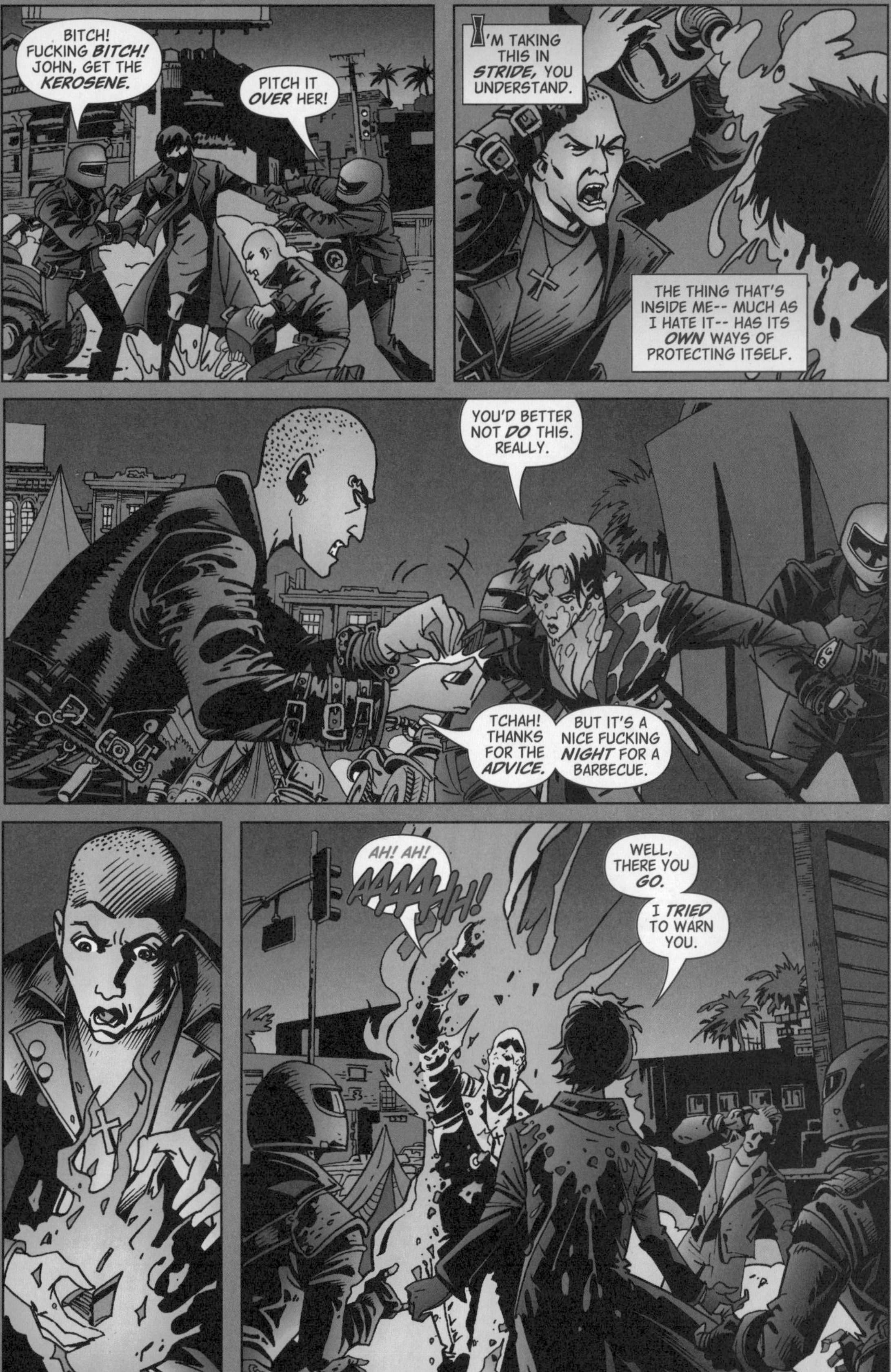
BITCH! FUCKING BITCH! JOHN, GET THE KEROSENE.
PITCH IT OVER HER!
I'M TAKING THIS IN STRIDE, YOU UNDERSTAND.
THE THING THAT'S INSIDE ME-- MUCH AS I HATE IT-- HAS ITS OWN WAYS OF PROTECTING ITSELF.
YOU'D BETTER NOT DO THIS. REALLY.
TCHAH! THANKS FOR THE ADVICE.
BUT IT'S A NICE FUCKING NIGHT FOR A BARBECUE.
AH! AH! AAAAHH!
WELL, THERE YOU GO.
I TRIED TO WARN YOU.

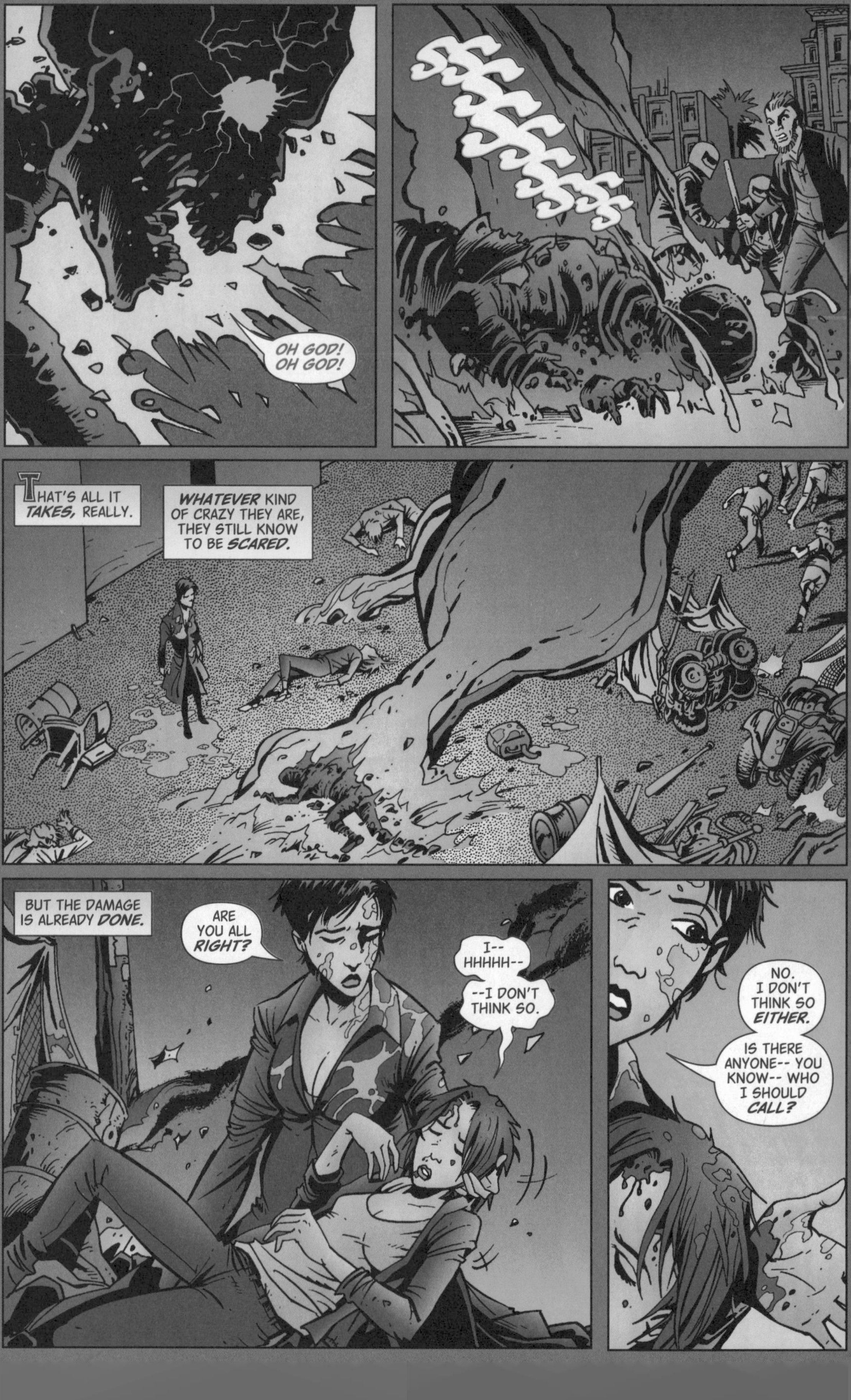
OH GOD! OH GOD!
SSSSSSSSS
THAT'S ALL IT TAKES, REALLY.
WHATEVER KIND OF CRAZY THEY ARE, THEY STILL KNOW TO BE SCARED.
BUT THE DAMAGE IS ALREADY DONE.
ARE YOU ALL RIGHT?
I-- HHHHH--
--I DON'T THINK SO.
NO. I DON'T THINK SO EITHER.
IS THERE ANYONE-- YOU KNOW-- WHO I SHOULD CALL?

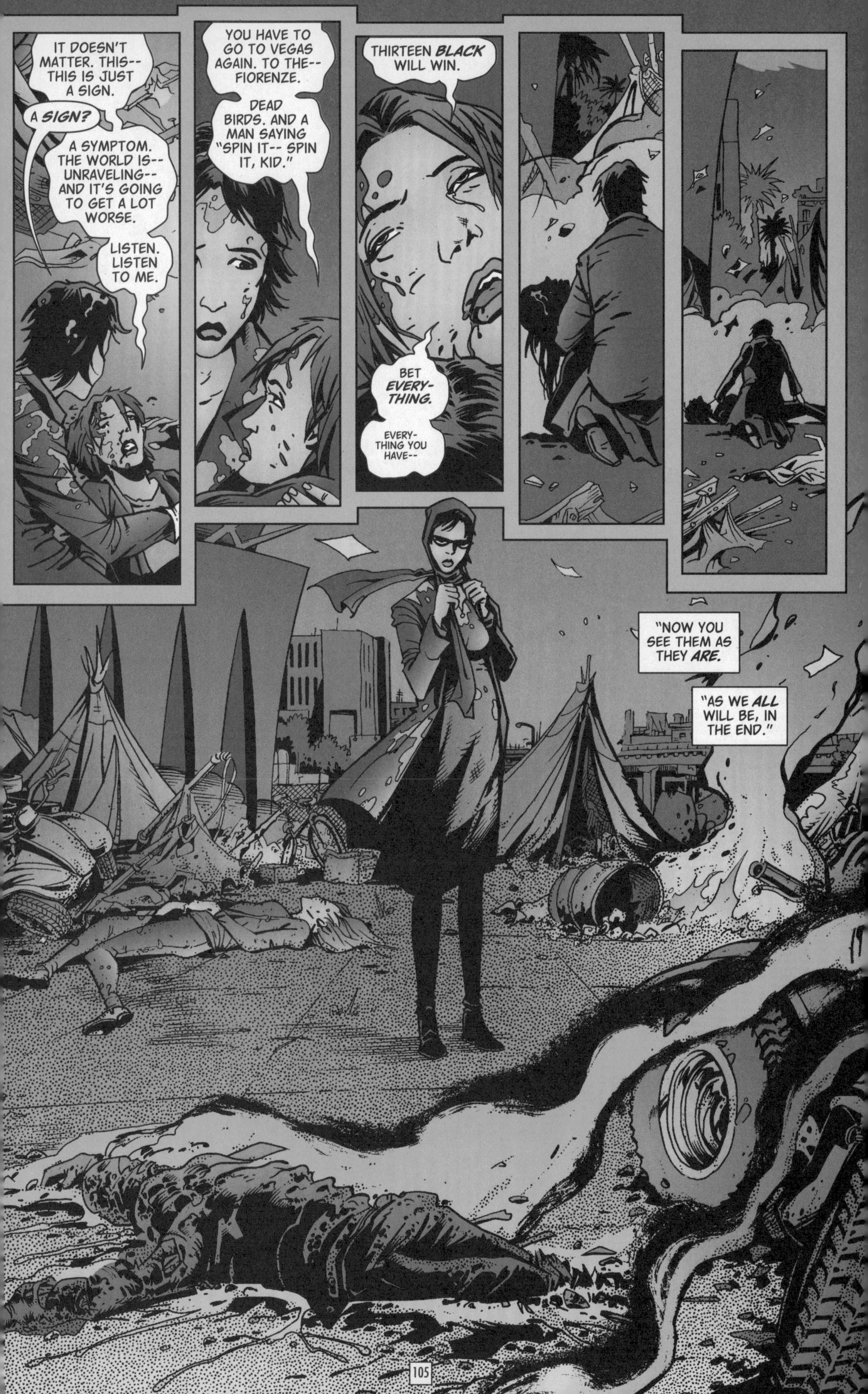
IT DOESN'T MATTER. THIS-- THIS IS JUST A SIGN.
A SIGN?
A SYMPTOM. THE WORLD IS-- UNRAVELING-- AND IT'S GOING TO GET A LOT WORSE.
LISTEN. LISTEN TO ME.
YOU HAVE TO GO TO VEGAS AGAIN. TO THE-- FIORENZE.
DEAD BIRDS. AND A MAN SAYING "SPIN IT-- SPIN IT, KID."
THIRTEEN BLACK WILL WIN.
BET EVERYTHING.
EVERYTHING YOU HAVE--
"NOW YOU SEE THEM AS THEY ARE.
"AS WE ALL WILL BE, IN THE END."

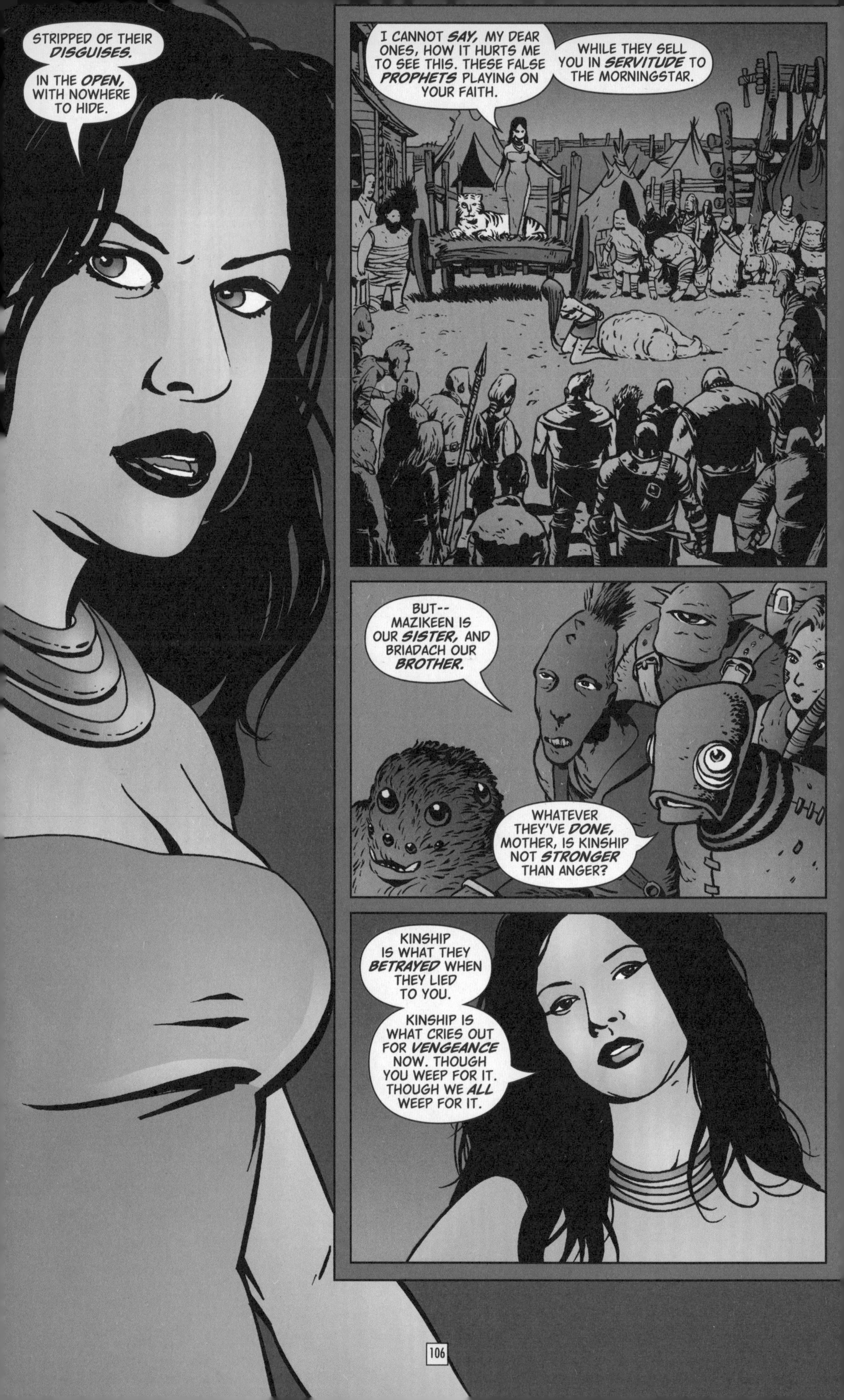
STRIPPED OF THEIR DISGUISES.
IN THE OPEN, WITH NOWHERE TO HIDE.
I CANNOT SAY, MY DEAR ONES, HOW IT HURTS ME TO SEE THIS. THESE FALSE PROPHETS PLAYING ON YOUR FAITH.
WHILE THEY SELL YOU IN SERVITUDE TO THE MORNINGSTAR.
BUT-- MAZIKEEN IS OUR SISTER, AND BRIADACH OUR BROTHER.
WHATEVER THEY'VE DONE, MOTHER, IS KINSHIP NOT STRONGER THAN ANGER?
KINSHIP IS WHAT THEY BETRAYED WHEN THEY LIED TO YOU.
KINSHIP IS WHAT CRIES OUT FOR VENGEANCE NOW. THOUGH YOU WEEP FOR IT. THOUGH WE ALL WEEP FOR IT.

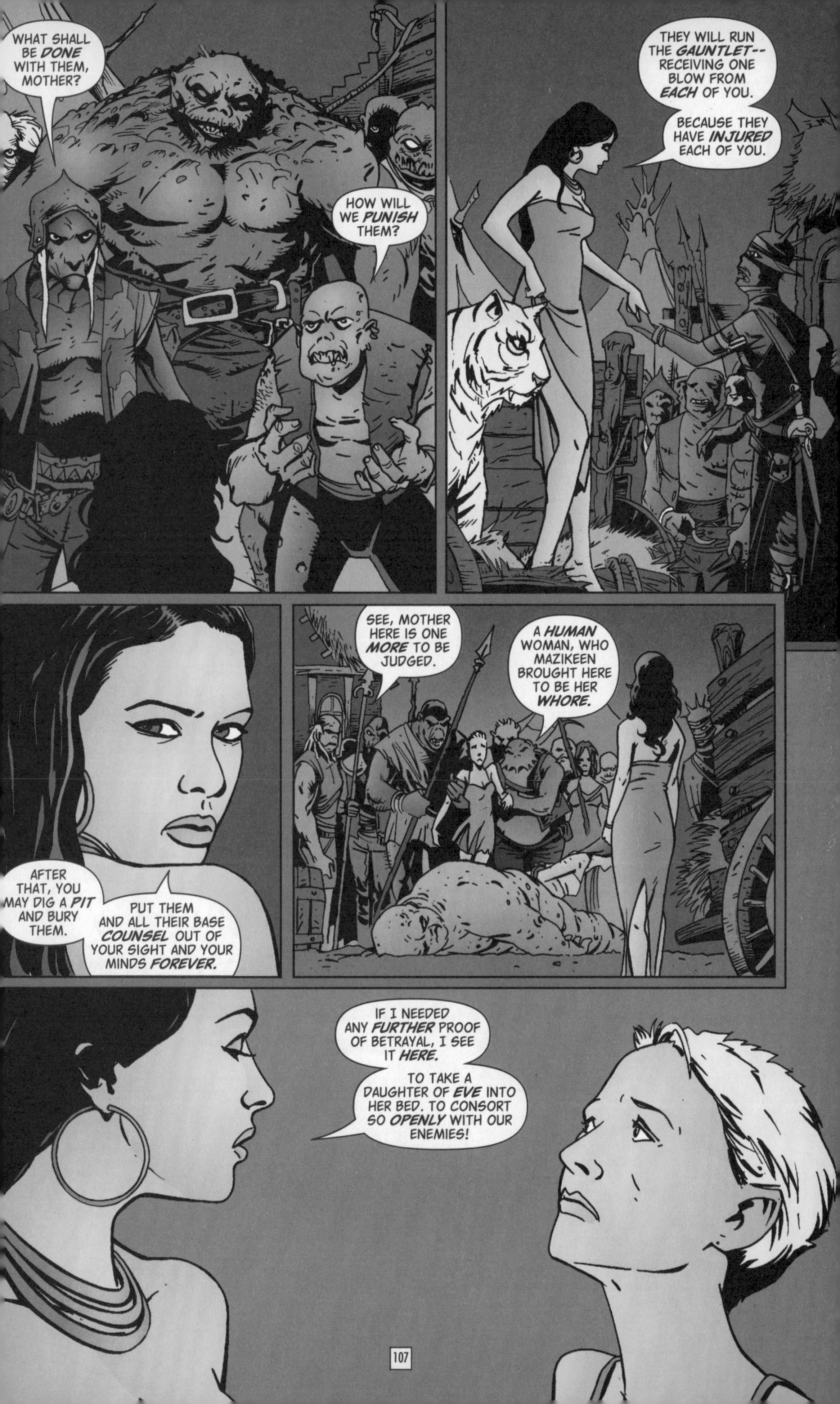
WHAT SHALL BE *DONE* WITH THEM, MOTHER?
HOW WILL WE *PUNISH* THEM?
THEY WILL RUN THE *GAUNTLET*-- RECEIVING ONE BLOW FROM *EACH* OF YOU.
BECAUSE THEY HAVE *INJURED* EACH OF YOU.
AFTER THAT, YOU MAY DIG A *PIT* AND BURY THEM.
PUT THEM AND ALL THEIR BASE *COUNSEL* OUT OF YOUR SIGHT AND YOUR MINDS *FOREVER.*
SEE, MOTHER HERE IS ONE *MORE* TO BE JUDGED.
A *HUMAN* WOMAN, WHO MAZIKEEN BROUGHT HERE TO BE HER *WHORE.*
IF I NEEDED ANY *FURTHER* PROOF OF BETRAYAL, I SEE IT *HERE.*
TO TAKE A DAUGHTER OF *EVE* INTO HER BED. TO CONSORT SO *OPENLY* WITH OUR ENEMIES!

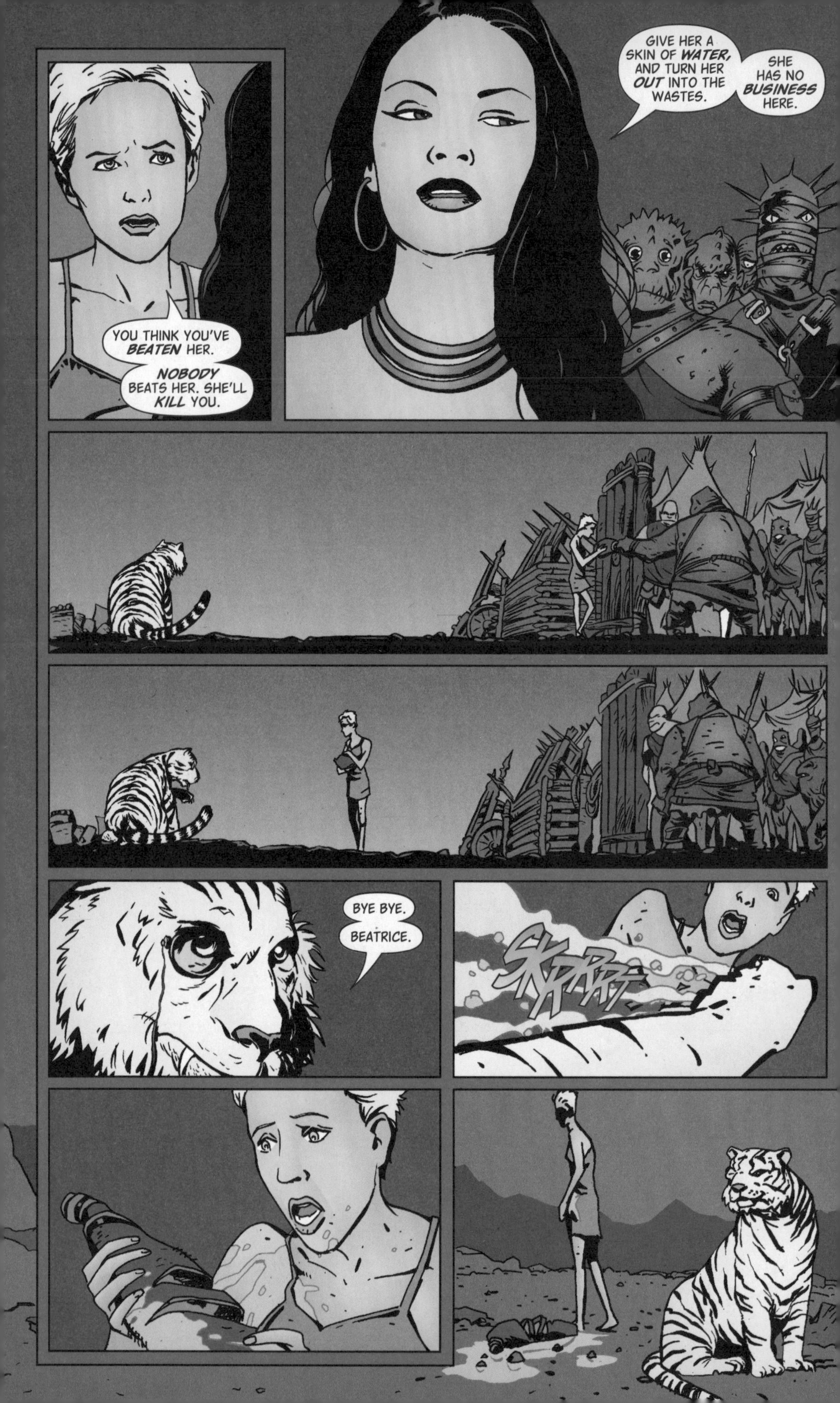
YOU THINK YOU'VE BEATEN HER.
NOBODY BEATS HER. SHE'LL KILL YOU.
GIVE HER A SKIN OF WATER, AND TURN HER OUT INTO THE WASTES.
SHE HAS NO BUSINESS HERE.
BYE BYE.
BEATRICE.
SKRRRF

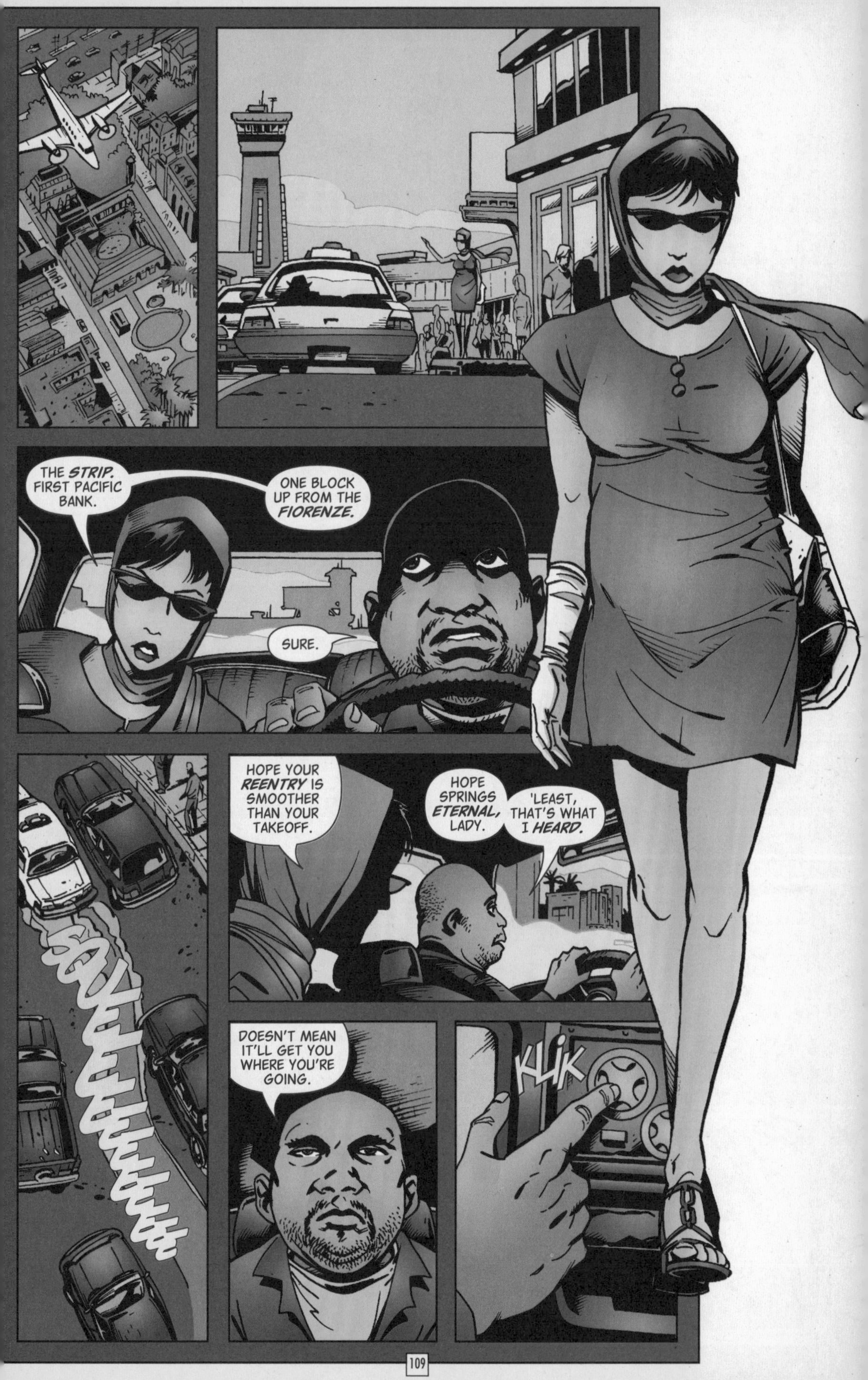
THE STRIP. FIRST PACIFIC BANK.
ONE BLOCK UP FROM THE FIORENZE.
SURE.
HOPE YOUR REENTRY IS SMOOTHER THAN YOUR TAKEOFF.
HOPE SPRINGS ETERNAL, LADY.
'LEAST, THAT'S WHAT I HEARD.
DOESN'T MEAN IT'LL GET YOU WHERE YOU'RE GOING.
KLIK

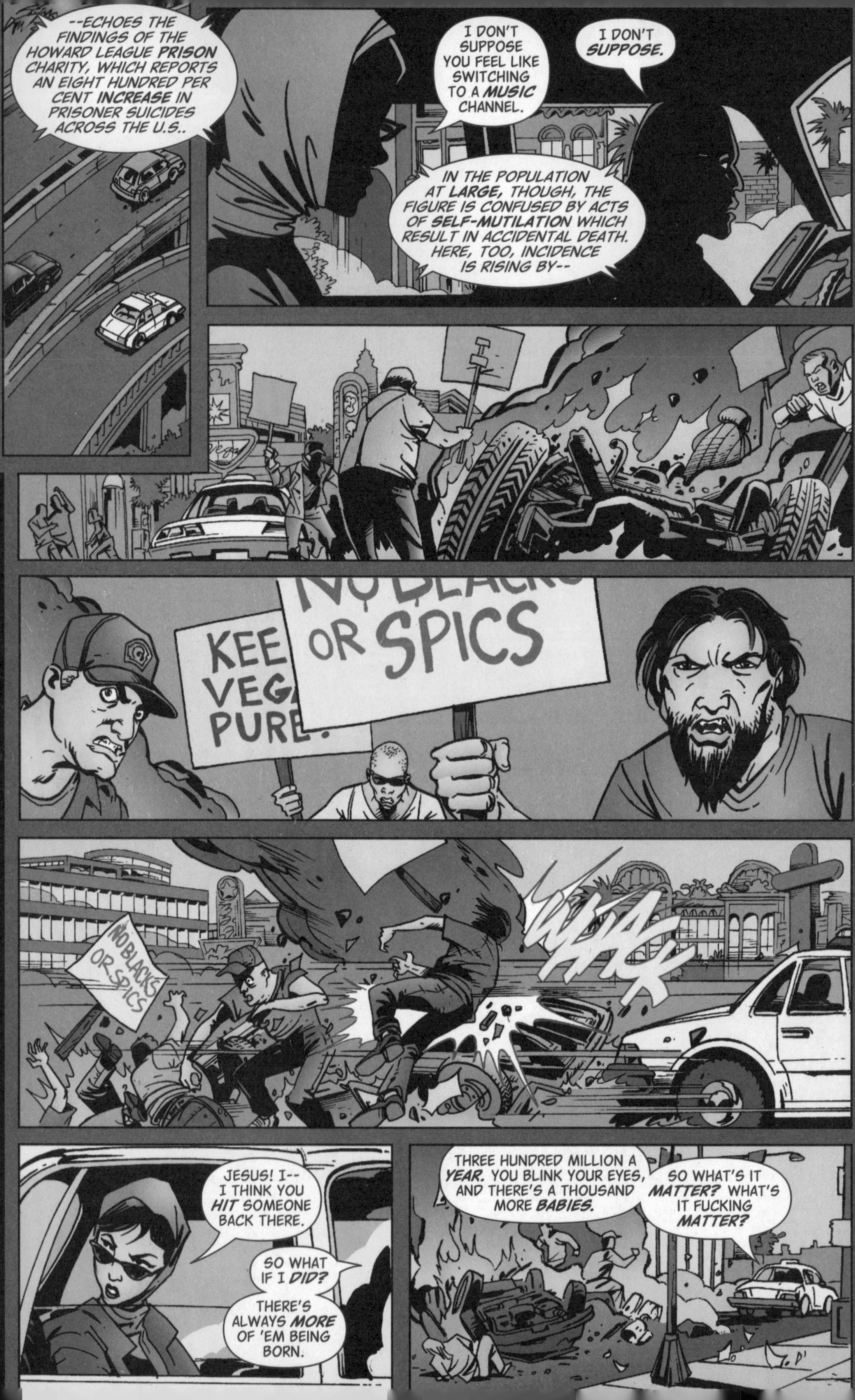

--ECHOES THE FINDINGS OF THE HOWARD LEAGUE PRISON CHARITY, WHICH REPORTS AN EIGHT HUNDRED PER CENT INCREASE IN PRISONER SUICIDES ACROSS THE U.S..
I DON'T SUPPOSE YOU FEEL LIKE SWITCHING TO A MUSIC CHANNEL.
I DON'T SUPPOSE.
IN THE POPULATION AT LARGE, THOUGH, THE FIGURE IS CONFUSED BY ACTS OF SELF-MUTILATION WHICH RESULT IN ACCIDENTAL DEATH. HERE, TOO, INCIDENCE IS RISING BY--
KEE VEGA PURE
OR SPICS
NO BLACKS OR SPICS
WHACK
JESUS! I-- I THINK YOU HIT SOMEONE BACK THERE.
SO WHAT IF I DID?
THERE'S ALWAYS MORE OF 'EM BEING BORN.
THREE HUNDRED MILLION A YEAR. YOU BLINK YOUR EYES, AND THERE'S A THOUSAND MORE BABIES.
SO WHAT'S IT MATTER? WHAT'S IT FUCKING MATTER?

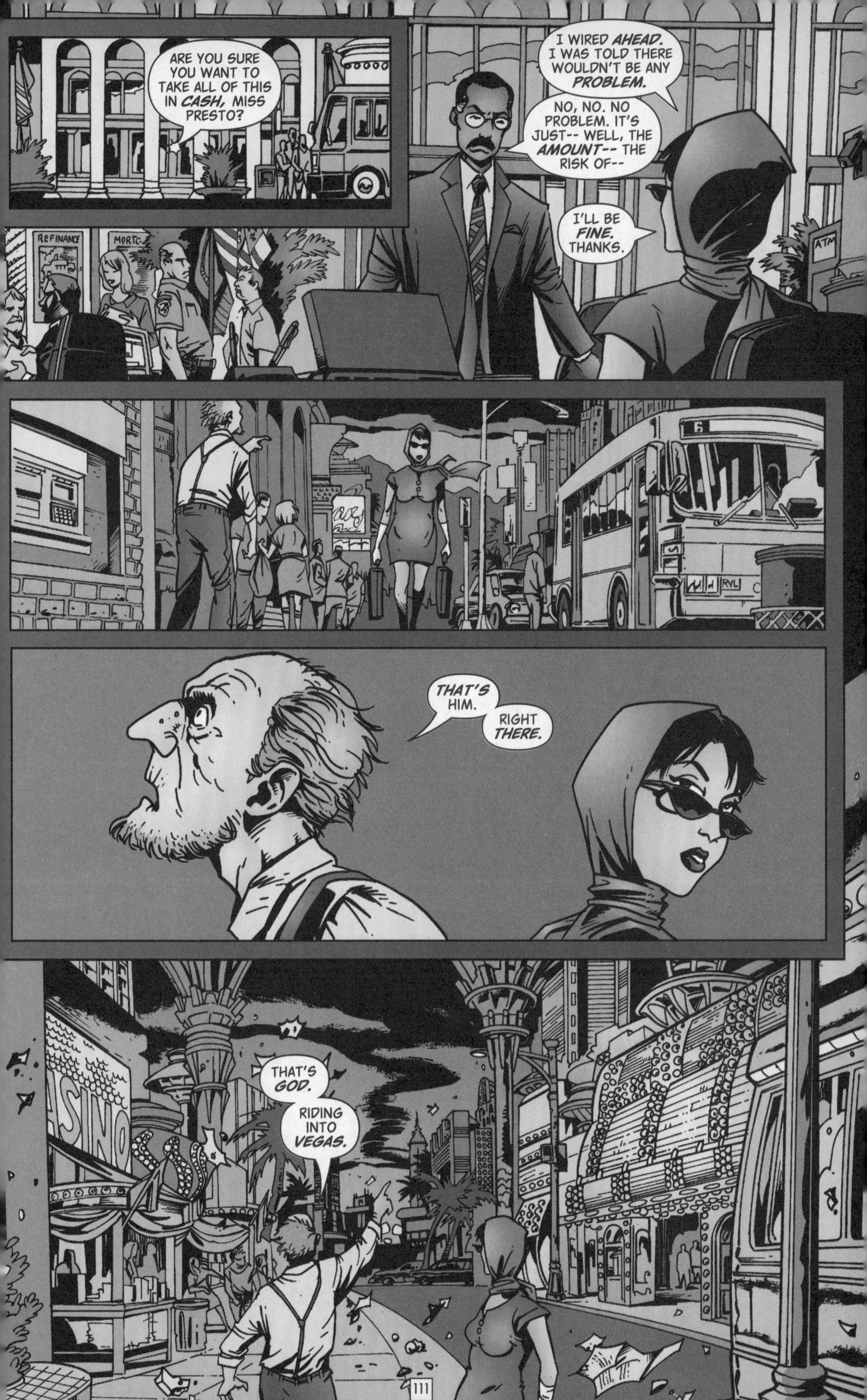
ARE YOU SURE YOU WANT TO TAKE ALL OF THIS IN CASH, MISS PRESTO?
I WIRED AHEAD. I WAS TOLD THERE WOULDN'T BE ANY PROBLEM.
NO, NO. NO PROBLEM. IT'S JUST-- WELL, THE AMOUNT-- THE RISK OF--
I'LL BE FINE. THANKS.
REFINANCE
MORTG
ATM
THAT'S HIM.
RIGHT THERE.
THAT'S GOD.
RIDING INTO VEGAS.
ASINO

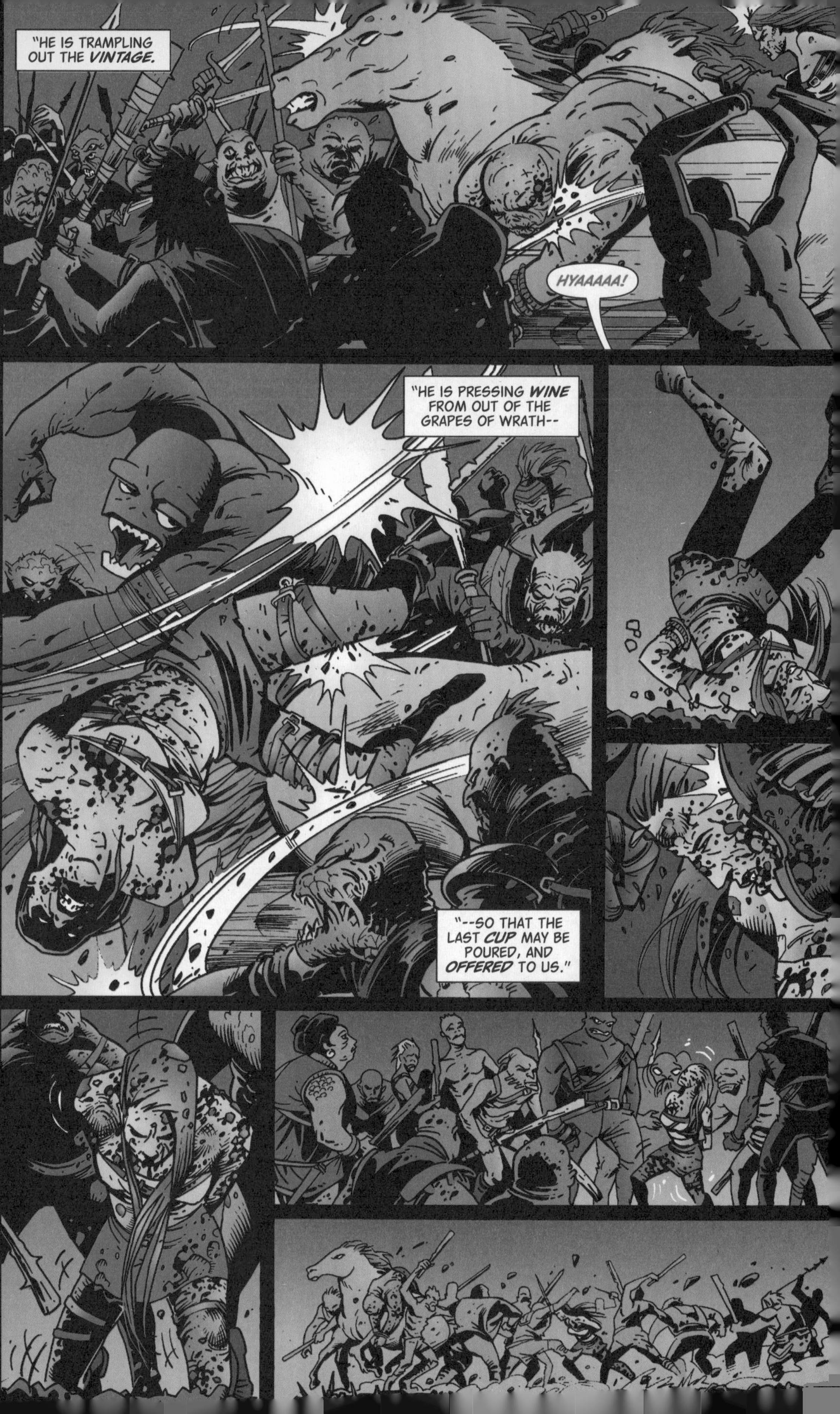
"HE IS TRAMPLING OUT THE VINTAGE.
HYAAAAA!
"HE IS PRESSING WINE FROM OUT OF THE GRAPES OF WRATH--
"--SO THAT THE LAST CUP MAY BE POURED, AND OFFERED TO US."

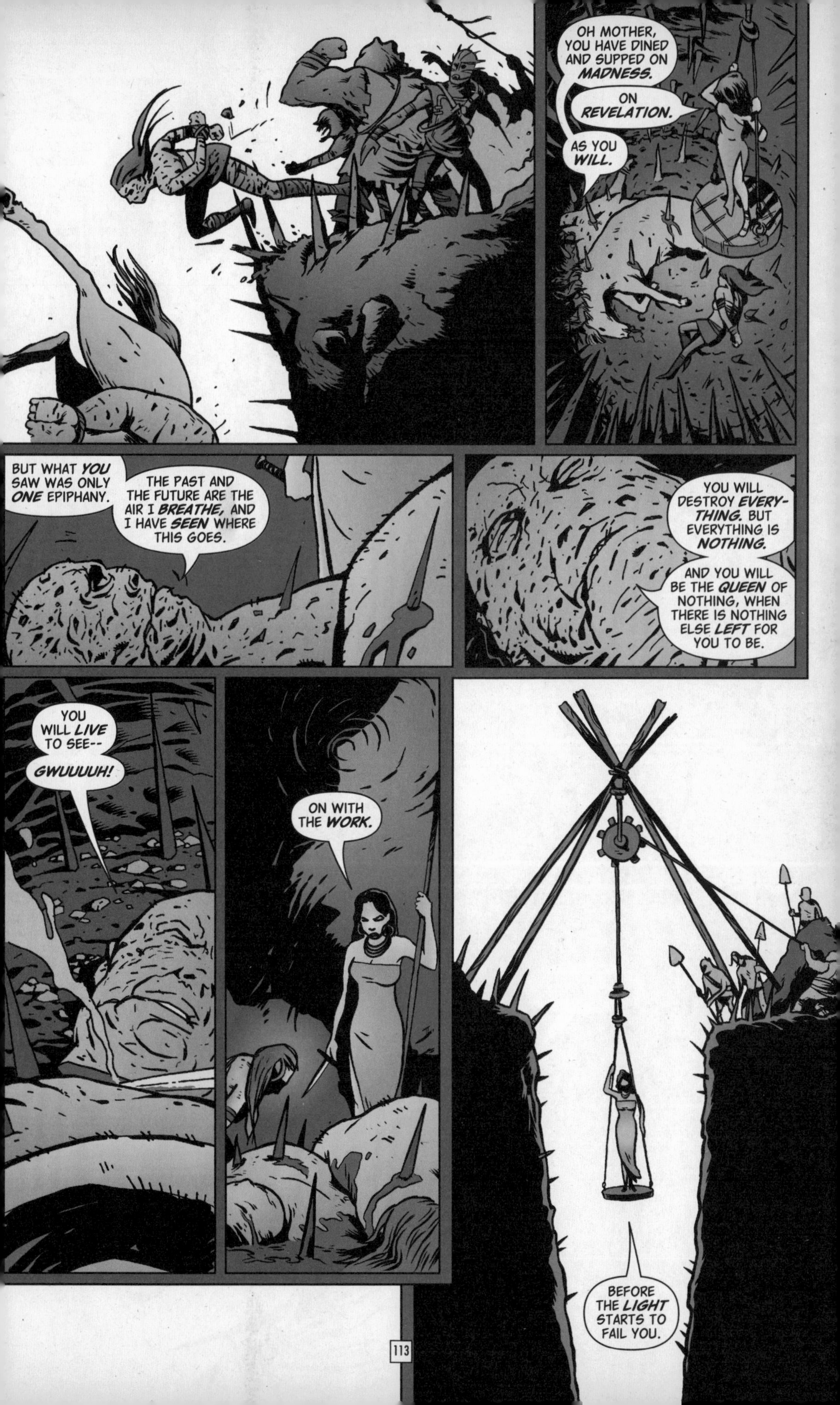

OH MOTHER, YOU HAVE DINED AND SUPPED ON MADNESS.
ON REVELATION.
AS YOU WILL.
BUT WHAT YOU SAW WAS ONLY ONE EPIPHANY.
THE PAST AND THE FUTURE ARE THE AIR I BREATHE, AND I HAVE SEEN WHERE THIS GOES.
YOU WILL DESTROY EVERYTHING. BUT EVERYTHING IS NOTHING.
AND YOU WILL BE THE QUEEN OF NOTHING, WHEN THERE IS NOTHING ELSE LEFT FOR YOU TO BE.
YOU WILL LIVE TO SEE--
GWUUUUH!
ON WITH THE WORK.
BEFORE THE LIGHT STARTS TO FAIL YOU.

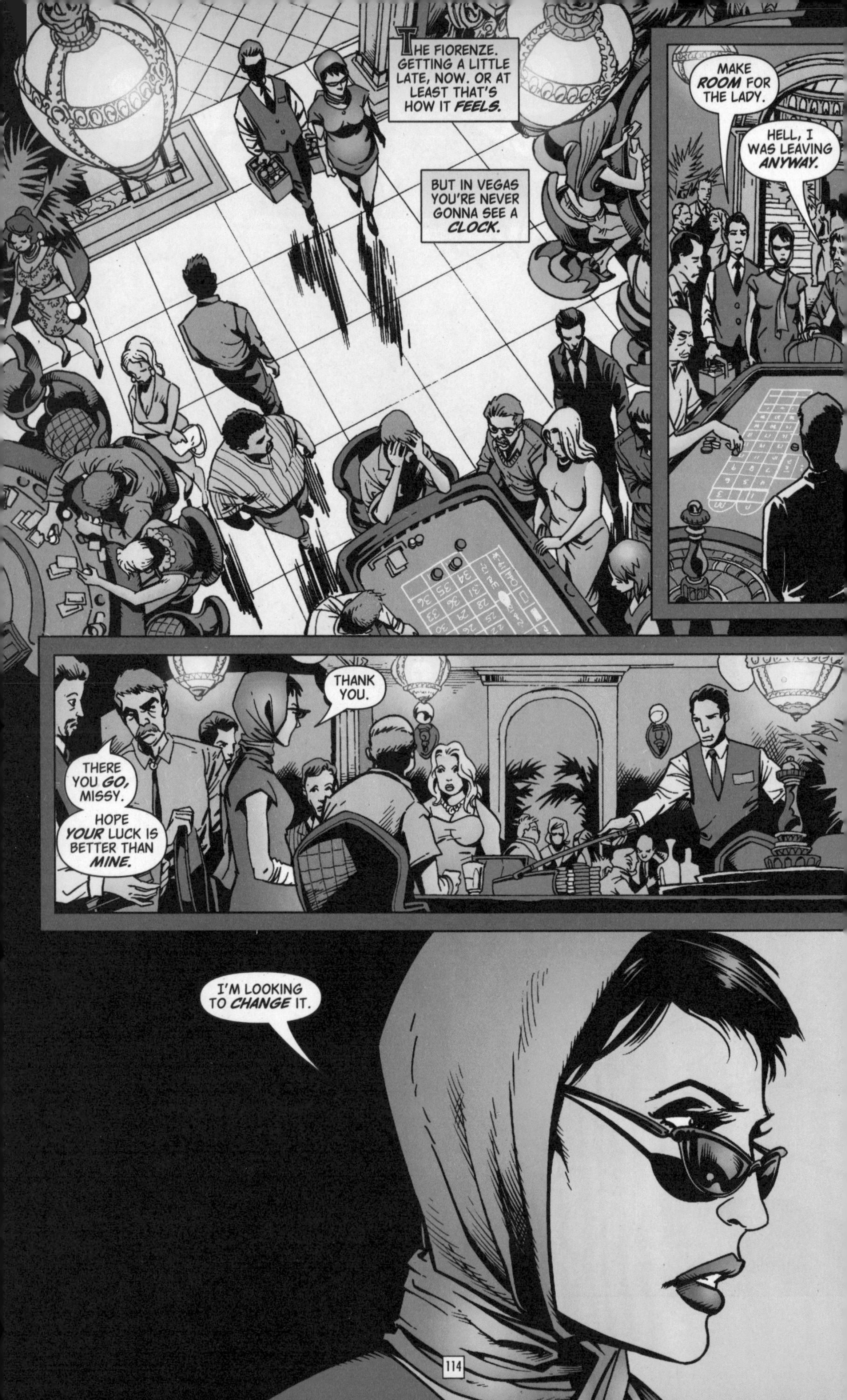
THE FIORENZE. GETTING A LITTLE LATE, NOW. OR AT LEAST THAT'S HOW IT FEELS.
BUT IN VEGAS YOU'RE NEVER GONNA SEE A CLOCK.
MAKE ROOM FOR THE LADY.
HELL, I WAS LEAVING ANYWAY.
THANK YOU.
THERE YOU GO, MISSY.
HOPE YOUR LUCK IS BETTER THAN MINE.
I'M LOOKING TO CHANGE IT.

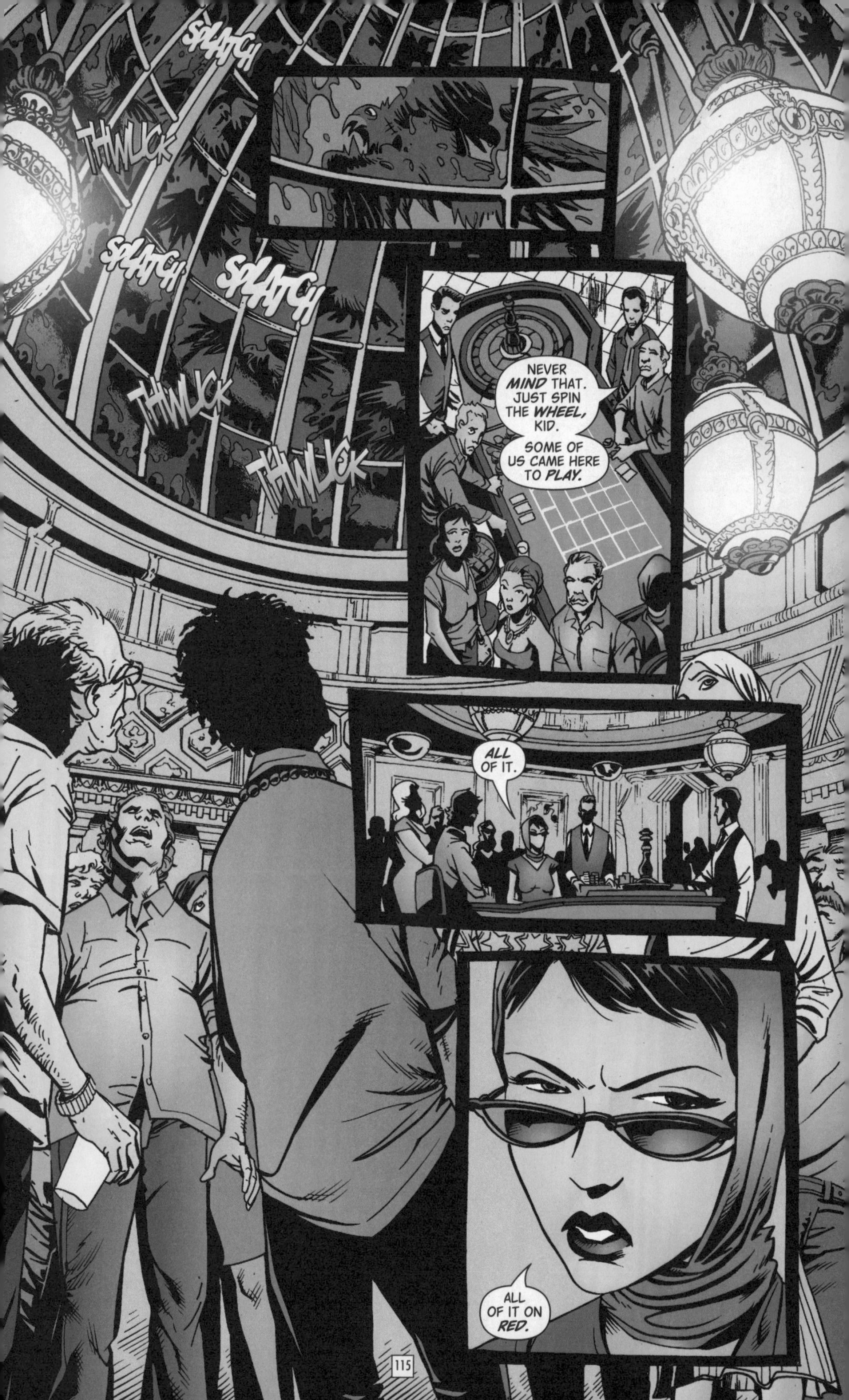
SPLATCH
THWUCK
SPLATCH
SPLATCH
THWUCK
THWUCK
NEVER MIND THAT. JUST SPIN THE WHEEL, KID.
SOME OF US CAME HERE TO PLAY.
ALL OF IT.
ALL OF IT ON RED.

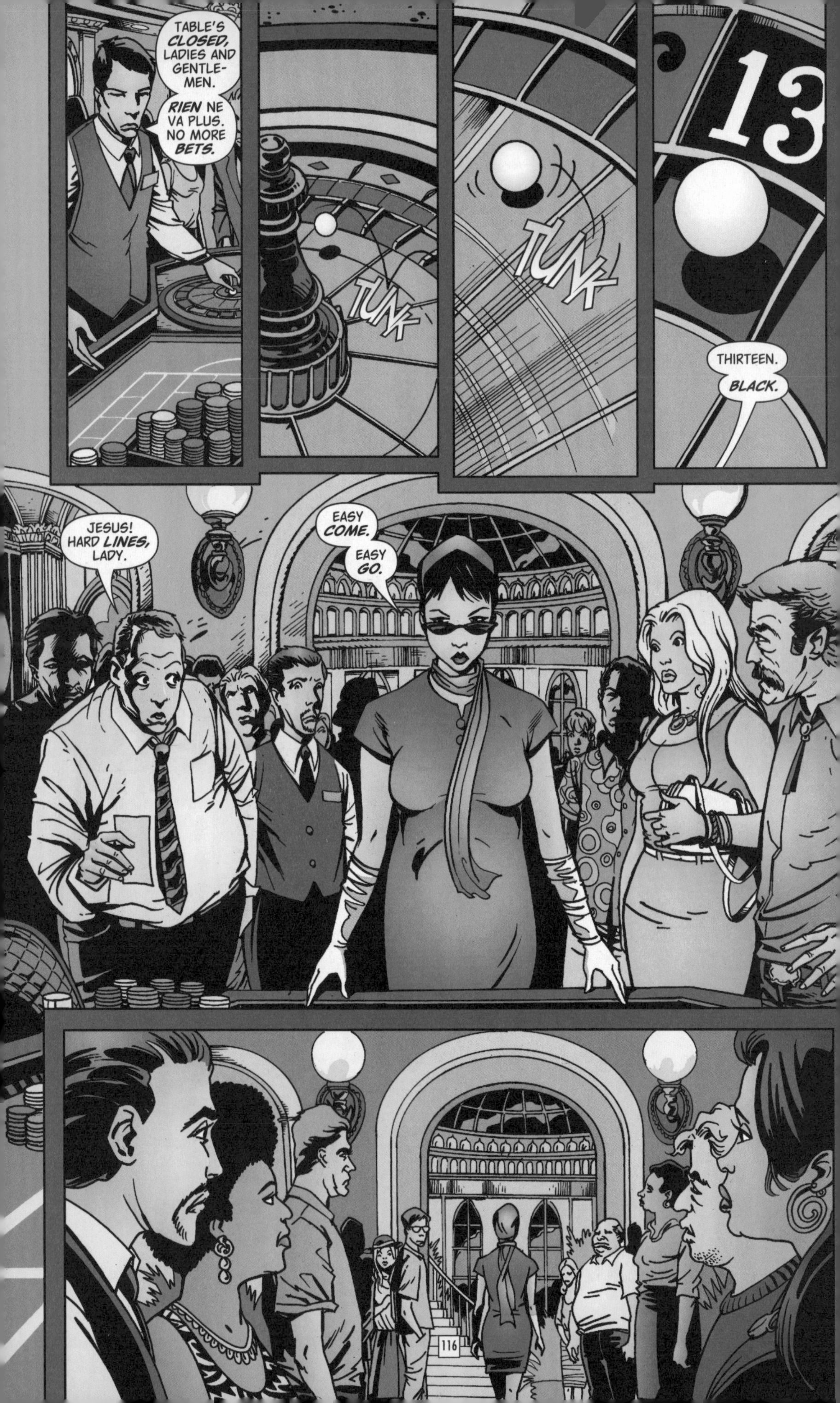

TABLE'S CLOSED, LADIES AND GENTLE-MEN.
RIEN NE VA PLUS. NO MORE BETS.
TUNK
TUNK
THIRTEEN. BLACK.
JESUS! HARD LINES, LADY.
EASY COME.
EASY GO.

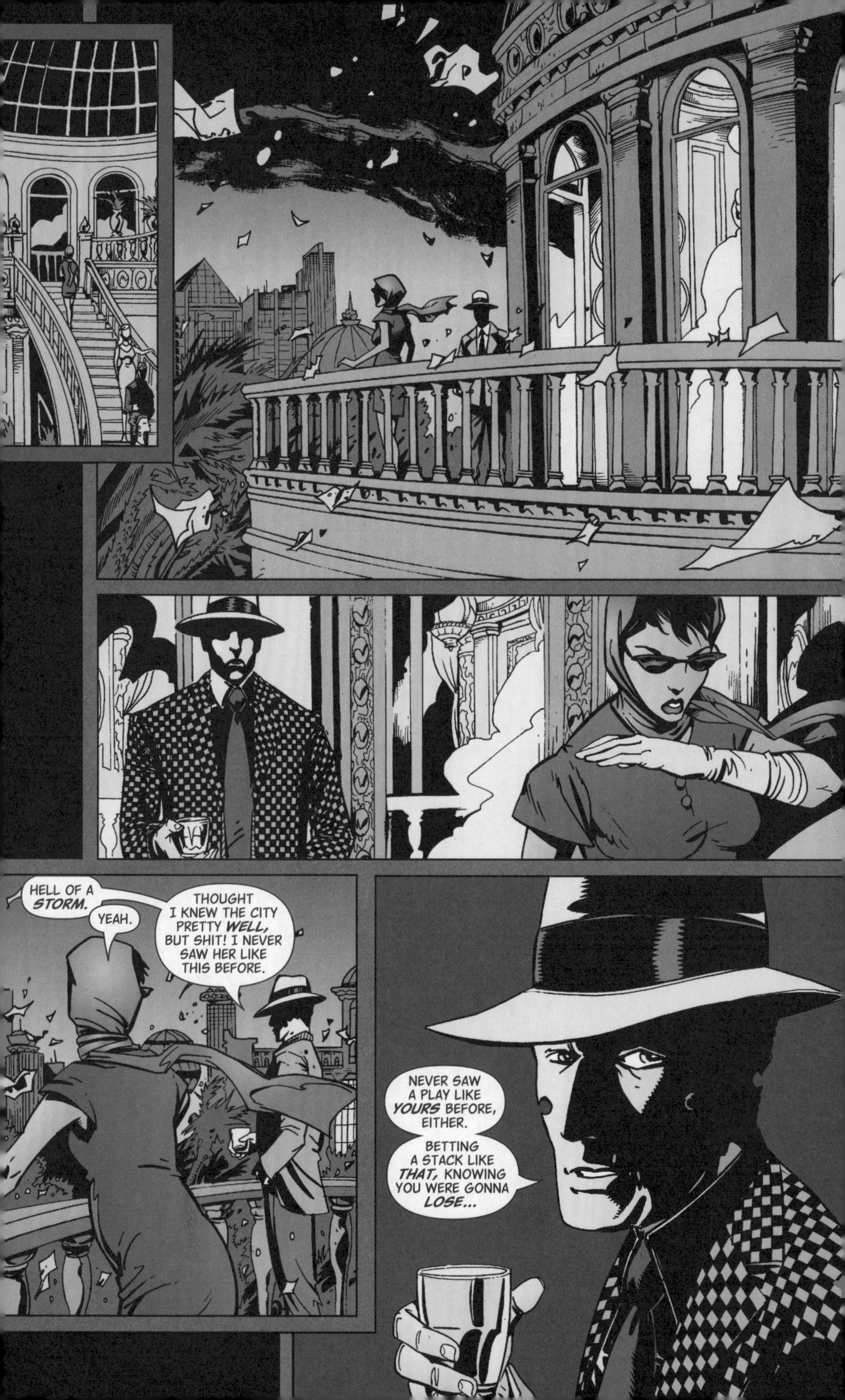
HELL OF A STORM.
YEAH.
THOUGHT I KNEW THE CITY PRETTY WELL, BUT SHIT! I NEVER SAW HER LIKE THIS BEFORE.
NEVER SAW A PLAY LIKE YOURS BEFORE, EITHER.
BETTING A STACK LIKE THAT, KNOWING YOU WERE GONNA LOSE...

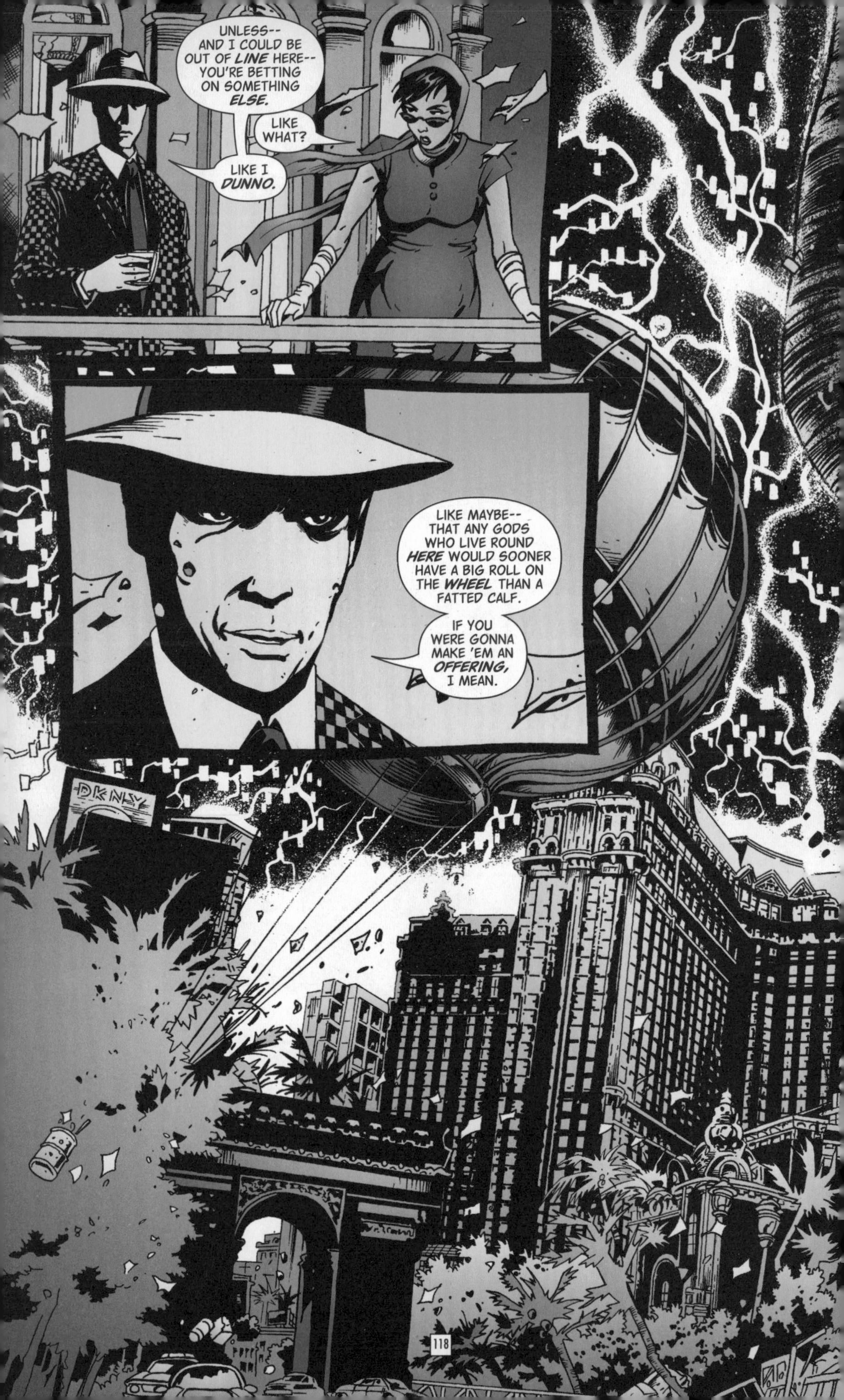

UNLESS-- AND I COULD BE OUT OF LINE HERE-- YOU'RE BETTING ON SOMETHING ELSE.
LIKE WHAT?
LIKE I DUNNO.
LIKE MAYBE-- THAT ANY GODS WHO LIVE ROUND HERE WOULD SOONER HAVE A BIG ROLL ON THE WHEEL THAN A FATTED CALF.
IF YOU WERE GONNA MAKE 'EM AN OFFERING, I MEAN.
DKNY

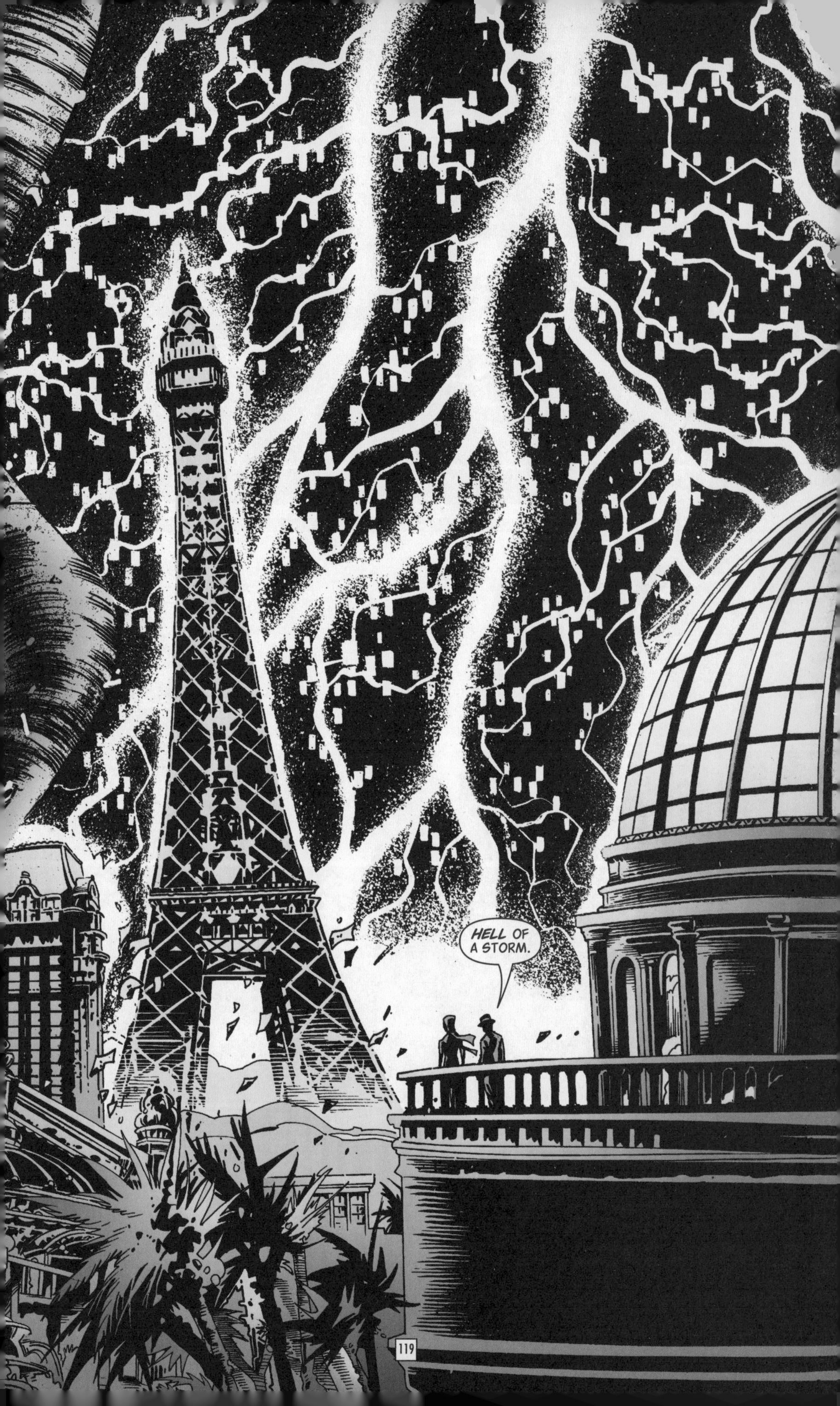
HELL OF A STORM.

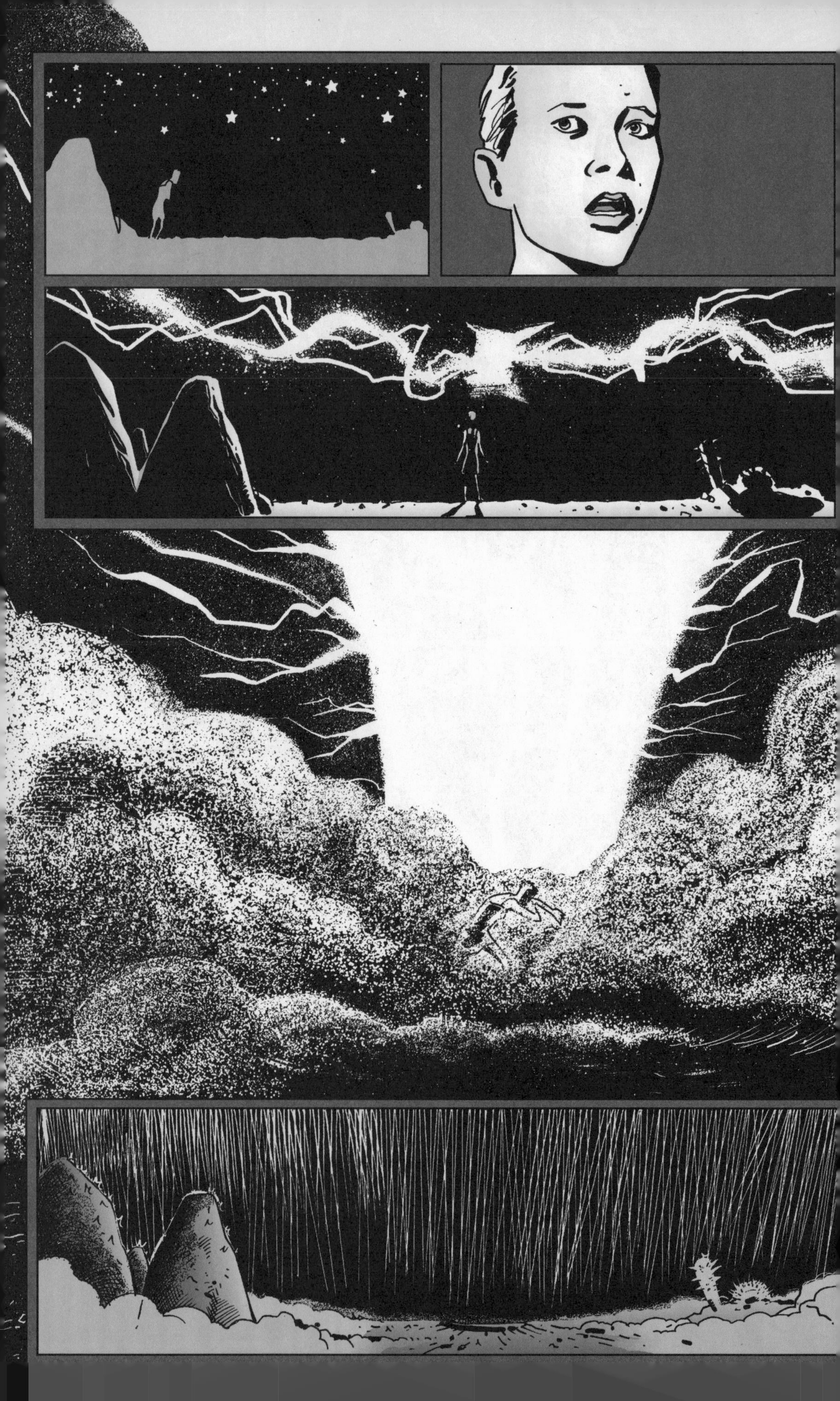

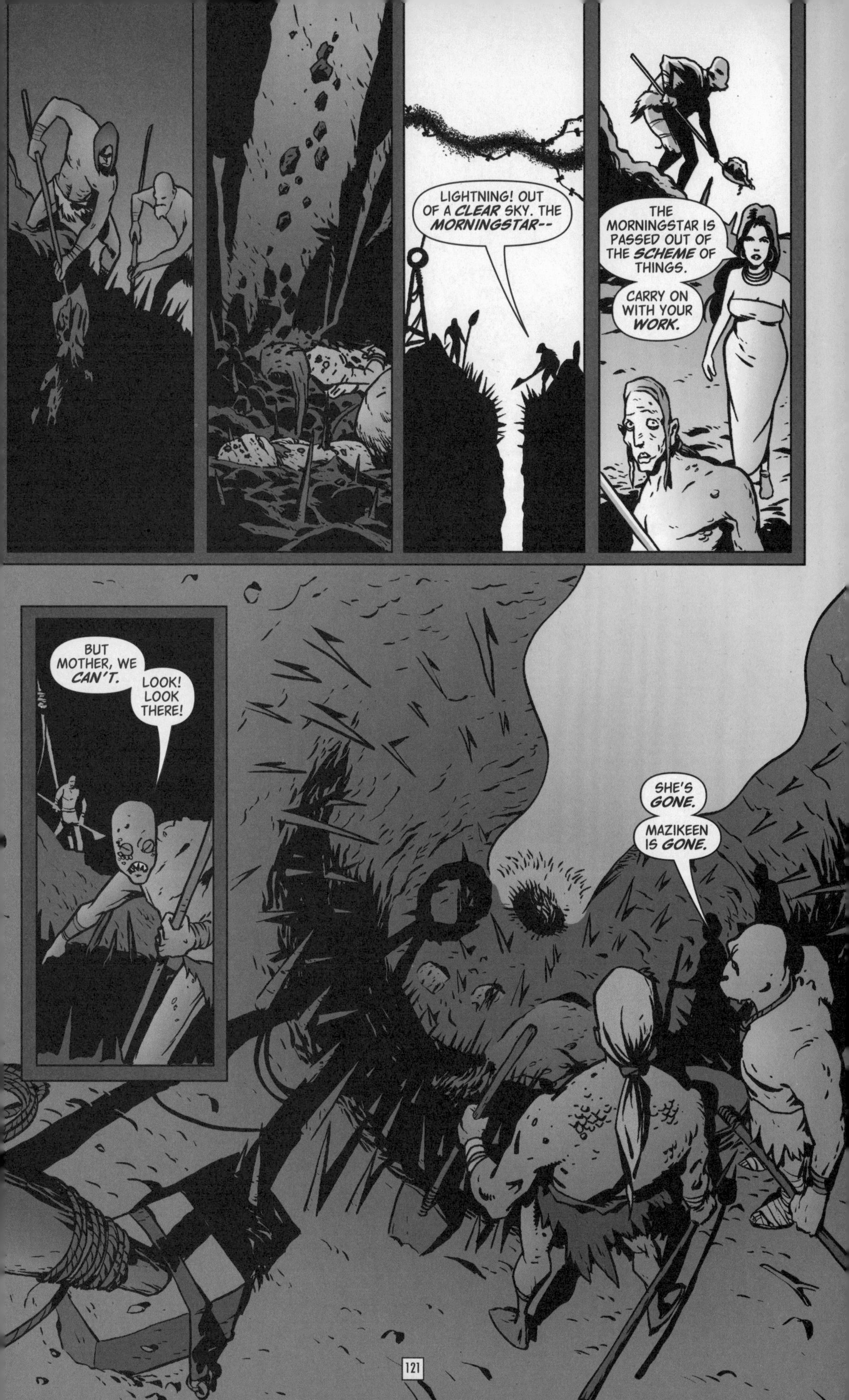
LIGHTNING! OUT OF A CLEAR SKY. THE MORNINGSTAR--
THE MORNINGSTAR IS PASSED OUT OF THE SCHEME OF THINGS.
CARRY ON WITH YOUR WORK.
BUT MOTHER, WE CAN'T.
LOOK! LOOK THERE!
SHE'S GONE.
MAZIKEEN IS GONE.

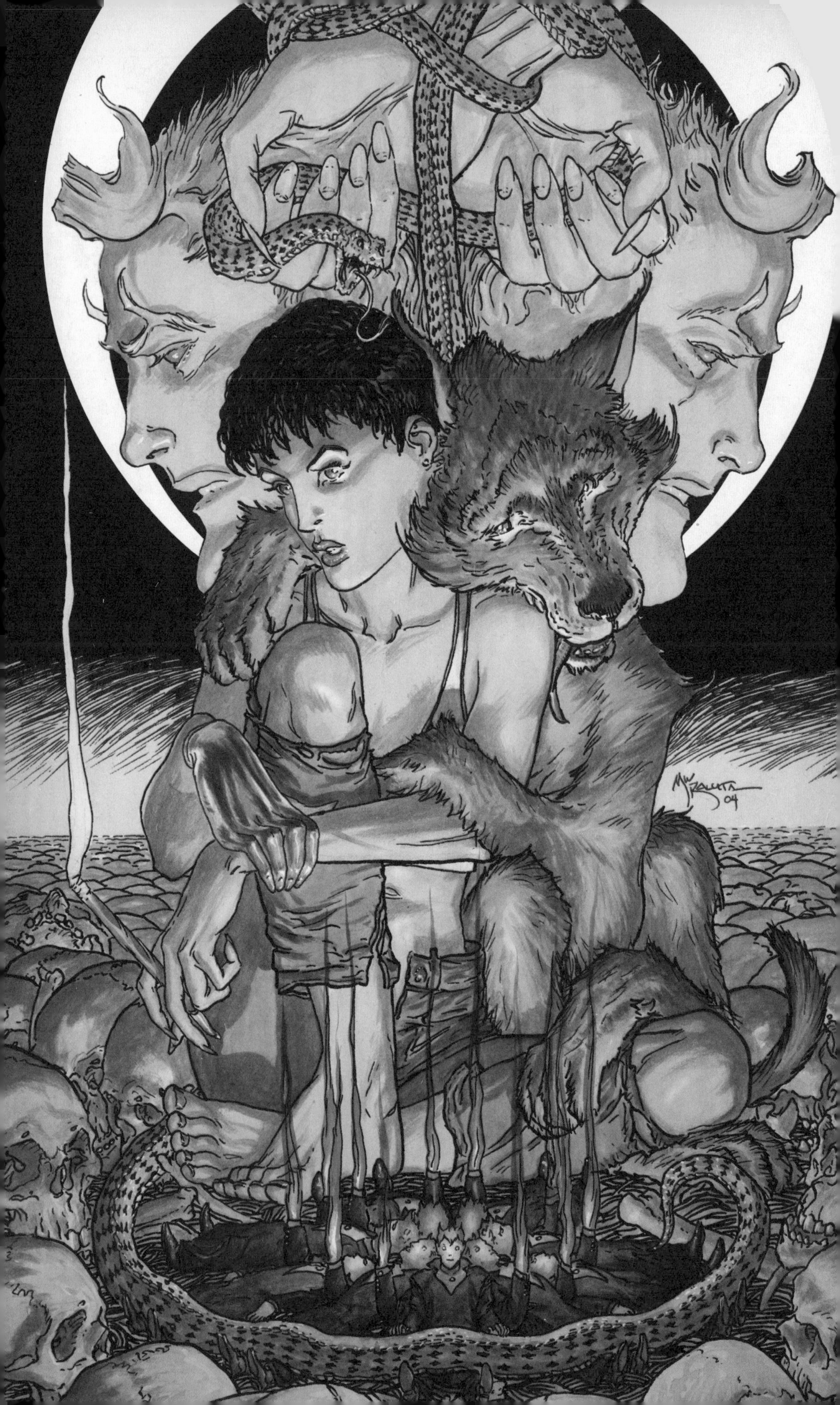

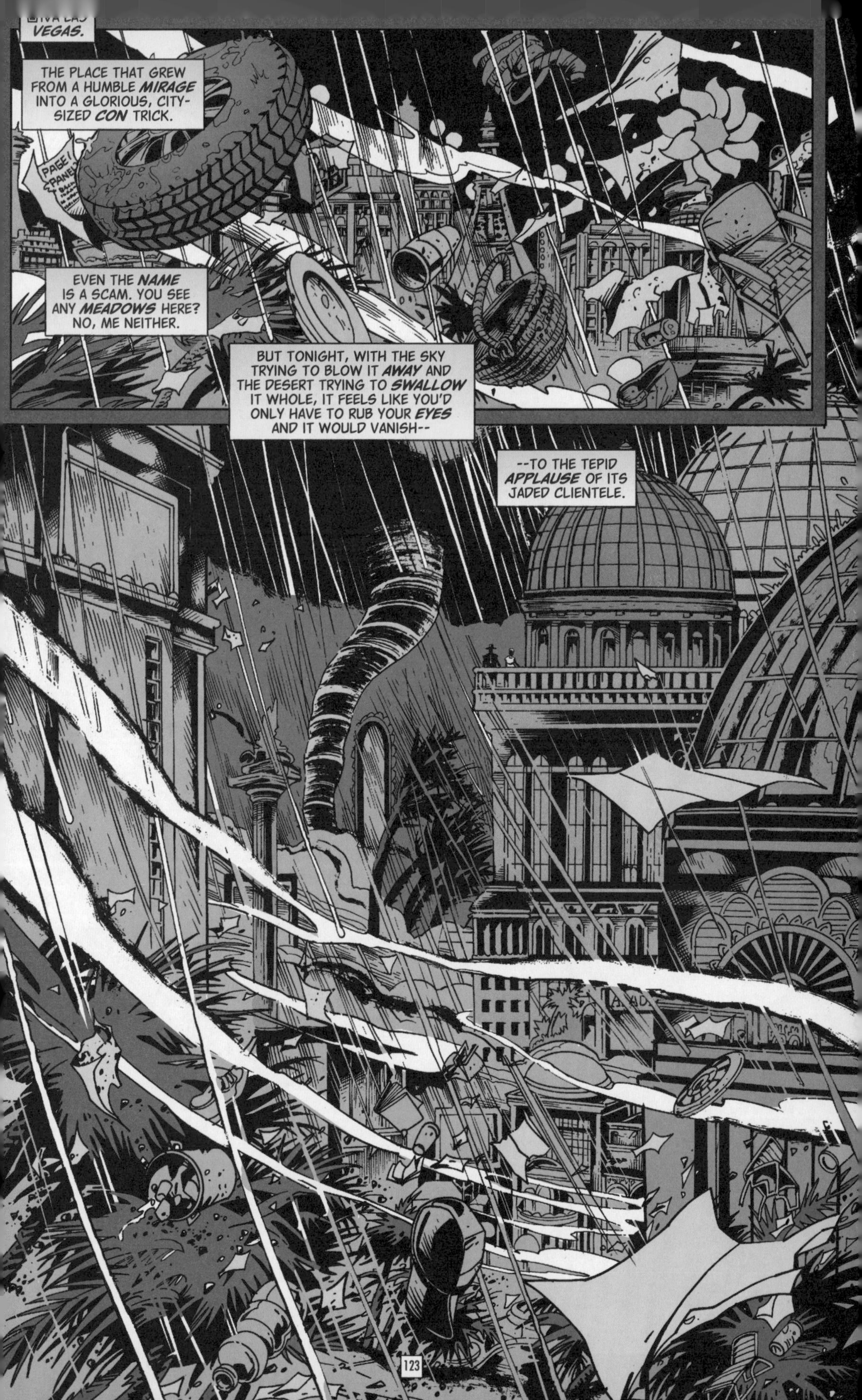
VEGAS.
THE PLACE THAT GREW FROM A HUMBLE *MIRAGE* INTO A GLORIOUS, CITY-SIZED *CON* TRICK.
EVEN THE *NAME* IS A SCAM. YOU SEE ANY *MEADOWS* HERE? NO, ME NEITHER.
BUT TONIGHT, WITH THE SKY TRYING TO BLOW IT *AWAY* AND THE DESERT TRYING TO *SWALLOW* IT WHOLE, IT FEELS LIKE YOU'D ONLY HAVE TO RUB YOUR *EYES* AND IT WOULD VANISH--
--TO THE TEPID *APPLAUSE* OF ITS JADED CLIENTELE.

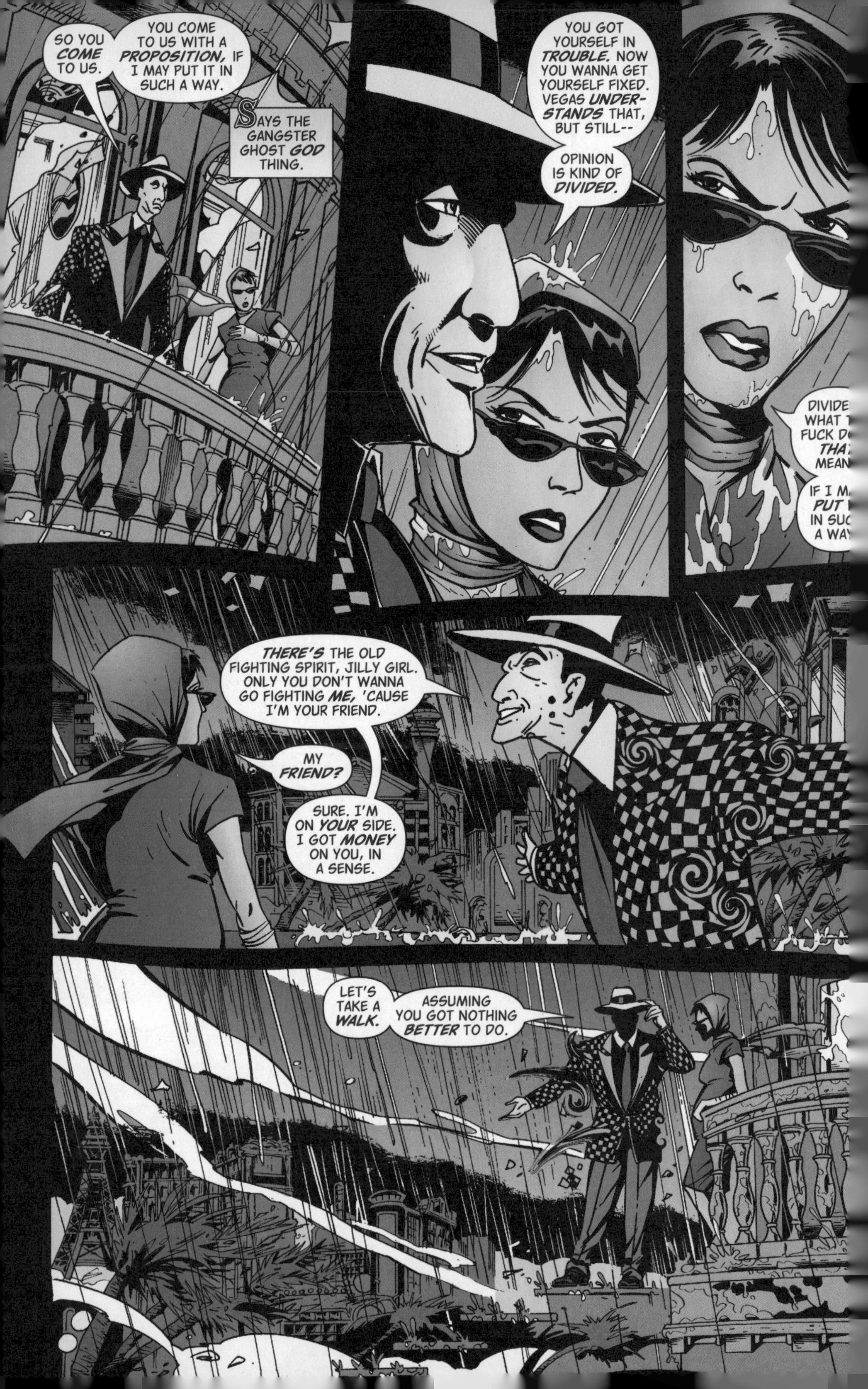
SO YOU COME TO US.
YOU COME TO US WITH A PROPOSITION, IF I MAY PUT IT IN SUCH A WAY.
SAYS THE GANGSTER GHOST GOD THING.
YOU GOT YOURSELF IN TROUBLE. NOW YOU WANNA GET YOURSELF FIXED. VEGAS UNDER-STANDS THAT, BUT STILL--
OPINION IS KIND OF DIVIDED.
DIVIDE WHAT FUCK D MEAN
IF I M PUT IN SU A WAY
THERE'S THE OLD FIGHTING SPIRIT, JILLY GIRL. ONLY YOU DON'T WANNA GO FIGHTING ME, 'CAUSE I'M YOUR FRIEND.
MY FRIEND?
SURE. I'M ON YOUR SIDE. I GOT MONEY ON YOU, IN A SENSE.
LET'S TAKE A WALK.
ASSUMING YOU GOT NOTHING BETTER TO DO.

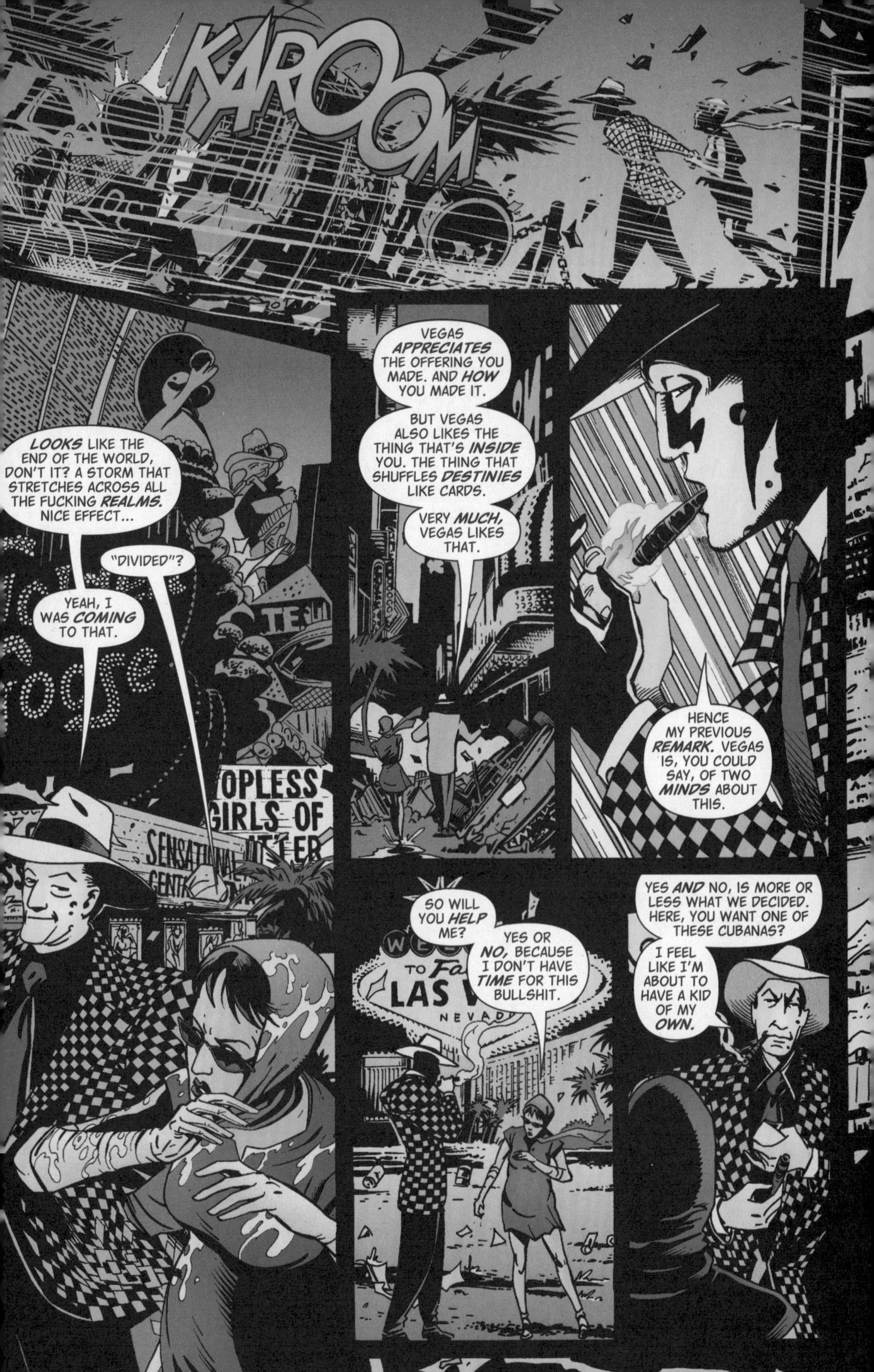
KAROOM
LOOKS LIKE THE END OF THE WORLD, DON'T IT? A STORM THAT STRETCHES ACROSS ALL THE FUCKING REALMS. NICE EFFECT...
"DIVIDED"?
YEAH, I WAS COMING TO THAT.
OPLESS GIRLS OF
SENSATIONAL
VEGAS APPRECIATES THE OFFERING YOU MADE. AND HOW YOU MADE IT.
BUT VEGAS ALSO LIKES THE THING THAT'S INSIDE YOU. THE THING THAT SHUFFLES DESTINIES LIKE CARDS.
VERY MUCH, VEGAS LIKES THAT.
HENCE MY PREVIOUS REMARK. VEGAS IS, YOU COULD SAY, OF TWO MINDS ABOUT THIS.
SO WILL YOU HELP ME?
YES OR NO, BECAUSE I DON'T HAVE TIME FOR THIS BULLSHIT.
LAS
NEVAD
YES AND NO, IS MORE OR LESS WHAT WE DECIDED. HERE, YOU WANT ONE OF THESE CUBANAS?
I FEEL LIKE I'M ABOUT TO HAVE A KID OF MY OWN.

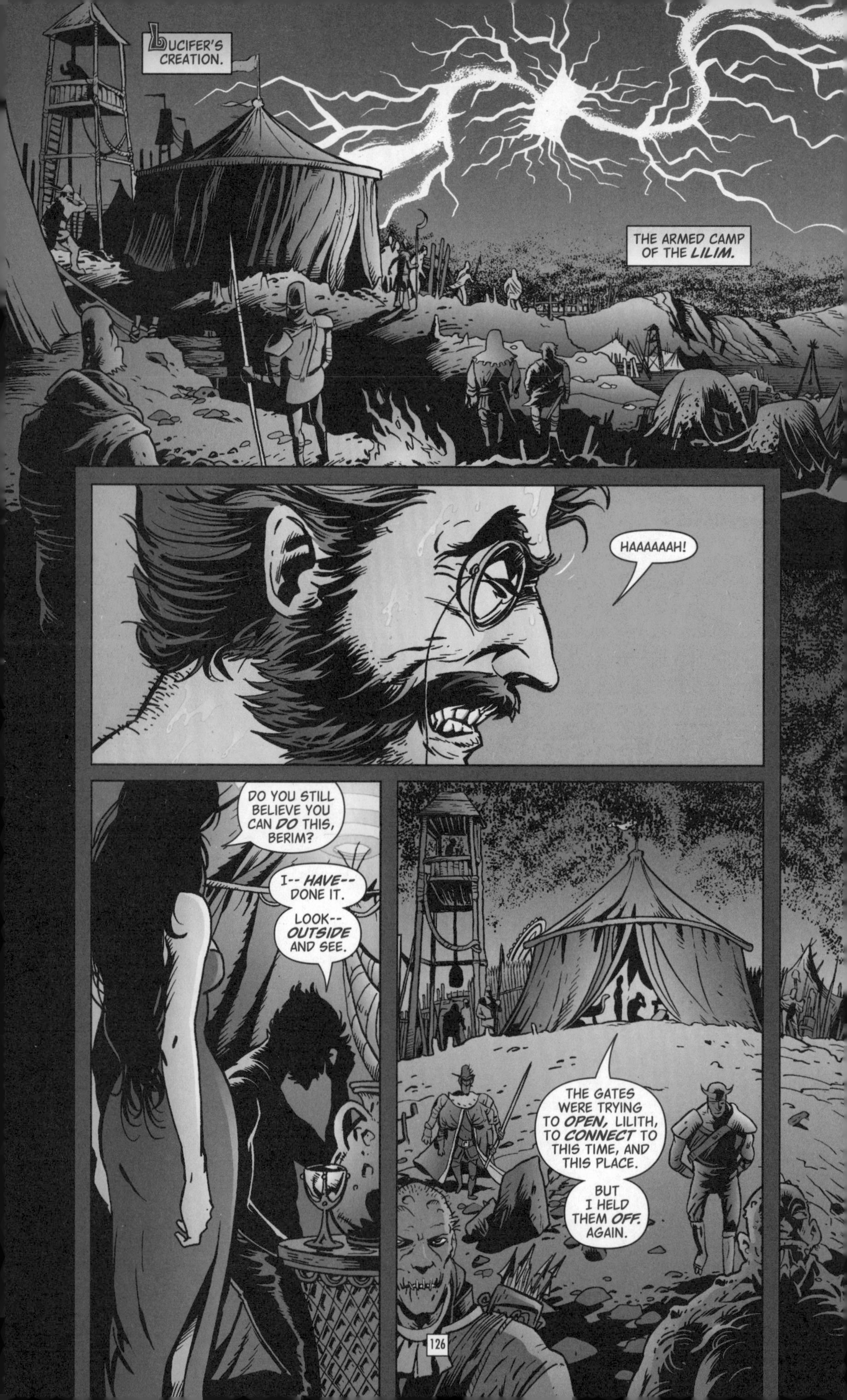
LUCIFER'S CREATION.
THE ARMED CAMP OF THE LILIM.
HAAAAAAH!
DO YOU STILL BELIEVE YOU CAN DO THIS, BERIM?
I-- HAVE-- DONE IT.
LOOK-- OUTSIDE AND SEE.
THE GATES WERE TRYING TO OPEN, LILITH, TO CONNECT TO THIS TIME, AND THIS PLACE.
BUT I HELD THEM OFF. AGAIN.

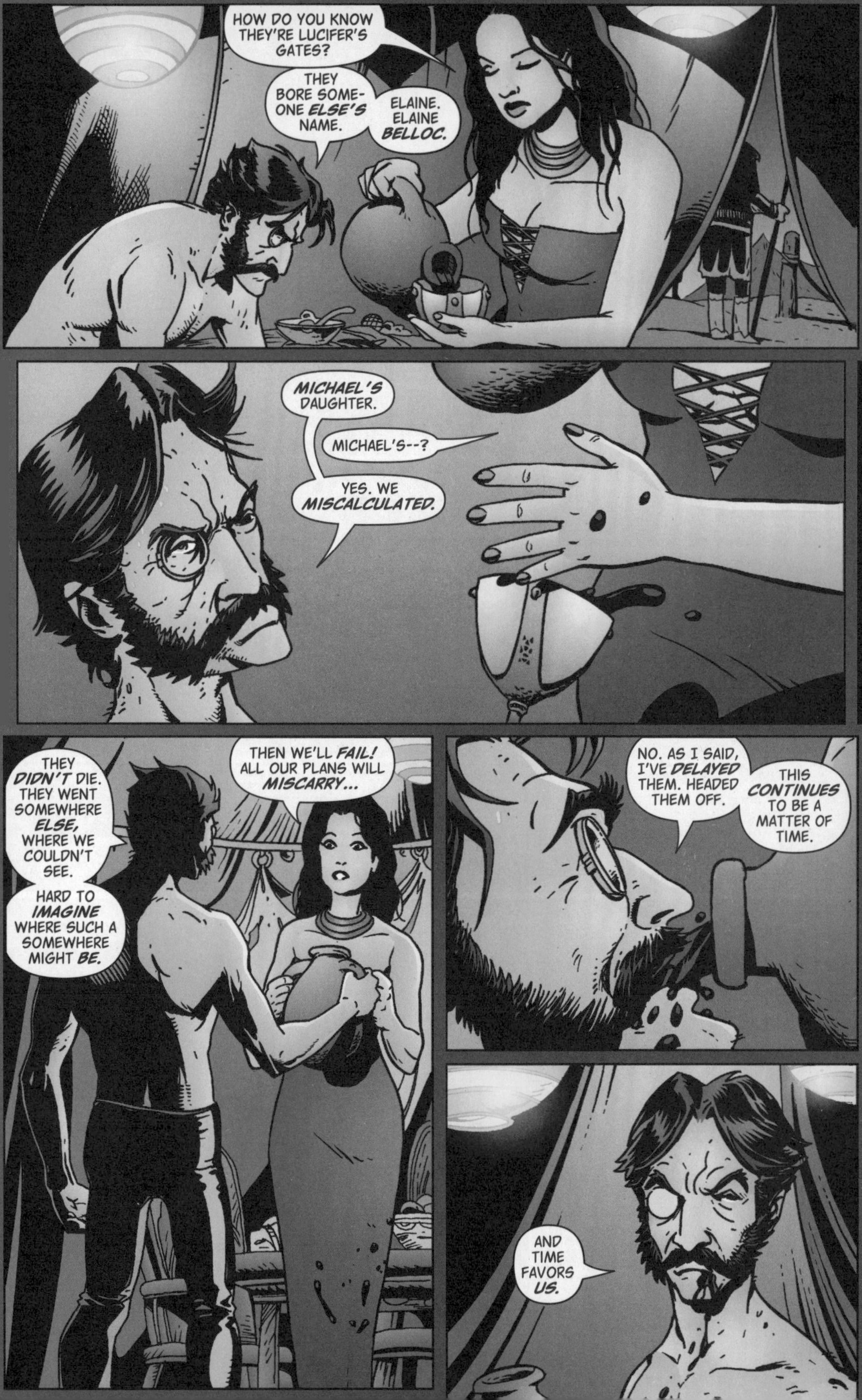

HOW DO YOU KNOW THEY'RE LUCIFER'S GATES?
THEY BORE SOME-ONE ELSE'S NAME.
ELAINE. ELAINE BELLOC.
MICHAEL'S DAUGHTER.
MICHAEL'S--?
YES. WE MISCALCULATED.
THEY DIDN'T DIE. THEY WENT SOMEWHERE ELSE, WHERE WE COULDN'T SEE.
HARD TO IMAGINE WHERE SUCH A SOMEWHERE MIGHT BE.
THEN WE'LL FAIL! ALL OUR PLANS WILL MISCARRY...
NO. AS I SAID, I'VE DELAYED THEM. HEADED THEM OFF.
THIS CONTINUES TO BE A MATTER OF TIME.
AND TIME FAVORS US.

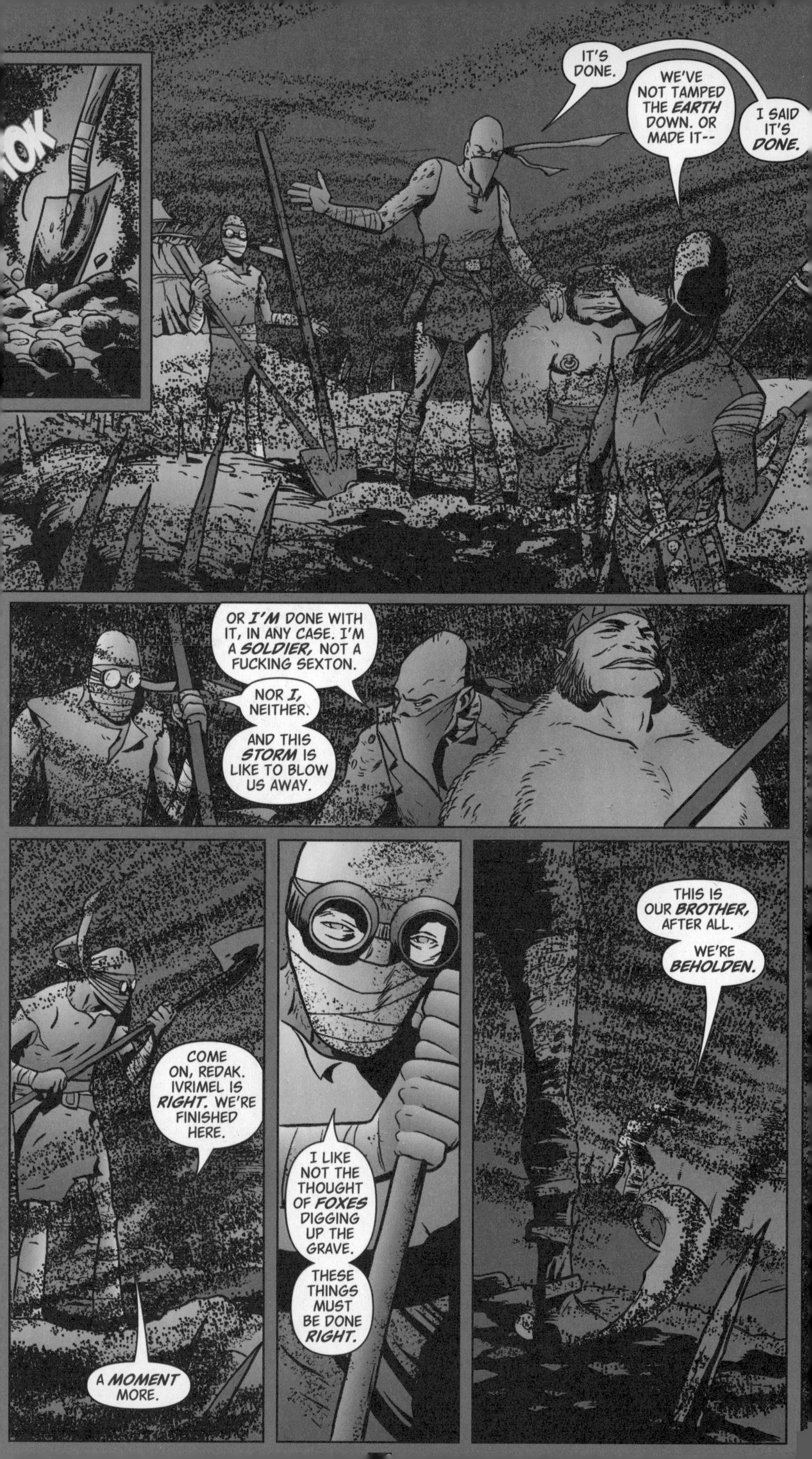

CHOK
IT'S DONE.
WE'VE NOT TAMPED THE EARTH DOWN. OR MADE IT--
I SAID IT'S DONE.
OR I'M DONE WITH IT, IN ANY CASE. I'M A SOLDIER, NOT A FUCKING SEXTON.
NOR I, NEITHER.
AND THIS STORM IS LIKE TO BLOW US AWAY.
COME ON, REDAK. IVRIMEL IS RIGHT. WE'RE FINISHED HERE.
A MOMENT MORE.
I LIKE NOT THE THOUGHT OF FOXES DIGGING UP THE GRAVE.
THESE THINGS MUST BE DONE RIGHT.
THIS IS OUR BROTHER, AFTER ALL.
WE'RE BEHOLDEN.

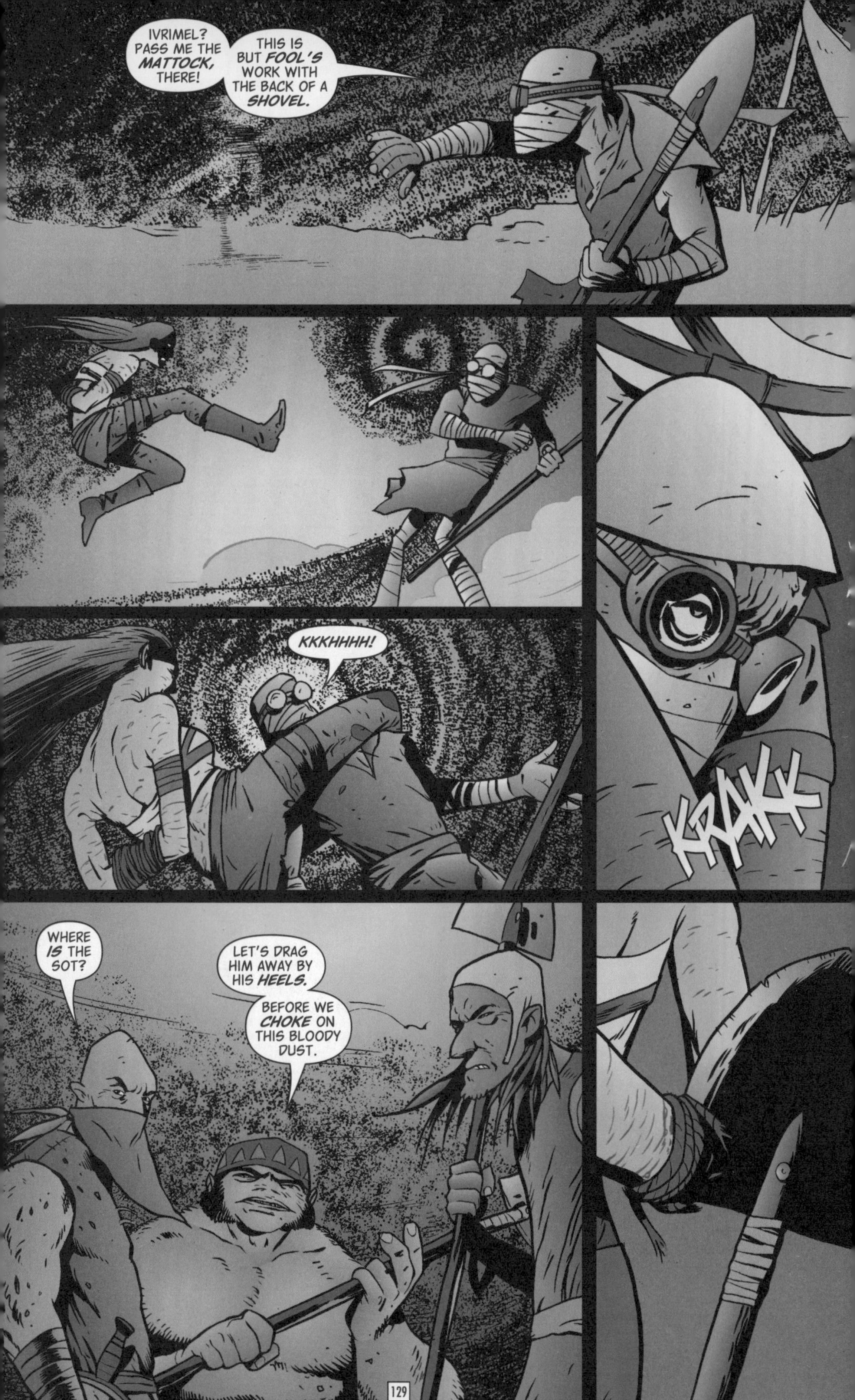
IVRIMEL? PASS ME THE *MATTOCK,* THERE!
THIS IS BUT *FOOL'S* WORK WITH THE BACK OF A *SHOVEL.*
KKKHHHH!
KRAKK
WHERE *IS* THE SOT?
LET'S DRAG HIM AWAY BY HIS *HEELS.*
BEFORE WE *CHOKE* ON THIS BLOODY DUST.

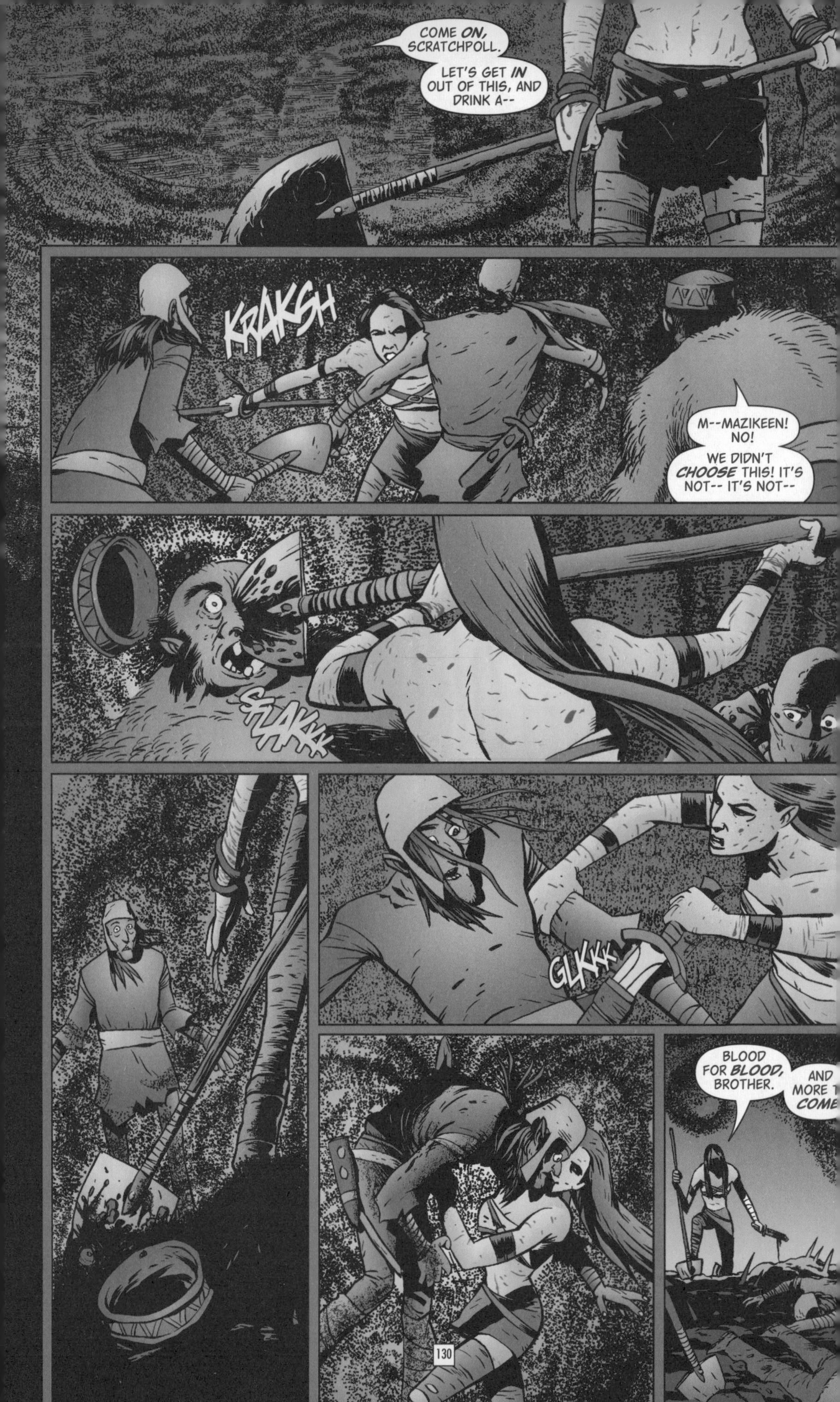
COME ON, SCRATCHPOLL.
LET'S GET IN OUT OF THIS, AND DRINK A--
KRAKSH
M--MAZIKEEN! NO!
WE DIDN'T CHOOSE THIS! IT'S NOT-- IT'S NOT--
SFLAKKK
GLKKK
BLOOD FOR BLOOD, BROTHER.

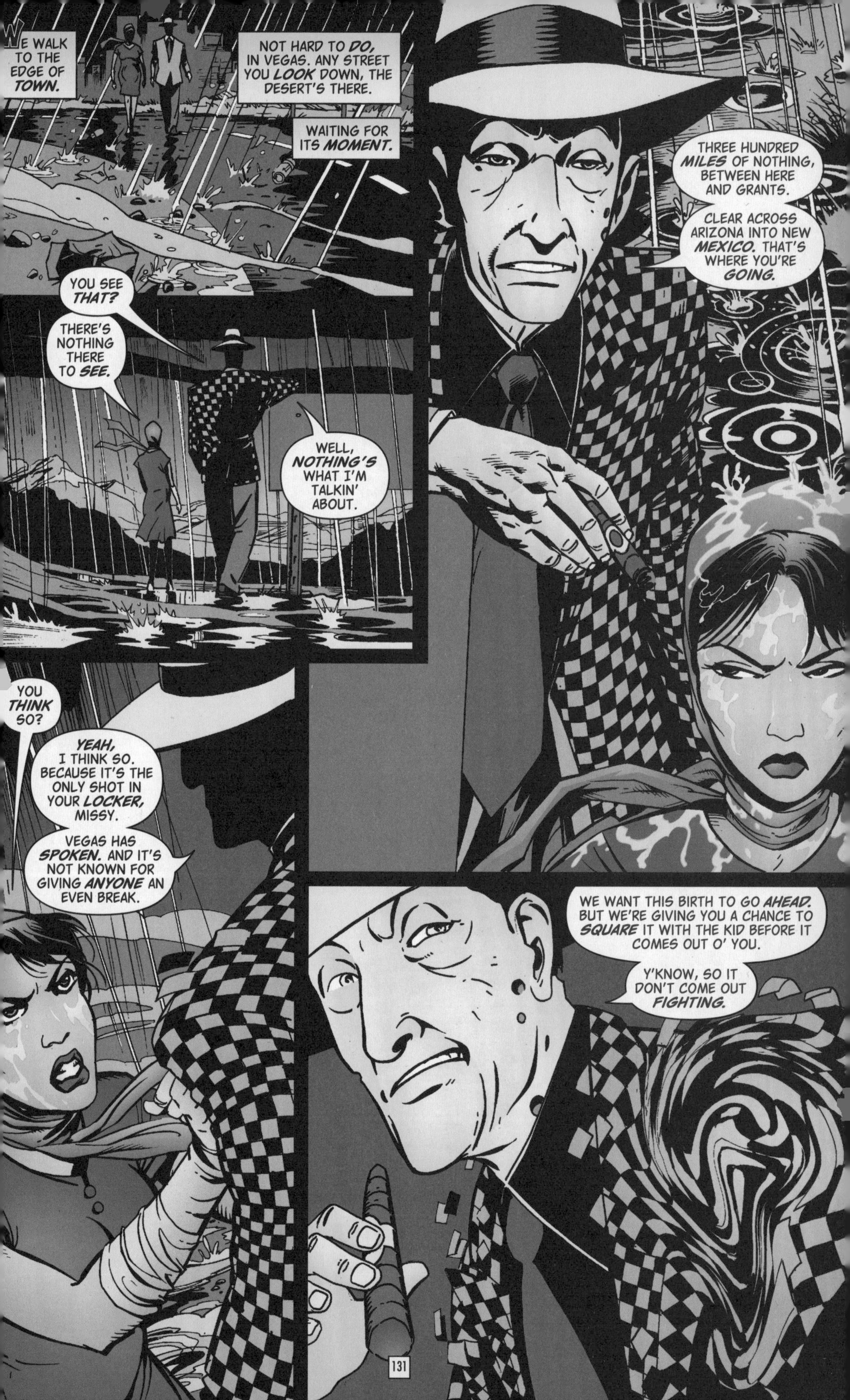

WE WALK TO THE EDGE OF TOWN.
NOT HARD TO DO, IN VEGAS. ANY STREET YOU LOOK DOWN, THE DESERT'S THERE.
WAITING FOR ITS MOMENT.
THREE HUNDRED MILES OF NOTHING, BETWEEN HERE AND GRANTS.
CLEAR ACROSS ARIZONA INTO NEW MEXICO. THAT'S WHERE YOU'RE GOING.
YOU SEE THAT?
THERE'S NOTHING THERE TO SEE.
WELL, NOTHING'S WHAT I'M TALKIN' ABOUT.
YOU THINK SO?
YEAH, I THINK SO. BECAUSE IT'S THE ONLY SHOT IN YOUR LOCKER, MISSY.
VEGAS HAS SPOKEN. AND IT'S NOT KNOWN FOR GIVING ANYONE AN EVEN BREAK.
WE WANT THIS BIRTH TO GO AHEAD. BUT WE'RE GIVING YOU A CHANCE TO SQUARE IT WITH THE KID BEFORE IT COMES OUT O' YOU.
Y'KNOW, SO IT DON'T COME OUT FIGHTING.

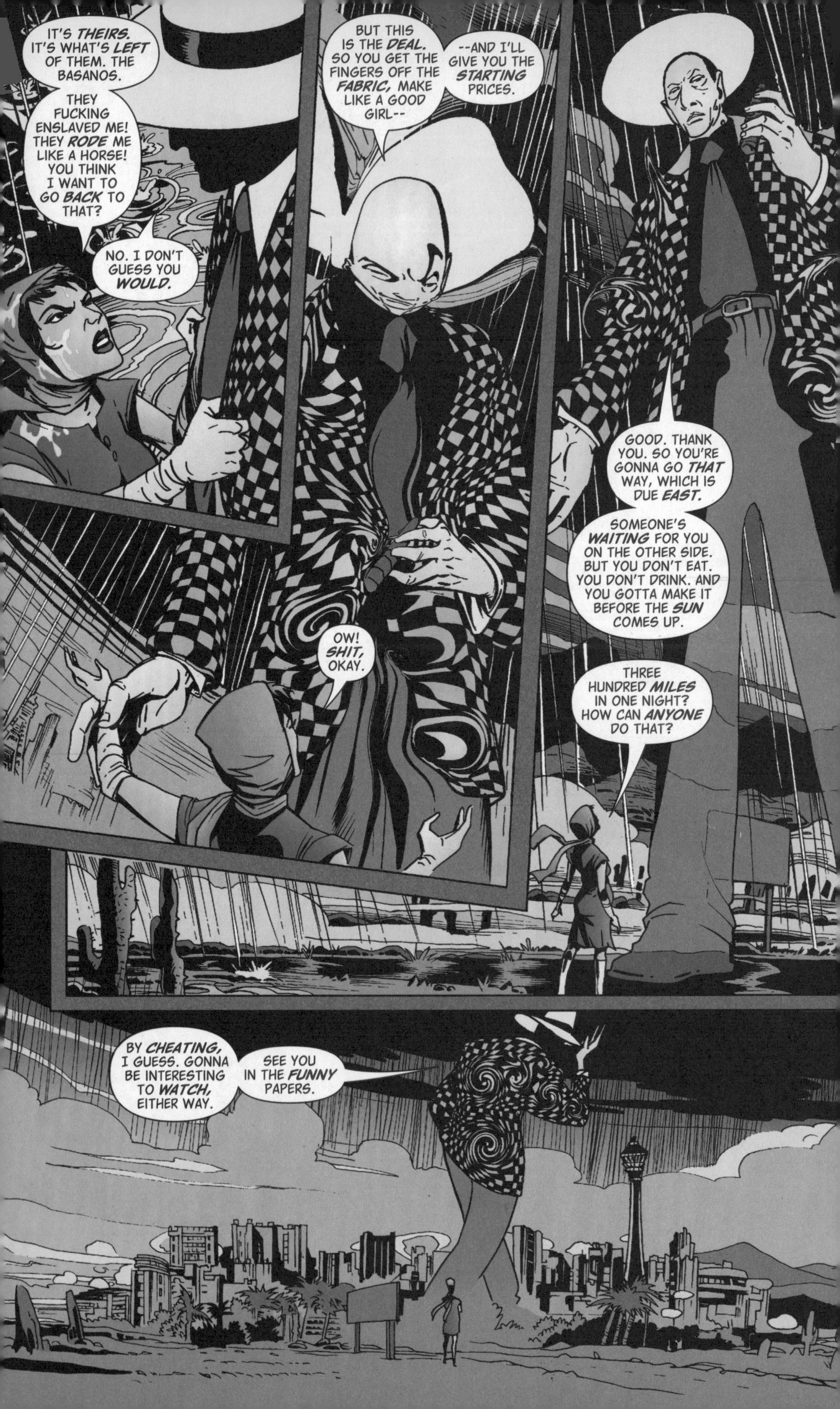
IT'S THEIRS. IT'S WHAT'S LEFT OF THEM. THE BASANOS.
THEY FUCKING ENSLAVED ME! THEY RODE ME LIKE A HORSE! YOU THINK I WANT TO GO BACK TO THAT?
NO. I DON'T GUESS YOU WOULD.
BUT THIS IS THE DEAL. SO YOU GET THE FINGERS OFF THE FABRIC, MAKE LIKE A GOOD GIRL--
--AND I'LL GIVE YOU THE STARTING PRICES.
OW! SHIT, OKAY.
GOOD. THANK YOU. SO YOU'RE GONNA GO THAT WAY, WHICH IS DUE EAST.
SOMEONE'S WAITING FOR YOU ON THE OTHER SIDE. BUT YOU DON'T EAT. YOU DON'T DRINK. AND YOU GOTTA MAKE IT BEFORE THE SUN COMES UP.
THREE HUNDRED MILES IN ONE NIGHT? HOW CAN ANYONE DO THAT?
BY CHEATING, I GUESS. GONNA BE INTERESTING TO WATCH, EITHER WAY.
SEE YOU IN THE FUNNY PAPERS.

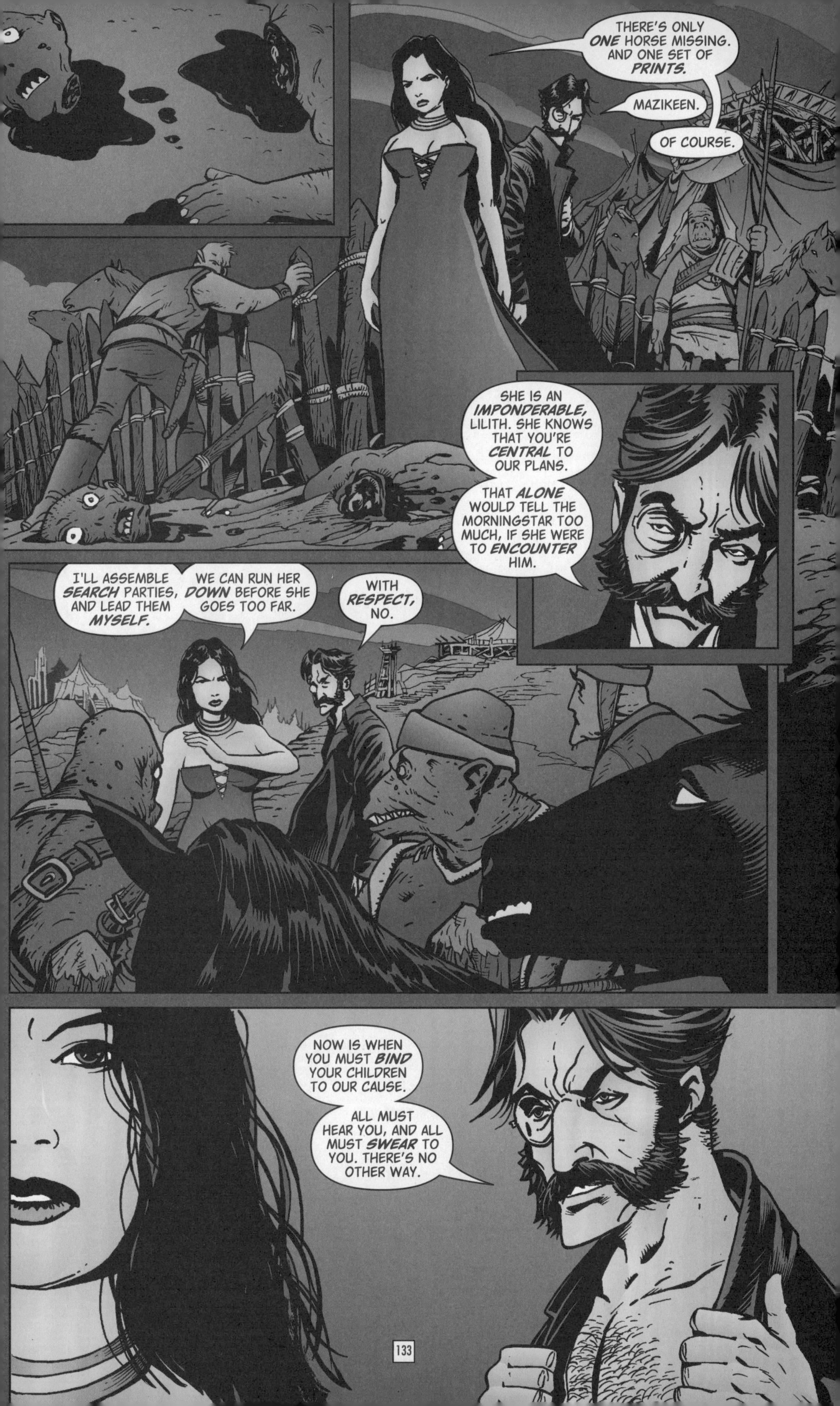

THERE'S ONLY ONE HORSE MISSING. AND ONE SET OF PRINTS.
MAZIKEEN.
OF COURSE.
SHE IS AN IMPONDERABLE, LILITH. SHE KNOWS THAT YOU'RE CENTRAL TO OUR PLANS.
THAT ALONE WOULD TELL THE MORNINGSTAR TOO MUCH, IF SHE WERE TO ENCOUNTER HIM.
I'LL ASSEMBLE SEARCH PARTIES, AND LEAD THEM MYSELF.
WE CAN RUN HER DOWN BEFORE SHE GOES TOO FAR.
WITH RESPECT, NO.
NOW IS WHEN YOU MUST BIND YOUR CHILDREN TO OUR CAUSE.
ALL MUST HEAR YOU, AND ALL MUST SWEAR TO YOU. THERE'S NO OTHER WAY.

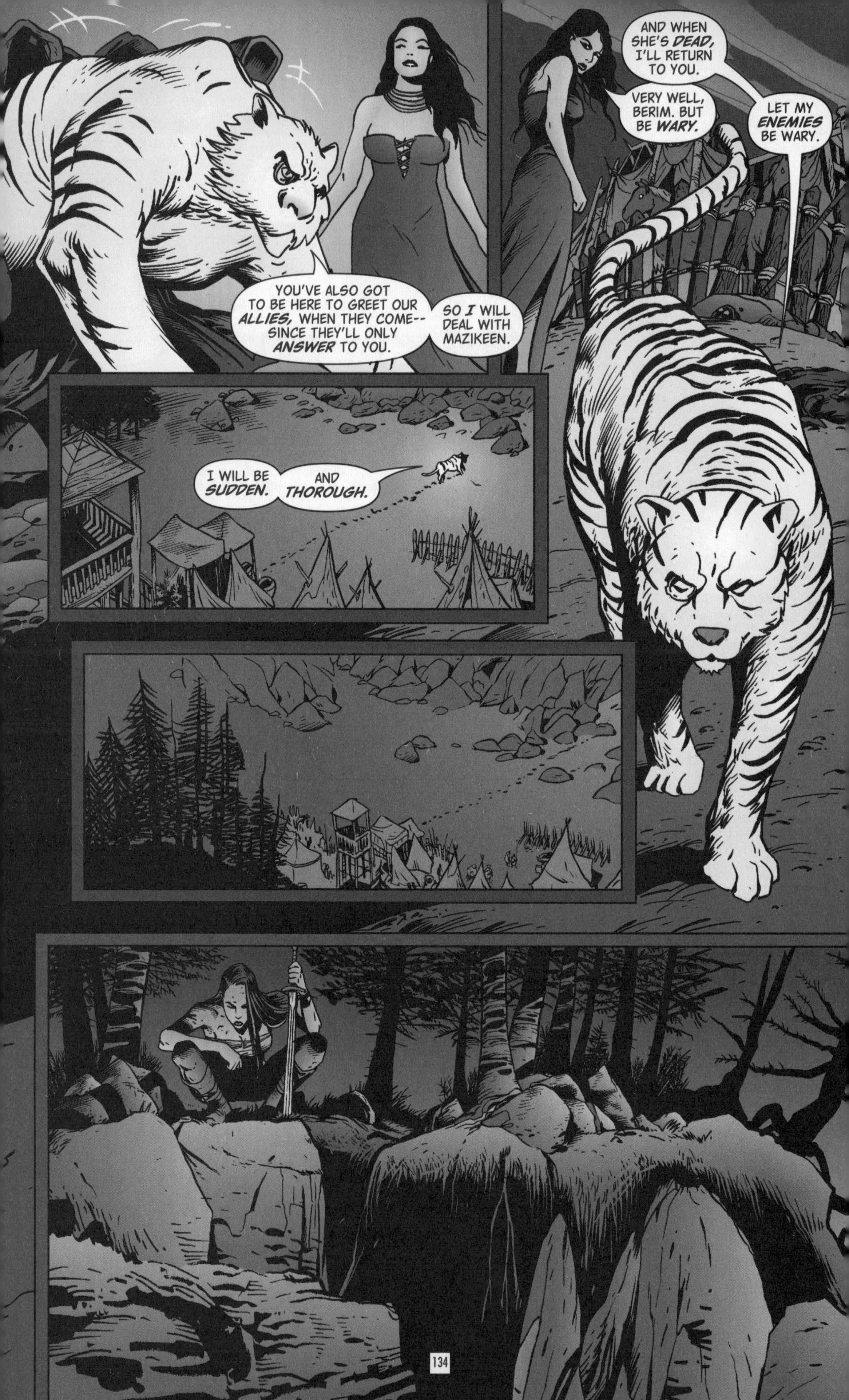
YOU'VE ALSO GOT TO BE HERE TO GREET OUR ALLIES, WHEN THEY COME--SINCE THEY'LL ONLY ANSWER TO YOU.
SO I WILL DEAL WITH MAZIKEEN.
VERY WELL, BERIM. BUT BE WARY.
AND WHEN SHE'S DEAD, I'LL RETURN TO YOU.
LET MY ENEMIES BE WARY.
I WILL BE SUDDEN.
AND THOROUGH.

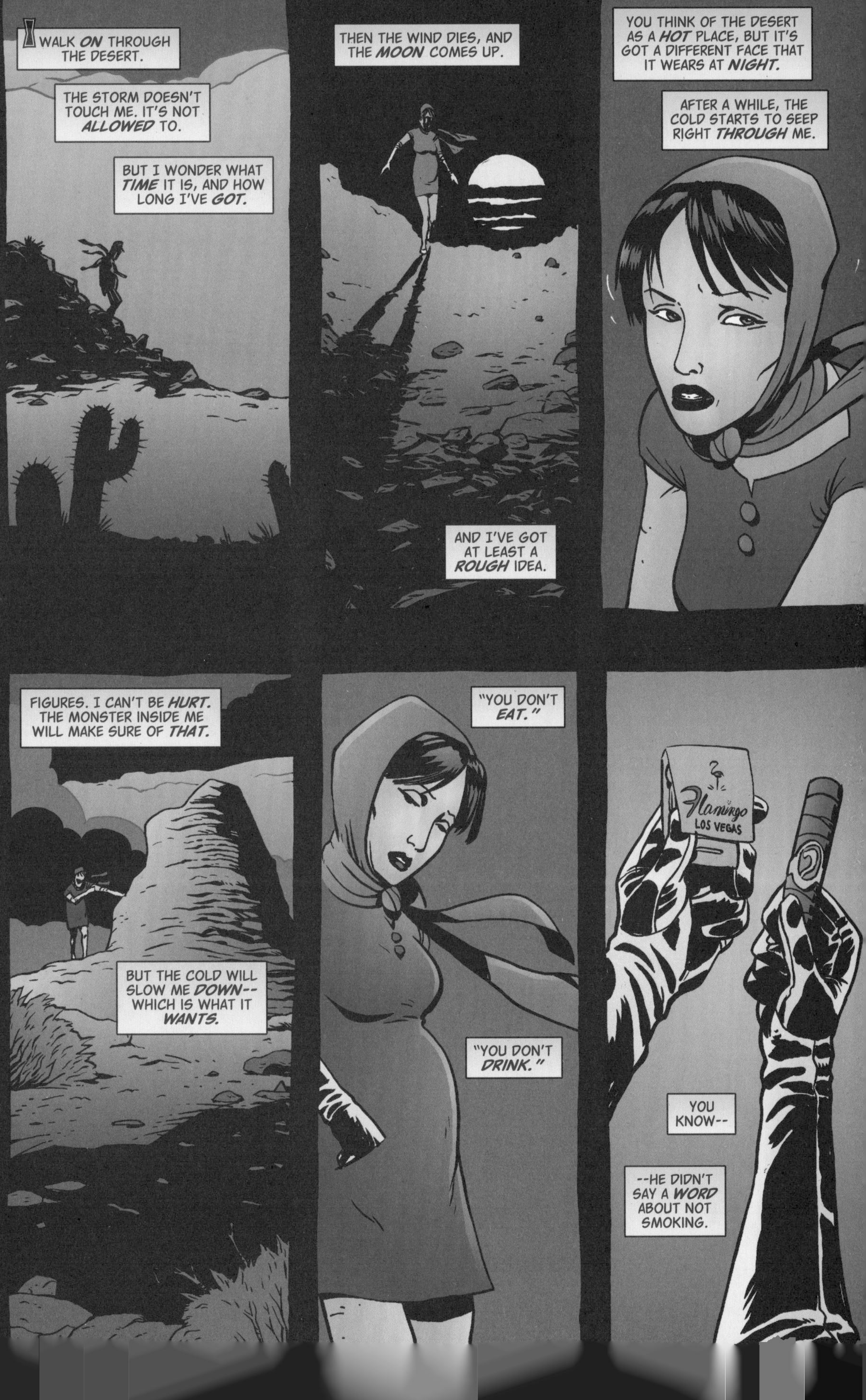
I WALK ON THROUGH THE DESERT.
THE STORM DOESN'T TOUCH ME. IT'S NOT ALLOWED TO.
BUT I WONDER WHAT TIME IT IS, AND HOW LONG I'VE GOT.
THEN THE WIND DIES, AND THE MOON COMES UP.
AND I'VE GOT AT LEAST A ROUGH IDEA.
YOU THINK OF THE DESERT AS A HOT PLACE, BUT IT'S GOT A DIFFERENT FACE THAT IT WEARS AT NIGHT.
AFTER A WHILE, THE COLD STARTS TO SEEP RIGHT THROUGH ME.
FIGURES. I CAN'T BE HURT. THE MONSTER INSIDE ME WILL MAKE SURE OF THAT.
BUT THE COLD WILL SLOW ME DOWN-- WHICH IS WHAT IT WANTS.
"YOU DON'T EAT."
"YOU DON'T DRINK."
Flamingo
LOS VEGAS
YOU KNOW--
--HE DIDN'T SAY A WORD ABOUT NOT SMOKING.

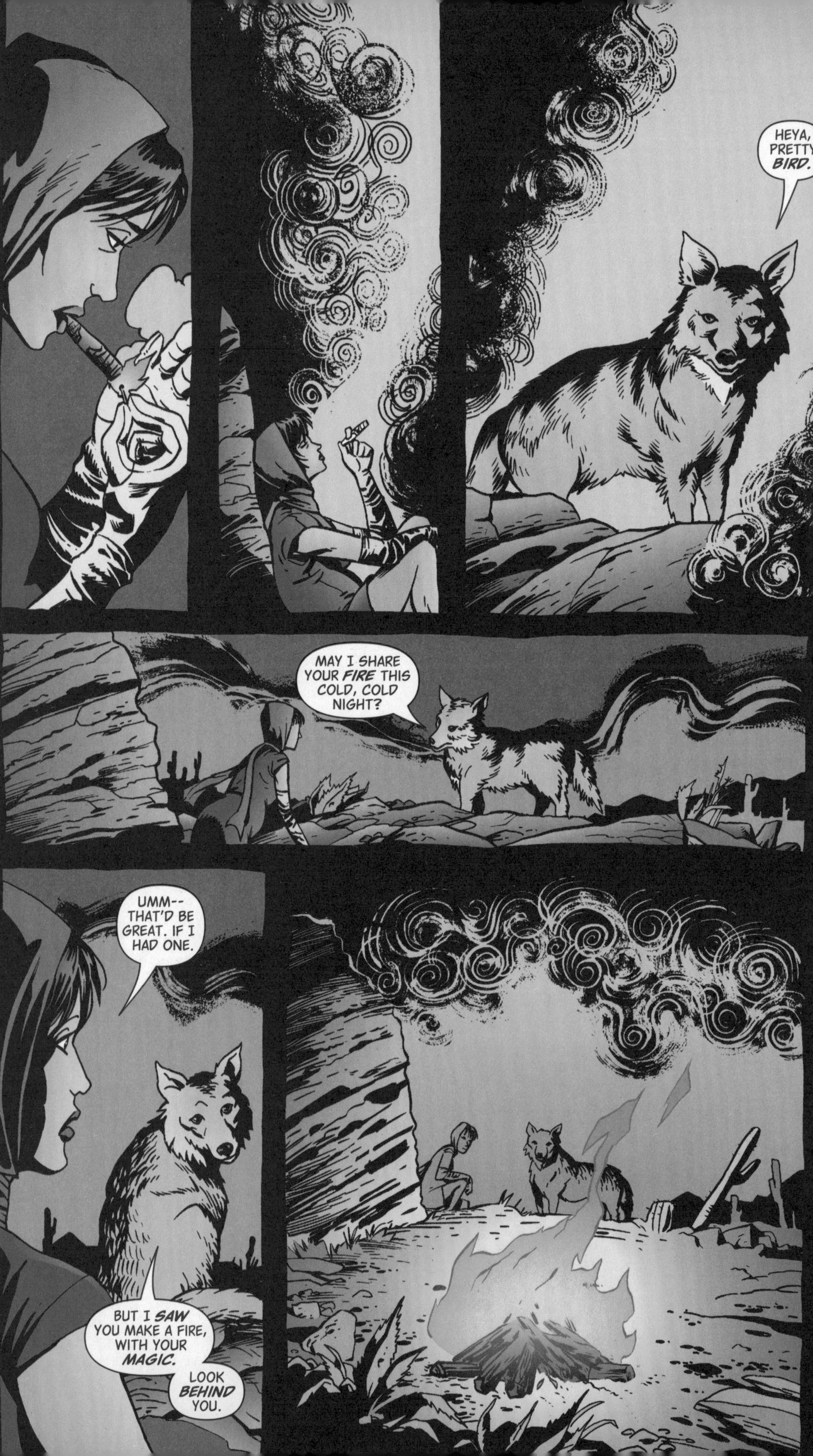
HEYA, PRETTY *BIRD.*
MAY I SHARE YOUR *FIRE* THIS COLD, COLD NIGHT?
UMM-- THAT'D BE GREAT. IF I HAD ONE.
BUT I *SAW* YOU MAKE A FIRE, WITH YOUR *MAGIC.*
LOOK *BEHIND* YOU.

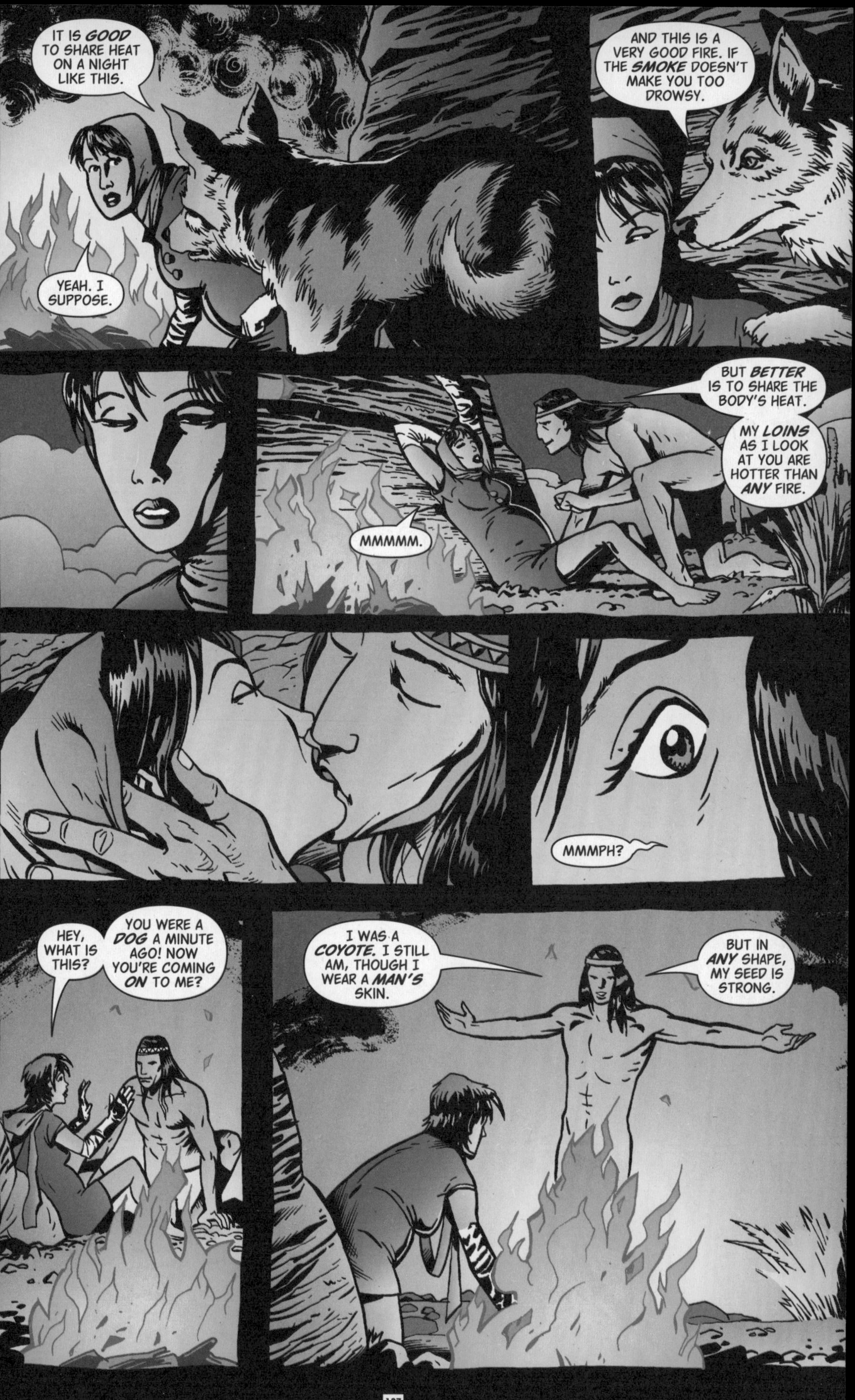
IT IS GOOD TO SHARE HEAT ON A NIGHT LIKE THIS.
YEAH. I SUPPOSE.
AND THIS IS A VERY GOOD FIRE. IF THE SMOKE DOESN'T MAKE YOU TOO DROWSY.
BUT BETTER IS TO SHARE THE BODY'S HEAT.
MY LOINS AS I LOOK AT YOU ARE HOTTER THAN ANY FIRE.
MMMMM.
MMMPH?
HEY, WHAT IS THIS?
YOU WERE A DOG A MINUTE AGO! NOW YOU'RE COMING ON TO ME?
I WAS A COYOTE. I STILL AM, THOUGH I WEAR A MAN'S SKIN.
BUT IN ANY SHAPE, MY SEED IS STRONG.

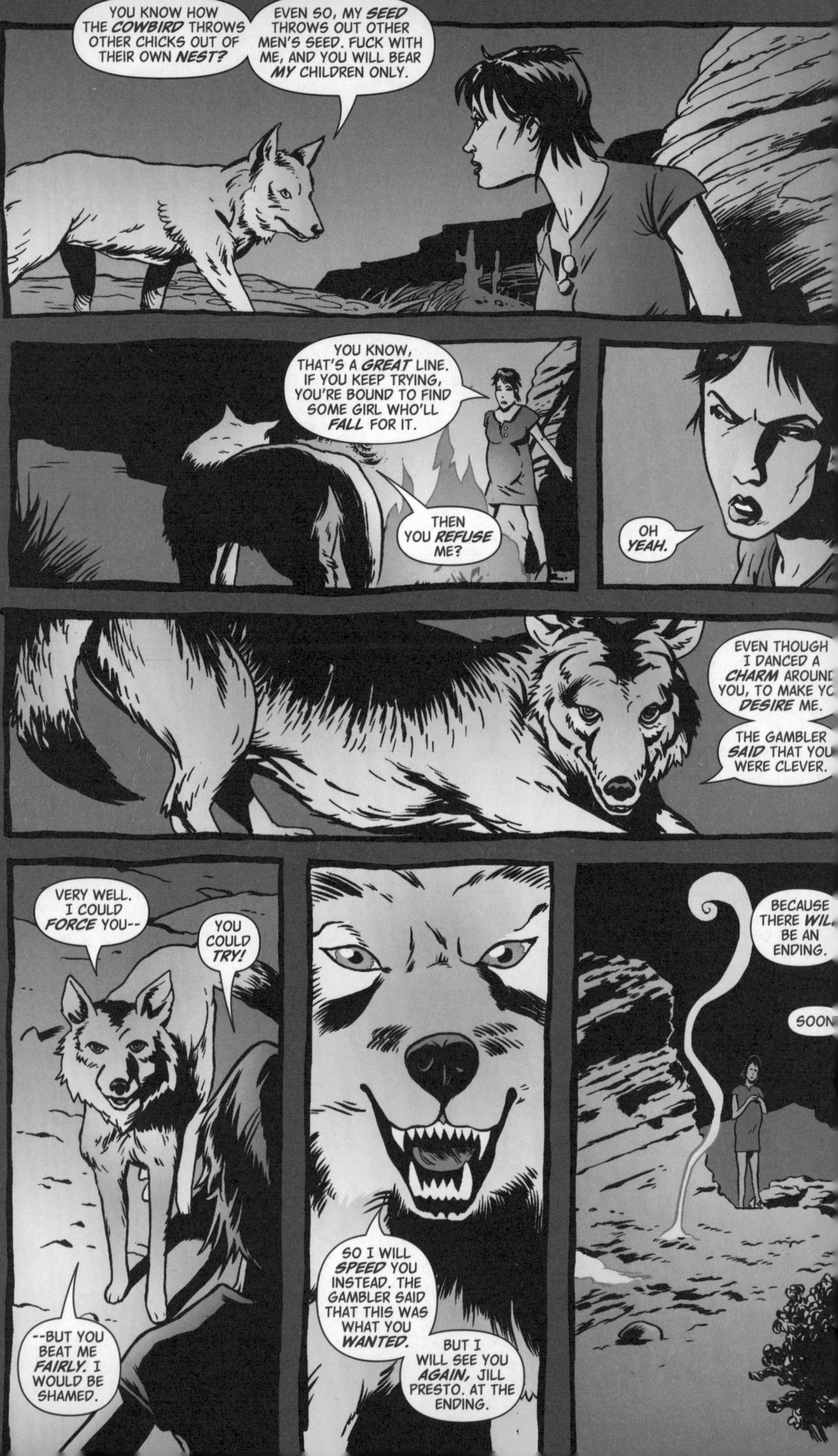

YOU KNOW HOW THE COWBIRD THROWS OTHER CHICKS OUT OF THEIR OWN NEST?
EVEN SO, MY SEED THROWS OUT OTHER MEN'S SEED. FUCK WITH ME, AND YOU WILL BEAR MY CHILDREN ONLY.
YOU KNOW, THAT'S A GREAT LINE. IF YOU KEEP TRYING, YOU'RE BOUND TO FIND SOME GIRL WHO'LL FALL FOR IT.
THEN YOU REFUSE ME?
OH YEAH.
EVEN THOUGH I DANCED A CHARM AROUND YOU, TO MAKE YO DESIRE ME.
THE GAMBLER SAID THAT YOU WERE CLEVER.
VERY WELL. I COULD FORCE YOU--
YOU COULD TRY!
--BUT YOU BEAT ME FAIRLY. I WOULD BE SHAMED.
SO I WILL SPEED YOU INSTEAD. THE GAMBLER SAID THAT THIS WAS WHAT YOU WANTED.
BUT I WILL SEE YOU AGAIN, JILL PRESTO. AT THE ENDING.
BECAUSE THERE WIL BE AN ENDING.
SOON

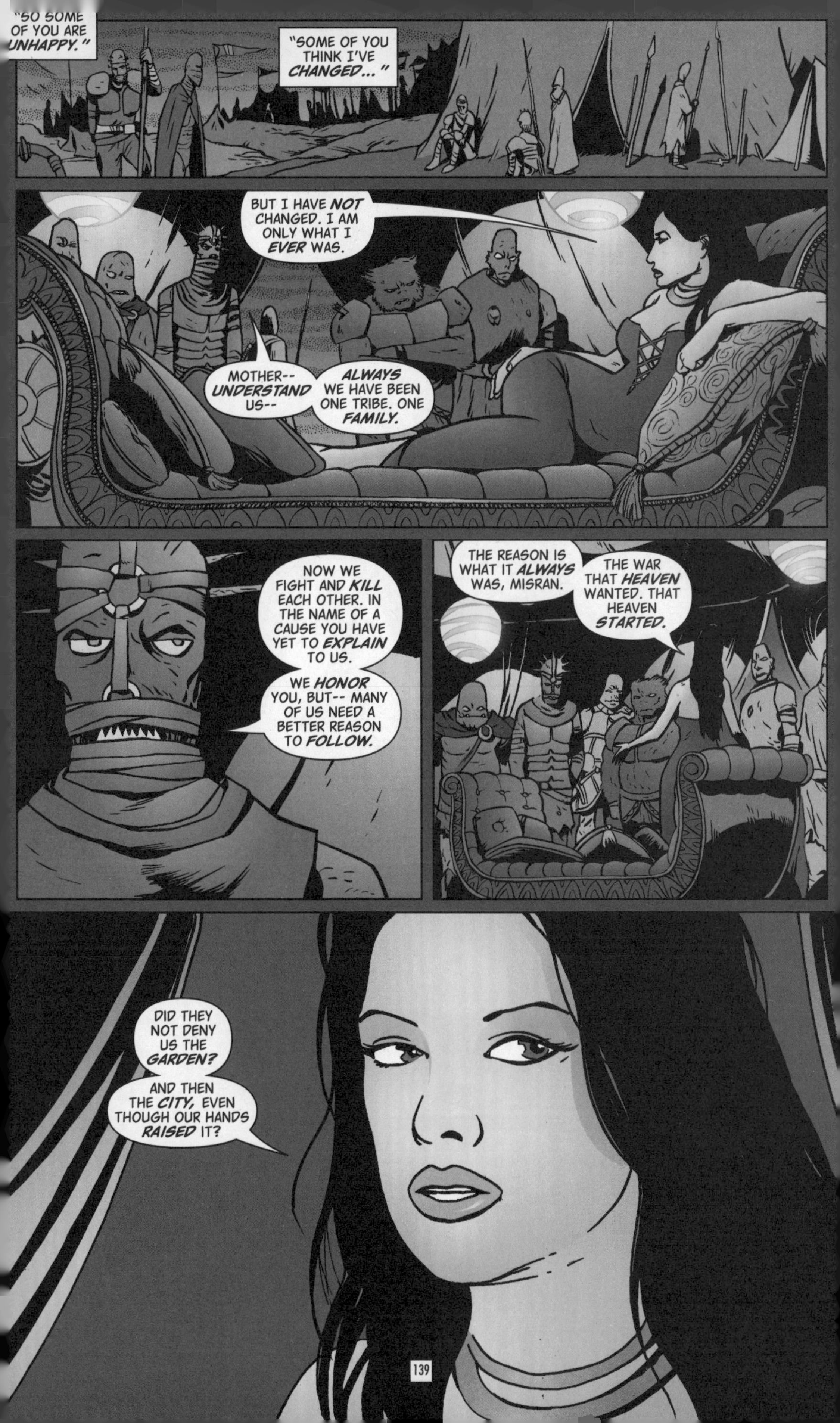
"SO SOME OF YOU ARE UNHAPPY."
"SOME OF YOU THINK I'VE CHANGED..."
BUT I HAVE NOT CHANGED. I AM ONLY WHAT I EVER WAS.
MOTHER-- UNDERSTAND US--
ALWAYS WE HAVE BEEN ONE TRIBE. ONE FAMILY.
NOW WE FIGHT AND KILL EACH OTHER. IN THE NAME OF A CAUSE YOU HAVE YET TO EXPLAIN TO US.
WE HONOR YOU, BUT-- MANY OF US NEED A BETTER REASON TO FOLLOW.
THE REASON IS WHAT IT ALWAYS WAS, MISRAN.
THE WAR THAT HEAVEN WANTED. THAT HEAVEN STARTED.
DID THEY NOT DENY US THE GARDEN?
AND THEN THE CITY, EVEN THOUGH OUR HANDS RAISED IT?

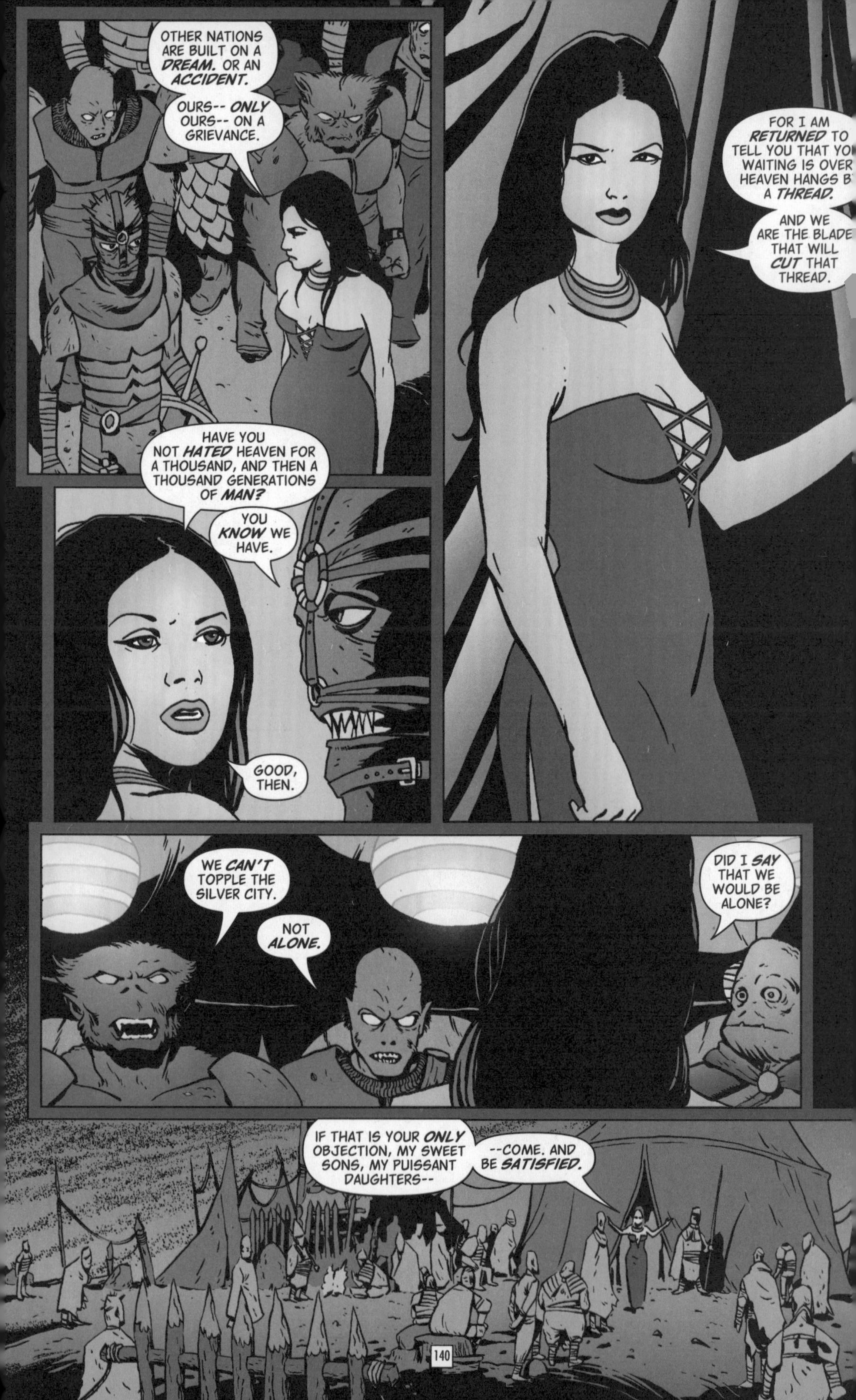
OTHER NATIONS ARE BUILT ON A DREAM. OR AN ACCIDENT.
OURS-- ONLY OURS-- ON A GRIEVANCE.
HAVE YOU NOT HATED HEAVEN FOR A THOUSAND, AND THEN A THOUSAND GENERATIONS OF MAN?
YOU KNOW WE HAVE.
GOOD, THEN.
FOR I AM RETURNED TO TELL YOU THAT YO WAITING IS OVER HEAVEN HANGS B A THREAD.
AND WE ARE THE BLADE THAT WILL CUT THAT THREAD.
WE CAN'T TOPPLE THE SILVER CITY.
NOT ALONE.
DID I SAY THAT WE WOULD BE ALONE?
IF THAT IS YOUR ONLY OBJECTION, MY SWEET SONS, MY PUISSANT DAUGHTERS--
--COME. AND BE SATISFIED.

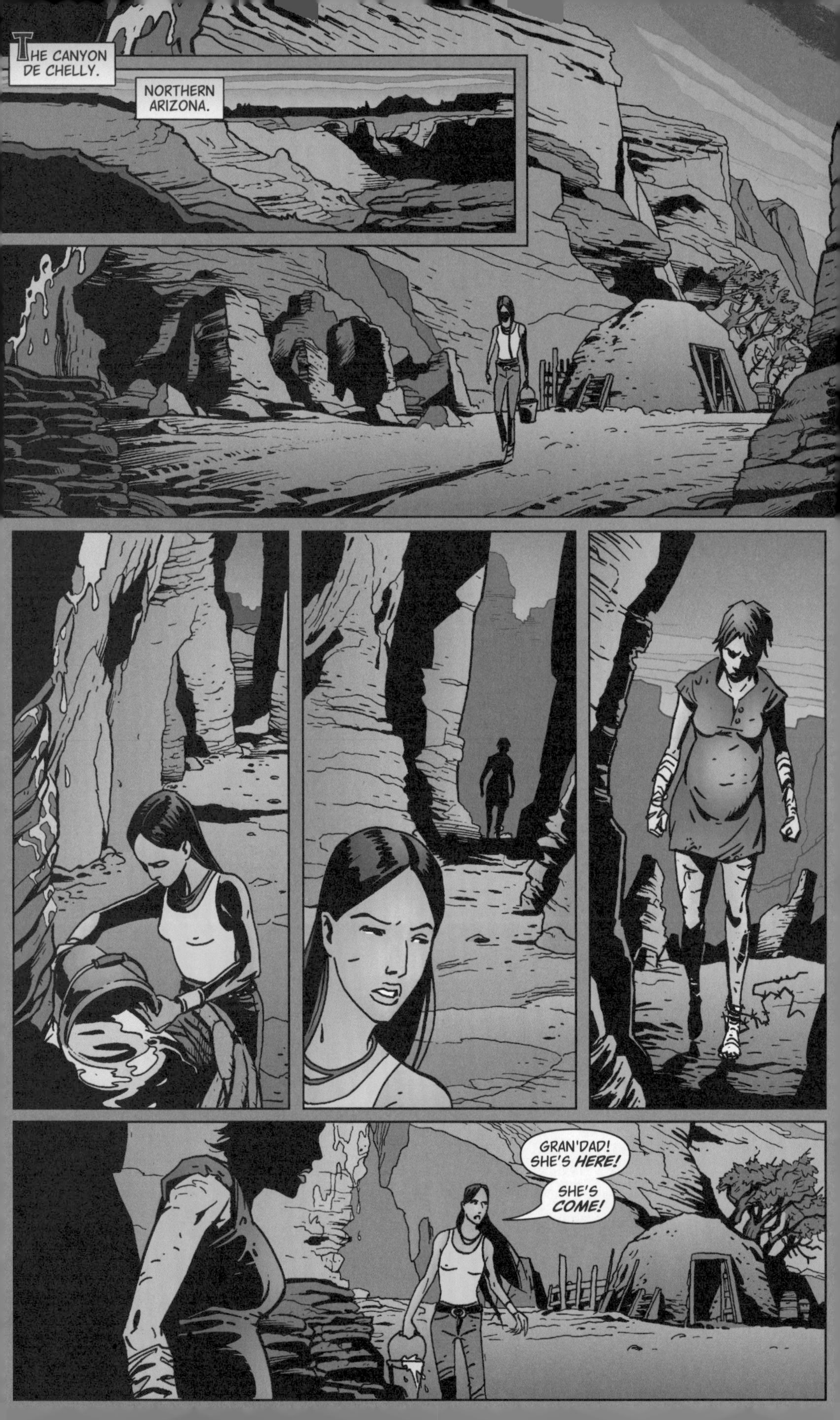
THE CANYON DE CHELLY.
NORTHERN ARIZONA.
GRAN'DAD! SHE'S *HERE!*
SHE'S *COME!*

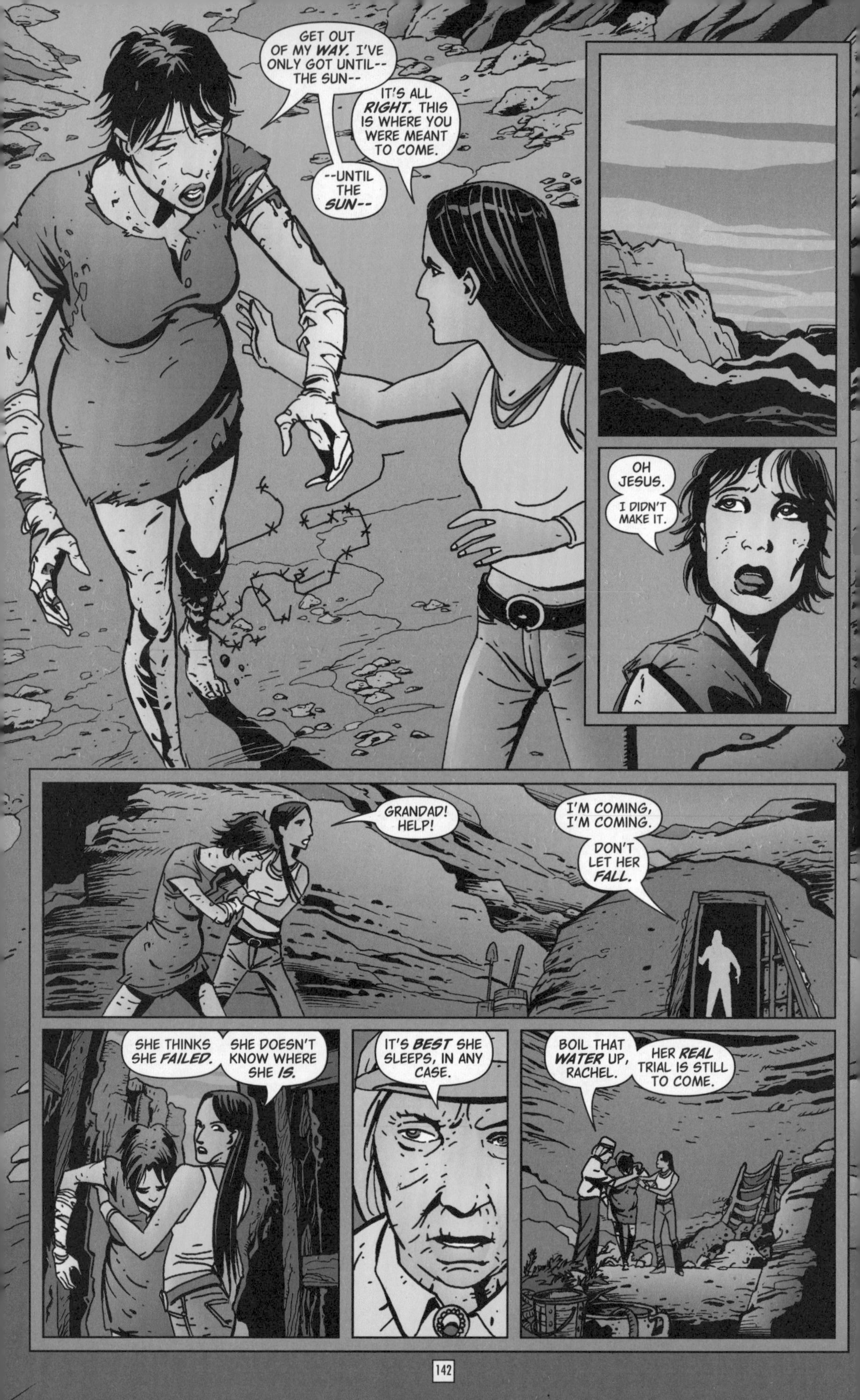
GET OUT OF MY WAY. I'VE ONLY GOT UNTIL-- THE SUN--
IT'S ALL RIGHT. THIS IS WHERE YOU WERE MEANT TO COME.
--UNTIL THE SUN--
OH JESUS.
I DIDN'T MAKE IT.
GRANDAD! HELP!
I'M COMING, I'M COMING.
DON'T LET HER FALL.
SHE THINKS SHE FAILED.
SHE DOESN'T KNOW WHERE SHE IS.
IT'S BEST SHE SLEEPS, IN ANY CASE.
BOIL THAT WATER UP, RACHEL.
HER REAL TRIAL IS STILL TO COME.

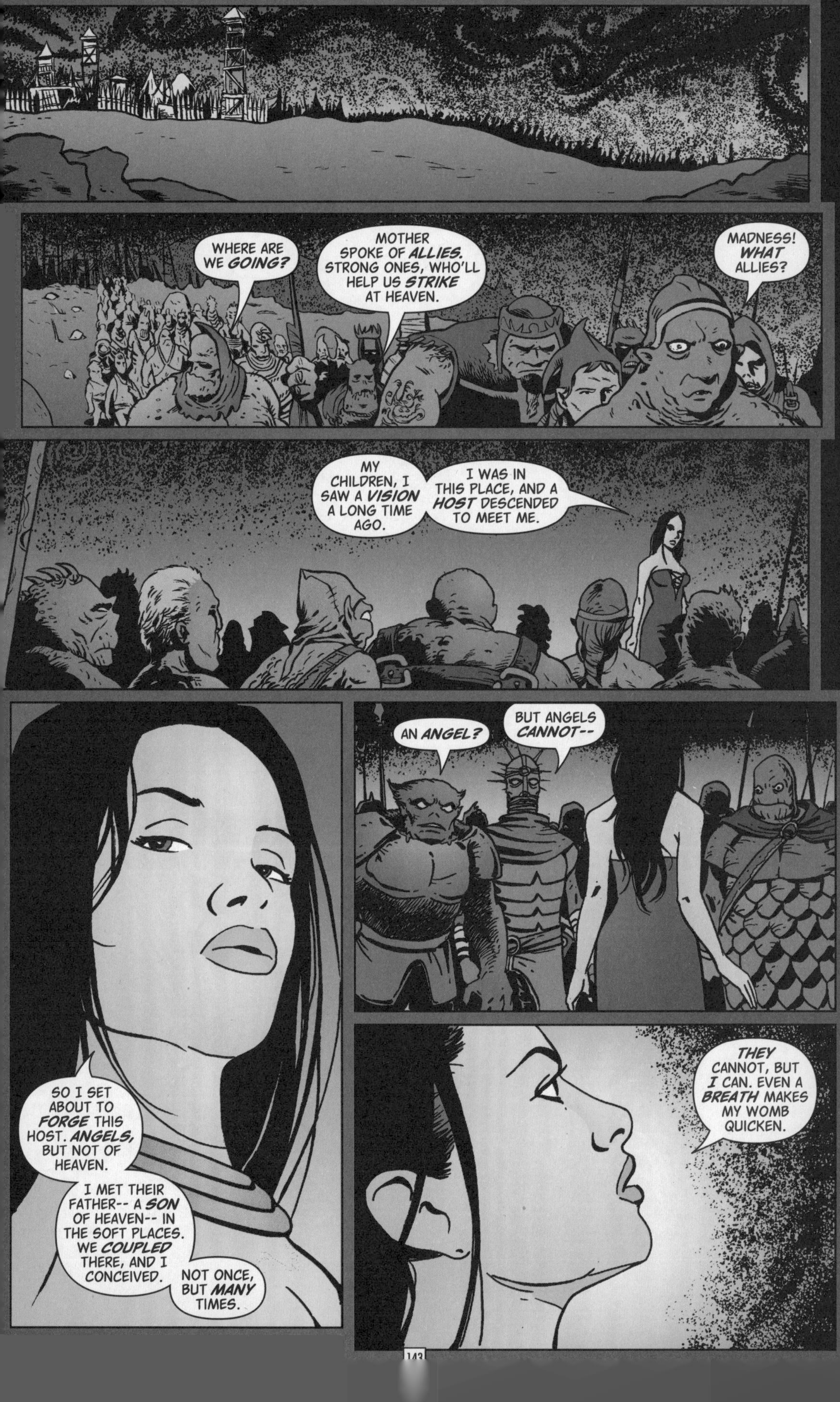
WHERE ARE WE GOING?
MOTHER SPOKE OF ALLIES. STRONG ONES, WHO'LL HELP US STRIKE AT HEAVEN.
MADNESS! WHAT ALLIES?
MY CHILDREN, I SAW A VISION A LONG TIME AGO.
I WAS IN THIS PLACE, AND A HOST DESCENDED TO MEET ME.
SO I SET ABOUT TO FORGE THIS HOST. ANGELS, BUT NOT OF HEAVEN.
I MET THEIR FATHER-- A SON OF HEAVEN-- IN THE SOFT PLACES. WE COUPLED THERE, AND I CONCEIVED.
NOT ONCE, BUT MANY TIMES.
AN ANGEL?
BUT ANGELS CANNOT--
THEY CANNOT, BUT I CAN. EVEN A BREATH MAKES MY WOMB QUICKEN.

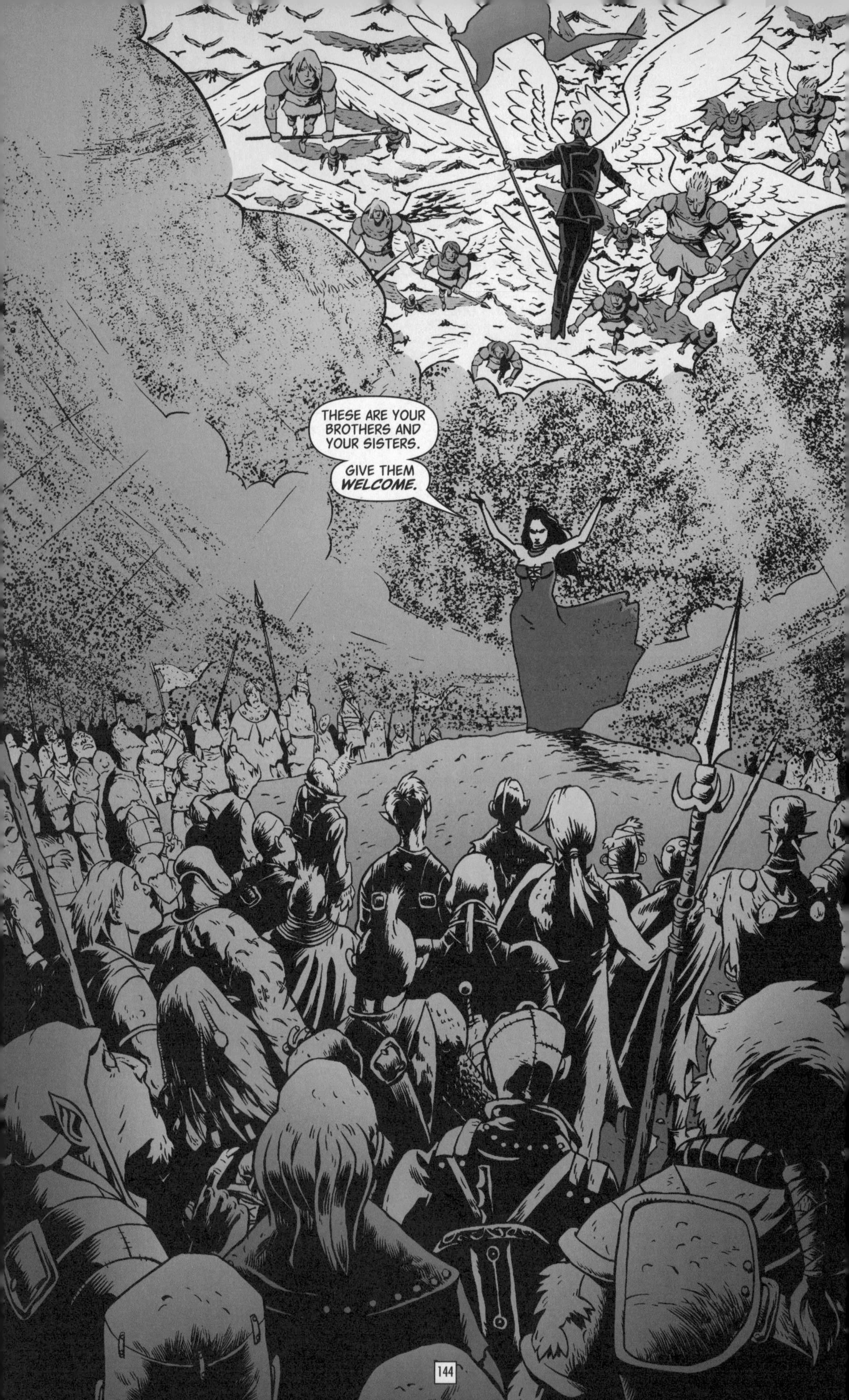
THESE ARE YOUR BROTHERS AND YOUR SISTERS.
GIVE THEM **WELCOME.**

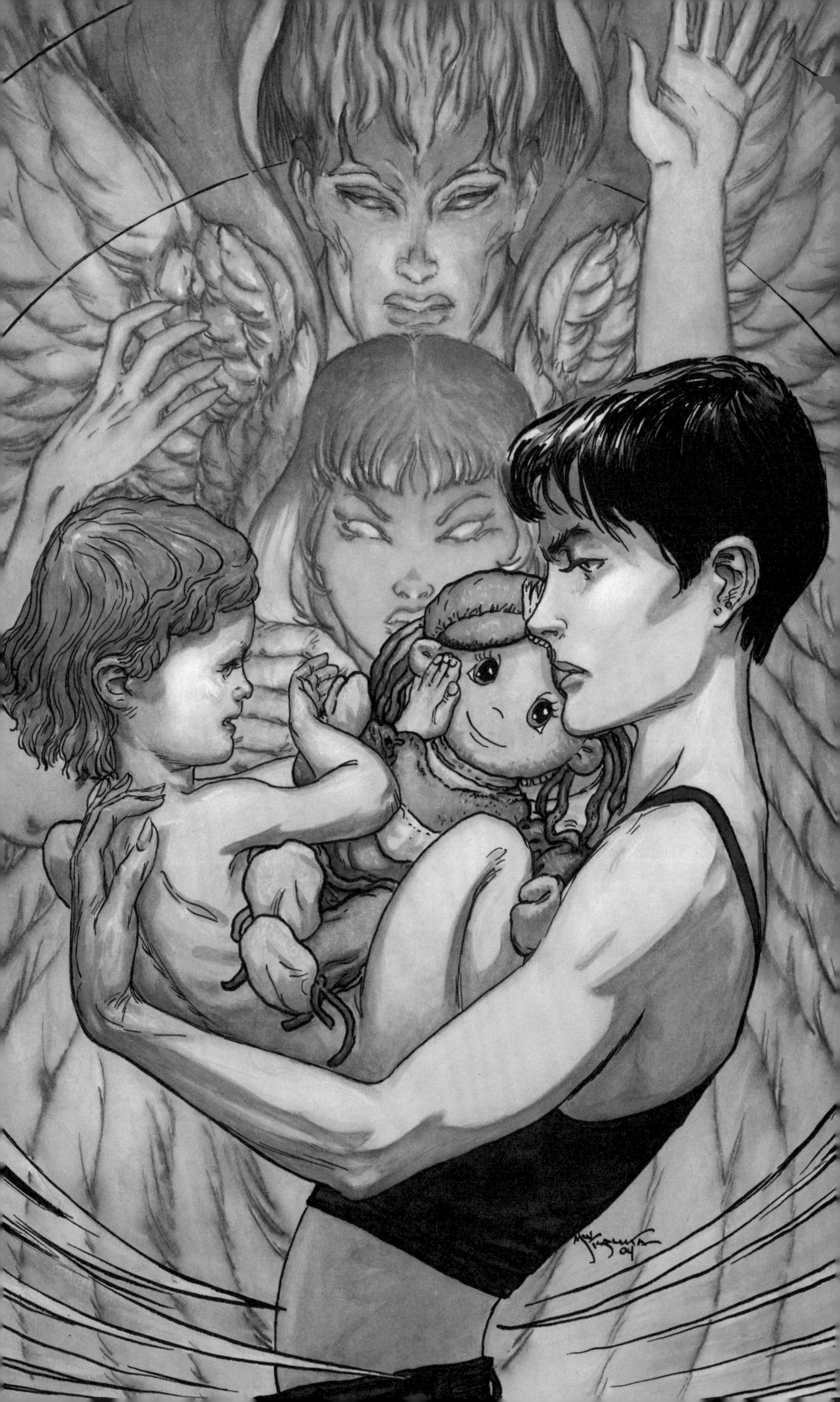

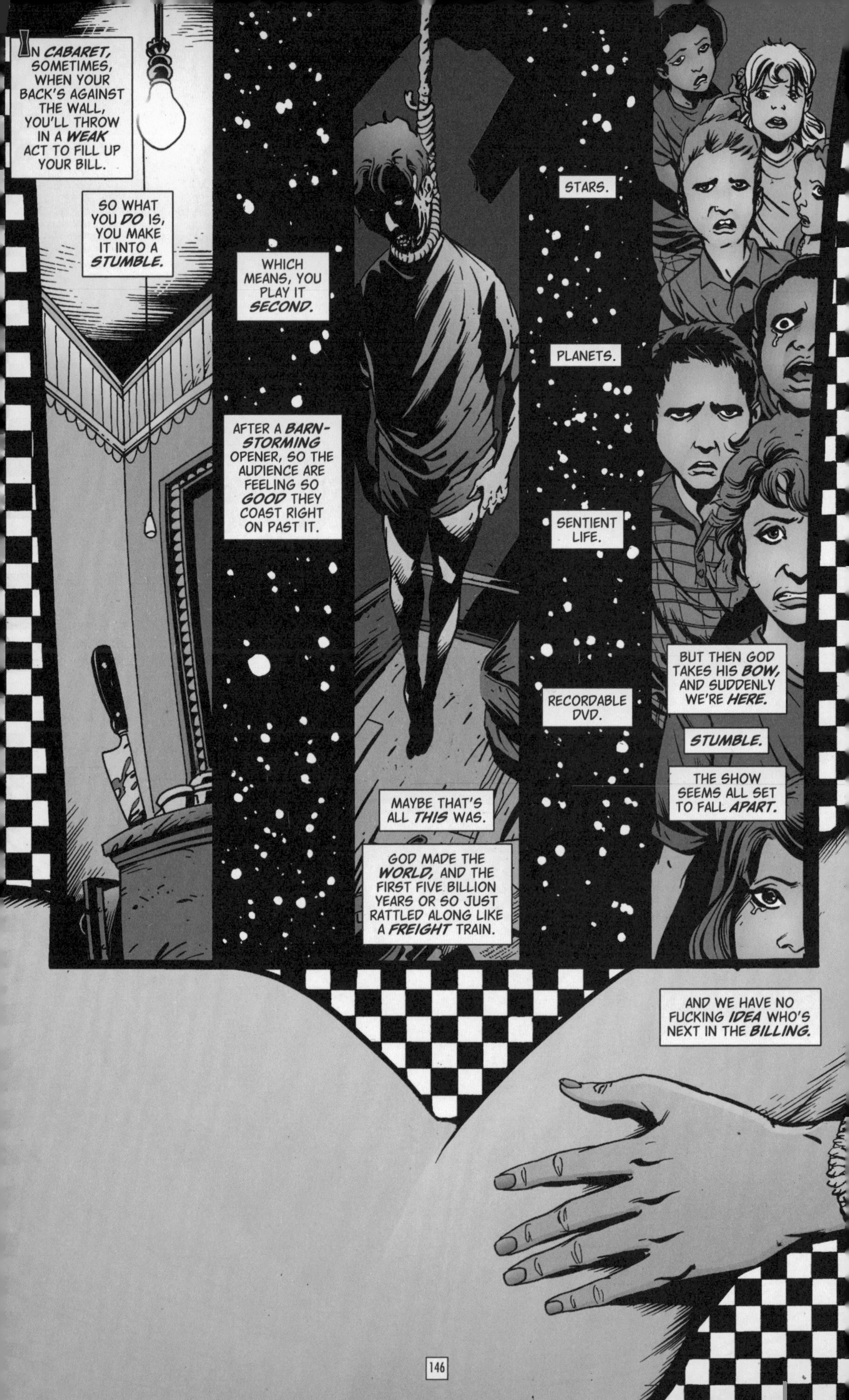
IN CABARET, SOMETIMES, WHEN YOUR BACK'S AGAINST THE WALL, YOU'LL THROW IN A WEAK ACT TO FILL UP YOUR BILL.
SO WHAT YOU DO IS, YOU MAKE IT INTO A STUMBLE.
WHICH MEANS, YOU PLAY IT SECOND.
AFTER A BARN-STORMING OPENER, SO THE AUDIENCE ARE FEELING SO GOOD THEY COAST RIGHT ON PAST IT.
MAYBE THAT'S ALL THIS WAS.
GOD MADE THE WORLD, AND THE FIRST FIVE BILLION YEARS OR SO JUST RATTLED ALONG LIKE A FREIGHT TRAIN.
STARS.
PLANETS.
SENTIENT LIFE.
RECORDABLE DVD.
BUT THEN GOD TAKES HIS BOW, AND SUDDENLY WE'RE HERE.
STUMBLE.
THE SHOW SEEMS ALL SET TO FALL APART.
AND WE HAVE NO FUCKING IDEA WHO'S NEXT IN THE BILLING.

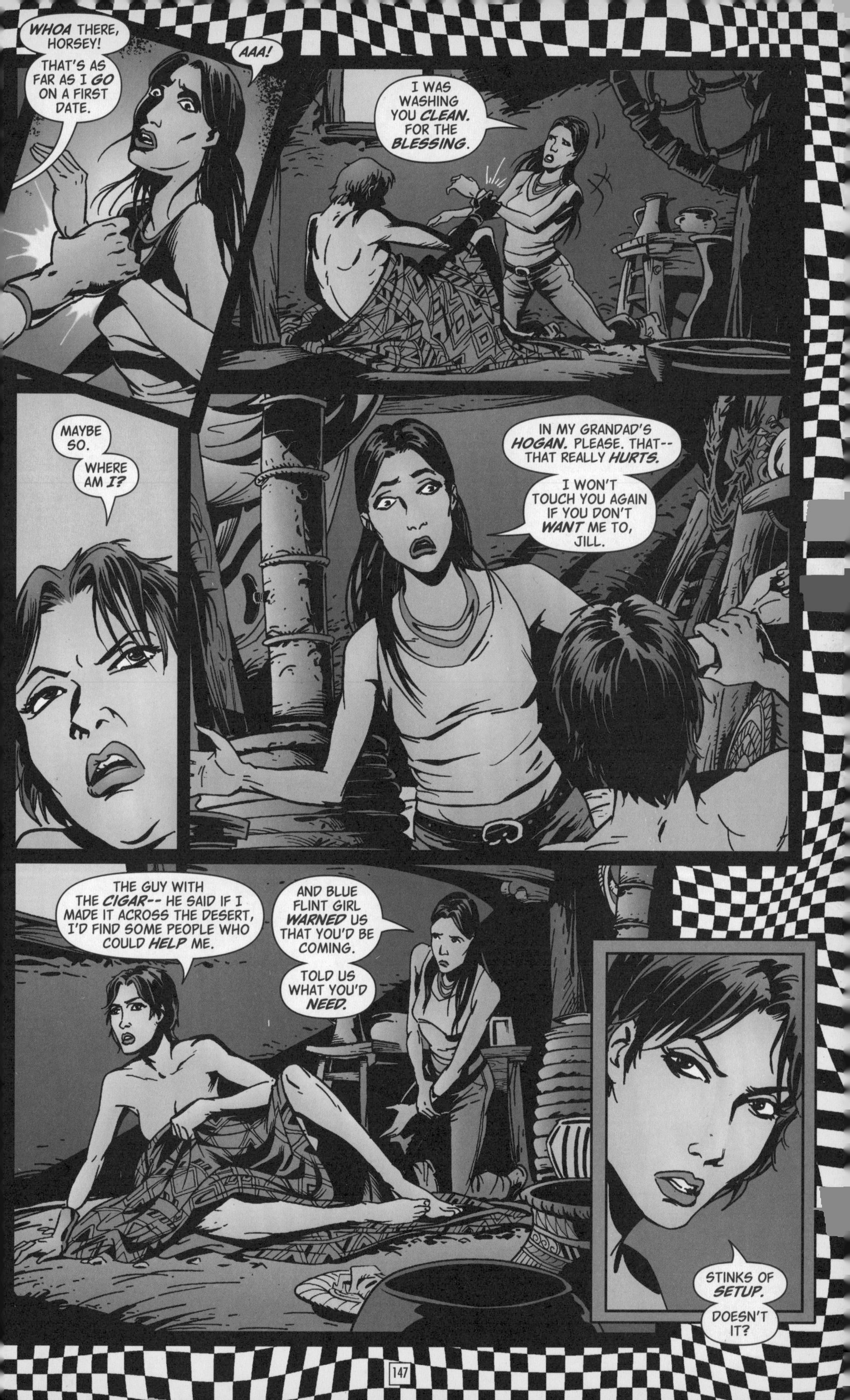
WHOA THERE, HORSEY!
THAT'S AS FAR AS I GO ON A FIRST DATE.
AAA!
I WAS WASHING YOU CLEAN. FOR THE BLESSING.
MAYBE SO.
WHERE AM I?
IN MY GRANDAD'S HOGAN. PLEASE. THAT-- THAT REALLY HURTS.
I WON'T TOUCH YOU AGAIN IF YOU DON'T WANT ME TO, JILL.
THE GUY WITH THE CIGAR-- HE SAID IF I MADE IT ACROSS THE DESERT, I'D FIND SOME PEOPLE WHO COULD HELP ME.
AND BLUE FLINT GIRL WARNED US THAT YOU'D BE COMING.
TOLD US WHAT YOU'D NEED.
STINKS OF SETUP.
DOESN'T IT?

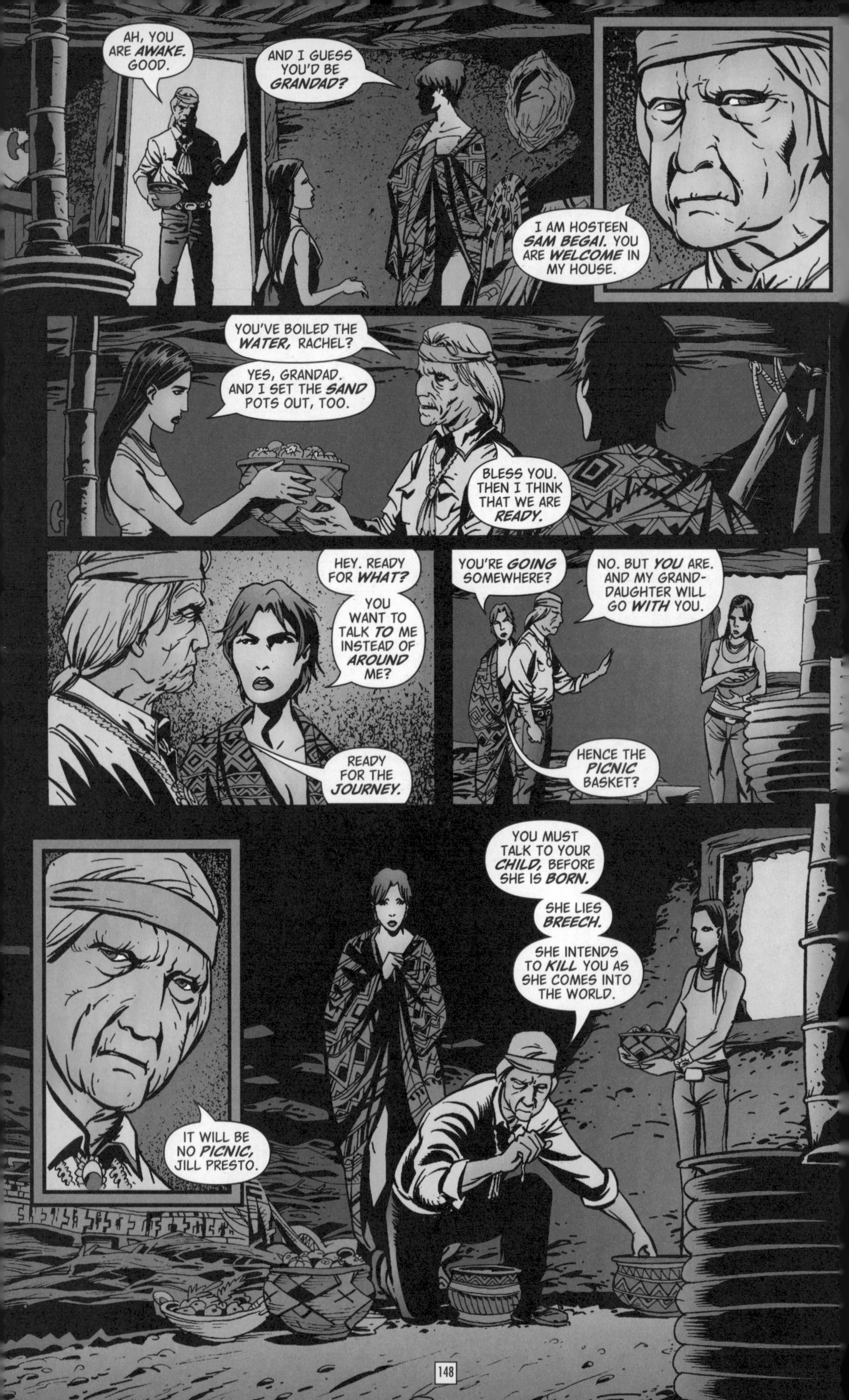
AH, YOU ARE AWAKE. GOOD.
AND I GUESS YOU'D BE GRANDAD?
I AM HOSTEEN SAM BEGAI. YOU ARE WELCOME IN MY HOUSE.
YOU'VE BOILED THE WATER, RACHEL?
YES, GRANDAD. AND I SET THE SAND POTS OUT, TOO.
BLESS YOU. THEN I THINK THAT WE ARE READY.
HEY. READY FOR WHAT?
YOU WANT TO TALK TO ME INSTEAD OF AROUND ME?
READY FOR THE JOURNEY.
YOU'RE GOING SOMEWHERE?
NO. BUT YOU ARE. AND MY GRAND-DAUGHTER WILL GO WITH YOU.
HENCE THE PICNIC BASKET?
IT WILL BE NO PICNIC, JILL PRESTO.
YOU MUST TALK TO YOUR CHILD, BEFORE SHE IS BORN.
SHE LIES BREECH.
SHE INTENDS TO KILL YOU AS SHE COMES INTO THE WORLD.

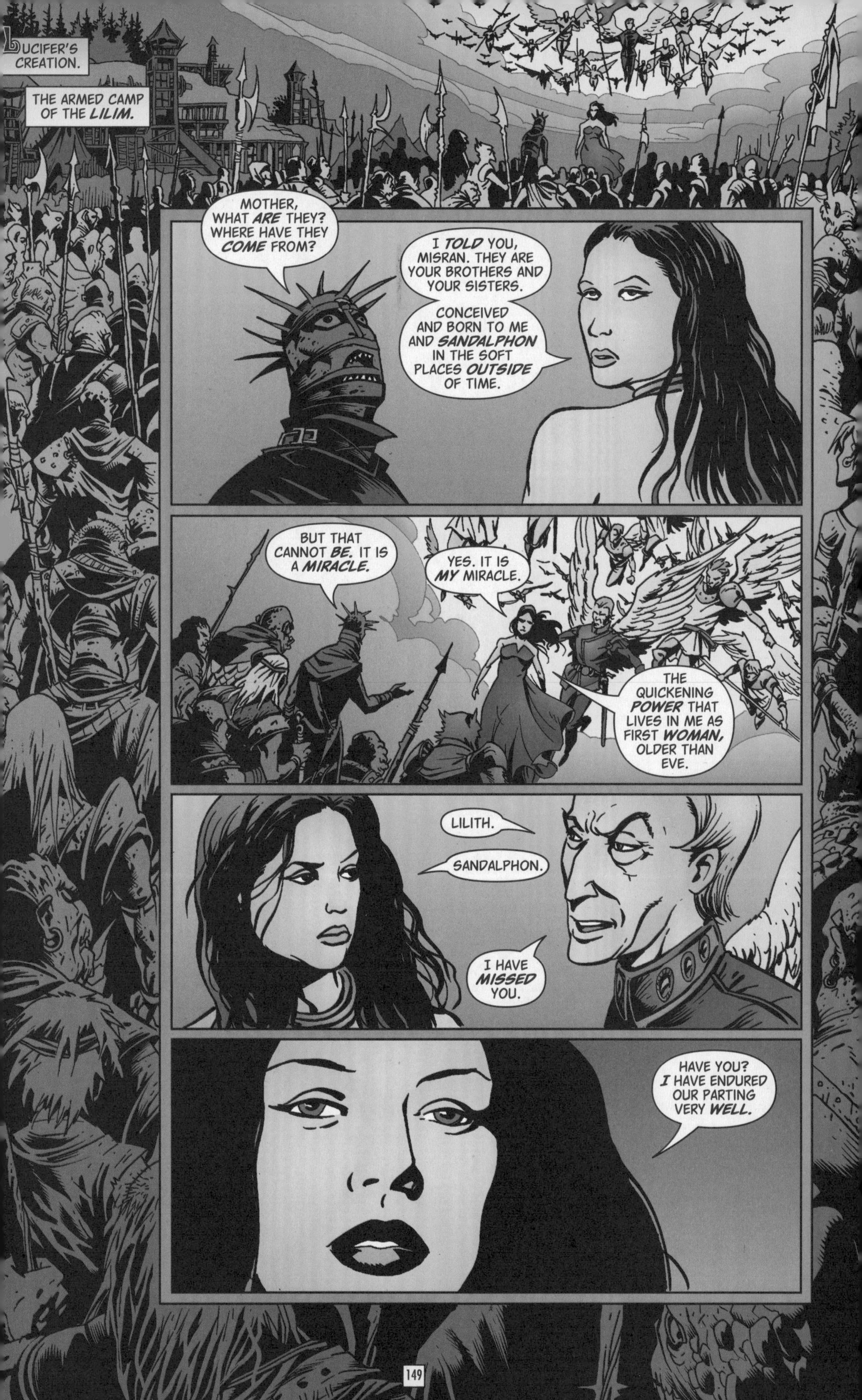
LUCIFER'S CREATION.
THE ARMED CAMP OF THE LILIM.
MOTHER, WHAT ARE THEY? WHERE HAVE THEY COME FROM?
I TOLD YOU, MISRAN. THEY ARE YOUR BROTHERS AND YOUR SISTERS.
CONCEIVED AND BORN TO ME AND SANDALPHON IN THE SOFT PLACES OUTSIDE OF TIME.
BUT THAT CANNOT BE. IT IS A MIRACLE.
YES. IT IS MY MIRACLE.
THE QUICKENING POWER THAT LIVES IN ME AS FIRST WOMAN, OLDER THAN EVE.
LILITH.
SANDALPHON.
I HAVE MISSED YOU.
HAVE YOU? I HAVE ENDURED OUR PARTING VERY WELL.

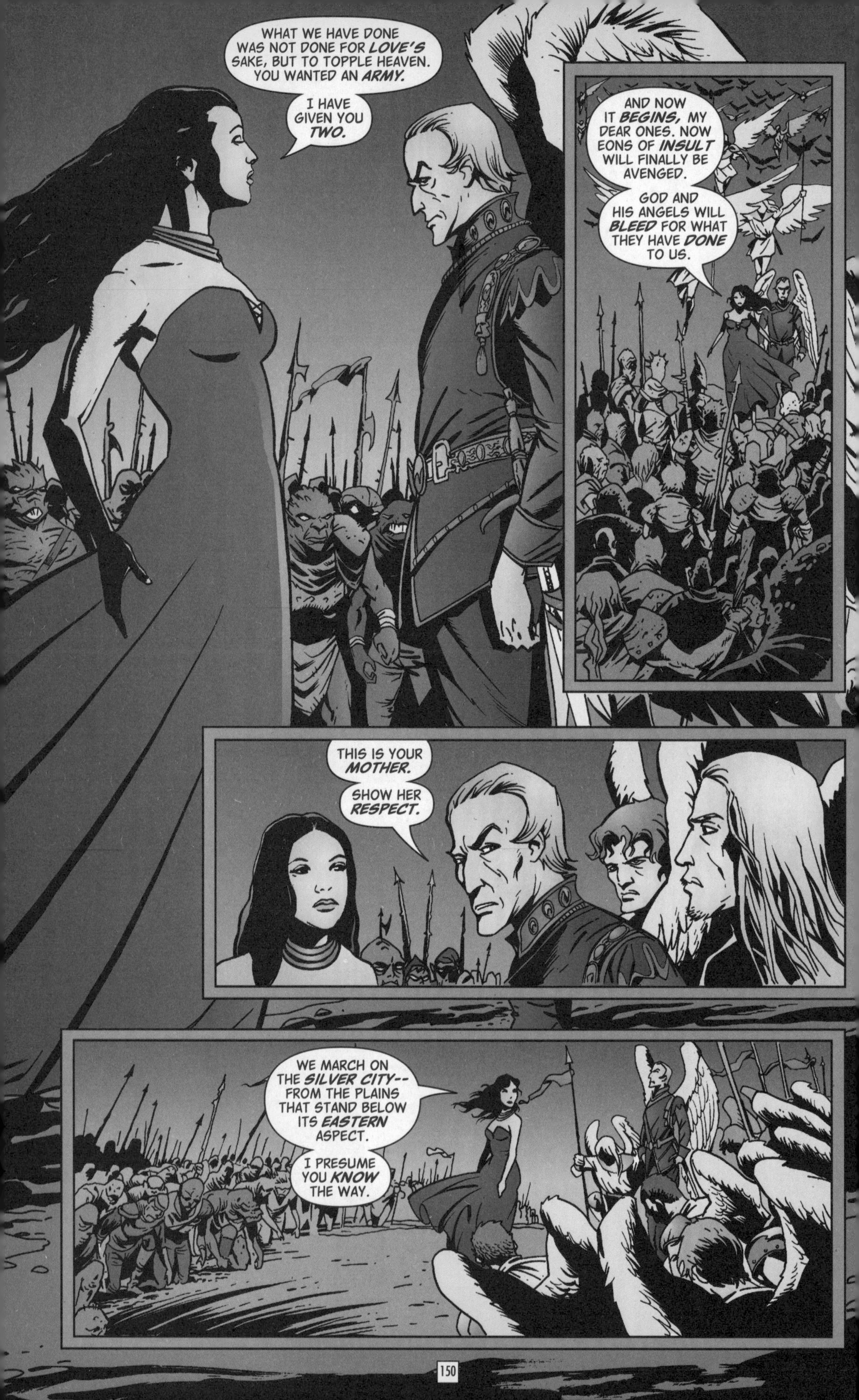
WHAT WE HAVE DONE WAS NOT DONE FOR LOVE'S SAKE, BUT TO TOPPLE HEAVEN. YOU WANTED AN ARMY.
I HAVE GIVEN YOU TWO.
AND NOW IT BEGINS, MY DEAR ONES. NOW EONS OF INSULT WILL FINALLY BE AVENGED.
GOD AND HIS ANGELS WILL BLEED FOR WHAT THEY HAVE DONE TO US.
THIS IS YOUR MOTHER.
SHOW HER RESPECT.
WE MARCH ON THE SILVER CITY-- FROM THE PLAINS THAT STAND BELOW ITS EASTERN ASPECT.
I PRESUME YOU KNOW THE WAY.

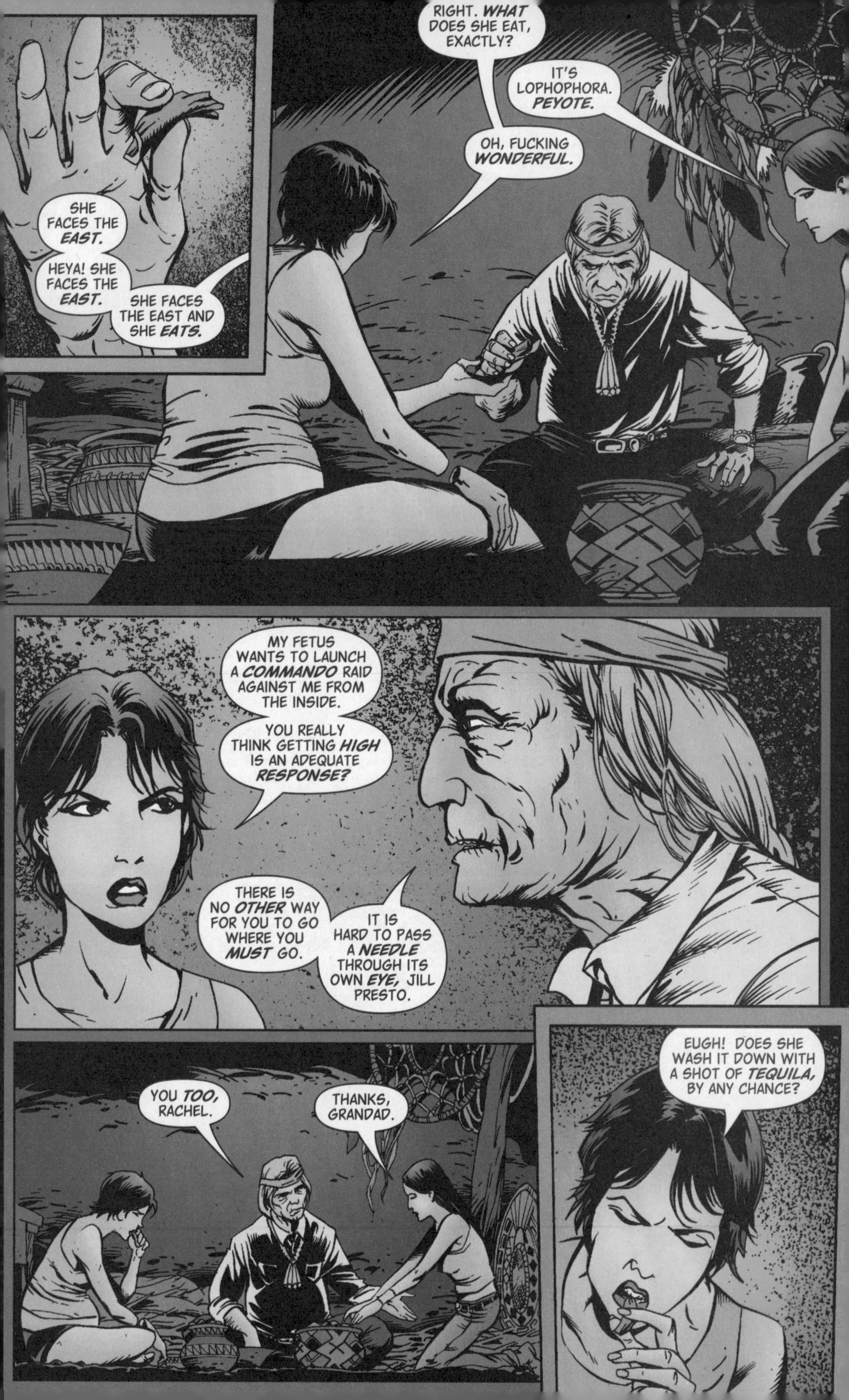
SHE FACES THE EAST.
HEYA! SHE FACES THE EAST.
SHE FACES THE EAST AND SHE EATS.
RIGHT. WHAT DOES SHE EAT, EXACTLY?
IT'S LOPHOPHORA. PEYOTE.
OH, FUCKING WONDERFUL.
MY FETUS WANTS TO LAUNCH A COMMANDO RAID AGAINST ME FROM THE INSIDE.
YOU REALLY THINK GETTING HIGH IS AN ADEQUATE RESPONSE?
THERE IS NO OTHER WAY FOR YOU TO GO WHERE YOU MUST GO.
IT IS HARD TO PASS A NEEDLE THROUGH ITS OWN EYE, JILL PRESTO.
YOU TOO, RACHEL.
THANKS, GRANDAD.
EUGH! DOES SHE WASH IT DOWN WITH A SHOT OF TEQUILA, BY ANY CHANCE?

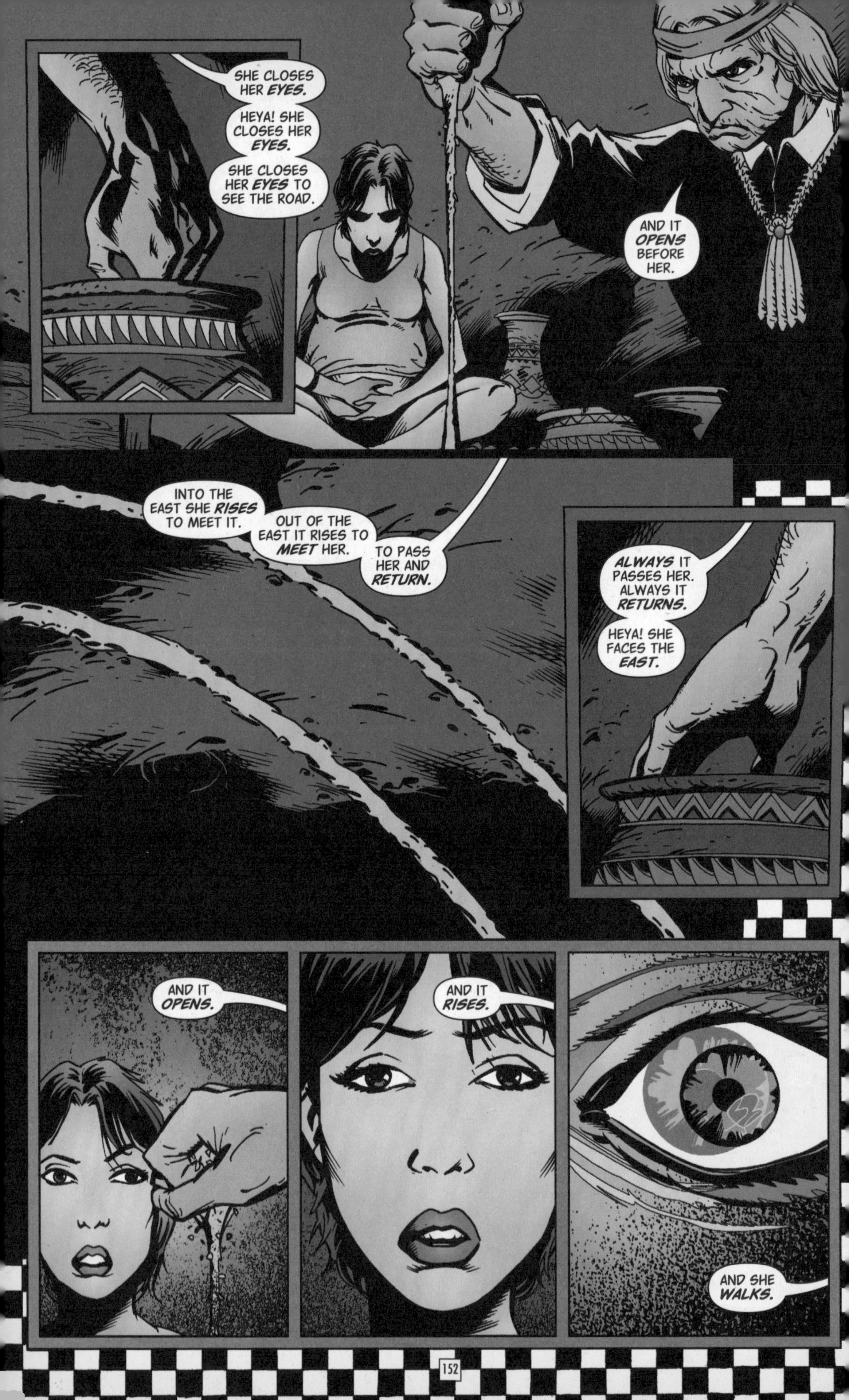
SHE CLOSES HER *EYES.*
HEYA! SHE CLOSES HER *EYES.*
SHE CLOSES HER *EYES* TO SEE THE ROAD.
AND IT *OPENS* BEFORE HER.
INTO THE EAST SHE *RISES* TO MEET IT.
OUT OF THE EAST IT RISES TO *MEET* HER.
TO PASS HER AND *RETURN.*
ALWAYS IT PASSES HER. ALWAYS IT *RETURNS.*
HEYA! SHE FACES THE *EAST.*
AND IT *OPENS.*
AND IT *RISES.*
AND SHE *WALKS.*

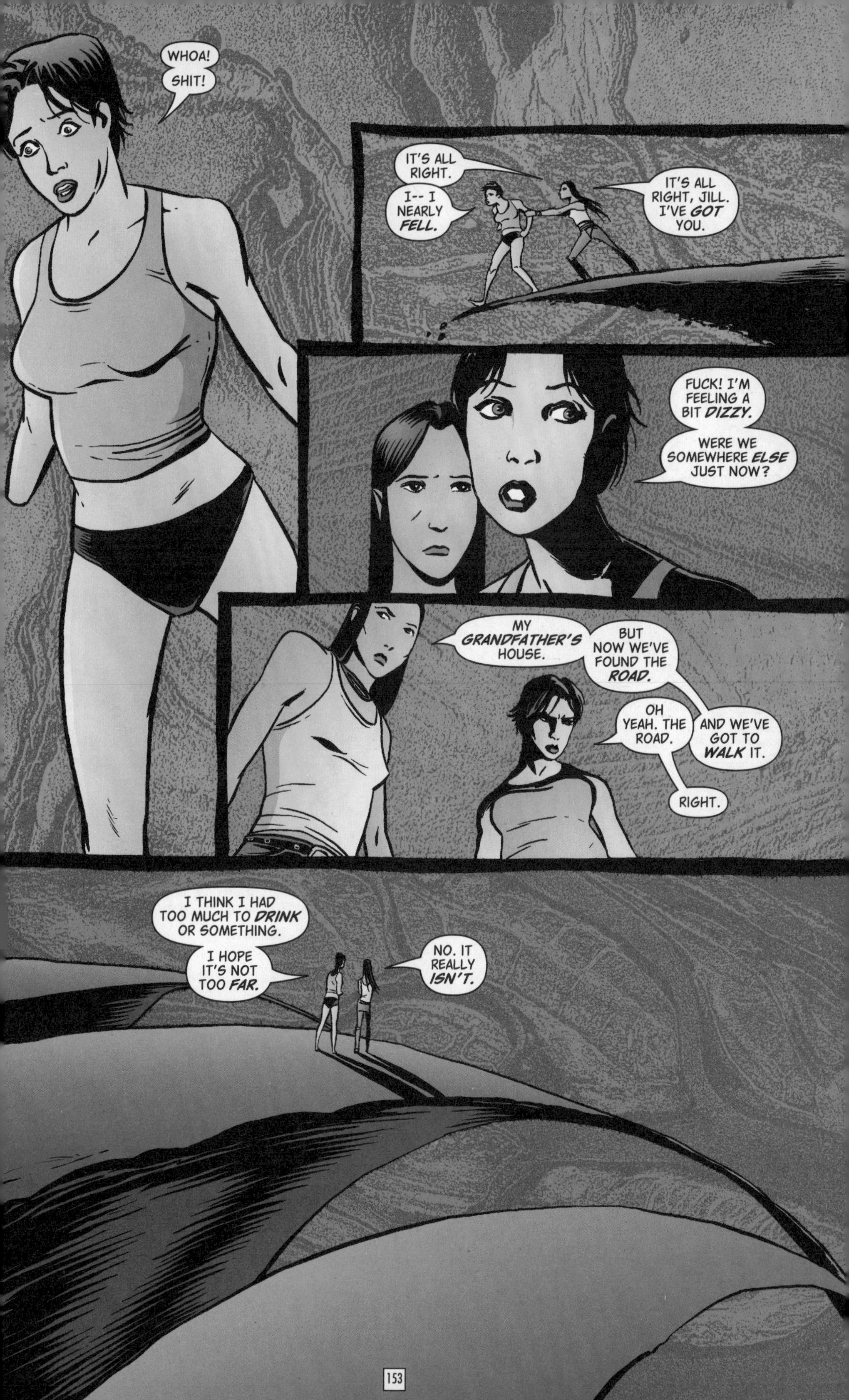
WHOA! SHIT!
IT'S ALL RIGHT.
I-- I NEARLY FELL.
IT'S ALL RIGHT, JILL. I'VE GOT YOU.
FUCK! I'M FEELING A BIT DIZZY.
WERE WE SOMEWHERE ELSE JUST NOW?
MY GRANDFATHER'S HOUSE.
BUT NOW WE'VE FOUND THE ROAD.
OH YEAH. THE ROAD.
AND WE'VE GOT TO WALK IT.
RIGHT.
I THINK I HAD TOO MUCH TO DRINK OR SOMETHING.
I HOPE IT'S NOT TOO FAR.
NO. IT REALLY ISN'T.

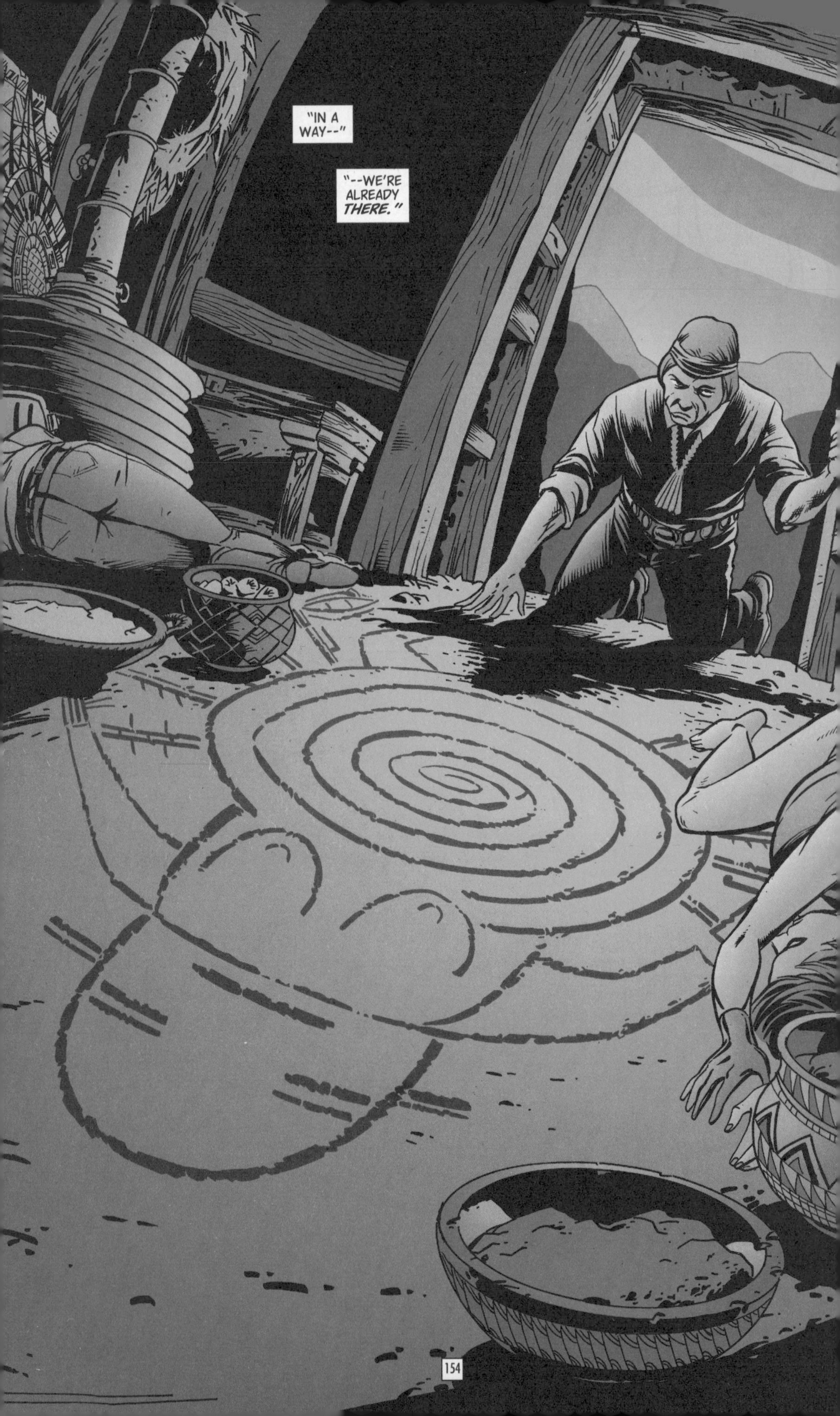
"IN A WAY--"
"--WE'RE ALREADY *THERE.*"

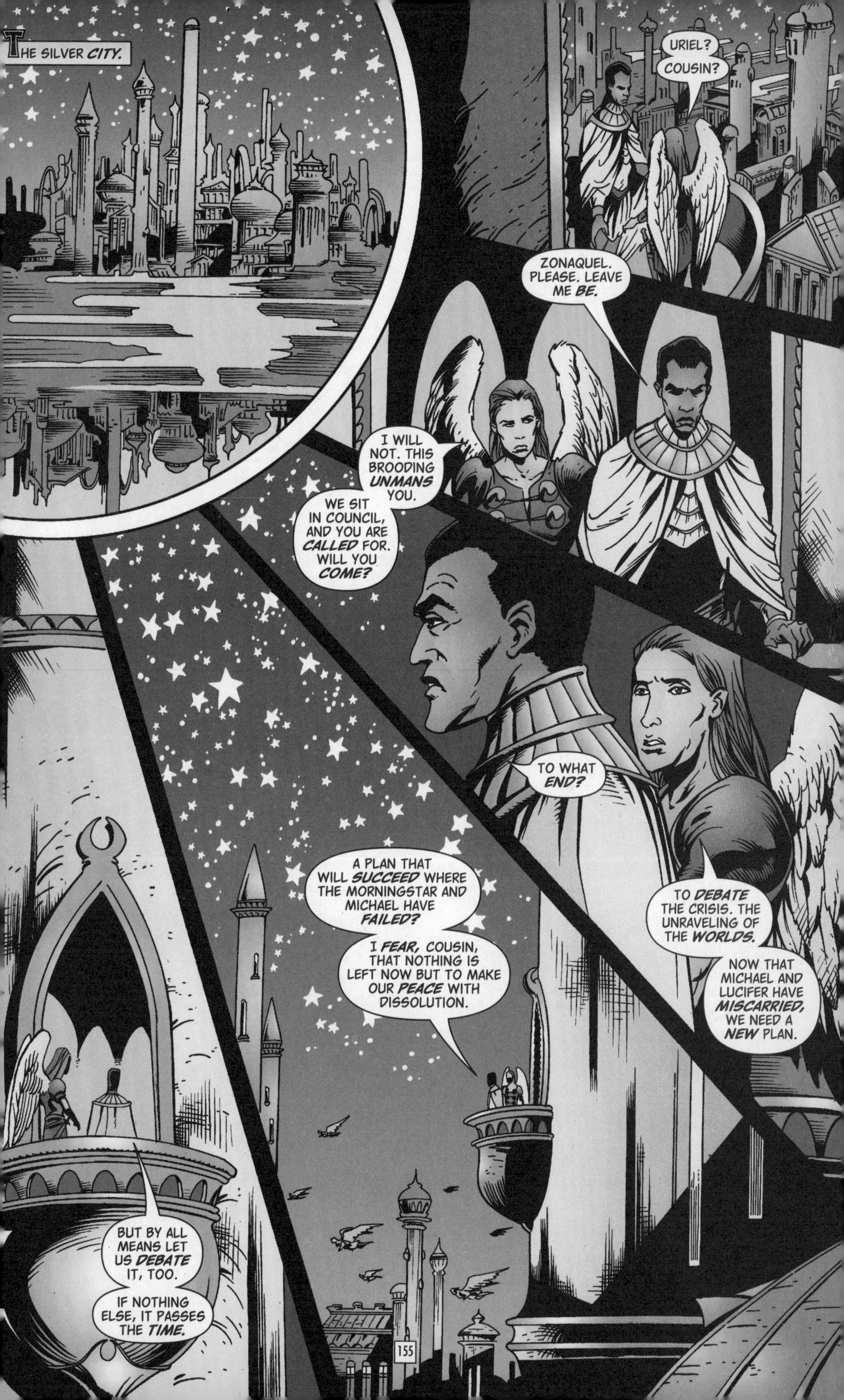
THE SILVER CITY.
URIEL? COUSIN?
ZONAQUEL. PLEASE. LEAVE ME BE.
I WILL NOT. THIS BROODING UNMANS YOU.
WE SIT IN COUNCIL, AND YOU ARE CALLED FOR. WILL YOU COME?
TO WHAT END?
TO DEBATE THE CRISIS. THE UNRAVELING OF THE WORLDS.
NOW THAT MICHAEL AND LUCIFER HAVE MISCARRIED, WE NEED A NEW PLAN.
A PLAN THAT WILL SUCCEED WHERE THE MORNINGSTAR AND MICHAEL HAVE FAILED?
I FEAR, COUSIN, THAT NOTHING IS LEFT NOW BUT TO MAKE OUR PEACE WITH DISSOLUTION.
BUT BY ALL MEANS LET US DEBATE IT, TOO.
IF NOTHING ELSE, IT PASSES THE TIME.

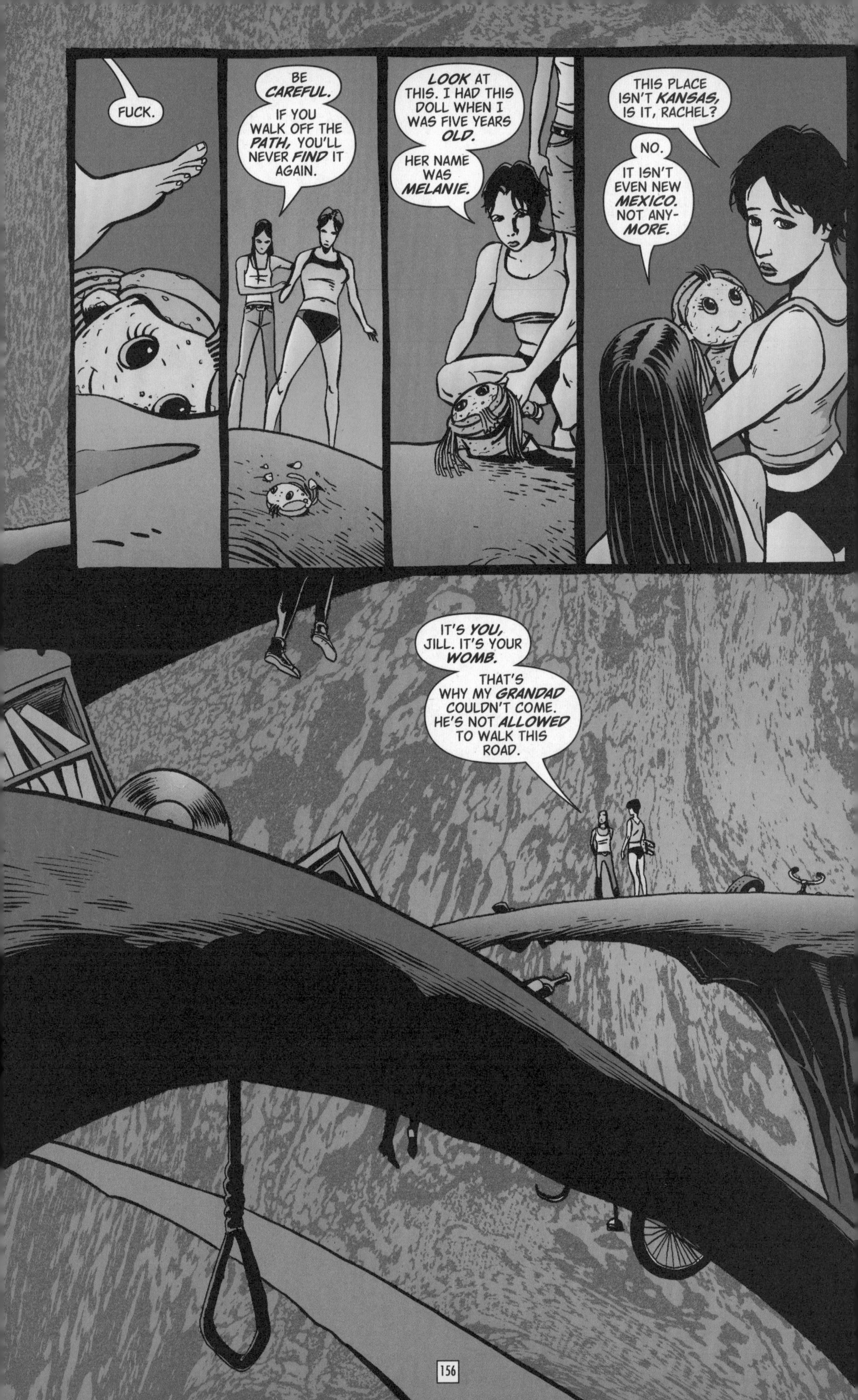
FUCK.
BE CAREFUL.
IF YOU WALK OFF THE PATH, YOU'LL NEVER FIND IT AGAIN.
LOOK AT THIS. I HAD THIS DOLL WHEN I WAS FIVE YEARS OLD.
HER NAME WAS MELANIE.
THIS PLACE ISN'T KANSAS, IS IT, RACHEL?
NO.
IT ISN'T EVEN NEW MEXICO. NOT ANY-MORE.
IT'S YOU, JILL. IT'S YOUR WOMB.
THAT'S WHY MY GRANDAD COULDN'T COME. HE'S NOT ALLOWED TO WALK THIS ROAD.

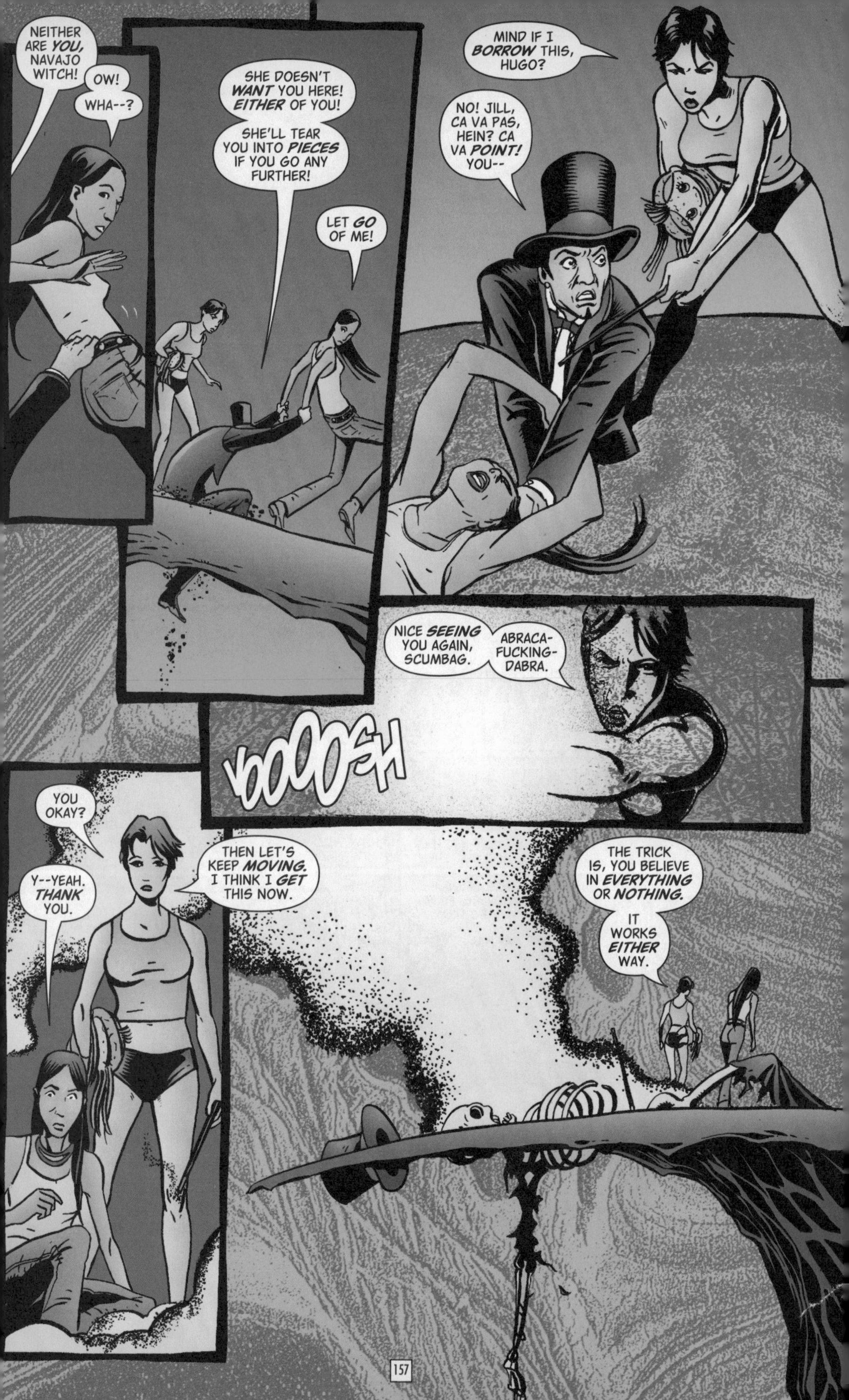
NEITHER ARE *YOU*, NAVAJO WITCH!
OW!
WHA--?
SHE DOESN'T *WANT* YOU HERE! *EITHER* OF YOU!
SHE'LL TEAR YOU INTO *PIECES* IF YOU GO ANY FURTHER!
LET *GO* OF ME!
MIND IF I *BORROW* THIS, HUGO?
NO! JILL, CA VA PAS, HEIN? CA VA *POINT!* YOU--
NICE *SEEING* YOU AGAIN, SCUMBAG.
ABRACA-FUCKING-DABRA.
VOOOOSH
YOU OKAY?
Y--YEAH. *THANK* YOU.
THEN LET'S KEEP *MOVING*. I THINK I *GET* THIS NOW.
THE TRICK IS, YOU BELIEVE IN *EVERYTHING* OR *NOTHING*.
IT WORKS *EITHER* WAY.

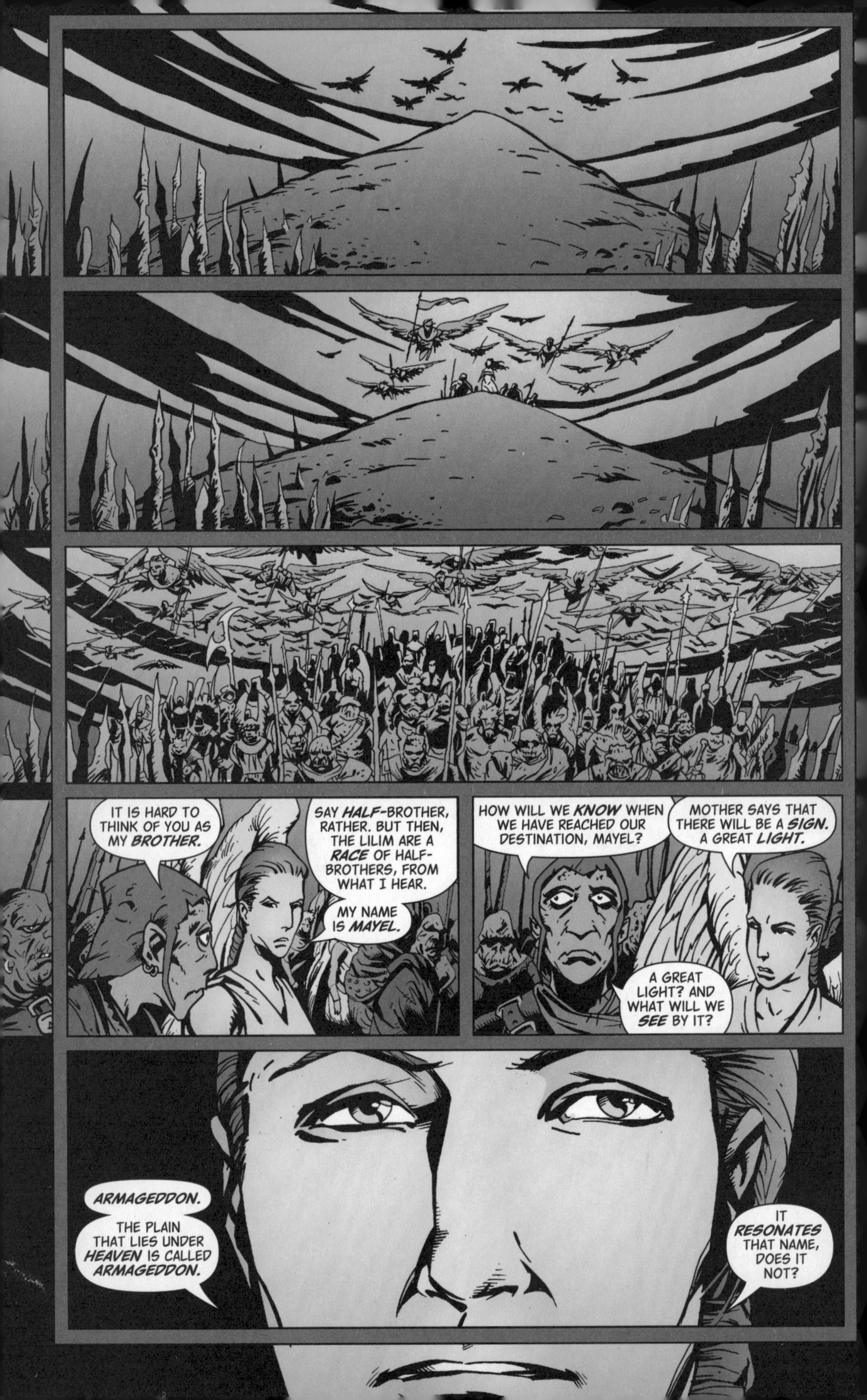
IT IS HARD TO THINK OF YOU AS MY BROTHER.
SAY HALF-BROTHER, RATHER. BUT THEN, THE LILIM ARE A RACE OF HALF-BROTHERS, FROM WHAT I HEAR.
MY NAME IS MAYEL.
HOW WILL WE KNOW WHEN WE HAVE REACHED OUR DESTINATION, MAYEL?
MOTHER SAYS THAT THERE WILL BE A SIGN. A GREAT LIGHT.
A GREAT LIGHT? AND WHAT WILL WE SEE BY IT?
ARMAGEDDON.
THE PLAIN THAT LIES UNDER HEAVEN IS CALLED ARMAGEDDON.
IT RESONATES THAT NAME, DOES IT NOT?

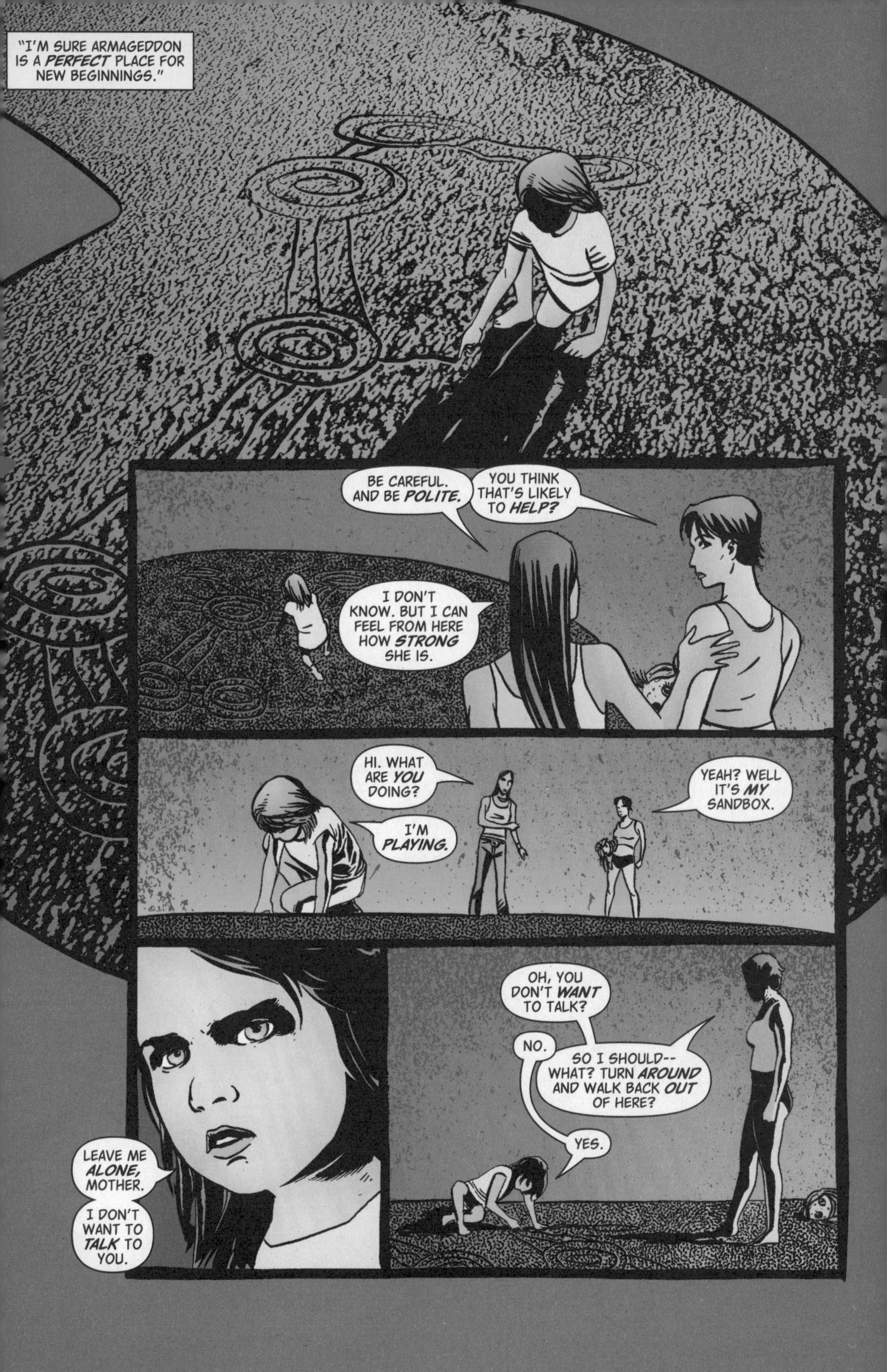
"I'M SURE ARMAGEDDON IS A PERFECT PLACE FOR NEW BEGINNINGS."
BE CAREFUL. AND BE POLITE.
YOU THINK THAT'S LIKELY TO HELP?
I DON'T KNOW. BUT I CAN FEEL FROM HERE HOW STRONG SHE IS.
HI. WHAT ARE YOU DOING?
I'M PLAYING.
YEAH? WELL IT'S MY SANDBOX.
LEAVE ME ALONE, MOTHER.
I DON'T WANT TO TALK TO YOU.
OH, YOU DON'T WANT TO TALK?
NO.
SO I SHOULD-- WHAT? TURN AROUND AND WALK BACK OUT OF HERE?
YES.

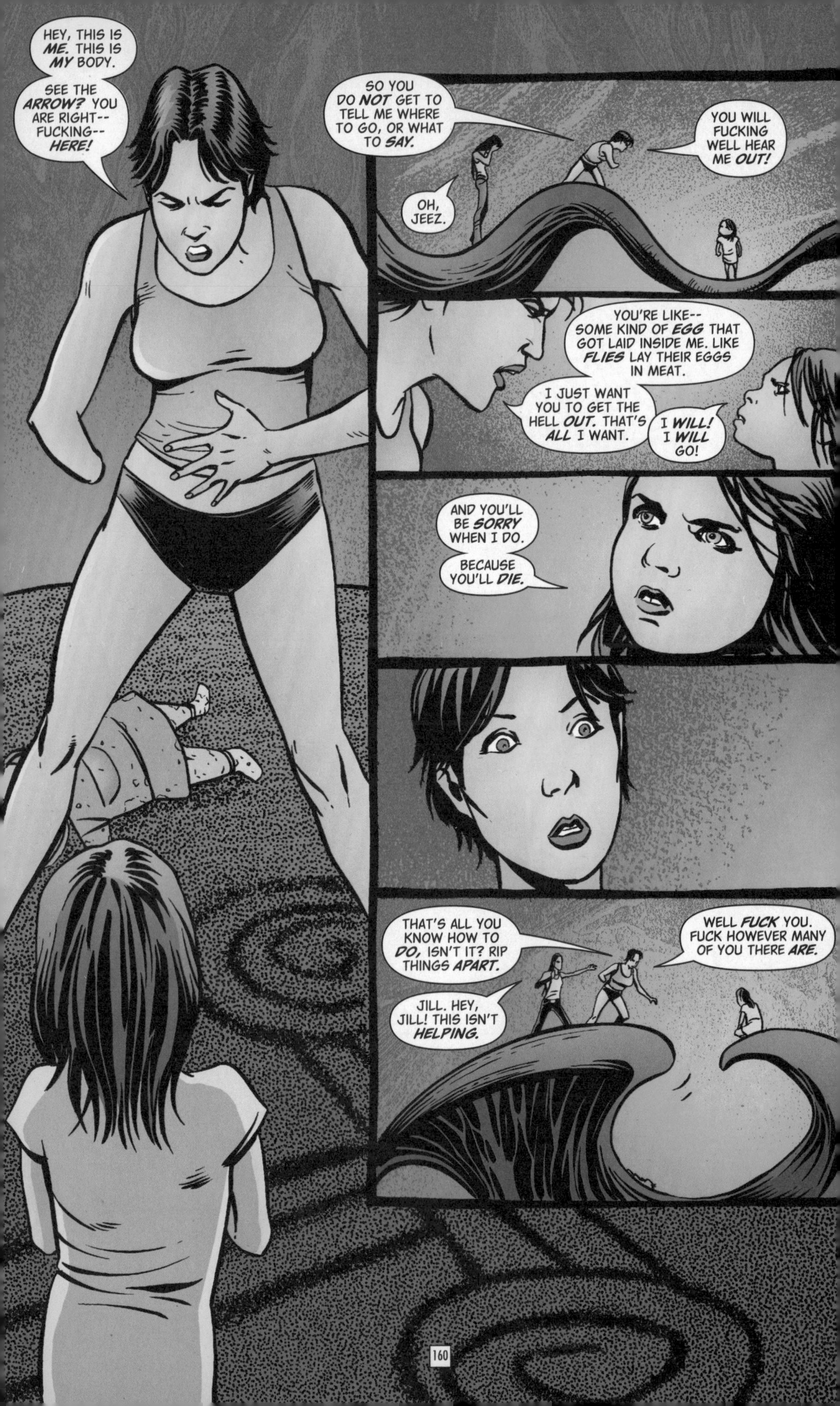

HEY, THIS IS ME. THIS IS MY BODY.
SEE THE ARROW? YOU ARE RIGHT-- FUCKING-- HERE!
SO YOU DO NOT GET TO TELL ME WHERE TO GO, OR WHAT TO SAY.
YOU WILL FUCKING WELL HEAR ME OUT!
OH, JEEZ.
YOU'RE LIKE-- SOME KIND OF EGG THAT GOT LAID INSIDE ME. LIKE FLIES LAY THEIR EGGS IN MEAT.
I JUST WANT YOU TO GET THE HELL OUT. THAT'S ALL I WANT.
I WILL! I WILL GO!
AND YOU'LL BE SORRY WHEN I DO.
BECAUSE YOU'LL DIE.
THAT'S ALL YOU KNOW HOW TO DO, ISN'T IT? RIP THINGS APART.
WELL FUCK YOU. FUCK HOWEVER MANY OF YOU THERE ARE.
JILL. HEY, JILL! THIS ISN'T HELPING.

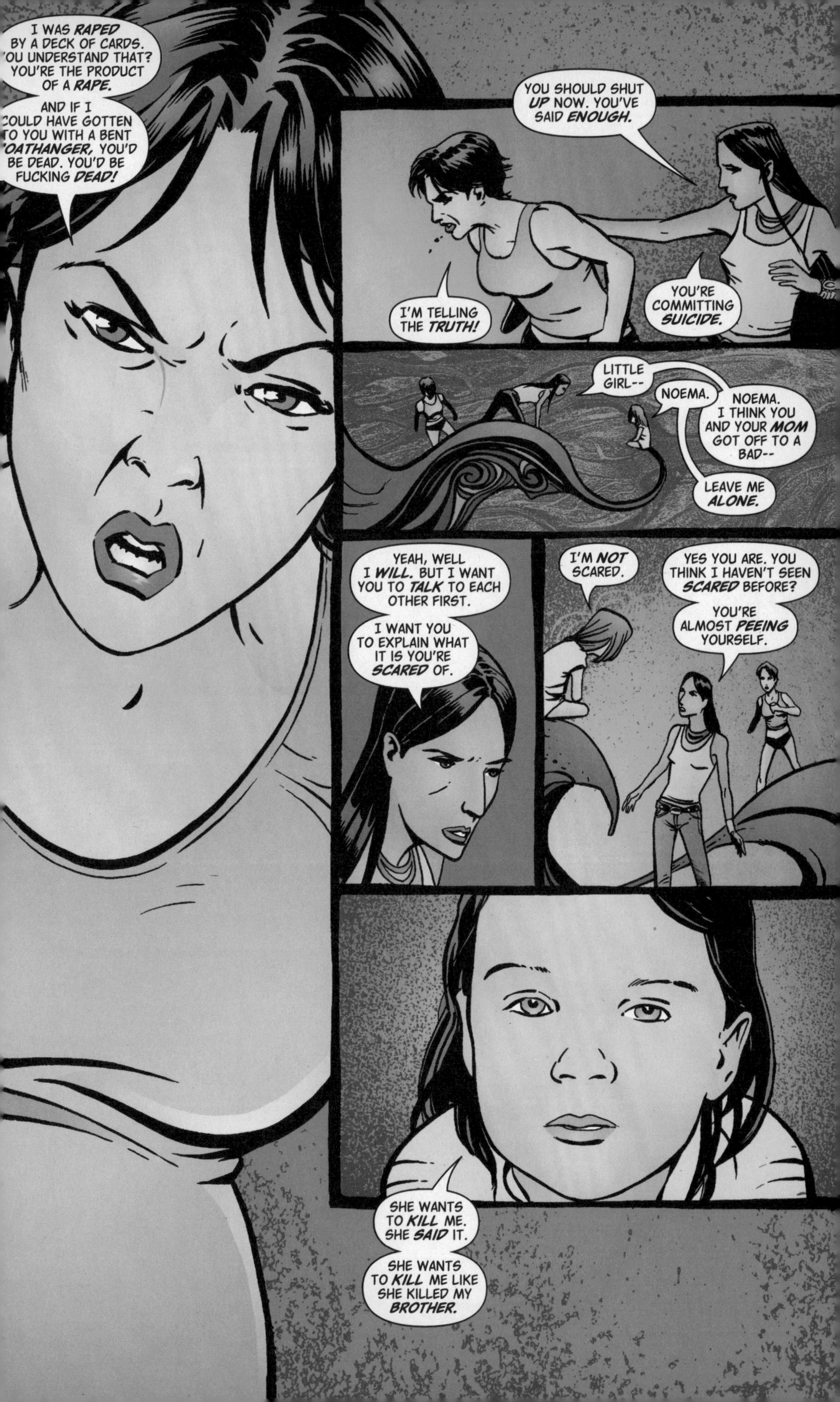
I WAS RAPED BY A DECK OF CARDS. YOU UNDERSTAND THAT? YOU'RE THE PRODUCT OF A RAPE.
AND IF I COULD HAVE GOTTEN TO YOU WITH A BENT COATHANGER, YOU'D BE DEAD. YOU'D BE FUCKING DEAD!
YOU SHOULD SHUT UP NOW. YOU'VE SAID ENOUGH.
I'M TELLING THE TRUTH!
YOU'RE COMMITTING SUICIDE.
LITTLE GIRL--
NOEMA.
NOEMA. I THINK YOU AND YOUR MOM GOT OFF TO A BAD--
LEAVE ME ALONE.
YEAH, WELL I WILL. BUT I WANT YOU TO TALK TO EACH OTHER FIRST.
I WANT YOU TO EXPLAIN WHAT IT IS YOU'RE SCARED OF.
I'M NOT SCARED.
YES YOU ARE. YOU THINK I HAVEN'T SEEN SCARED BEFORE?
YOU'RE ALMOST PEEING YOURSELF.
SHE WANTS TO KILL ME. SHE SAID IT.
SHE WANTS TO KILL ME LIKE SHE KILLED MY BROTHER.

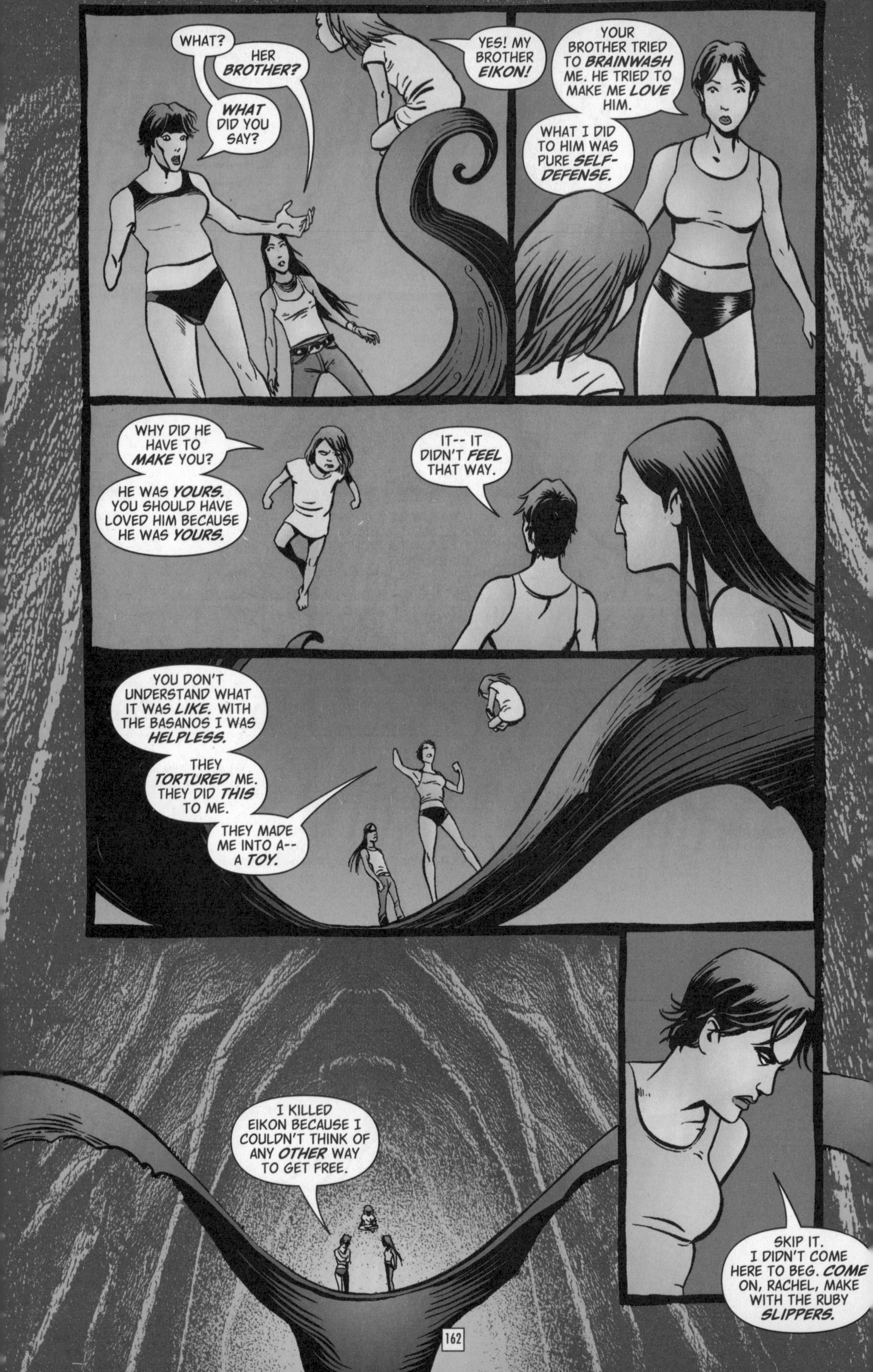

WHAT?
HER BROTHER?
WHAT DID YOU SAY?
YES! MY BROTHER EIKON!
YOUR BROTHER TRIED TO BRAINWASH ME. HE TRIED TO MAKE ME LOVE HIM.
WHAT I DID TO HIM WAS PURE SELF-DEFENSE.
WHY DID HE HAVE TO MAKE YOU?
HE WAS YOURS. YOU SHOULD HAVE LOVED HIM BECAUSE HE WAS YOURS.
IT-- IT DIDN'T FEEL THAT WAY.
YOU DON'T UNDERSTAND WHAT IT WAS LIKE. WITH THE BASANOS I WAS HELPLESS.
THEY TORTURED ME. THEY DID THIS TO ME.
THEY MADE ME INTO A-- A TOY.
I KILLED EIKON BECAUSE I COULDN'T THINK OF ANY OTHER WAY TO GET FREE.
SKIP IT. I DIDN'T COME HERE TO BEG. COME ON, RACHEL, MAKE WITH THE RUBY SLIPPERS.

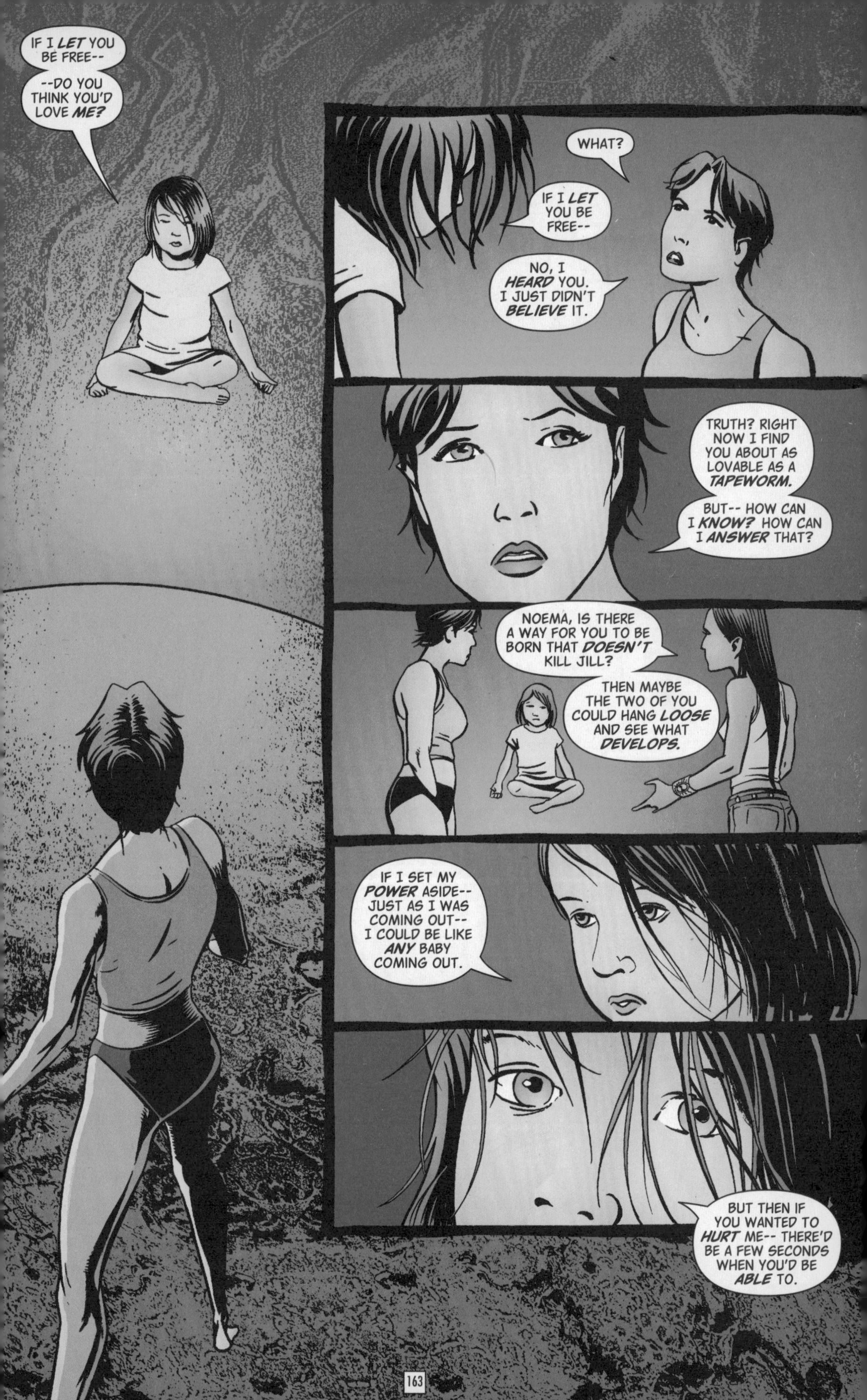

IF I LET YOU BE FREE--
--DO YOU THINK YOU'D LOVE ME?
WHAT?
IF I LET YOU BE FREE--
NO, I HEARD YOU. I JUST DIDN'T BELIEVE IT.
TRUTH? RIGHT NOW I FIND YOU ABOUT AS LOVABLE AS A TAPEWORM.
BUT-- HOW CAN I KNOW? HOW CAN I ANSWER THAT?
NOEMA, IS THERE A WAY FOR YOU TO BE BORN THAT DOESN'T KILL JILL?
THEN MAYBE THE TWO OF YOU COULD HANG LOOSE AND SEE WHAT DEVELOPS.
IF I SET MY POWER ASIDE-- JUST AS I WAS COMING OUT-- I COULD BE LIKE ANY BABY COMING OUT.
BUT THEN IF YOU WANTED TO HURT ME-- THERE'D BE A FEW SECONDS WHEN YOU'D BE ABLE TO.

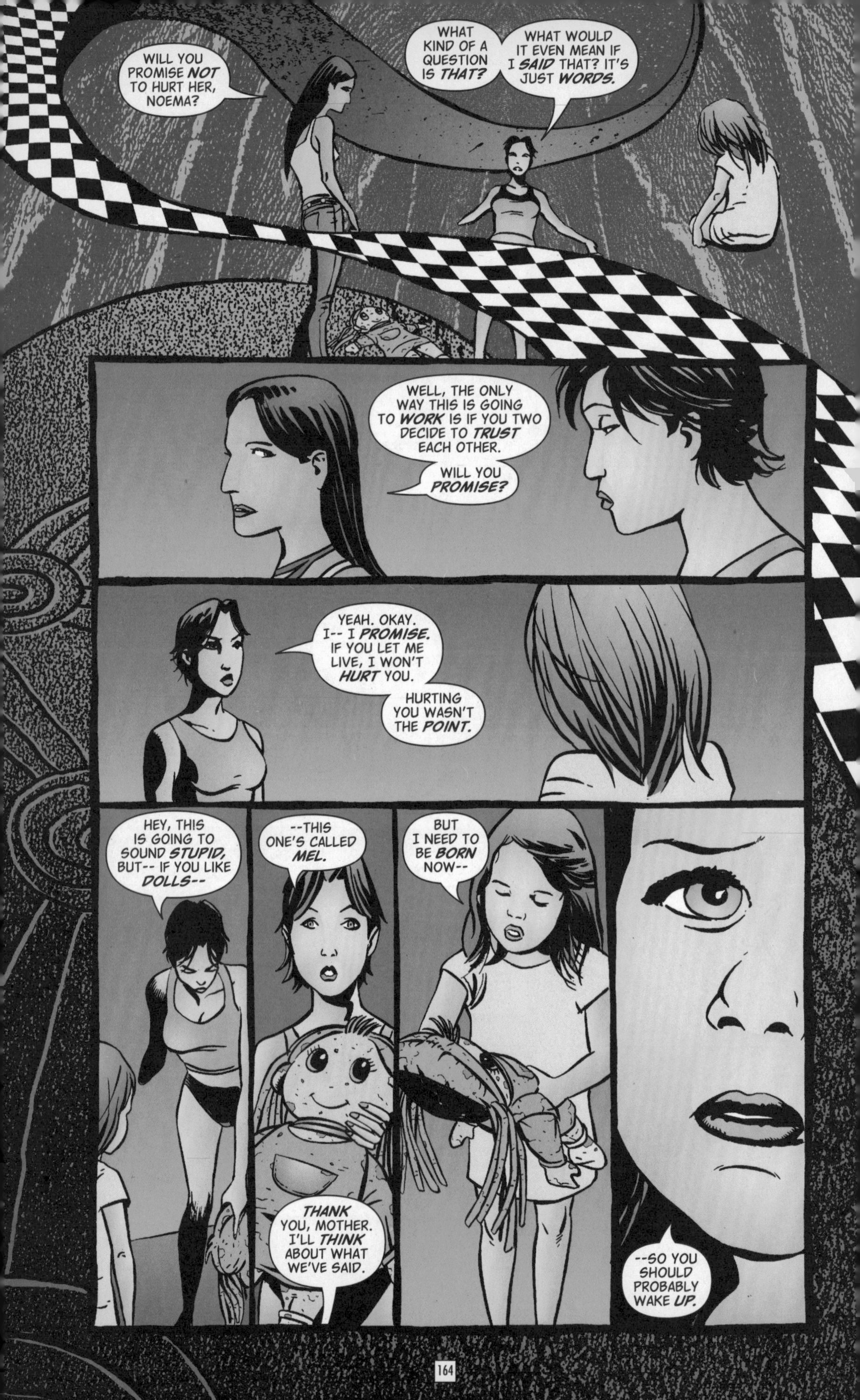
WILL YOU PROMISE NOT TO HURT HER, NOEMA?
WHAT KIND OF A QUESTION IS THAT?
WHAT WOULD IT EVEN MEAN IF I SAID THAT? IT'S JUST WORDS.
WELL, THE ONLY WAY THIS IS GOING TO WORK IS IF YOU TWO DECIDE TO TRUST EACH OTHER.
WILL YOU PROMISE?
YEAH. OKAY. I-- I PROMISE. IF YOU LET ME LIVE, I WON'T HURT YOU.
HURTING YOU WASN'T THE POINT.
HEY, THIS IS GOING TO SOUND STUPID, BUT-- IF YOU LIKE DOLLS--
--THIS ONE'S CALLED MEL.
THANK YOU, MOTHER. I'LL THINK ABOUT WHAT WE'VE SAID.
BUT I NEED TO BE BORN NOW--
--SO YOU SHOULD PROBABLY WAKE UP.

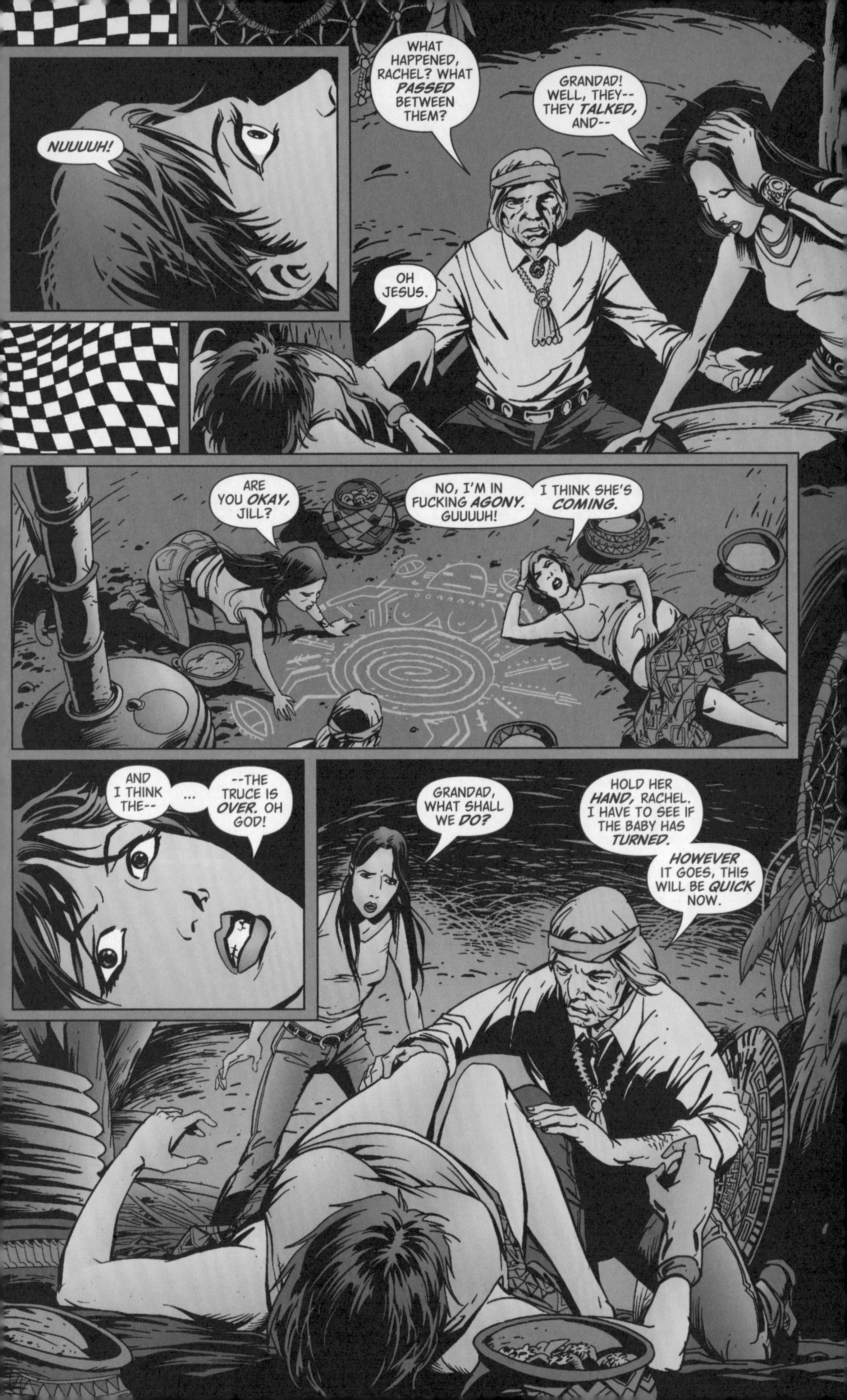
NUUUUH!
WHAT HAPPENED, RACHEL? WHAT PASSED BETWEEN THEM?
GRANDAD! WELL, THEY-- THEY TALKED, AND--
OH JESUS.
ARE YOU OKAY, JILL?
NO, I'M IN FUCKING AGONY. GUUUUH!
I THINK SHE'S COMING.
AND I THINK THE--
...
--THE TRUCE IS OVER. OH GOD!
GRANDAD, WHAT SHALL WE DO?
HOLD HER HAND, RACHEL. I HAVE TO SEE IF THE BABY HAS TURNED.
HOWEVER IT GOES, THIS WILL BE QUICK NOW.

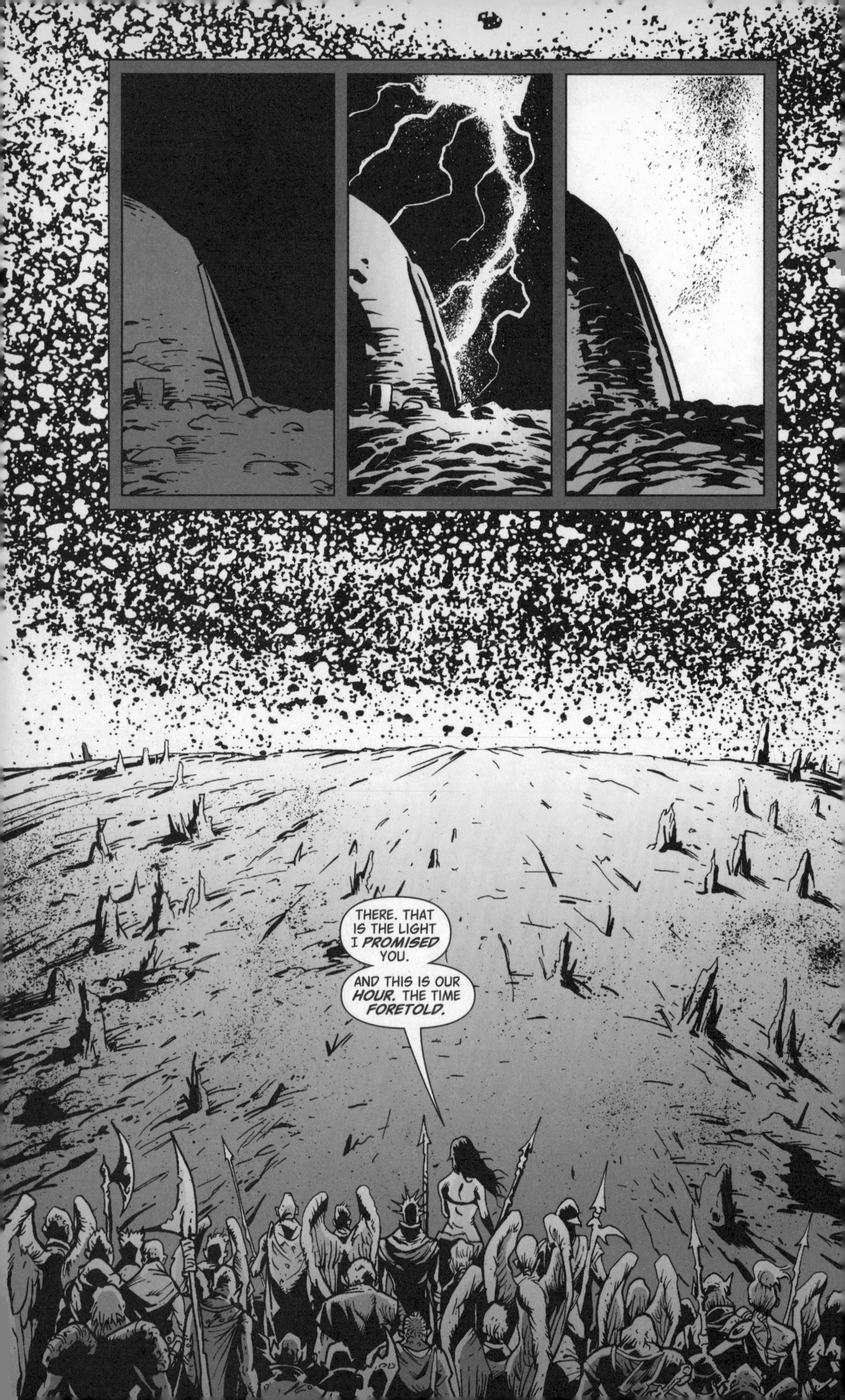
THERE. THAT IS THE LIGHT I PROMISED YOU.
AND THIS IS OUR HOUR. THE TIME FORETOLD.

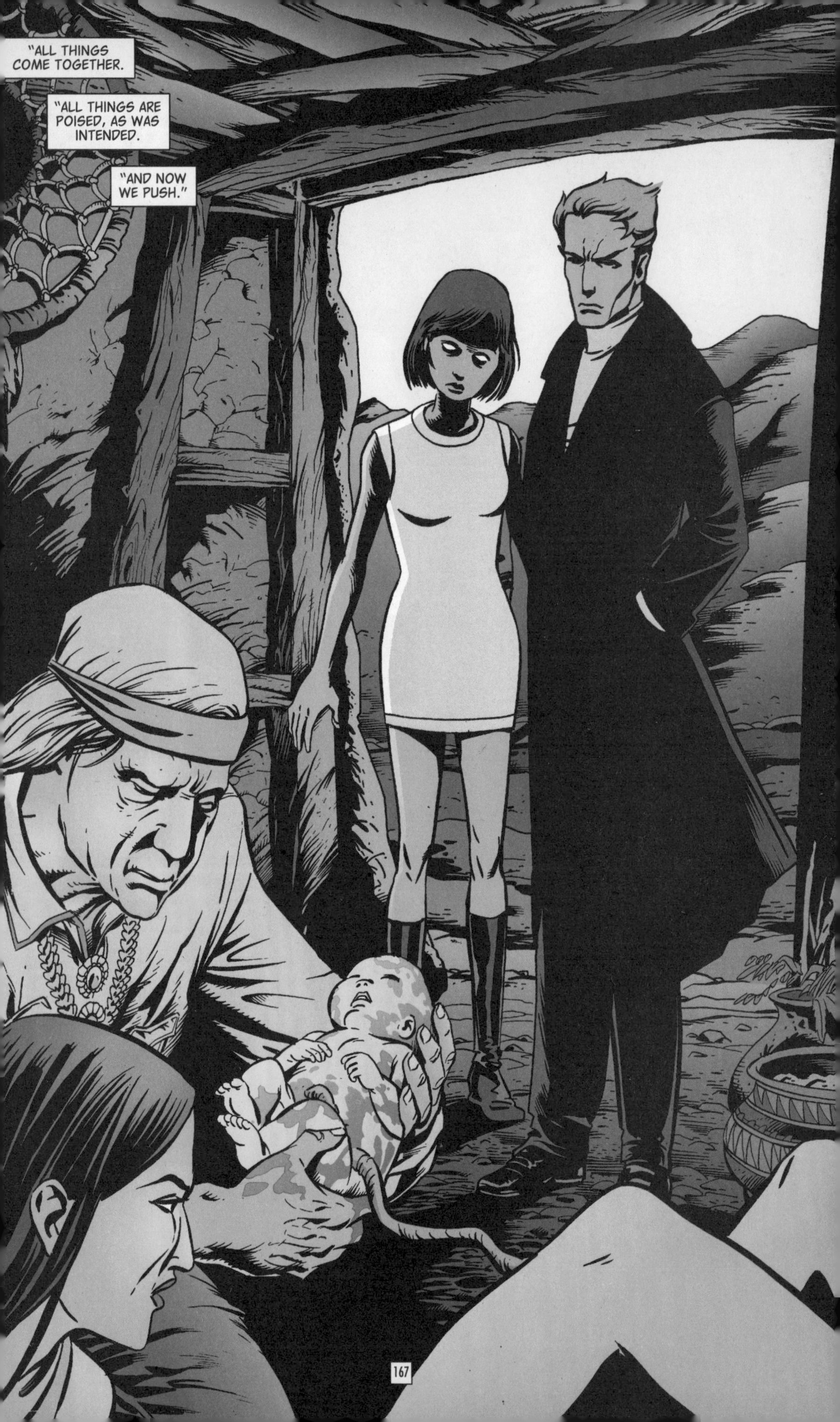
"ALL THINGS COME TOGETHER.
"ALL THINGS ARE POISED, AS WAS INTENDED.
"AND NOW WE PUSH."

... PAGES OF **THE SANDMAN**), AN AMBITIOUS
LUCIFER MORNINGSTAR CREATES A NEW
COSMOS MODELLED AFTER HIS OWN IMAGE
IN THESE COLLECTIONS FROM WRITER
MIKE CAREY AND **VERTIGO:**

Lucifer

VOLUME 1:
DEVIL IN THE GATEWAY

ALSO AVAILABLE:
Vol. 2: CHILDREN AND MONSTERS
Vol. 3: A DALLIANCE WITH
THE DAMNED
Vol. 4: THE DIVINE COMEDY
Vol. 5: INFERNO
Vol. 6: MANSIONS OF THE SILENCE
Vol. 7: EXODUS
Vol. 8: THE WOLF BENEATH THE TREE
Vol. 9: CRUX

VERTIGO

Lucifer
Devil in the Gateway

"Mike Carey's Lucifer is even more manipulative, charming
and dangerous than I could have hoped."
— *Neil Gaiman, from his Foreword*

Mike Carey
Scott Hampton
Chris Weston
James Hodgkins
Warren Pleece
Dean Ormston

"THE BEST FANTASY COMIC AROUND."
— **COMICS INTERNATIONAL**

"AN ORIGINAL TAKE ON THE FORCES OF GOOD, EVIL AND BEYOND EVIL."
— **PUBLISHERS WEEKLY**

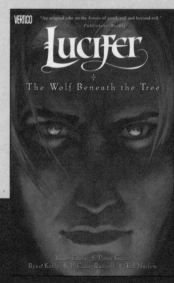

ALL TITLES ARE SUGGESTED FOR MATURE READERS.

SEARCH THE GRAPHIC NOVELS SECTION OF
www.VERTIGOCOMICS.com
FOR ART AND INFORMATION ON ALL OF OUR BOOKS